Gradual Institutional Change in Japan

This book analyses institutional reforms implemented by Japanese Prime Minister Abe Shinzō, under his second administration from 2012 to 2020. Also examined is the evolution in the role of such actors in Japanese politics as bureaucrats, Liberal Democratic Party (LDP) factions, and backbenchers of the ruling party.

Chapters offer multi-dimensional explanations for the preconditions of successful gradual institutional change in political systems, characterized by relatively strong veto players, rigid governmental structures, and numerous unofficial decision-making rules. It is argued that enhancement of the prime minister's position was implemented through the creative use of preexisting policy venues, coupled with minor institutional changes in decision-making bodies. Using three illustrated case studies, it is demonstrated how the prime minister managed to centralize the decision-making process: a result of strategic appointment of ministers, empowerment of the Cabinet Secretariat and also taking advantage of wider advisory organs, largely circumventing deliberations on key policies in the ruling party. Seemingly minor changes thus manifested in a major redefinition of decision-making patterns: a result of the long-term perspective of the Abe administration.

Gradual Institutional Change in Japan: Kantei Leadership under the Abe Administration will be useful for students seeking to understand the process of successful gradual institutional change and for scholars of Japanese studies and political science.

Karol Zakowski is Associate Professor at the University of Lodz. He specializes in the politics and foreign policy of Japan. His recent books include *Decision-Making Reform in Japan: The DPJ's Failed Attempt at a Politician-Led Government* (2015) and *Japan's Foreign Policy Making* (2018).

The Nissan Institute/Routledge Japanese Studies Series

Series Editors:
Roger Goodman, Nissan Professor of Modern Japanese Studies, University of Oxford, Fellow, St Antony's College

J.A.A. Stockwin, formerly Nissan Professor of Modern Japanese Studies and former Director of the Nissan Institute of Japanese Studies, University of Oxford, Emeritus Fellow, St Antony's College

Understanding Japanese Society
Fifth edition
Joy Hendry

Japan and the New Silk Road
Diplomacy, Development and Connectivity
Nikolay Murashkin

The Liberal Democratic Party of Japan
The Realities of 'Power'
Nakakita Kōji

Japan's New Ruralities
Coping with Decline in the Periphery
Edited by Wolfram Manzenreiter, Ralph Lützeler and Sebastian Polak-Rottmann

New Directions in Japan's Security
Non-U.S. Centric Evolution
Edited by Paul Midford and Wilhelm Vosse

Child Guidance Centres in Japan
Alternative Care and the Family
Michael Rivera King

Gradual Institutional Change in Japan
Kantei Leadership under the Abe Administration
Karol Zakowski

For more information about this series, please visit: www.routledge.com/Nissan-Institute-Routledge-Japanese-Studies/book-series/SE0022

Gradual Institutional Change in Japan

Kantei Leadership under the Abe Administration

Karol Zakowski

LONDON AND NEW YORK

First published 2021
by Routledge
2 Park Square, Milton Park, Abingdon, Oxon OX14 4RN

and by Routledge
52 Vanderbilt Avenue, New York, NY 10017

Routledge is an imprint of the Taylor & Francis Group, an informa business

© 2021 Karol Zakowski

The right of Karol Zakowski to be identified as author of this work has been asserted by him in accordance with sections 77 and 78 of the Copyright, Designs and Patents Act 1988.

All rights reserved. No part of this book may be reprinted or reproduced or utilized in any form or by any electronic, mechanical, or other means, now known or hereafter invented, including photocopying and recording, or in any information storage or retrieval system, without permission in writing from the publishers.

Trademark notice: Product or corporate names may be trademarks or registered trademarks, and are used only for identification and explanation without intent to infringe.

British Library Cataloguing-in-Publication Data
A catalogue record for this book is available from the British Library

Library of Congress Cataloging-in-Publication Data
A catalog record has been requested for this book

ISBN: 978-0-367-62336-4 (hbk)
ISBN: 978-1-003-10898-6 (ebk)

Typeset in Times New Roman
by KnowledgeWorks Global Ltd.

To my wife Magdalena

Contents

List of figures viii
List of tables ix
List of abbreviations x
Acknowledgements xii

Introduction 1

1 Prime ministerial leadership in Japan 12

2 Remaining in power 54

3 Reforming governmental institutions 89

4 Reforming the LDP 132

5 Abenomics 164

6 Postponement of the VAT hike 186

7 Revision of interpretation of Article 9 of the Constitution 206

Summary and conclusions 234

Index 244

Figures

1.1	Cabinet and LDP support rates under the first Abe administration	25
1.2	Evolution of the number of LDP faction members in 1975–2006	42
2.1	Reasons for support or non-support of the first Abe administration	57
2.2	Reasons for support or non-support of the second Abe administration	58
2.3	Cabinet and LDP support rates under the second Abe administration	63
2.4	Evolution of the number of LDP faction members in 2006–2019	68
2.5	Difference in the sizes of the first, second, and third parties in the House of Representatives	78
3.1	The Cabinet Secretariat's structure as of March 31, 2020	99
3.2	Average cabinet meeting duration and percentage of round-robin cabinet meetings	102
3.3	Number of special tasks and ministers therewith in the Japanese government after the administrative reform	103
3.4	Number of National Security Council meetings in four-member and nine-member formats	118
3.5	Number of meetings of the Council on Economic and Fiscal Policy and the Headquarters for Japan's Economic Revitalization under the second Abe administration	123
4.1	Traditional two-track decision-making process	133
4.2	Number of LDP members of the House of Representatives according to the number of terms	141
4.3	Two-track decision-making process under the Abe administration	152

Tables

3.1 Composition of the Abe Cabinet, except for the ministers of state for special missions, in September 2019   105
4.1 Special committees established directly under LDP president as of January 2020   155

Abbreviations

APEC	Asia-Pacific Economic Cooperation
ASEAN	Association of Southeast Asian Nations
BOJ	Bank of Japan
CCS	Chief cabinet secretary
CDPJ	Constitutional Democratic Party of Japan (Rikken Minshutō)
CEFP	Council on Economic and Fiscal Policy
DP	Democratic Party (Minshintō)
DPJ	Democratic Party of Japan (Minshutō)
DPP	Democratic Party For the People (Kokumin Minshutō)
FY	Fiscal year
GDP	Gross domestic product
GNP	Gross national product
IMF	International Monetary Fund
JA Zenchū	Central Union of Agricultural Cooperatives
JCP	Japanese Communist Party (Nihon Kyōsantō)
JIP	Japan Innovation Party (Ishin no Tō)
JRA	Japan Restoration Association (Nippon Ishin no Kai)
JSP	Japan Socialist Party (Nihon Shakaitō)
LDP	Liberal Democratic Party (Jiyū Minshutō)
LP	Liberal Party (Jiyūtō)
MAFF	Ministry of Agriculture, Forestry and Fisheries
METI	Ministry of Economy, Trade and Industry
MITI	Ministry of International Trade and Industry
MOD	Ministry of Defense
MOF	Ministry of Finance
MOFA	Ministry of Foreign Affairs
NFP	New Frontier Party (Shinshintō)
NSC	National Security Council
ODA	Official Development Assistance
PFG	Party for Future Generations (Jisedai no Tō)
PH	Party of Hope (Kibō no Tō)
PLP	People's Life Party (Seikatsu no Tō)

SDF	Self-Defense Forces
SDP	Social Democratic Party (Shakai Minshutō)
SEALDs	Students Emergency Action for Liberal Democracy
SMEs	Small and medium-sized enterprises
TPP	Trans-Pacific Partnership
UK	United Kingdom
UN	United Nations
UP	Unity Party (Yui no Tō)
US	United States
VAT	Value-added tax
YP	Your Party (Minna no Tō)

Acknowledgements

Writing this book would not have been possible without the generous support and help from many people and institutions. This study is a result of research conducted as part of the project "Evolution of the Core Executive under Prime Minister Abe's Government in Japan" financed by the National Science Centre, Poland (DEC-2016/23/B/HS5/00059). Many of the interviews cited in the book were conducted during a research stay at the University of Tokyo in autumn of 2019.

Different parts of this study were presented during conferences and research meetings at the University of Lodz, Seikei University, Kansai University, University of Turku, University of Copenhagen, University of Sheffield, and Paris Diderot University. I am grateful for all the comments provided by the panelists. I would like to express my particular gratitude to Professor Maeda Yukio and Professor Iio Jun without whose advice and guidance completing this book would have been much more difficult.

I am especially indebted to my wife Magdalena for her relentless encouragement and understanding.

Introduction

In September 2018, Prime Minister Abe Shinzō was elected as Liberal Democratic Party (LDP) president for the third term in a row, which paved the way for him to become the longest-serving head of government in Japanese history. Under his second administration (2012–2020), Abe led the LDP to three victories in House of Representatives (in 2012, 2014, and 2017), and three in House of Councilors elections (in 2013, 2016, and 2019), which enabled the ruling coalition to maintain a stable majority in both houses. He announced his intention to resign due to health reasons in August 2020, only few days after renewing the record of longest tenure, which had previously belonged to his great uncle Satō Eisaku, prime minister from 1964 to 1972.

The objective of this book is to analyze decision-making reforms in Japan's government under the second Abe administration. Thanks to the weakening of veto players, exploitation of propitious political conditions, and gradual institutional reforms, the prime minister managed to display stronger leadership than most of his predecessors. Interestingly, Abe's success in redefining the balance of power between the head of government, ruling party backbenchers, and bureaucrats was achieved without a comprehensive administrative reform. Rather than rushing his ambitious plans, Abe put emphasis on remaining in power, and implemented institutional changes incrementally. Rather than replacing the existing institutions with new ones, he redefined their role or simply bypassed them. Rather than fighting all veto players at once, he played one group of them off against another.

The book analyzes the major effects of these seemingly minor changes. It relies on a theory of gradual institutional change to explain the factors necessary to enhance the prime minister's powers in Japan – a country characterized by relatively strong veto players, rigid governmental structures, and numerous unofficial decision-making rules. It is argued that thanks to the long-term perspective of the Abe cabinet, the head of government succeeded in transforming bureaucratic ethics and LDP backbenchers' political culture in an incremental manner, so as to become an unquestioned arbiter in all policy affairs.

Evolution of prime minister's position in Japan

At least until the 1990s, the decision-making process at the central government level in Japan had been characterized by the existence of strong veto players – bureaucrats and ruling party backbenchers – who limited the power of prime ministers. As defined by Tsebelis (1995: 293), a veto player is "an individual or collective actor whose agreement is required for a policy decision." Extensive research has been conducted on the protection of sectoral interests, bottom-up *ringi* system, or time-consuming inter-ministerial coordination processes within the bureaucratic structures (Campbell 1980; Inoguchi 1983; Nakano 1993; Matsushita 1998; Iio 2008). Equally numerous scholars have analyzed the principles of advance screening of all bill projects by LDP decision-making bodies, strength of parliamentary tribes (*zoku giin*, influential backbenchers specializing in a given legislative field), and influence of LDP factions on distribution of cabinet portfolios (Fukui 1969; Satō & Matsuzaki 1986; Inoguchi & Iwai 1987; Curtis 1988). In this light, the role of the prime minister used to be interpreted as ritualistic (Van Wolferen 1986/1987: 289–290), prevalently reactive (Hayao 1993: 184–210), "un-Westminster" (George Mulgan 2003: 91), or "ranging from weak to moderately effective" (Stockwin 2008: 139).

After the political (mainly electoral system) reform in 1994 and administrative (mainly central government) reform that was drafted in the 1990s and entered into force in 2001, the interest of Japan scholars shifted toward institutional changes in political leadership. Surveys among civil servants conducted by Muramatsu (2010: 266) and his team indicated that the bureaucrats started paying more attention to the prime ministers' policy agenda at the expense of the stance of LDP parliamentary tribes. Analysis of the prime ministers' daily schedules by Machidori (2012: 113–126) proved that after the administrative reforms, the heads of government intensified contacts with their closest entourages at the expense of consulting other actors. According to Krauss and Nyblade (2005: 357–368), the longer-term trend of increase in media coverage of the prime ministers contributed to the "presidentialization" of Japanese politics. All these findings confirmed that under the new system, it became much easier for the heads of government to display a top-down leadership against veto players.

To describe the abovementioned power shifts, political scientists started relying on the concept of the core executive. As defined by Dunleavy and Rhodes (1990: 4), core executive refers to "all those organizations and structures which primarily serve to pull together and integrate central government policies, or act as final arbiters within the executive of conflicts between different elements of the government machine." While the concept of core executive had been initially created to analyze political leadership in the UK, it was quickly adapted for examination of the political systems of other countries. According to Shinoda (2005: 800–821), in the case of Japan, it is the Cabinet Secretariat that emerged as a core executive after the political and administrative reforms of the 1990s. Thanks to newly acquired competences, this important decision-making organ started acting as an arbiter in inter-ministerial conflicts, thus bolstering the role played by the prime minister and the chief cabinet secretary (CCS).

Yet, most scholars agreed that development of the core executive in Japan was still limited by structural determinants. As indicated by Krauss and Pekkanen (2011: 258), the reforms conducted in the 1990s enabled a shift toward a "partially centralized but partially decentralized, non-Westminster but not un-Westminster system." According to George Mulgan (2018: 3), due to the fact that policymaking was centralized in the prime minister and his closest staff rather than in the cabinet, no Westminster-like core executive has been ever established in Japan. As indicated by Shinoda (2013: 229), to successfully utilize the new instruments of power, the prime minister still had "to balance between centralized institutions and bureaucratic support." Among the constraints on top-down leadership in the 21st century, the most frequently cited were such factors as lack of full cabinet control over the legislative process, shortness of parliamentary sessions, relative ease of taking control over the upper house by the opposition parties, high frequency of LDP presidential elections, fluidity in public support for the government, and political culture based on the bureaucrats' and ruling party backbenchers' influence on the decision-making process (George Mulgan 2002; Woodall 2014; Ochi 2015: 83–107; Takenaka 2015: 46–82; Zakowski 2015).

The institutional reforms implemented under the second Abe administration attracted considerable interest from political scientists. A comprehensive analysis of the prime ministerial executive under the Abe administration was conducted by George Mulgan (2018: 87–95), who drew attention to the collective character of the Kantei (Prime Minister's Residence) leadership. Other scholars examined different aspects of Abe's top-down leadership style. Tazaki (2014) emphasized the gravity of unofficial daily meetings by a group of core decision makers in the Kantei, Nakakita (2017) saw the reasons for Abe's ability to impose his will on the ruling party in the weakening of parliamentary tribes and the use of new LDP organs under the party president's direct control, Sunohara (2014) compared the organizational structure of the National Security Council (NSC) to its US counterpart, Makihara (2016) described the impact of new institutions on strengthening the Cabinet Secretariat's coordinating capabilities, Asakura (2016) paid special attention to the gradual, though not complete, enhancement of the prime minister's abilities to control the bureaucrats, while Mikuriya (2015) embedded the discourse on Prime Minister Abe's strengthened position vis-à-vis the ruling party in a broader context of the weakening of LDP factions. Burret (2017: 400–429) claimed that while Abe displayed better leadership skills under his second administration than during his first cabinet, it was the contextual factors, such as increased support for security reforms due to tensions with China, weakness of opposition parties, or lack of significant rivals inside the LDP, that contributed to a greater extent to his relative success. Mark (2016: 9–94) stressed that Abe's ambition to lead Japan's restoration in political, economic, and strategic dimensions, coupled with the weakness of LDP factions and opposition parties, enabled him to completely dominate policy agenda setting. Stockwin and Ampiah (2017) analyzed the impact of Abe's nationalism on the distortion of Japan's democracy. Hughes (2015) described contradictions in Abe's foreign and security policy agenda, such as appealing to liberal values while promoting historical revisionism. Pugliese (2017: 158), in turn, found the source of Abe's success in gaining direct control over foreign policy making in a "hybrid leadership" consisting of a "forceful micromanagement of bureaucratic and Cabinet appointments."

While prior studies have contributed greatly to understanding the evolution of political leadership in Japan, they have failed to give a clear answer regarding the factors necessary for strengthening the prime minister's powers under the structural constraints characteristic of the Japanese political system. The occasional emergence of strong prime ministers, such as Nakasone Yasuhiro in 1982–1987, Koizumi Jun'ichirō in 2001–2006, and Abe Shinzō in 2012–2020, has been mostly attributed to their leadership skills or their ability to take full advantage of the institutional tools at their disposal (Gaunder 2007; Uchiyama 2007; Shinoda 2013; George Mulgan 2018). Without denying the salience of agency-related factors, this study refers to the theory of gradual institutional change to explain in a more systematic way the preconditions for successful top-down leadership in a seemingly unfavorable environment. Instead of examining the level of "Westministerization" of the Japanese government, the book analyzes the strategies of layering and conversion aimed at long-term redefinition of decision-making mechanisms. It is argued that Prime Minister Abe, aware of the structural constraints to his powers, initiated a process of gradual institutional reforms. Thanks to a prolonged term in office, he managed to bypass some of the policy venues used by veto players, while partly redefining policymaking rules in an incremental manner.

Gradual institutional change directed by the Kantei

To explain the determinants of decision-making reforms implemented by the second Abe administration, this study refers to historical institutionalism. When analyzing institutional change in a path-dependent reality, historical institutionalists often rely on the concept of critical junctures, which is "relatively short periods of time during which there is a substantially heightened probability that agents' choices will affect the outcome of interest" (Capoccia & Kelemen 2007: 348). Nevertheless, as pointed out by Mahoney and Thelen (2010: 2–14), it is more common for change and stability to be inextricably linked, and for reforms to be implemented through gradual evolution rather than through exogenous shocks.

Mahoney and Thelen (2010: 15–28), in their theory of gradual institutional change, distinguished four modes of institutional change: displacement (replacement of the old rules with new ones), conversion (change in "enactment of existing rules due to their strategic redeployment"), layering (establishment of new institutional arrangements "on top of or alongside existing ones"), as well as drift (alteration of "impact of existing rules due to shifts in the environment"). The first two options are most efficient in the case of a weak *status quo* bias, and the remaining two apply whenever the opponents of change enjoy strong veto possibilities. The existence of numerous institutional constraints on reforms discourages change agents from overtly challenging the old system, and instead prompts them to preserve the preexisting rules while circumventing them or waiting for them to stagnate due to contextual shifts. At the same time, the higher the level of discretion in interpretation or enforcement of rules, the easier it is to conduct conversion or drift. In the light of the gradual institutional change theory, a proper adaptation to the strength of veto players as well as a skillful use of the ambiguities of rules can decide about the success of reforms.

The theory of gradual institutional change has been criticized for excessive rigidity, lack of clarity and explanatory power, ambiguity, or the risk of concept stretching. The boundaries between the four modes of institutional change often overlap, and it is not uncommon for one of them to be accompanied by or lead to another (van der Heijden & Kuhlmann 2017: 535–554). In particular, as indicated by Boas (2007: 50–51), layering is interconnected with conversion, as the former provides the means by which the latter ultimately occurs. While layering serves to overcome lock-in effects of distinct components of the whole system, the macro-level institutional change is often implemented through conversion. In one of the first analyses of layering, Schickler examined the evolution of the US Congress through the creation of new institutions without dismantling the old ones. As he stressed, "New coalitions may design novel institutional arrangements but lack the support, or perhaps the inclination, to replace preexisting institutions established to pursue other ends" (Schickler 2001: 15). According to the theory of gradual institutional change, while layering is most useful in systems characterized by strong veto players and low discretion in interpretation or enforcement of rules, conversion is situated at the opposite pole of both axes. Nevertheless, in her later work, Thelen herself linked conversion with "political settings that make authoritative change more difficult," thus admitting it can occur in systems with strong veto players (Hacker, Pierson & Thelen 2013: 11). The level of discretion in interpretation or enforcement of rules, in turn, may vary depending on distinct elements of the institutional setting in question.

Despite its weaknesses, the theory of gradual institutional change offers a convincing analytical framework for examining decision-making reforms in Japan. In particular, it draws attention to the fact that long-term efforts are crucial for the institutional change to materialize. As pointed out by

Hacker, Pierson, and Thelen (2013: 29), long time-horizons are particularly important in the cases of conversion and drift, as change actors need "to monitor policies and institutions across multiple venues," as well as possess "the organizational prowess to prevent the updating of existing rules or to shape the way such rules are enacted on the ground." In politics, just as in poker, what differentiates repeat players from one-shotters is long-term planning and experience. While avoiding the worst scenarios, the professionals "play the odds strategically across a number of cases" and focus on cumulative gains. Over time, they acquire expertise, build their reputation, and establish relationships with institutional players that gradually become assets themselves (Hacker, Pierson & Thelen 2013: 32). Similarly, prime ministers who remain in office long enough, in a natural way, gain advantage over veto players.

As already mentioned, the Japanese political system has been traditionally characterized by the existence of two kinds of veto players – bureaucrats and ruling party backbenchers – whose influence on decision making has been gradually weakening as an effect of the reforms conducted in the 1990s. The level of discretion in interpretation or enforcement of rules, in turn, has varied in different fields. On the one hand, decision-making patterns in Japan, especially regarding bureaucratic appointments and policy-making traditions in the ruling party, have been, to a great extent, based on unwritten codes of conduct sanctioned by custom rather than formal regulations (Ishikawa & Hirose 1989: 222; Iio 2008: 40–42). On the other hand, the legislation process and governmental structures have been highly formalized and difficult to change (Shindō 2012: 90–93; Kawato 2015: 25–45). This complex nature of the Japanese political system created a favorable environment for applying both layering and conversion strategies.

The main problem was the fact that prime ministers rarely remained in office long enough to conduct bold reforms. Since 1945, the head of the Japanese government changed as many as 36 times, and between 2006 and 2012, there were six prime ministers, each serving only one year. As indicated by Kawato (2015: 3–5), while in the UK or Germany, the heads of government usually enjoyed a stable position after victorious parliamentary elections, in Japan, they were deprived of this luxury. The reasons for short-lived cabinets included frequent dissolutions of the Diet, short terms in office of the presidents of major parties, elections to the House of Councilors held separately from the lower house elections, and the mass media's tendency to blame the prime minister for all the negative news, such as a difficult economic situation, results of local elections, or disputes in the Diet. This political instability prevented the Kantei from using layering and conversion strategies in reforming the decision-making process.

Due to numerous structural constraints on the prime minister's powers, the historic alternation of power in 2009 did not lead to a durable institutional change. As the Democratic Party of Japan (DPJ) was the first, and so far the only, party that managed to perform better in a lower house election than the LDP, its victory can be considered a potential critical juncture that did not materialize. Despite full control over the Diet and initially strong popular support, the DPJ failed to change decision-making rules through displacement and suffered a crushing electoral defeat in December 2012.[1] Paradoxically, the scale of DPJ's fiasco in modifying the general institutional setting for policymaking prepared a favorable ground for Abe to generally return to the old decision-making patterns while strengthening the Kantei in an evolutionary manner. In contrast to the DPJ government, the second Abe administration adjusted the pace of reforms to the capacities of the political system. At the same time, fragmentation of the DPJ and other opposition parties paved the way for the revival of LDP's domination, despite the lack of a significant increase in the popularity of that party. DPJ's fiasco and Abe's success seem to confirm Mahoney's and Thelen's finding that reforms are more often implemented through incremental reforms rather than through exogenous shocks.

This book analyzes the preconditions for a successful gradual institutional change in political systems characterized by relatively strong veto players, rigid governmental structures, and numerous unofficial decision-making rules. It is argued that enhancement of the Kantei's position in Japan has been implemented through a mixture of layering and conversion strategies, possible thanks to the long-term perspective of the Abe administration. The prime minister took full advantage of the preexisting institutional instruments to strengthen the coordinating capacities of the Kantei. In parallel, Abe created new decision-making bodies, such as the NSC, the Cabinet Bureau of Personnel Affairs, and numerous advisory organs under the cabinet and in the LDP, to dilute the significance of the policy venues controlled by the bureaucrats and LDP backbenchers. The weakening of veto players, in turn, enabled the government to exploit a high level of discretion in the interpretation of unofficial decision-making rules to gradually undermine some of the unwritten practices. While the formal institutions have been to some extent bypassed through layering, the ambiguous informal decision-making rules have been gradually reinterpreted through the conversion strategy.

Structure of the book and methodology

The book is composed of seven chapters. The first one describes the prime minister's competences as well as the constraints on top-down leadership in Japan. The chapter analyzes, from a historical perspective, the institutional, personal, and situational factors that decided about the successes and failures of the heads of government in remaining in power. In this light, it examines the dynamics of prolonged prime ministership that was a necessary prerequisite for conducting gradual institutional reforms. The second chapter analyzes how Abe, having learnt his lesson after the failure of his first administration, did not repeat the same mistakes after regaining power in 2012. Abe's policy agenda, efforts in maintaining the high popularity of the cabinet, intra-party balancing techniques, as well as strategy toward the coalition partner and the opposition parties were the factors that ensured the stability of his government, which, in turn, created favorable conditions for initiating a gradual institutional change. Chapters 3 and 4 describe the institutional reforms conducted by the Abe Kantei both in the government and in the ruling party. They draw attention not only to the changes in the official decision-making bodies, but also to the revision of the informal mechanisms through a mixture of layering and conversion strategies.

Case studies and decision-making methods are used to evaluate the efficiency of the gradual institutional change initiated by Abe. Chapters 5–7 describe three theory-driven case studies: formulation and implementation of Abe's economics (so-called Abenomics), postponement of a consumption tax increase in 2014 and 2016, as well as the revision of interpretation of Article 9 of the Constitution to allow collective self-defense. These cases were selected to cover the most important and most controversial policies that encountered opposition from different veto players. Each of them examines the level of involvement of distinct actors within the Kantei and the government (prime minister, CCS and Cabinet Secretariat, prime minister's executive secretary, key cabinet members), the strategies of layering and conversion employed by policy initiators, the use of the preexisting and newly established institutions, the methods for coordinating contradictory interests of the parties involved (various ministries, pressure groups, ruling party parliamentary tribes), as well as the management of the legislative process. The case studies show that instead of overtly challenging the old decision-making venues, Abe either circumvented them or redefined their role. It is described how, without antagonizing all veto players, the prime minister tactically played one ministry or group of LDP backbenchers off against another.

The book relies on an institutional analysis to examine both the legal aspects and the unofficial rules of conduct of Japanese decision-making bodies in the government and the LDP. The study refers to primary and secondary sources, including interviews with Japanese politicians and bureaucrats, to evaluate the adaptation of the Kantei's strategy to the strength of veto players and the level of discretion in interpretation or enforcement of rules. In this light, it is concluded that a gradual institutional change provides the most efficient means for conducting a decision-making reform in Japan.

Note on conventions

The author uses the modified Hepburn transcription for Japanese terms and titles. The original order of Japanese, Chinese, and Korean names is preserved with family names preceding given names. In the case of English-language sources published by Asian authors, the version that appeared in the referred title is used.

Note

1. For a detailed analysis of the DPJ's failed attempt at decision-making reforms, see the author's earlier monograph (Zakowski 2015).

References

Asakura, Hideo (2016) *Kantei Shihai* [Kantei's Supremacy], Tokyo: Īsuto Puresu.
Boas, Taylor C. (2007) "Conceptualizing Continuity and Change. The Composite-Standard Model of Path Dependence," *Journal of Theoretical Politics*, 19, 1: 33–54.
Burret, Tina (2017) "Abe Road: Comparing Japanese Prime Minister Shinzo Abe's Leadership of His First and Second Governments," *Parliamentary Affairs*, 70, 2: 400–429.
Campbell, John Creighton (1980) *Contemporary Japanese Budget Politics*, Berkeley: University of California Press.
Capoccia, Giovanni & Kelemen, R. Daniel (2007) "The Study of Critical Junctures: Theory, Narrative, and Counterfactuals in Historical Institutionalism," *World Politics*, 59, 3: 341–369.
Curtis, Gerald L. (1988) *Japanese Way of Politics*, New York: Columbia University Press.
Dunleavy, Patrick & Rhodes, R. A. W. (1990) "Core Executive Studies in Britain," *Public Administration*, 68, 1: 3–28.
Fukui, Haruhiro (1969) *Jiyū Minshutō to Seisaku Kettei* [Liberal Democratic Party and Policy Decisions], Tokyo: Fukumura Shuppan.
Gaunder, Alisa (2007) *Political Reform in Japan. Leadership Looming Large*, London and New York: Routledge.
George Mulgan, Aurelia (2002) *Japan's Failed Revolution: Koizumi and the Politics of Economic Reforms*, Canberra: Asia Pacific Press.
George Mulgan, Aurelia (2003) "Japan's 'Un-Westminster' System: Impediments to Reform in a Crisis Economy," *Government and Opposition*, 38, 1: 73–91.
George Mulgan, Aurelia (2018) *The Abe Administration and the Rise of the Prime Ministerial Executive*, London and New York: Routledge.
Hacker, Jacob S., Pierson, Paul & Thelen, Kathleen (2013) "Drift and Conversion: Hidden Faces of Institutional Change," American Political Science Association 2013 Annual Meeting Paper Chicago. Online. Available: https://papers.ssrn.com/sol3/papers.cfm?abstract_id=2303593 (accessed December 24, 2019).
Hayao, Kenji (1993) *The Japanese Prime Minister and Public Policy*, Pittsburgh and London: University of Pittsburgh Press.
Hughes, Christopher W. (2015) *Japan's Foreign and Security Policy Under the "Abe Doctrine": New Dynamism or New Dead End?*, London: Palgrave Macmillan.
Iio, Jun (2008) *Nihon No Tōchi Kōzō* [Structure of Government in Japan], Tokyo: Chūō Kōron Shinsha.
Inoguchi, Takashi & Iwai, Tomoaki (1987) *"Zoku Giin" no Kenkyū* [A Study on "Parliamentary Tribes"], Tokyo: Nihon Keizai Shinbunsha.
Inoguchi, Takashi (1983) *Gendai Nihon Seiji Keizai no Kōzu* [Contemporary Japanese Political Economy: Government and Market], Tokyo: Tōyō Keizai Shinpōsha.
Ishikawa, Masumi & Hirose, Michisada (1989) *Jimintō – Chōki Shihai no Kōzō* [LDP – Structure of Long-Term Supremacy], Tokyo: Iwanami Shoten.

Kawato, Sadafumi (2015) *Giin Naikakusei* [Parliamentary Government], Tokyo: Tōkyō Daigaku Shuppankai.
Krauss, Ellis S. & Nyblade, Benjamin (2005) "'Presidentialization' in Japan? The Prime Minister, Media and Elections in Japan," *British Journal of Political Science*, 35, 2: 357–368.
Krauss, Ellis S. & Pekkanen, Robert J. (2011) *The Rise and Fall of Japan's LDP. Political Party Organizations as Historical Institutions*, Ithaca and London: Cornell University Press.
Machidori, Satoshi (2012) *Shushō Seiji no Seido Bunseki. Gendai Nihon Seiji no Kenryoku Kiban Keisei*, [The Japanese Premiership: An Institutional Analysis of the Power Relations], Tokyo: Chikura Shobō.
Mahoney, James & Thelen, Kathleen (2010) "A Theory of Gradual Institutional Change," in James Mahoney & Kathleen Thelen (eds), *Explaining Institutional Change: Ambiguity, Agency, and Power*, Cambridge: Cambridge University Press, 1–37.
Makihara, Izuru (2016) *"Abe Ikkyō" no Nazo* [The Mystery of "Abe's Unilateral Strength"], Tokyo: Asahi Shinbun Shuppan.
Mark, Craig (2016) *The Abe Restoration. Contemporary Japanese Politics and Reformation*, Lanham–Boulder–New York–London: Lexington Books.
Matsushita, Keiichi (1998) *Seiji Gyōsei no Kangaekata* [Philosophy of Politics and Administration], Tokyo: Iwanami Shoten.
Mikuriya, Takashi (2015) *Abe Seiken wa Hontō ni Tsuyoi noka* [Is the Abe Administration Really Powerful?], Tokyo: PHP Kenkyūjo.
Muramatsu, Michio (2010) *Sei-Kan Sukuramu-gata Rīdāshippu no Hōkai* [The Breakdown of Leadership based on the Politico-Bureaucratic Scrum], Tokyo: Tōyō Keizai Shinpōsha.
Nakakita, Kōji (2017) *Jimintō – Ikkyō no Jitsuzō* [LDP – Real Image of Unilateral Strength], Tokyo: Chūō Kōron Shinsha.
Nakano, Minoru (1993) *Nihon no Seiji Rikigaku. Dare ga Seisaku o Kimeru noka* [Dynamics of the Japanese Politics. Who Makes Policy Decisions?], Tokyo: Nihon Hōsō Shuppan Kyōkai.
Ochi, Takao (2015) "Party Politics and Leadership Change in Japan: The Prime Ministerial Relay," in Sahashi Ryo & James Gannon (eds), *Looking for Leadership: The Dilemma of Political Leadership in Japan*, Tokyo and New York: Japan Center for International Exchange, 83–107.
Pugliese, Giulio (2017) "Kantei Diplomacy? Japan's Hybrid Leadership in Foreign and Security Policy," *The Pacific Review*, 30, 2: 152–168.
Satō, Seizaburō & Matsuzaki, Tetsuhisa (1986) *Jimintō Seiken* [LDP Government], Tokyo: Chūō Kōronsha.
Schickler, Eric (2001) *Disjointed Pluralism. Institutional Innovation and the Development of the U.S. Congress*, Princeton, NJ: Princeton University Press.
Shindō, Muneyuki (2012) *Seiji Shudō. Kanryōsei o Toinaosu* [Politician-Led Government. Reexamination of the Bureaucratic System], Tokyo: Chikuma Shobō.
Shinoda, Tomohito (2005) "Japan's Cabinet Secretariat and Its Emergence as Core Executive," *Asian Survey*, 45, 5: 800–821.
Shinoda, Tomohito (2013) *Contemporary Japanese Politics: Institutional Changes and Power Shifts*, New York: Columbia University Press.
Stockwin, Arthur & Ampiah, Kweku (2017) *Rethinking Japan. The Politics of Contested Nationalism*, Lanham–Boulder–New York–London: Lexington Books.

Stockwin, J. A. A. (2008) *Governing Japan. Divided Politics in a Resurgent Economy*, Malden–Oxford–Carlton: Blackwell Publishing.
Sunohara, Tsuyoshi (2014) *Nihon-ban NSC towa Nanika* [What is Japanese NSC?], Tokyo: Shinchōsha.
Takenaka, Harukata (2015) "The Frequent Turnover of Japanese Prime Ministers: Still a Long Way to a Westminster Model," in Sahashi Ryo & James Gannon (eds.), *Looking for Leadership: The Dilemma of Political Leadership in Japan*, Tokyo and New York: Japan Center for International Exchange, 46–82.
Tazaki, Shirō (2014) *Abe Kantei no Shōtai* [The True Image of the Abe Kantei], Tokyo: Kōdansha.
Tsebelis, George (1995) "Decision Making in Political Systems: Veto Players in Presidentialism, Parliamentarism, Multicameralism and Multipartyism," *British Journal of Political Science*, 25, 3: 289–325.
Uchiyama, Yū (2007) *Koizumi Seiken* [Koizumi Government], Tokyo: Chūō Kōron Shinsha.
Van der Heijden, Jeroen & Kuhlmann, Johanna (2017) "Studying Incremental Institutional Change: A Systematic and Critical Meta-Review of the Literature from 2005 to 2015," *The Policy Studies Journal*, 45, 3: 535–554.
Van Wolferen, Karel G. (1986/1987) "The Japan Problem," *Foreign Affairs*, 65, 2: 288–303.
Woodall, Brian (2014) *Growing Democracy in Japan: The Parliamentary Cabinet System Since 1868*, Lexington: The University Press of Kentucky.
Zakowski, Karol (2015) *Decision-Making Reform in Japan: The DPJ's Failed Attempt at a Politician-Led Government*, London and New York: Routledge.

1 Prime ministerial leadership in Japan

While prime ministers in Japan boasted broad constitutional competences, their ability to lead in a top-down manner was subject to many institutional constraints. Some of these obstacles were eliminated or weakened by electoral and administrative reforms, but the Japanese political system still remained different from the Westminster system that had been the model for the authors of the 1946 Constitution. This chapter briefly analyzes how Japanese prime ministers tried to overcome the official and unofficial constraints on their leadership in the post-war period, and due to what factors most of them failed and only a handful succeeded. In this light, the main characteristics of a prolonged prime ministership, as a necessary prerequisite for an effective top-down leadership, are analyzed.

Prime minister's competences and constraints on leadership

Theoretically, the Japanese Constitution vests broad prerogatives in the prime minister. The heads of government nominate and dismiss cabinet members and act as superior decision makers in all legislative fields. Serving concurrently as the president of the ruling party, the prime minister theoretically maintains control over a majority of parliamentarians. Additionally, he/she possess the right to dissolve the House of Representatives, which gives him/her a convenient instrument of putting pressure on both the opposition and ruling parties. Moreover, on behalf of the emperor, the prime minister nominates a range of high-ranking state officials, such as the Supreme Court chief justice, as well as appointing the chairpersons of crucial advisory councils (Neary 2002: 111). The head of government has at his/her disposal a direct staff, popularly referred to as the Kantei (Prime Minister's Residence). This closest entourage of the prime minister largely overlaps with the Cabinet Secretariat and the Cabinet Office, and includes the chief cabinet secretary (CCS), three deputy CCSs, three assistant CCSs, prime minister's special advisers and executive secretaries, as well as special advisers to the cabinet (George Mulgan 2018: 2).

Despite numerous formal prerogatives, the leadership of Japanese prime ministers was subject to considerable unofficial and institutional constraints.

The rule of dispersed management (*buntan kanri gensoku*) prohibited them from direct initiation of policies that fell within the jurisdiction of one of the ministries. Moreover, due to the principle of unanimity among cabinet members, a single minister was able to obstruct the decision-making process (Shinoda 2000: 47). Although the head of government could dismiss the opposing cabinet member, the political cost of such a decision often turned out to be too high. Instead of focusing on implementing their policy agenda in a top-down manner, Japanese prime ministers usually had to consider maintaining harmony between various factions in the ruling party and keeping balance between distinct ministries that were actually ruled by the bureaucrats. As pointed out by Van Wolferen (1986/1987: 289), the head of government played only a ritualistic, passive role, and was unable to freely steer the semiautonomous groups in the government. According to Hayao (1993: 184–210), Japanese prime ministers appeared to be reactive leaders because instead of imposing their own policy vision on other political actors, they usually merely supervised the enactment of the issues decided upon by their subordinates in the bureaucracy and the ruling party. These two institutional actors were the strongest veto players that could easily block structural reforms.

Catering for the privileges of their home ministries, the bureaucrats were characterized by strong sectionalism (Shinoda 2000: 5–10; Iio 2008: 39). Recruitment from among the graduates of top universities, the policy of life-time employment, fixed stages of career, and lack of flow between ministries resulted in the collectiveness, solidarity, and elitist self-esteem of the administrative staff in each ministry. In addition, the extreme rigidity of the organizational structure of the Japanese government strengthened the sense of independence of the bureaucrats from politicians. In order to establish or abolish a ministry, and until 1983, even a single bureau, the prime minister had to prepare and have passed through the Diet a separate law, which necessitated a lot of effort (Shindō 2012: 90–93). The tradition of frequent cabinet reshuffles further distorted the relationship between the bureaucrats and their political superiors. The ministers were changed annually, as there was a limited number of cabinet portfolios to fulfill the ambitions of all senior parliamentarians of the ruling party (Kohno 1997: 110). Prime ministers did not stay in office for long, either. Until the modification of the party constitution in 2002, the Liberal Democratic Party (LDP) leader's tenure was limited to only two consecutive two-year terms. Afterwards, the length of term was changed to three years, and under the Abe cabinet in 2017, the maximum number of terms was increased to three. Due to these factors, the bureaucrats rarely identified themselves with the changeable policy agenda of the prime minister or their own minister, and simply followed the pre-established policy line of their ministry.

In addition, it was not uncommon for the bureaucrats to sabotage the efforts of reform-minded prime ministers and cabinet members. Civil servants did not hesitate to resort to such measures as changing the meaning of new regulations through making seemingly minor modifications to their contents, playing one politician off against another, or denying their expertise to their political superiors during Diet proceedings to discredit them in the eyes of the public. Bureaucrats could also simply wait for the next cabinet reshuffle, while prolonging procedures in the ministry, for instance by concealing important documents. In addition, conspiracy theories about "suicide attacks" committed by the administrative staff against their superiors abound in Japan. By leaking information on internal problems in the ministry to the media, the bureaucrats could effectively undermine the position of their minister or even, depending on the gravity of the problem, of the head of the government (Zakowski 2015: 20–21). Perhaps Prime Minister Abe Shinzō himself fell victim to such a "conspiracy." In 2007, the employees of the Ministry of Health, Labor and Welfare presumably leaked to the media and opposition politicians information on missing pension records. According to journalists sympathizing with Abe, the bureaucrats' aim was to impede the Kantei's plan to prohibit *amakudari* practices.[1] As indicated by Abiru (2016: 113), Ministry of Health, Labor and Welfare employees felt additional resentment against Abe due to his plans for privatizing the Social Insurance Agency. The bureaucrats could afford such behavior as they knew it would be their political superior to take the blame for their actions.

Another veto player were the ruling party backbenchers. Until the electoral reform of 1994, shifting alliances between faction bosses remained a decisive factor behind the election of LDP presidents. In order to avoid defections of separate groups, a set of unwritten rules was established in the dominant party. The prime minister traditionally distributed party and governmental portfolios according to recommendations from faction leaders (Uchida 1983: 134–139; Iseri 1988: 124–129). The offices of ministers or membership of the LDP General Council and the LDP Policy Research Council Board were assigned proportionally according to each faction's size, while some posts, e.g. LDP deputy secretaries-general, or vice-chairpersons of the LDP General Council and the LDP Policy Research Council Board, were distributed in equal number to each faction (Satō & Matsuzaki 1986: 63). As a result, decision-making bodies both in the government and in the ruling party were composed of politicians representing various factions and interest groups rather than of the loyal executioners of the prime minister's policy agenda.

Along with the vertical structure of factions, the LDP was horizontally divided into parliamentary tribes (*zoku giin*) – informal groups of lawmakers who boasted considerable experience in a single legislative field and represented the interests of the corresponding pressure group and ministry (Yuasa 1986: 10–16). In particular, specialization in three fields – agriculture, construction, and commerce and industry – was considered the most profitable because it enabled protectionism toward influential groups of the electorate through farming subsidies, infrastructural projects, and development policies, respectively (Inoguchi & Iwai 1987: 133). The parliamentary tribes gained in prominence due to the institutionalization of the two-track decision-making process conducted in the government and in the LDP. No bill project could be approved as a cabinet decision nor submitted to the Diet unless it had been authorized by the LDP General Council (Sōmukai) and the LDP Policy Research Council (Seimu Chōsakai). Policy Research Council policy divisions (*bukai*) hosted different parliamentary tribes that almost monopolized decisions in their corresponding legislative fields. Together with bureaucrats from the corresponding ministry and companies from a particular industrial sector, each *zoku* formed a small "iron triangle" of vested interests (Stockwin 2008: 138). While the divisions between separate tribes blurred from the 1990s, parliamentary tribes survived and continued to affect the decision-making process.

Contrary to the veto players, the prime ministers possessed very weak institutional backing. Until 2001, only a limited staff of about 200 bureaucrats served in the Prime Minister's Office (Sōrifu) and the Cabinet Secretariat (Naikaku Kanbō). Moreover, most of the employees of these two bodies were only temporarily dispatched to them and still placed their loyalty in their home ministries rather than in the Kantei. On a regular basis, the bureaucrats informed their ministries about the prime minister's plans, which facilitated veto players in delaying or sabotaging any reforms orchestrated by the head of government (Makihara 2009: 60).

In addition to the administrative staff, the prime minister was directly assisted only by a handful of politicians. Among them, the CCS (*naikaku kanbō chōkan*) played the most important role. According to Article 13 of the Cabinet Law, he/she supervised the affairs of the Cabinet Secretariat and oversaw the duties of various offices within it (Ministry of Internal Affairs and Communications 2019). Originally, the CCS post had been entrusted to a promising mid-ranking politician, but over time, it gained in prominence. In 1966, the CCS received the status of a fully-fledged cabinet member. The rising gravity of the CCS was symbolized by the fact that two former CCSs, Abe Shinzō in 2006 and Fukuda Yasuo in 2007, became prime ministers without having served as the heads of any ministry. The CCS handled various policies entrusted to her/him by the head of government and acted as a spokesperson for the prime minister and the cabinet. Depending on personal skills, he/she could more or less efficiently overcome the bureaucratic and parliamentary tribes' sectionalisms while coordinating the implementation of the Kantei's policy agenda (Shinoda 2000: 72). Gotōda Masaharu (1989: 2), who had served as the CCS under the Nakasone cabinet, noted that, due to the proximity to the prime minister, the CCS was often dubbed the "housewife" (*nyobō yaku*) of the head of government. Interestingly, one of the CCS's sources of power was a special fund amounting to more than one billion yen that could be freely used without keeping strict documentation. It is presumed that this money was spent on mitigating the opposition parties' resistance against government-sponsored bills or on conducting backstage diplomacy (Hoshi 2014: 139–145). While the CCSs were overloaded with responsibilities, they were directly assisted only by four staffers – one private secretary and three civil servants dispatched from the Ministry of Foreign Affairs (MOFA), Ministry of Finance (MOF), and the National Police Agency (Eda & Ryūzaki 2002: 86–90).

The administrative deputy CCS (*jimu kanbō fukuchōkan*), in turn, was considered as the top bureaucratic post. It remained an unwritten tradition to appoint him/her from among the former administrative vice-ministers of one of the institutions that originated from the powerful pre-war Ministry of Home Affairs, such as the Ministries of Interior, Labor, Health and Welfare, or from the National Police Agency. These central institutions were considered as more concerned about the national interests than other ministries, and thus less partial regarding the prime minister's policy agenda. The administrative deputy CCS was in charge of daily policy coordination between the Kantei and the ministerial bureaucrats (Shinoda 2000: 72–73). What symbolized his/her influence on decision-making process was the fact that she/he presided over the Administrative Vice-Ministers' Council (Jimujikantō Kaigi). This organ, which functioned based on tradition rather than official regulations, was composed of the top bureaucrats from all ministries who gathered on Mondays and Thursdays. Importantly, while the Administrative Vice-Ministers' Council remained a largely ceremonial body, only the decisions authorized by it were submitted for the cabinet's approval. For that reason, it was not uncommon to portray the administrative deputy CCS as a shadow eminence behind the prime minister.

Although administrative deputy CCSs often changed when a new prime minister assumed office, sometimes they were reappointed by successive administrations, which ensured stability of the decision-making process. In particular, Administrative Deputy CCS Ishihara Nobuo became famous for the fact that he served seven heads of government from 1987 to 1995. His successor, Furukawa Teijirō, remained in office even longer, under five administrations from 1995 to 2003. Reflecting on his role in the decision-making process, Ishihara stressed that, paradoxically, while cabinet meetings could take place without the presence of the prime minister, the administrative deputy CCS could hardly be replaced, as it was he who explained the agenda of each meeting (Ishihara, Mikuriya & Watanabe 1997: 191). Furukawa (2015: 114), in turn, emphasized that, as he was overloaded with work, he hoped to resign when Koizumi Jun'ichirō assumed office in 2001. Nevertheless, Furukawa was persuaded to continue his duties by the new prime minister and his entourage, who needed the administrative deputy CCS's experience to conduct structural reforms. These testimonies account to the importance of this post in ensuring a good flow of information in the government and efficient communication between the Kantei and the bureaucrats.

Initially, there was only one politically nominated (parliamentary) deputy CCS (*seimu kanbō fukuchōkan*). Out of consideration for the House of Councilors, however, in 1998, their number was raised to two, each representing one house of the Diet. At the same time, an additional post of deputy CCS for crisis management (*naikaku kiki kanrikan*) was created. Just like the CCS office, the post of political deputy CCS gained in prominence over time. Initially, she/he was selected from among third or fourth-term lawmakers. From the end of the 1980s, however, it became more common to nominate for this position more experienced politicians, who had already served as ministers. Being observers in the meetings of LDP executives, political deputy CCSs coordinated the Kantei's policies with the parliament and the ruling parties. They also assisted the head of government and the CCS in daily matters, for instance by acting as on-the-spot spokespersons for the prime minister during his/her visits abroad (Eda & Ryūzaki 2002: 90–97).

In addition, five secretaries (*naikaku sōri daijin hishokan*) – one political and four administrative – were charged with clerical work for the head of government. The political secretaries, often called "senior," "chief," or "executive," were usually selected from among private staffers, relatives, or journalists who enjoyed the full trust of the prime minister. Their responsibilities often exceeded ordinary administrative work, such as preparing daily schedules for the head of government. Political secretaries acted as liaisons between their superior and her/his faction, as well as attending numerous ceremonies and meetings on his/her behalf. Accompanying the prime minister on a daily basis, they often became influential advisers. The four posts of administrative secretaries, in turn, were divided among the representatives of the MOF, Ministry of International Trade and Industry (MITI, Ministry of Economy, Trade and Industry – METI – since 2001), MOFA, and the National Police Agency. They acted as liaisons between the head of government and their home ministries. Administrative secretaries accompanied the prime minister in shifts, carrying all the documents necessary to provide him/her with information on current issues (Shinoda 2000: 77–78; Eda & Ryūzaki 2002: 106–109).

The prime minister's powers were considerably strengthened in the 1990s. The electoral reform of 1994 introduced a mixed system of single-seat districts and proportional representation together with state subsidies for political parties. As a result, individual candidates from one party no longer had to compete against each other, which weakened factionalism. Central party authorities' better control over candidate endorsements and party finances, accompanied by stricter rules on private donations to separate politicians, provided the ruling party president and the secretary-general with new tools for disciplining backbenchers (Krauss & Pekkanen 2011: 235–236; Shinoda 2013: 55–58). In the 1990s, Koizumi Jun'ichirō had opposed electoral reform as he claimed it would lead to the suppression of free exchange of opinions in the LDP. Paradoxically, he later admitted that he became the main beneficiary of the reform after becoming prime minister in 2001, as under the old system, it would have been unthinkable for him to impose such a daring decision as the privatization of Japan Post on the ruling party (Koizumi & Tokoi 2018: 132–161).

The central government reform, which entered into force in 2001, further strengthened the prime minister's powers. To weaken bureaucratic sectionalism, the number of ministries and central agencies was reduced from 23 to 12. At the same time, the number of political appointees in the government rose considerably due to the replacement of political vice-ministers (*seimujikan*) with vice-ministers (*fukudaijin*) and the creation of new posts of parliamentary vice-ministers (*daijin seimukan*). The Prime Minister's Office was restructured into the Cabinet Office (Naikakufu), together with the agencies for economic planning, management and coordination, science and technology, as well as Okinawa development. The new body was placed above all ministries, thus gaining easier access to all the information necessary to efficiently run the government. In addition, four "important policy councils" (*jūyō seisaku kaigi*) were placed directly under the prime minister to assist him/her with decision-making on economic and fiscal policy, science and technology, gender equality, and disaster prevention (Neary 2002: 124–127; Woodall 2014: 174–176). The revised Cabinet Law clarified both the head of government's right to propose new policies during cabinet meetings and the Cabinet Secretariat's leading role in drafting and coordinating "important policies" (*jūyō seisaku*) (Ministry of Internal Affairs and Communications 2019). To deal with the new tasks, the Cabinet Secretariat staff was increased from 186 to 648 between 2000 and 2005 (Makihara 2009: 56). Thanks to the new powers and stronger administrative backing, the prime minister could more efficiently control all the ministries, thus overcoming the limitations stemming from the rule of dispersed management.

Furthermore, the number of high-ranking officials in the prime minister's entourage was raised considerably. In particular, apart from the ten regular ministers and the CCS, the head of government could fill the remaining positions in the cabinet with ministers of state for special missions (*tokumei tantō daijin*). Serving in the Cabinet Office, they were less prone to ministerial sectionalisms, which enabled them to focus on the tasks prioritized by individual prime ministers. Such policy areas included those dealt with by the four "important policy councils," as well as other pending problems, e.g. Okinawa and Northern Territories affairs, consumer and food safety, measures for the declining birthrate, or regulatory reform. Most often, one minister was entrusted with several portfolios of this kind (Woodall 2014: 177). The head of government also gained the possibility of issuing an executive order to hire more than five secretaries and to establish *ad hoc* policy offices that dealt with different issues. The prime minister's policymaking initiatives in various fields were additionally supported by special advisers (*naikaku sōri daijin hosakan*), whose maximum number was raised from three to five. Moreover, posts of assistant CCSs (*naikaku kanbō fukuchōkanho*) in charge of domestic, international, and security affairs were created in the Cabinet Secretariat. All three were placed in a single office, which, to some extent, weakened turf battles between them (Shinoda 2007: 70–76).

The electoral and administrative reforms considerably facilitated, but did not guarantee, strong prime ministerial leadership. Both in pre- and post-reform periods, the efficiency of the Kantei depended on the personal skills of the heads of government and their direct entourages. While some prime ministers succeeded in taking advantage of the institutional tools at their disposal, others failed to remain in office long enough to establish an effective top-down leadership.

How prime ministers have failed

Taking into account the strength of veto players and the relative institutional weakness of the Kantei, it is not surprising that most heads of government were unable to successfully pursue bold policy initiatives, especially in the pre-reform period. Most importantly, short terms in office impeded them in initiating and implementing more profound institutional changes. Even after the electoral and administrative reforms of the 1990s, short-lived administrations abounded. Among the factors that decided about the prime ministers' inability to remain in office for longer periods of time, one can enumerate the existence of strong political contenders for power, backstage dependence on powerful faction leaders, low popularity among the public, lack of charisma or a clear policy agenda, overly ambitious policy goals, as well as poor performance of the ruling party in the upper house elections.

Strong political rivalry

Factional divisions in the ruling parties often fueled competition for the prime ministerial post. At the beginning of the postwar period, the camps led by two strong statespersons – Yoshida Shigeru and Hatoyama Ichirō – dominated the Japanese political landscape. After the parliamentary election in 1946, the American occupation authorities purged from public offices the leader of the victorious Japanese Liberal Party, Hatoyama, who was thus forced to ask former MOFA bureaucrat Yoshida to become prime minister. Following implementation of the San Francisco Peace Treaty of 1951, Hatoyama was allowed to return to politics, but Yoshida had no intention of ceding leadership back to him. Before Hatoyama's return, Yoshida had created a powerful faction in the ruling party, whose members were recruited mainly from among former high-ranking bureaucrats. A large part of prewar politicians, in turn, supported Hatoyama. The rivalry between the two camps was underwritten by an ideological confrontation. While the former group eagerly embraced the pacifist Constitution that allowed Japan to focus on economic recovery under an American security umbrella, the latter demanded a revision of the Constitution and a more equal alliance with the US. In 1954, the Hatoyama camp defected from Yoshida's Liberal Party, established the Japanese Democratic Party, and grasped power thanks to extra-governmental cooperation with the Socialists (Fukunaga 2004: 183–186).

In subsequent years, the LDP, which was created in 1955 as a result of the merger of the Yoshida and Hatoyama camps, was frequently shaken by factional struggles that tested prime ministerial leadership. Hatoyama resigned in 1956, after the normalization of diplomatic relations with the Soviet Union. In order to achieve this diplomatic success, he had to please other faction bosses by promising to step down from office. Such a pattern of sacrificing one's prime ministership for the sake of realizing an unpopular policy agenda would be later repeated by several heads of government, baptized "kamikaze fighters" by Shinoda (2000: 208–209). Examples of Japanese prime ministers who had to face strong intra-party contenders in the golden era of factionalism were Kishi Nobusuke (1957–1960), Miki Takeo (1974–1976), Fukuda Takeo (1976–1978), and Ōhira Masayoshi (1978–1980). It is symptomatic that in order to assuage intra-party opposition against the new security treaty with the US in 1960, Abe Shinzō's grandfather, Kishi, probably promised succession as LDP leader to as many as four other faction bosses: Ōno Banboku, Ikeda Hayato, Ishii Mitsujirō, and Fujiyama Aiichirō (Ōno 1962: 145–149; Kishi 1983: 455–456; Uchida 1983: 55–59; Tsuchiya 2000: 191–192). As he admitted, his tenure ended prematurely, which prevented him from realizing most of his policy plans (Kishi 1983: 639–640). In 1976, Prime Minister Miki had to face similar pressure from faction leaders. Despite relatively high popularity among the public, Miki stepped down from office, taking responsibility for the poor performance of the LDP in parliamentary elections (Iyasu 1983: 266–269; Tsuchiya 2000: 208–209). Only two years later, his successor, Fukuda Takeo, was defeated by Ōhira Masayoshi in the first primaries among rank-and-file LDP members. Ōhira owed his success less to his popularity among the public than to institutional support from the powerful Tanaka faction and its funds needed to recruit new LDP members (Iyasu 1983: 287–288). In 1980, the Fukuda and Miki factions repaid Ōhira by abstaining from voting on a no-confidence motion, thus ensuring its passage. The intense factional struggle eventually contributed to Ōhira's death from overwork during the electoral campaign that ensued (Tsuchiya 2000: 212). Despite fierce factional struggles, the LDP avoided major splits and managed to remain in power until the beginning of the 1990s. Nevertheless, in June 1993, the Hata/Ozawa faction supported the motion of no confidence against the Miyazawa cabinet and defected from the LDP, which led to the loss of power by the dominant party (Morita 1993: 15–16).

While intra-party divisions were most severe before the electoral reform in 1994, also in the post-reform period, the existence of strong anti-mainstream groups in the ruling party could force the prime minister to resign. For example, both Kan Naoto and Noda Yoshihiko had to face a challenge from the powerful Ozawa camp in the DPJ. Accusing Kan of mishandling the Fukushima Daiichi Nuclear Power Plant crisis, the Ozawa and Hatoyama factions planned to support a motion of no-confidence against the prime minister in June 2010. Kan managed to avoid the passage of the motion in exchange for promising to resign after the compilation of the second supplementary budget and the passage of the Reconstruction Basic Law. His successor, Noda Yoshihiko, in turn, clashed with the Ozawa camp over taxation reform. Protesting against the VAT hike, in July 2012, Ozawa defected from the DPJ together with 49 Diet members who established a party called People's Life First (Kokumin no Seikatsu ga Daiichi). This and subsequent splits weakened the ruling party, which lost power in the December 2012 parliamentary election (Zakowski 2015: 128–173).

Existence of strong contenders for power in the ruling party naturally undermined the position of the prime minister, forcing him/her to waste time and energy on intra-party struggles. While the electoral reform weakened factionalism, faction bosses still waited for a good opportunity to challenge the leadership of the head of government, which often destabilized the government.

Backstage dependence on a powerful faction boss

Another reason for weak prime ministerial leadership was the excessive dependence of the head of government on a powerful faction boss who influenced policymaking from behind the scenes. Suzuki Zenkō (1980–1982), Kaifu Toshiki (1989–1991), and Hatoyama Yukio (2009–2010) had to share power with "shadow shoguns" Tanaka Kakuei, Takeshita Noboru, and Ozawa Ichirō, respectively.

Former prime ministers usually enjoyed great authority in the ruling party and often continued their political careers as senior party advisers (Ochi 2015: 102). In extreme cases, they preserved their role as power brokers. Despite being involved in the Lockheed corruption scandal, former Prime Minister Tanaka Kakuei remained the leader of the largest faction in the LDP at the beginning of the 1980s.[2] It was his support that decided about the election of Suzuki as LDP leader in 1980. Analogically, former Prime Minister Takeshita Noboru, who had to resign due to the Recruit scandal in 1989, continued influencing politics from behind the scenes as a power broker behind the Kaifu government.[3] The phenomenon of "puppeteers" (*kuromaku*) was characteristic not only of the LDP. Prime Minister Hatoyama Yukio was elected as DPJ leader in 2009 thanks to support from his predecessor Ozawa Ichirō, who was accused of taking bribes from a construction company.

The prime ministers who assumed office in lieu of real power brokers had limited room for maneuver in promoting their own policy agenda. In reality, it was not the head of government, but the leader of the biggest faction, who remained the main decision maker. By avoiding running in the LDP presidential election, the boss of an intra-party group that gathered one-eighth of the parliamentarians could theoretically control the government. After all, control of over half of the politicians of the intra-party mainstream ensured control over the inner circle of power in the LDP, which gave domination over the whole ruling party and meant that the backstage boss kept half of the Diet in check, thus steering the government from behind the scenes (Iseri 1988: 170–171). Relying on the *kuromaku*, the prime minister could display leadership only in the fields that did not excessively infringe on the political interests of his patron.

The fate of such heads of government was to a great extent dependent on the political strategy of their "puppeteers." For instance, in 1991, the Takeshita faction suddenly decided to switch their support to Miyazawa Kiichi, which forced Prime Minister Kaifu to step down from office. Despite relatively high popularity among the public, Kaifu was thus unable to implement political reforms (Asahi Shinbun Seijibu 1992: 16–51). As Kaifu (2010: 147–156) admitted, until the last moment, he planned to dissolve the House of Representatives and use the public support to impose reforms on the ruling party. Nevertheless, after the Takeshita faction voiced their opposition to the dissolution, he preferred to resign rather than to revive factional struggles in the LDP.

Due to the fact that prime ministers were not always real power brokers in Japanese politics, they often had limited possibilities to pursue their own policy agenda. Similarly to strong intra-party rivalry, however, dependence on *kuromaku* became less common after the demise of factionalism.

Low popularity

While strong intra-party rivalry and backstage dependence on powerful faction bosses were characteristic particularly of the pre-reform period, from the 1990s, it was the support rate for the cabinet among the public that gained in prominence as a factor undermining or bolstering the position of the head of government. Tanaka Kakuei (1972–1974), Takeshita Noboru (1987–1989), Uno Sōsuke (1989), Mori Yoshirō (2000–2001), Abe Shinzō (2006–2007), Asō Tarō (2008–2009), and Hatoyama Yukio (2009–2010) were all prime ministers who had to resign or lost an election due to low popularity.

When Tanaka assumed prime ministerial office in 1972, he enjoyed high popularity as a young "self-made man" and the first head of government without higher education. Nevertheless, accusations of "money politics" – buying political support – caused a dramatic drop in the government support rate (from 60.5% in October 1972 to 21.2% in June 1974) and Tanaka's resignation in 1974. A similar fate awaited Tanaka's successor as faction leader. Takeshita Noboru had to step down from office in 1989 due to accusations of corruption in the Recruit scandal. Another factor that contributed to an abrupt decrease in government popularity was the introduction of a 3% consumption tax in 1988. As a result, while in November 1987, the Takeshita cabinet enjoyed the support of 51.5% of respondents, in April 1989, this percentage dropped to a record-low 8%. Both Tanaka and Takeshita had to resign despite being leaders of the most powerful factions in the LDP.

Prime ministerial leadership in Japan 23

Low popularity of the government forced the even faster stepping down from office of those prime ministers who did not possess similarly strong factional bases of support in the ruling party. Takeshita's successor, Uno Sōsuke, resigned after only two months as prime minister due to accusations of having a mistress (in June 1989, his cabinet was supported by 22.8%, and in July 1989, by only 12.9% of respondents) (Yomiuri Shinbunsha Yoron Chōsabu 2002: 486–490).

As the strength of LDP factions weakened due to the 1994 electoral reform, the public image of the prime minister gained in prominence. For example, Mori Yoshirō had bad press from the very beginning of his term in office. He was elected as LDP leader in 2000 through backstage negotiations between the representatives of intra-party factions, which met with strong criticism from the media as a revival of old politics. Frequent slips of the tongue of the head government, such as calling Japan "a country of gods with the emperor at the center," worsened the situation even further. Criticism of the cabinet peaked when Mori failed to stop playing golf to react to the sinking of the Japanese ship *Ehime Maru* that was rammed by an American submarine near Hawaii (Honda 2008: 257–259). Mori's popularity dropped from 41.9% in April 2000 to merely 8.6% in February 2001, which forced the prime minister to resign (Yomiuri Shinbunsha Yoron Chōsabu 2002: 493).

A sudden decrease in popularity was also one of the main reasons of the failure of the first Abe administration. Paradoxically, Abe to a great extent owed his victory in the September 2006 LDP presidential election to opinion polls. As reported by *Yomiuri Shinbun* in June 2006, he was considered the most suitable successor to Prime Minister Koizumi by 43.7% of respondents, well ahead of Fukuda Yasuo (19.3%), Asō Tarō (4%), and Tanigaki Sadakazu (1.9%) (Satō 2008: 298). High popularity among the public facilitated Abe in gathering a large, supra-factional group of supporters in the LDP. Abe himself admitted that without the opinion polls it would have been unthinkable for him to become an LDP presidential candidate at that stage (Satō 2008: 297). Aged 52, he was the youngest head of government ever and the first prime minister born after the Second World War. Moreover, he assumed office after only a 13-year parliamentary career, which was much shorter than his predecessors: Koizumi's 28 years, Mori's 30 years, Obuchi's 34 years, and Hashimoto's 32 years. Initially, the Abe cabinet enjoyed the third highest rate of support in Japanese history – 63% according to *Asahi Shinbun*, 67% according to *Mainichi Shinbun*, and 70% according to *Yomiuri Shinbun*. According to *Nihon Keizai Shinbun*, the Abe cabinet ranked the second highest with 71% of support (Satō 2008: 301).

Nevertheless, just like many other heads of government, Abe quickly wasted his initial political capital. At the end of 2006, he allowed 11 defectors who had opposed the privatization of Japan Post to return to the LDP, which was interpreted by the public as the beginning of the abandonment of the neoliberal policy that had been massively supported by the electorate in the 2005 parliamentary election (Yomiuri Shinbun Yoron Chōsabu 2009: 163–164). Moreover, Abe quickly developed conflicts with journalists. Immediately after assuming office, he reduced the number of press conferences and treated reporters he knew preferentially. The journalists reciprocated by showing the prime minister in a bad light. A series of corruption scandals of government officials further exacerbated the image of the government. In December 2006, Research Commission on the Tax System Chairperson Honma Masaaki resigned after the media reported that he allowed a female friend to live in an apartment for civil servants (Ōsaka 2014: 303–305). In the same month, Minister in Charge of Administrative Reform Sata Gen'ichirō stepped down from office due to allegations of having received funds for the maintenance of a fictitious office. At the same time, Minister of Agriculture, Forestry and Fisheries, Matsuoka Toshikatsu, was found guilty of financial abuse, but Abe refused to dismiss him. After Matsuoka committed suicide in May 2007, Akagi Norihiko, who became the new agriculture minister, was quickly accused of similar illegal practices. To make things worse, cabinet members made slips of the tongue that were broadly commented on by the media. In January 2007, Minister of Health, Labor and Welfare Yanagisawa Hakuo called women "birth-giving machines," and in June 2007, Defense Minister Kyūma Fumio stated that the US "had no choice" but to drop atomic bombs on Hiroshima and Nagasaki. However, the severest blow to the government was the missing pension scandal. In the spring of 2007, the media and opposition parties reported serious problems in the functioning of the social security system. It was revealed that the annuities payment history of millions of Japanese had vanished during the digitalization of pension records (Yomiuri Shinbun Seijibu 2008: 30–60).

As a result of these unfortunate events, the cabinet support rate started nose diving only two months after the inauguration of the Abe administration. As shown in Figure 1.1, in February 2007, the percentage of respondents who opposed the Abe cabinet surpassed that of those who supported the government. Afterwards, the support rate stabilized for several months at a decent level of 40%, but before the July 2007 upper house election it once more started to fall, mostly due to the missing pension records issue. The LDP support rate followed the government's popularity. According to an opinion poll conducted by *Asahi Shinbun* immediately after the electoral defeat, the cabinet support rate dropped to a mere 26%, LDP's to 21%, while the number of those who declared a lack of support for the government rose to 60%. The *Yomiuri Shinbun* opinion poll indicated similar results – when Abe stepped down from office in September 2007, he was supported by only 29% of respondents, less than half of the percentage from one year earlier (Yomiuri Shinbun Seijibu 2008: 382).

The support rate for the cabinets of Abe's successors followed a similar pattern. Most significantly, the low popularity of Asō Tarō, who became prime minister in September 2008, buried LDP's chances of remaining in

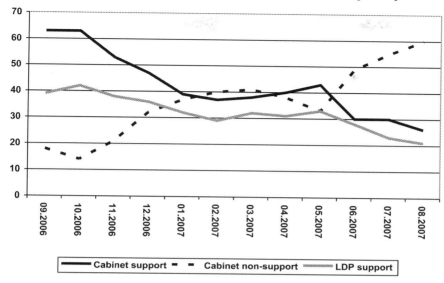

Figure 1.1 Cabinet and LDP support rates under the first Abe administration.

Source: Compiled by the author, based on *Asahi Shinbun*.

power. Asō's popularity as a manga fan quickly turned out to be limited to relatively small groups of *otaku* subculture (Sugawara 2009: 126–142). His frequent gaffes, funny slips of the tongue, and lavish lifestyle put into question his competence to be prime minister. Moreover, Asō was criticized for selecting cabinet members from among his closest friends instead of paying attention to the expertise of potential ministers. For instance, Nakagawa Shōichi was appointed as finance minister despite his alcohol problems. Asō accepted his resignation only after Nakagawa held a scandalous press conference when drunk during the G-7 meeting in Rome. For these reasons, the support rate for the Asō cabinet fell from 49.5% in September 2008 to about 20% at the moment of Diet dissolution in August 2009 (Yomiuri Shinbun Seijibu 2009: 17–222).

The alternation of power in 2009 did not change the pattern of abrupt drops in cabinet support rate only a few months after the formation of a new government. In fact, DPJ leader Hatoyama Yukio lost in popularity even faster than his LDP predecessors. As well as an inability to fulfill electoral promises, the DPJ administration was criticized for two troublesome scandals. While DPJ Secretary-General Ozawa Ichirō faced charges of corruption, the prime minister himself was accused of having taken illegal donations amounting to 15 million yen per month from his mother – a successor to the fortune of the founder of the Bridgestone company. As a result, within only eight months, the government support rate fell from 75% in September 2009 to a mere 19% at the time of Hatoyama's resignation in June 2010 (Yomiuri Shinbun Seijibu 2010: 106–286).

Theses numerous examples of prime ministers who resigned because they lost credibility in the eyes of the public indicate how important it was for the head of government to maintain high popularity. Whenever the government support rate fell to approximately 30%, anti-mainstream politicians intensified their efforts to change the balance of power in the ruling party, and a 20% level of support was usually considered the border line for stepping down from office.

Lack of charisma or a clear policy agenda

Prime ministers who lacked charisma or did not manage to offer a convincing policy agenda to the public, such as Suzuki Zenkō (1980–1982), Fukuda Yasuo (2007–2008), and Kan Naoto (2010–2011), were also prone to fail. Charisma is an ambiguous term. According to Weber (1968: 48), it is "a certain quality of an individual personality, by virtue of which he is set apart from ordinary men and treated as endowed with supernatural, superhuman, or at least specifically exceptional powers or qualities." In line with this classical definition, charismatic leaders attracted popular support thanks to their non-routine behavior rather than their skills in using state apparatus.

It was difficult for uncharismatic prime ministers to arouse the masses, especially if they lacked a clear policy agenda. After assuming office in 1980, Suzuki Zenkō proclaimed a "policy of harmony" (*wa no seiji*) aimed at assuaging frictions in the LDP (Uji 1983: 40–41). While this consensus-seeking attitude constituted a remedy against previous factional struggles, the prime minister failed to present a coherent policy program that would appeal to the voters. Trying to please veto players, he was unable to make bold decisions necessary to reduce the budget deficit. Discouraged by the risk of exacerbating factional struggles, Suzuki surprisingly announced he would not seek re-election as LDP president in 1982 (Shinoda 2000: 209). A similar conciliatory posture characterized Fukuda Yasuo, who was known for his tendency to seek balance between various groups in the LDP (Kabashima & Steel 2010: 85). In November 2007, the prime minister tried to form a grand coalition with the DPJ, but his endeavors ended in a failure. Eventually, discouraged by the unceasing quarrels with the opposition parties who held a majority of seats in the upper house, Fukuda suddenly stepped down from office in September 2008.

Contrary to Suzuki and Fukuda, DPJ leader Kan Naoto was considered as an ill-tempered, quarrelsome, and potentially even charismatic politician. Yet, just like the two consensus-seeking prime ministers, "fretful Kan" (*ira Kan*), as he was dubbed by the media, failed to appeal to the public with a consistent policy agenda. He initiated his tenure with VAT hike plans in late spring and early summer 2010, subsequently started insisting on liberalization of trade through accession to the Trans-Pacific Partnership (TPP) in autumn 2010, and eventually focused on promoting a vision of a nuclear-free society after the Fukushima Daiichi Nuclear Power Plant crisis in March 2011. These frequent shifts in policy priorities undermined Prime Minister Kan's credibility and contributed to a gradual decrease in his popularity, which led to his resignation in August 2011 (Zakowski 2015: 118–119).

Although charisma was not a necessary prerequisite for a successful prime ministership, a lack of it required the head of government to at least boast technocratic skills or appeal to the public with a convincing policy agenda. Leaders who failed to demonstrate their abilities in any of these fields usually did not survive long in office.

Overly ambitious policy goals

On the other hand, a clear, but overloaded and overly ambitious policy agenda could also decrease the chances for the prime minister to succeed. Both Abe Shinzō under his first administration (2006–2007) and Hatoyama Yukio (2009–2010) miscalculated their abilities to hastily conduct bold reforms without taking into consideration the strength of veto players.

After assuming office in 2006, Abe promoted an ambitious policy of "breaking out of the postwar regime" (*sengo rejīmu kara no dakkyaku*). His endeavors focused on establishing the Ministry of Defense (MOD), introducing patriotic education to schools, and plans for constitutional revision. These goals were not only difficult to realize in a short period of time, but they also did not address the daily needs of the ordinary Japanese, such as the social security system or employment policy reforms. Due to his eagerness to promote right-wing initiatives instead of focusing on the economic agenda, Abe was ironically called by the media a prime minister who "can't read the moods" (KY, abbreviation from *kūki ga yomenai*) (Honda 2008: 272). Even Administrative Deputy CCS Matoba Junzō, who shared the ideological stance of the prime minister, admitted that instead of selecting priorities, Abe tried to implement too many reforms in too short a period of time. Matoba (2013: 23–26) deplored the fact that among the Abe cabinet members, there were no veteran politicians who would understand that successful policy-making should resemble a marathon, not a 100-meter sprint race.

In addition, Abe pursued an ambitious goal of institutional reform. In particular, persuaded by Minister of State for Regulatory Reform Watanabe Yoshimi, he put much effort into passing the anti-*amakudari* law in June 2007. This revolutionary bill prohibited the practice of arranging post-retirement employment for bureaucrats by their home ministries. As the new law endangered the interests of all bureaucrats, it encountered strong opposition from the administrative staff, including Administrative Deputy CCS Matoba. While the legislation project was rejected by the Administrative Vice-Ministers' Council, Abe arbitrarily ordered it to be submitted for the cabinet's approval, thus ignoring a 120-year-old unwritten rule that cabinet meetings' schedules should be arranged through a unanimous decision by the administrative vice-ministers (Shinoda 2013: 110). It is probable that the leaking of information on missing pension records by the Ministry of Health, Labor and Welfare bureaucrats was aimed at impeding implementation of the controversial law.

The policy agenda of Prime Minister Hatoyama Yukio went even further. The DPJ came to power in September 2009 with plans to completely overhaul the decision-making process and strengthen the political leadership over the bureaucrats. Nevertheless, it quickly turned out that changing all policy-making practices in a fortnight was impossible. While refusing to use the bodies that had effectively served as policy venues for the LDP government, such as the Council on Economic and Fiscal Policy (CEFP), Hatoyama was unable to provide a sufficient legal underpinning to the new organs that he established: the National Strategy Unit and the Government Revitalization Unit. Due to the complexity of the legislative process that can sustain only a limited number of important bills in a single session, the Bill Establishing Political Leadership was never passed by the Diet. Overwhelmed with tasks and antagonized by their administrative staff, the political appointees in each ministry could not work properly. As a result, instead of conducting bold reforms, Hatoyama gave the impression of a powerless leader who could not even control his own government (Zakowski 2015: 64–90).

Moreover, during the electoral campaign in 2009, Hatoyama made an unwise vow, which he was unable to fulfill. When he visited Okinawa, he promised to relocate the US Marine Corps Air Station Futenma outside of Japan, or at least outside of the prefecture. Because this base caused severe safety issues for the inhabitants of Ginowan City, in 2006, Tokyo and Washington had agreed on its relocation to the Henoko Bay near Nago City. However, local citizens and ecologists demanded the complete removal of the base from Okinawa. As the 2006 agreement had been the result of 10-year long negotiations between Japan and the US, it was extremely difficult to persuade the Obama administration to make any concessions on that matter. In addition, MOFA and MOD bureaucrats sabotaged the efforts of their political superiors. Eventually, in May 2010, Hatoyama had to give consent to the initial plans of relocation to the Henoko Bay, which prompted the Social Democratic Party (SDP, Shakai Minshutō) to leave the ruling coalition and led to Hatoyama's resignation (Zakowski 2015: 97–104).

Excessive hastiness in implementing one's policy agenda usually did not end well for Japanese prime ministers. Due to the strength of veto players and the limitations of the legislative procedures, the heads of government who failed to carefully choose their priorities simply bottlenecked the decision-making process, which undermined their credibility as effective leaders.

Upper house electoral defeat

Another factor behind prime ministers' stepping down from office, often in conjunction with those already mentioned, was a defeat in the House of Councilors election. Uno Sōsuke (1989), Hashimoto Ryūtarō (1996–1998), and Abe Shinzō (2006–2007) had to resign, taking responsibility for the LDP's poor performance in upper house elections.

Loss of control over the House of Councilors put a great constraint on prime ministerial leadership. The upper house election was held every three years when half of its members were chosen for six-year long terms. Contrary to the House of Representatives, the upper house could not be dissolved by the head of government, but it enjoyed almost equal powers to the lower house. In only a few cases (voting on the budget, international treaties, no-confidence motions, and election of the prime minister) did the decisions of the House of Representatives prevail. All other bills, including supplementary budget laws, had to be passed by both houses. The House of Representatives needed two thirds of the votes to overrule the House of Councilors' decision. The upper house could vote censure motions (*monseki ketsugi an*) against the head of government or individual ministers, but they were not legally binding, unlike the lower house's no-confidence motions (*naikaku fushin'nin an*) (Takenaka 2010: 5–20).

Due to the electoral system that combined single- and multimember districts, it was more difficult for the LDP to maintain a majority of votes in the upper than in the lower house. The so-called "twisted Diet" (*nejire Kokkai*), when opposition parties assumed control over the House of Councilors, occurred for the first time since 1956 in July 1989. At that time, the LDP faced strong criticism even from its traditional electorate for the Recruit scandal, introduction of VAT, and liberalization of trade in agricultural products. Prime Minister Uno's affair with a geisha additionally tarnished the image of the ruling party, while the Japan Socialist Party (JSP, Nihon Shakaitō), chaired by first female party leader, Doi Takako, gained in popularity. As a result, although the LDP remained the biggest party with 109 seats in the 252-member house, it won only 36 seats, far fewer than the JSP's 46 seats. Immediately after the election, Uno stepped down from office (Honda 2008: 181–183).

The LDP did not manage to regain independent control over the House of Councilors until 2016, which forced it to enter into temporary policy agreements or ruling coalitions with smaller parties. As pointed out by Takenaka (2010: 184–186), this situation contributed to a gradual increase in the importance of the LDP House of Councilors Caucus chairs who gained more influence on the decision-making process. In the July 1998 election, the LDP once more performed much worse than anticipated, winning only 44 seats, far fewer than the 61 seats won six years earlier. The main reasons were the popular criticism of an increase in consumption tax from 3% to 5% just before the Asian financial crisis of 1997, as well as the nomination of Satō Kōko, who in the 1980s had been sentenced for corruption, as minister for central government reform. Prime Minister Hashimoto Ryūtarō took full responsibility for the poor electoral result and stepped down from office at the end of July 1998. As Koizumi stressed, the fate of the government was often decided in the years of upper house elections. When Koizumi was chosen as LDP president in April 2001, his opponents hoped to challenge his leadership after the House of Councilors election, but, thanks to a landslide victory, he was easily reelected as party leader in August 2001 (Koizumi & Tokoi 2018: 180–181).

When Abe assumed the prime ministerial post for the first time, in 2006, the LDP–Kōmeitō coalition enjoyed a comfortable majority in both houses. However, Administrative Deputy CCS Matoba Junzō warned Abe that he should fulfill his electoral pledges at a "slow pace," not to encounter too strong opposition that could endanger the LDP's chances of winning the House of Councilors election in July 2007. According to Matoba (2013: 24–25), it would have been sufficient to focus on a single important issue, such as education reform, and proceed with the other goals after the electoral victory. However, Abe did not intend to wait with the realization of his ambitious policy agenda, which, along with illegal donations scandals of his ministers and the missing pension records issue, damaged his public image. In fact, paradoxically, the strong position of the LDP House of Councilors Caucus to some extent exacerbated the upper house electoral defeat. It was LDP House of Councilors Caucus Chair Aoki Mikio who persuaded Abe to restore party membership to the incumbent members of parliament that had defected from the LDP in 2005. Aoki's motivation was to strengthen party structures before the upper house election, but this move only contributed to a further decrease in the support rate for Abe cabinet. As a result, the LDP won only 37 seats, far fewer than the 64 seats won six years earlier. The DPJ, in turn, received 60 seats. In total, the DPJ possessed 109 seats, 6 more than the LDP. As the largest party in the chamber, the DPJ elected Eda Satsuki as House of Councilors speaker and Nishioka Takeo as the chair of the Steering Committee, thus gaining complete control over scheduling the house's proceedings (Takenaka 2010: 266–273). According to an *Asahi Shinbun* (2007a: 3) opinion poll, the biggest reasons for LDP's defeat were the missing pension records problem (44%), scandals of ministers (38%), and a widening gap between the rich and the poor (12%).

Despite the electoral defeat, Abe initially refused to resign. In August 2007, he conducted a cabinet reshuffle, which indicated that he was determined to continue his government. However, voices of discontent increased to the point that even Mori Yoshirō, leader of the faction from which Abe originated, started putting pressure on the prime minister to assume full responsibility for the poor electoral result. Adding to that his health problems that emerged in the summer of 2007, Abe announced his resignation on September 12, and stepped down from office on September 26, 2007, exactly on the first anniversary of his cabinet's inauguration. The public felt disappointed with the Abe administration. According to an *Asahi Shinbun* (2007b: 3) opinion poll, 51% of respondents were content with the resignation (29% were not), but 70% deemed that its timing, only two days after a policy speech in the Diet, was irresponsible (22% thought otherwise). Only 4% evaluated highly the achievements of the Abe cabinet, 33% had a mildly positive opinion on its results, while 45% held a moderately, and 15% a decisively negative judgment on the fruits of the Abe administration. At that point, Abe had wasted all the political capital he had inherited from Koizumi after the 2005 parliamentary election. When he stepped down from office, 50% of respondents demanded a swift dissolution of the House of Representatives (43% thought otherwise), and the percentage of the supporters of a DPJ-led government (41%) surpassed that of those who wanted continuation of LDP's domination (33%).

Because it was the lower house that selected the prime minister, the heads of Japanese government did not necessarily attach sufficient importance to the upper house election. They probably did not want to constantly operate in the mode of electoral campaign, as it largely complicated realization of any decisions that were perceived as controversial by voters. Nevertheless, the failure to grasp control over the House of Councilors irreparably tarnished the image of the prime minister as a successful leader, which often forced him to resign.

The abovementioned examples show that remaining in office longer than two or three years was a daring task for the prime minister. Until the 1990s, frequent change of the head of government could be attributed mostly to factional struggles in the ruling party, and afterward to the problems with maintaining high popularity of the government. It is natural that the heads of government who assumed office for short periods of time did not have the time to draft and implement profound reforms against veto players. Also, Abe's first prime ministership ended after merely one year due to a sudden decrease in his cabinet's popularity, overly ambitious policy agenda, upper house electoral defeat, and health problems.

How prime ministers have succeeded

The factors that decided about prime ministers' successes were mirror images of the causes of their failures. In order to remain in office for a longer period of time, the head of government had to maintain either a solid basis of factional support in the ruling party or a high popularity among the public. Instrumental in achieving these tasks were personal charisma, bold economic policy agenda, and leading the ruling party to successive electoral victories.

Exploitation of factional base of support

During the era of strong factionalism, the crucial method for being elected as LDP president and remaining in office was maintaining a powerful support base in the ruling party. Yoshida Shigeru (1946–1947, 1948–1954), Ikeda Hayato (1960–1964), and Satō Eisaku (1964–1972) succeeded in establishing stable mainstreams in the LDP that became the foundations for their leadership.

Yoshida assumed office under the exceptional conditions of American occupation, but he still owed his long term in office, to a great extent, to a stable support base in the ruling party. After the purge of prewar politicians imposed by the US, Yoshida recruited into politics many high-ranking bureaucrats, such as Ikeda Hayato from the Ministry of the Treasury and Satō Eisaku from the Ministry of Railways. The strength of the "Yoshida school" explains why it was so difficult for Hatoyama, who returned to politics in 1951, to successfully challenge Yoshida's domination. Subsequently, it was the two leading followers of Yoshida who exploited the power of this "conservative mainstream" (*hoshu honryū*) in the LDP (Iseri 1988: 111–116). Until the Abe era, Ikeda and Satō proved the most successful prime ministers in seeking reelection as LDP leaders – Ikeda achieved this feat twice, and Satō three times.

Ikeda assumed office in 1960, thanks to an alliance with the Satō and Kishi factions. However, once his rivalry with Satō escalated, he switched to an agreement with the Kōno, Miki/Matsumura, Ōno, and Kawashima groups in 1962. The same mainstream decided about the reelection of Ikeda for a third term in 1964. Unfortunately, the prime minister resigned only two months later due to a diagnosis of laryngeal cancer. Ikeda's authority became unquestioned to the point that, under these exceptional circumstances, he was entrusted with the decision on who should become his successor. He used this privilege and nominated Satō Eisaku as LDP leader (Tsuchiya 2000: 193–198).

While Yoshida and Ikeda, despite possessing a solid base of support in the LDP, faced challenges from strong contenders for the prime ministership, Abe's great uncle Satō was in a much more convenient position. As most of high-profile faction bosses had died before or at the beginning of his term in office (Ōno Banboku in 1964, Kōno Ichirō and Ikeda Hayato in 1965), for several years, there were no serious rivals that could endanger his leadership of the LDP. Under these conditions, an alliance with the Fukuda faction, patronized by Satō's brother Kishi, ensured Satō's reelection in 1966, 1968, and 1970. Satō became famous for his power-balancing abilities. During his bureaucratic career, he had dealt with negotiations with railway trade unions, through which he learned to respond flexibly to the arguments of the other side (Gotō, Uchida & Ishikawa 1994: 56–57). Thanks to this experience, after becoming a politician, Satō knew how to balance different factions and make friends through backstage deals and the careful selection of associates. To approach individual politicians, Satō even read and memorized lists of lawmakers that included their CVs (Senda 1987: 182–183). Thanks to that practice, he was dubbed "Satō for personnel affairs" (*jinji no Satō*) (Uchida 1969: 60). This power-balancing style of leadership turned out very effective, but it was not highly valued by voters. The support rate for the Satō cabinet oscillated between 30% and 40% from 1964 to 1971, and dropped to about 20% at the end of Satō's prime ministership (Yomiuri Shinbunsha Yoron Chōsabu 2002: 486).

The long tenure in office by Satō prompted LDP faction leaders to introduce a limit of two terms as LDP leader in the 1970s. Tanaka Kakuei (1972–1974) and Takeshita Noboru (1987–1989), who took over leadership of the former Satō group, tried to emulate the success of their former faction boss, but due to corruption scandals they had to prematurely step down from office and rule from behind the scenes as *kuromaku*. Nevertheless, after the 1994 electoral reform, the significance of presiding over a strong intra-party group weakened, just like the solidarity among faction members.

High popularity among the public

As shown by the example of Kaifu Toshiki, during the period of strong factionalism, popularity among the public did not guarantee the prime minister's political survival. However, a high cabinet support rate, coupled with skilful balancing between factions, could be a recipe for success. Moreover, after the weakening of factions in the 1990s, the prime minister's popularity became a crucial factor that decided about his/her fate. Nakasone Yasuhiro (1982–1987) and Koizumi Jun'ichirō (2001–2006) are the best examples of heads of government who skillfully shaped their image in the media.

When Nakasone became prime minister in November 1982, his support base in the ruling party was rather weak. As a leader of one of the smaller factions, he owed his election as LDP president to an alliance with Tanaka Kakuei. Reliance on Tanaka severely limited Nakasone's ability to rule in a top-down manner. Not only was the prime minister dependent on the "shadow shogun's" political plans, but also his public image was tainted due to the backstage agreement with the corrupt politician. The media dubbed the Nakasone cabinet "Tanakasone" because many of its members, including the CCS, as well as LDP executives, such as the secretary-general, came from the Tanaka faction (Narai 1988: 195). For these reasons, at the beginning of Nakasone's term in office, the support rate for his cabinet was not overly high, amounting to 40.1%. However, after Tanaka suffered a stroke in 1985, Nakasone became more independent of the most powerful faction in the LDP. In 1985 and 1986, the support rate for his government almost always exceeded 50%, and in October 1987, before Nakasone stepped down from office, it remained at sound 48.8% (Yomiuri Shinbunsha Yoron Chōsabu 2002: 488–489). After five and half years as the prime minister, his authority was so strong that the leaders of the three largest LDP factions – Takeshita Noboru, Abe Shintarō, and Miyazawa Kiichi – entrusted to him the decision on who should become his successor.

Nakasone was perhaps the first Japanese prime minister who consciously utilized the media to shape his positive image among the public. As he said, his government could be compared to a "glider" – "without the wind of the people, the glider will fall. (...) The reason I held office for so long was the support of the people. I changed the performance of the government.

There is that expression 'television democracy.' I kept up with this phenomenon by utilizing my staff and 'the brains'" (Nakasone 1991: 46). Pharr (1986: 55–56) noted that the personal style of Nakasone consisted of three major characteristics. Firstly, he was "a master of the photo opportunity," who invited the media to report on his daily activities, such as meditation in a Zen temple. Secondly, Nakasone used his international activity to score points at home. Thanks to frequent participation in the summits of the most influential world leaders and ties of friendship with US President Ronald Reagan, dubbed the Ron–Yasu relationship, he made the Japanese feel that their country had become an important player in the international arena. Thirdly, Nakasone knew how to convey his message to the public in a straightforward and vivid fashion.

A similar strategy was employed by Koizumi Jun'ichirō, who won the LDP presidential election in 2001 thanks to high popularity among the public, not factional politics. Known as a maverick in the ruling party, Koizumi understood how to approach the media and convey his political vision directly to the voters. By issuing short statements full of catchy slogans, he effectively prevented journalists from distorting his message (Uchiyama 2007: 9). Koizumi took advantage of the media's tendency to report sensational news and he frequently declared that he would smash the "forces of resistance" (*teikō seiryoku*) against the reforms, even if he had to destroy the LDP. Contrary to the majority of his predecessors, he did not avoid appearances on entertainment shows, and in non-mainstream media, soft-news magazines, sports newspapers, and tabloids. At the same time, Koizumi allowed television reporters to cover his daily press briefings in the Kantei. Just like Nakasone, he also attracted media attention by frequent participation in high-level international summits. As indicated by Kabashima and Steel (2010: 79–104), the high television exposure of the prime minister contributed to his increased popularity. According to *Asahi Shinbun* opinion polls, at the beginning of the Koizumi administration in May 2001, the cabinet support rate was at a record high, exceeding 80%, and for most of Koizumi's long tenure, it fluctuated between 40% and 50% (Zakowski 2015: 33–34).

Another factor that enabled Koizumi to avoid an excessive decrease in popularity was his ability to influence agenda-setting by the media. When the prime minister faced criticism, he often made bold policy moves, especially in foreign policy, which attracted the interest of the media. For example, in May 2004, he suddenly announced a plan to visit North Korea on the same day the media reported that the prime minister had not paid his annuities in the past. As the leader of the main opposition party, DPJ, Kan Naoto had just resigned due to a similar problem, without diverting the media's attention to the North Korean issue, the prime minister would have probably been put under strong pressure to step down from office (Yomiuri Shinbun Seijibu 2006: 61–73).

The prime minister's high ratings among the public enabled him to assuage the voices of discontent in the ruling party and discouraged potential contenders from running against the head of government in party presidential elections. A popular leader not only created a sense of stability among LDP lawmakers, but he also attracted new voters in parliamentary elections.

Charisma

One of the factors that could ensure a high cabinet support rate was the charisma of the prime minister. Yoshida Shigeru (1946–1947, 1948–1954), Nakasone Yasuhiro (1982–1987), and Koizumi Jun'ichirō (2001–2006) were considered charismatic leaders, endowed with exceptional personal qualities that helped them to act in non-routine ways.

Despite his confrontation with the Hatoyama faction, Yoshida enjoyed considerable authority in the ruling party, stemming not only from his bureaucratic experience, but also from his personal qualities. Nicknamed "one man" for his determination in pursuing traditional values, Yoshida emanated the energy needed to lead the country in the difficult times of the US occupation (Davis 1996: 115–120). What helped him to gain respect from ruling party members, by whom he was initially treated as an outsider, was his ability to speak with the Americans in a straightforward way and oppose US initiatives whenever he felt they were detrimental for Japan. In particular, Yoshida remained relentless in rejecting American demands for Japan's remilitarization. It is this image as a tough negotiator that earned him a reputation as a charismatic leader (Shinoda 2000: 113, 207).

Being a professional politician, Nakasone was equally aware of the importance of charisma in leading the country. According to him, a good leader should be characterized by four traits: ability to anticipate the future situation in order to employ an appropriate political strategy, persuasion skills, power to combine human resources, information and necessary funds, as well as a "personal charm" to motivate subordinates and maximize their effectiveness. While all these factors were important, the last one was crucial. As Nakasone (2010: 145) pointed out, the "personal charm" was obtained not only through knowledge or education, but rather through the experience of overcoming various kinds of difficulties. Nakasone owed his image as a charismatic leader to his relentlessness in pursuing neoliberal reforms, coupled with a common perception of his role as an important player in world politics.

Koizumi possessed a personal charm similar to Nakasone's. Uchiyama (2007: 210–219) called him a "prime minister full of pathos" because he was often driven by emotions rather than rationality. As a former rock musician and an outsider in the LDP, Koizumi devoted his whole political career to pursuing policy goals that had never been popular in the ruling party. His determination in promoting structural reforms despite the hardships associated with them alienated him from most of his party colleagues, but it also coined his unyielding character that met with popular respect. Koizumi's extraordinary behavior earned him the reputation of a natural leader and a charismatic figure.

The lawmakers who acted extraordinarily were often treated as outsiders in the LDP, as the political culture of the ruling party valued collectiveness and factional loyalty above non-routine behavior. For that reason, it was difficult for eccentrics to assume top positions. It is symptomatic that all three heads of government mentioned above owed their initial success to propitious circumstances – Yoshida to the American occupation, Nakasone to the support of the Tanaka faction, and Koizumi to an increase in the importance of rank-and-file party members' votes in the 2001 LDP presidential election.[4] Yet, once charismatic politicians became prime ministers, they could more easily than their colleagues maintain high popularity, thus remaining in office longer than average.

Bold economic policy agenda

Another instrument for appealing to the public was an ambitious economic policy agenda. Ikeda Hayato (1960–1964), Nakasone Yasuhiro (1982–1987), and Koizumi Jun'ichirō (2001–2006) were skillful in inspiring voters through imposing on others and implementing bold challenges in the economic sphere.

Perhaps the first policy program that really inspired the masses in the postwar period was the "plan of doubling the income" (*shotoku baizō keikaku*), announced by Prime Minister Ikeda Hayato in 1960. Its aim was to increase the level of salaries in Japan by two times within a decade. In order to stimulate economic growth without inciting excessive inflation, Ikeda pursued an ambitious policy based on three pillars: public works projects, tax reductions, and social security system reform. He focused on building transportation infrastructure, power plants, schools and hospitals, promoting technological innovations, improving the health insurance system, decreasing income and corporate taxes, as well as reducing interest rates to encourage private investments (Itō 1985: 141–163). The results exceeded expectations. The average economic growth rate in the 1960s amounted to 11.6% – far above the scheduled 7.2%. The rapid increase in the level of salaries contributed to the creation of a strong middle class in Japan (Kusano 2012: 104–106).

Initially, Nakasone's policy agenda was not as focused on the economy as Ikeda's. Immediately after assuming office in 1982, the prime minister announced "a general settlement of post-war politics" (*sengo seiji no sōkessan*), which became the motto of his government. This slogan meant modification of the policies that had been effective in the past in order to adapt them to the needs of the next generation. It encompassed such ambitious goals as the shift from exclusively economic to more defense policy-oriented foreign policy and the privatization of inefficient state-owned companies

(Nakasone 2010: 131–132). Nevertheless, Nakasone adapted the details of the reforms to the possibilities of implementing them under his tenure. Most significantly, while he was an eager partisan of constitutional revision, he made no attempts at achieving this goal, as he knew it would be impossible in the political situation of the 1980s. Instead, he eventually focused on the economic dimension of the reforms. Nakasone gained popular support for rationalizing budget expenses, privatizing the Japanese National Railways, and stimulating private investments through deregulation. At the same time, he introduced partial reforms in the security field, for instance by abandoning the limitation of 1% of GNP for defense expenses.

Similarly, Koizumi appealed for "structural reforms without sanctuaries" (*seiiki naki kōzō kaikaku*). He based his policy on three pillars: elimination of bad loans, creation of a competitive economic system, and financial structural reforms aimed at a reduction of public debt. By proposing a fresh policy agenda, he gave hope to the public that Japan could overcome the economic stagnation of the "lost decade" that had started with the bursting of the bubble on the Tokyo Stock Exchange in 1990. While Koizumi did not cure all the ailments of Japan's economy, he managed to mitigate the bad loans problem, cut budget expenses for public works projects, pass the Japan Post privatization bill through the Diet, and improve the competitiveness of Japan's economy on world markets (Kusano 2012: 222–239). The slogan of structural reforms dominated the political debate to an extent that it overshadowed Koizumi's controversial endeavors in the diplomatic and security spheres. Public opinion was divided in its evaluation of sending Self-Defense Forces (SDF) to the Indian Ocean and Iraq and the annual visits to the Yasukuni Shrine, but these decisions had only a temporary impact on the popularity of the cabinet.[5]

The three abovementioned examples indicate that a bold policy agenda could contribute to strengthening prime ministerial leadership, if its realization was realistically planned. It is not insignificant that the heads of government who succeeded focused their efforts mainly on ensuring a high economic growth rate. The public would support structural reforms against veto players especially in the economic sphere, which was the legislative field most closely related to the daily lives of the Japanese people. As such, it remained the most efficient strategy to implement the other, less popular, policy goals, at a slower pace, after having gained considerable political capital on one's economic credentials.

Successive electoral victories

All the abovementioned factors increased the chances of the ruling party's winning parliamentary elections, which further reinforced the leadership of the prime minister. The main interest of lawmakers was to be reelected, so they valued those heads of government whose popularity and skills ensured their good electoral performance. Due to the high frequency of elections to both houses of the Diet, the leadership of the prime minister was almost constantly tested, which put on him/her pressure to polish the electoral agenda and wisely choose the moment of dissolution of the House of Representatives.

Prime Minister Satō Eisaku used to say that the power of the head of government was directly proportional to the number of elections and inversely proportional to the number of cabinet reshuffles under his leadership (Ishibashi 2019: 12). Indeed, each time the prime minister remained in power after a parliamentary election, his leadership strength increased. Only the strongest heads of government, in turn, could afford to postpone a cabinet reshuffle and overcome pressure from backbenchers who aimed at gaining governmental portfolios. Satō led the LDP to victories in two elections to the House of Representatives (in 1967 and 1969), as well as three to the House of Councilors (in 1965, 1968, and 1971), which remained a record number for an LDP leader until the second Abe administration. It is symptomatic that while, on average, Satō reshuffled his cabinet on an annual basis, the periods between reshuffles were generally longer at the end of his tenure, with the longest one amounting to 18 months from January 1970 to July 1971.

Prime Minister Nakasone, in turn, used his prerogative of Diet dissolution to maximize the scale of electoral victory. In June 1986, he dissolved the House of Representatives and called a lower house election on the same day as the scheduled upper house election. This move was aimed at raising voter turnout, which, coupled with the popularity of the Nakasone cabinet, ensured the good performance of the LDP. The ruling party managed to win as many as 300 seats in the 512-member lower house – 45 more than in the previous election. The JSP, in turn, maintained only 86 seats, thus losing 27. Thanks to the landslide victory, Nakasone was, exceptionally, allowed to extend his term in office as LDP president by an additional year. Especially for him, the Joint Plenary Meeting of Party Members of Both Houses of the Diet changed party rules (Ishikawa 2004: 157–160).

Dissolution of the House of Representatives by Prime Minister Koizumi in August 2005 was much riskier. The LDP seemed to be weakened due to expelling the lawmakers who opposed the Japan Post privatization bill from the party. In the constituencies of defectors, Koizumi endorsed competing candidates, who were baptized by the media as "assassins." As a result, the media's attention was diverted from analyzing the policy program differences between the LDP and its main rival, the DPJ, to reporting on duels between reform-minded candidates and anti-reform politicians in separate constituencies. Thanks to imposing the main topic of the electoral campaign, the ruling party achieved a landslide victory. The LDP managed to win as many as 296 out of 480 seats in the House of Representatives, much more than the 237 seats won in 2003. The DPJ, in turn, shrank from 177 to 113 lawmakers (Uchiyama 2007: 100–101, 253).

Thanks to successive electoral victories, the prime ministers strengthened their position vis-à-vis the bureaucrats and the ruling party. The massive popular support for the government's policy agenda provided a convenient argument for putting pressure on the administrative staff and backbenchers to fulfill electoral promises. In addition, large groups of newly elected first-term lawmakers generally felt obliged to remain loyal toward the prime minister.

While in the pre-reform period, the prime ministers owed their reputation as strong leaders mainly to stable factional bases of support in the ruling party, their popularity among the public gained in importance in the 1990s. Thanks to personal charisma and a bold economic policy agenda, the heads of government could inspire their closest entourage as well as the masses. However, the decisive factor that enabled prime ministers to remain in office longer than average was the myth of their invincibility. As evidenced by the prolongation of Nakasone's tenure until 1987, party rules could be easily bent or changed if only a majority of LDP lawmakers believed that the incumbent leader would ensure the best electoral performance for the ruling party.

Dynamics of prolonged prime ministership

The examples of failures and successes of prime ministers in implementing their policy agenda indicate that the most successful were those heads of government who managed to remain in office for a longer period of time. Shorter terms in office made realization of a single urgent policy goal possible, often at the expense of sacrificing one's prime ministership, but were usually insufficient to conduct more profound reforms. Extended tenure, in turn, enabled long-term planning, enhancing one's support base in the ruling party, strengthening the Kantei, and, eventually, implementing gradual institutional reforms.

Long-term planning

It is symptomatic that those prime ministers who remained in office more than one term did not rush the realization of their policy agenda. In the case of structural reforms that encountered strong opposition from veto players, long-term planning was a necessary measure. Successful prime ministers were aware of the fact that changing decision-making mechanisms and shaping political practices required a lot of time and flexibility. Just like regular poker players, they pursued cumulative gains rather than making decisions that could yield them a high one-time return, but were coupled with high risks.

Asked about what makes a person a leader, Nakasone Yasuhiro (1991: 40–41) said: "It's the same whether it's business or government. You must be able to set goals, persuade everyone, and have everyone participate.

And you have to help create enthusiasm. That is all." According to him, all statespersons who achieved great things were flexible regarding the methods of realizing their goals. As Nakasone often changed alliances and agreed to compromises and half-measures over his whole political career, he was dubbed a "weathercock" (*kazemidori*). Nevertheless, he claimed that he was not ashamed of that nickname, as he never lost sight of his ultimate plan of reforming Japan (Nakasone 2004: 27, 160–161). Nakasone emphasized that in order to succeed, it was crucial to plan the decision-making process over a longer term. Firstly, the prime minister would unofficially discuss selected policy ideas with his staff and ministers. It would take approximately half a year for the initial plans to ripen before establishing an official committee on the matter with academics, economists, and journalists. The committee would be then used as an effective medium for public relations, and the results of its deliberations would be publicized by the newspapers and television. Nakasone admitted that he failed to conduct tax reform because he hurried too much, without spending sufficient time on discussions. According to him, "In business or government, impatience can be a source of failure, even when the idea is sound" (Nakasone 1991: 48–49).

Koizumi Jun'ichirō was aware of the necessity of long-term planning as well. He deplored the fact that both Japanese prime ministers and the members of their cabinets changed too often, which made them prone to relying on bureaucrats in decision-making. Koizumi (1996: 87–92) claimed that the introduction of a general election of the head of government for a four-year tenure would enable the prime minister to focus on the realization of a longer-term policy agenda. Interestingly, Nakasone (2007: 522–524) had promoted a similar reform. Koizumi admitted that it was impossible to conduct real reforms in a short period of time. He started advocating the privatization of Japan Post when he was under 40- years old, became prime minister at 59, and managed to realize his plan at 64. According to Koizumi, while the powers of the head of government were extensive, one year was not enough to implement changes resisted by the whole ruling party (Koizumi & Tokoi 2018: 134–138). Just like Nakasone, Koizumi did not manage to introduce a prime minister's general election system, so he had to invest much energy into remaining in office. As Gaunder (2007: 122) pointed out, Koizumi's plan was "a progressive one, each reform building toward larger change." The prime minister knew how far he could proceed with the resources he had at his disposal at a given time. In order to promote the most difficult neoliberal reforms, Koizumi patiently waited until he had strengthened his position in the government and the ruling party after the third victory in the LDP presidential election in September 2003. It is this prudent posture that facilitated him in privatizing Japan Post despite resistance from veto players.

Nakasone and Koizumi probably learned patience as politicians who had spent most of their parliamentary careers outside of the LDP mainstream. Thanks to their profound knowledge of Japanese political culture, they were aware of the fact that, in order to succeed, the prime minister had to remain in office sufficiently long, which, depending on the situation, required agreeing to half-measures or even temporarily shelving one's policy agenda.

Enhancing the support base in the ruling party

The prime ministers who succeeded in extending their tenures could use the additional time to bolster their position in the ruling party. First-term lawmakers were most strongly attracted to the faction of the LDP leader. As a result, the intra-party group led by the head of government or the one from which he/she originated gradually gained in prominence. The more parliamentary elections were won under the incumbent prime minister, the more followers he/she gained.

Yoshida Shigeru was perhaps the first postwar prime minister who took full advantage of his position as the leader of the ruling party to introduce a large group of former bureaucrats into politics. Yoshida's followers would later form two powerful factions in the LDP, led by Ikeda Hayato and Satō Eisaku. Thanks to that, Yoshida exerted some influence from behind the scenes even after retiring from politics. Satō learned from his patron and gradually increased the size of his own faction over the years of his long prime ministership. While after the 1963 House of Representatives election, the Satō faction was composed of 91 members (46 from the lower and 45 from the upper house), following the subsequent lower house election victory under Satō's leadership in 1967, their number rose to 107 (53 from the lower and 54 from the upper house), and in 1971, one year before he stepped down from office, it still remained at a sound 105 (60 from the lower and 45 from the upper house) (Satō & Matsuzaki 1986: 243).

Similarly, Nakasone managed to attract new members to his faction when he was prime minister. As shown in Figure 1.2, at the beginning of his tenure in 1982, his group was composed of 49 lawmakers, but it swelled to 88 parliamentarians after the LDP's landslide victory in elections to both houses in July 1986. As a result, by 1987, it had advanced from fourth to second place in terms of members, slightly surpassing the factions led by Miyazawa Kiichi (87) and Abe Shinzō's father, Abe Shintarō (85). In addition, although the prime minister relied on an alliance with the powerful Tanaka–Takeshita faction, whose membership exceeded 100 lawmakers, thanks to his policy successes, he managed to gain supra-factional support in the LDP.

While Koizumi never became a faction leader and overtly ignored factional recommendations for cabinet posts, it was the Mori faction, from which he originated, that benefited most from his leadership. As shown in Figure 1.2, at the beginning of the Koizumi administration in 2001, the Mori faction was composed of 60 lawmakers, far fewer than the Hashimoto group's 99 members. In 2006, however, the balance of power between the two largest LDP factions was reversed – the Mori–Machimura group possessed

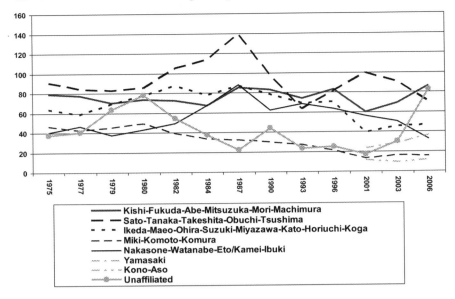

Figure 1.2 Evolution of the number of LDP faction members in 1975–2006.

Source: Compiled by the author, based on *Kokkai Binran* (1975–2006).

86 members, 16 more than the Tsushima (former Hashimoto) faction. Nevertheless, Koizumi was most interested in gaining supra-factional support. Thanks to his popularity, about 80 first-term LDP lawmakers entered the Diet as a result of the 2005 House of Representatives election. Baptized as "Koizumi's children" by the mass media, they generally remained loyal toward the prime minister and supported his neoliberal policy initiatives (Zakowski 2019: 85).

An extended tenure not only enabled the prime minister to introduce new politicians loyal toward him to the Diet, but it also strengthened the myth of his invincibility, which attracted additional followers. While in the pre-reform period, the heads of government used their position to increase the size of their factions, from the 1990s, they to a greater extent relied on supra-factional support in the LDP.

Strengthening the Kantei

Cautious long-term planning of the policy agenda and strengthening of the prime minister's position vis-à-vis backbenchers facilitated enhancement of the institutional backing to the head of government. Both Nakasone and Koizumi used their authority to redefine the role played by the Kantei.

Nakasone attached great importance to the recruitment of his administrative staff from the very beginning of his tenure. He instructed all ministries to select the prime minister's administrative secretaries from among the most promising bureaucrats who would aim at vice-ministerial posts in the future (Nakasone 2004: 40–41). Nakasone was the first prime minister who turned *ad hoc* advisory commissions into crucial policy venues of his government. In addition to the creative use of the preexisting bodies, Nakasone implemented some minor changes in the structure of the Kantei. In 1984, he established the Management and Coordination Agency charged with supervision of national personnel, policy coordination, administrative inspection, and administrative structure oversight. In 1985, the Subcommittee on the Functions of the Cabinet (Naikaku Kinō nado Bunkakai) was created under the umbrella of the Administrative Reform Promotion Committee. The Subcommittee proposed strengthening the coordination functions, administrative support, and intelligence collection abilities of the cabinet. As a result, the National Defense Council (Kokubō Kaigi) was replaced by the Security Council (Anzen Hoshō Kaigi), whose membership was broadened to include the CCS and the National Public Safety Commission chair (Angel 1988/1989: 594–600). What is important, the administration of the new council was to be handled by the National Security Office in the Cabinet Secretariat. Moreover, five new offices that dealt with information and research, public relations, internal affairs, security affairs, and external affairs were established in the Cabinet Secretariat led by CCS Gotōda Masaharu. The aim of the reforms was to enable a more active policy coordination by the Kantei (Shinoda 2007: 33–36).

Like Nakasone, Koizumi paid utmost attention to the selection of his administrative staff. Executive Secretary Iijima Isao carefully chose Cabinet Secretariat liaison office counselors. Without relying on the recommendations from separate ministries, he interviewed all the candidates to ensure that ties with their home ministries would not impede service to the head of government. Iijima (2006: 28–31) stressed that thanks to such a selection process, the counselors remained loyal toward the prime minister. They not only promoted Koizumi's policy initiatives as Cabinet Secretariat employees, but also acted as "shadow Kantei staff" after returning to their previous responsibilities. The prime minister also made full use of the experience, coordination skills, and personal connections among bureaucrats possessed by Administrative Deputy CCS Furukawa Teijirō, who "ensured that reform would not be accomplished at any drastic pace" (Makihara 2009: 69).

Thanks to strict control over the government, Koizumi managed to redefine the role played by bureaucratic organs. He even used the Administrative Vice-Ministers' Council – a bastion of bureaucratic power – to transmit instructions to civil servants in a top-down manner. The prime minister's intentions were often delivered by CCS Fukuda Yasuo to Administrative Deputy CCS Furukawa, who, in turn, directed them to top-level bureaucrats from all the ministries. At the same time, *ad hoc* policy offices were established under assistant CCSs to deal with the issues in question. The role of the administrative vice-ministers' meetings in the decision-making process was additionally weakened by the fact that the basic policies drafted by the CEFP – one of the four "important policy councils" created by the administrative reform – were not brought to its proceedings (Shinoda 2007: 68–78). The CEFP had been established under the Mori government, but it was Koizumi who fully used its potential. Just like *ad hoc* advisory commissions under the Nakasone cabinet, the CEFP became a vehicle for Koizumi's structural reforms.

Nakasone and Koizumi understood the importance of ensuring the policy coherence and institutional efficiency of the Kantei. In particular, they focused on empowering the Cabinet Secretariat as a central policy coordination organ in the government. Having loyal and competent staff at their disposal, the prime ministers could proceed to the implementation of their ambitious policy goals.

Conducting gradual institutional reforms and recognizing their limits

Enhancing one's position in the ruling party and strengthening the Kantei were the first steps toward a general redefinition of decision-making patterns. As backbenchers and bureaucrats saw that the prime minister's leadership was stable, they started to cooperate within the new institutional framework. What is interesting, however, is the fact that the heads of government who were the most successful in gradually redefining policymaking mechanisms during extended tenures made few institutional changes in the government and the ruling party. In fact, the two reforms that most strongly influenced the leadership of the prime minister – the change of the electoral system in 1994 and the administrative reform implemented in 2001 – were prepared by the short-lived cabinets of Hosokawa Morihiro (1993–1994) and Hashimoto Ryūtarō (1996–1998). It seems that it was more efficient to exploit and redefine the role of the preexisting decision-making bodies than waste one's political capital on trying to abolish them and replace them with new ones from scratch.

It is symptomatic that Prime Minister Yoshida Shigeru did not try to overhaul the political system imposed by the US occupation authorities, but rather adapted his leadership style to the new institutional setting. As Yoshida admitted, his aim was to make the Japanese parliamentarianism and bureaucracy approach the British model, in which the politicians put trust in the expert knowledge of the bureaucrats, and the administrative staff loyally implemented the decisions made by their political superiors. According to him, the ailment of Japan's post-war political system was the fact that those politicians who specialized in party politics had no administrative experience, while those who originated from the bureaucracy did not fully understand party affairs. In order to redress that situation, Yoshida stressed that he attached great importance to education. He appointed professional politicians as government members, and former bureaucrats as ruling party officials, thus enabling both groups to learn each other's work. Nevertheless, Yoshida knew that ensuring smooth cooperation between the politicians and the bureaucrats was a time-consuming process (Yoshida 1998: 301–203). While his policy did not necessarily make Japan's political system resemble the Westminster model, it contributed to the creation of many of the unwritten practices of the two-track decision-making process conducted in parallel in the ruling party and in the government, which survive until today.

Curiously, the political practices of each prime minister who ruled longer than average gradually became unwritten codes of conduct, even if the head of government did not really intend to implement any official institutional reforms. For instance, Prime Minister Satō's tendency to seek balance between various groups in the ruling party resulted in the establishment of the rule of seniority. By distributing governmental and party portfolios according to the number of times politicians had been elected, Satō avoided creating an impression that he favored one politician over another. Such objective rules of appointment facilitated the maintenance of solidarity of the prime ministerial faction and prevented the holding of grudges between politicians (Kitaoka 2008: 154–155). On the other hand, in subsequent years, seniority came to constrain the prime minister in the choice of his cabinet members. According to the standardized career path of LDP parliamentarians, in their first term, they became members of parliamentary committees and policy divisions in the LDP Policy Research Council, committee directors or division deputy chairpersons in their second term, political vice-ministers in their third term, LDP Policy Research Council policy division chairpersons in their fourth term, parliamentary committee chairpersons in their fifth term, and ministers in their sixth term (Inoguchi & Iwai 1987: 121). Such a system left little room for maneuver for the head of government to select suitable persons for appropriate tasks.

Because Japan experienced high economic growth during Satō's term in office, the prime minister was rarely faced with the necessity to challenge veto players. One of the most difficult tasks of the Satō cabinet was to fight the pollution of the natural environment, which became a grave problem as a result of rapid industrialization in the 1960s. Initially, Satō protected the interests of industrial circles, but eventually the public outcry forced him to act more decisively. Despite the risk of limiting economic growth, the government pushed through the Diet as many as fourteen environment-related laws in 1970, and it established the Environment Agency one year later (Barrett & Therivel 1991: 38–40). Satō's power-balancing techniques and inter-ministerial coordination skills proved helpful in promoting the reform.

As Nakasone and Koizumi became prime ministers under much less propitious economic circumstance than Satō, they shouldered the difficult task of conducting neoliberal reforms. Nakasone was proud of the fact that he managed to privatize the inefficient state-owned companies, such as the Japanese National Railways, Nippon Telegraph and Telephone Corporation, and Japan Tobacco, by a creative use of advisory councils that enjoyed only a weak legal foundation. The most significant role was played by the Second Provisional Administrative Reform Council (Daini Rinchō) presided over by former Japan Federation of Economic Organizations Chair Dokō Toshio. As Nakasone stressed, the Council successfully influenced even the budget compilation process, which had previously been under the exclusive jurisdiction of the Ministry of the Treasury (future MOF). While initially the bureaucrats from that ministry were unwilling to share their competences with the new body, they eventually became grateful that the Council managed to achieve a goal that had been vainly pursued by them for many years – a decrease in budget expenses. All administrative vice-ministers were simply instructed by the Council to uniformly cut the expenses of their ministries by 10%. Nakasone (2010: 134–144) emphasized that while he ruled in a top-down manner, he made maximum use of his personal connections to push ahead his policy agenda. For example, he directly asked high-ranking bureaucrats who had served together with him in the navy for cooperation. He also took advantage of the Tanaka faction's institutional strength to put pressure on those parliamentary tribes that opposed the reforms.

The administrative reform drafted by the Hashimoto cabinet, which entered into force in 2001, prepared the ground for Kantei leadership under the Koizumi administration. For that reason, Koizumi could strengthen his leadership without conducting radical institutional reforms. Due to considerable resistance from LDP backbenchers and coalition partner Kōmeitō, in 2002, he decided to reject most of the proposals of the LDP National Strategy Headquarters and the National Vision Planning Committee. The draft reforms postulated the abolition of advance screening of all bill projects by LDP decision-making organs and its replacement with a mere advance discussion without the necessity of acquiring the party's permission for realization of the cabinet's policy (Nakakita 2019: 186–187). Other recommendations included renunciation of holding regular meetings of administrative vice-ministers, nomination of cabinet members from among party executives, and a far-going civil service reform (Yasuoka 2008: 392–404). Instead of creating a new system from scratch, Koizumi preferred to take full advantage of the bodies created by the Hashimoto administrative reform and to invest his political capital in gradually redefining the role played by the preexisting institutions.

Similarly to Nakasone's reliance on the Second Provisional Administrative Reform Council, Koizumi took full advantage of the CEFP, supervised by Minister of State for Economic and Fiscal Policy Takenaka Heizō. Each year, the Council issued basic policies that imposed the general guidelines for the budget compilation process on all ministries, including the MOF (Iijima 2006: 21–23). Not to let veto players sabotage his efforts, Takenaka polished the Kantei's crucial initiatives in three-stages. The initial policy proposals were drafted in a small unit composed of reform-minded bureaucrats. Afterwards, the policy project gained support from the four private-sector CEFP members, and it was ultimately acknowledged by the prime minister. Such isolation of veto players from the decision-making process proved instrumental in ensuring the Kantei's control over the policy agenda (Takenaka 2006: 153–258). Nevertheless, just as in the case of the Second Provisional Administrative Reform Council under the Nakasone administration, it did not mean that MOF bureaucrats became openly antagonized with Koizumi. After all, budget cuts pursued by the government remained in line with their long-cherished goal of achieving budgetary balance (Uchiyama 2007: 52). The MOF maintained some connections with Koizumi through Prime Minister's Administrative Secretary, Tango Yasutake, and Assistant CCSs, Takeshima Kazuhiko and Fushiya Kazuhiko. The head of government remained relentless in pursuing his crucial policies, such as the Japan Post privatization, but he respected traditional decision-making patterns regarding other issues (Makihara 2018: 132–144).

The privatization of Japan Post was even more difficult than the privatization of the Japanese National Railways. After all, the railway trade unions were affiliated with the Socialists, while the postal employees provided considerable electoral support to the LDP. Koizumi entrusted the drafting of the plans of the reform to the CEFP, thus bypassing the Ministry of Internal Affairs and Communications bureaucrats and the LDP postal parliamentary tribe. The prime minister generally respected the principles of two-track decision-making and he made several concessions to veto players. In June 2005, the privatization of Japan Post was eventually authorized by the LDP General Council, though Koizumi ignored the unwritten tradition of unanimity. After passing the lower house, the privatization bill was rejected by the upper house in August 2005. In order to gain two-thirds of the votes necessary to overrule the House of Councilors' veto, Koizumi dissolved the House of Representatives. After a landslide victory, the LDP and Kōmeitō could easily pass the privatization bill (Uchiyama 2007: 94–102).

Nevertheless, institutional reforms did not always turn out to be durable. While Nakasone skillfully used the empowered Kantei to impose difficult reforms on veto players, his successors returned to traditional decision-making practices. For instance, the system of five offices established in the Cabinet Secretariat fell to the same sectionalism as all governmental institutions. Instead of cooperating, office directors refused to mutually share information received from their home ministries, and they often clashed over various policies (Eda & Ryūzaki 2002: 98–99). Similarly, after Koizumi stepped down from office, his successors failed to preserve the crucial role of the CEFP in the budget compilation process. Ōta Hiroko, Minister of State for Economic and Fiscal Policy under the first Abe administration, was not as skilful as Takenaka in managing the Council's proceedings. As a result, the bureaucrats and LDP backbenchers started regaining their influence on the decision-making process (Shinoda 2013: 110–111). These examples indicate how difficult it was for one prime minister to emulate the leadership style of another.

Most successful in overcoming resistance from veto players were the heads of government who remained in office sufficiently long to adapt their policy strategies to the institutional setting they encountered. It is the creative use of the preexisting policy venues, coupled with minor institutional changes in decision-making bodies under the prime minister's direct control, which enabled gradual redefinition of the rules of the game and the codes of conduct in the government and the ruling party.

Conclusion

The examples of prime ministers who failed and those who succeeded in creating a powerful Kantei confirm that in order to establish top-down decision-making mechanisms, the head of government had to create a strong support base in the ruling party and maintain a high support rate for the government, which, in turn, was facilitated by his/her charisma, bold policy agenda, and successive electoral victories. Due to the time-consuming nature of the decision-making process, prime ministers' initiatives rarely ended in success unless they were consistently promoted over a longer period of time. As such, a prolonged term in office was a necessary prerequisite to implement lasting reforms and to take advantage of the new institutional arrangements. It is symptomatic that the prime ministers who were the most successful in imposing their will on veto players – Nakasone Yasuhiro and Koizumi Jun'ichirō – made only minor changes in governmental and party structures. They privatized the Japanese National Railways and Japan Post, respectively, by creatively using the preexisting decision-making bodies rather than creating new ones from scratch. Their experience confirms that, due to the strength of veto players and the inflexibility of the official institutional structures, gradual institutional change remained the only viable method for implementing far-going reforms in Japan. It was simply more efficient to play one veto player off against another than to antagonize all of them and waste one's hard-gained political capital on overly ambitious goals. For instance, the fact that the aims of both Nakasone and Koizumi were largely consistent with the policy of the MOF, facilitated them in grasping control over the budget compilation process.

Contrary to Nakasone and Koizumi, Abe's first term in office abounded in strategic errors that undermined the prime minister's position in the government and the ruling party. Overconfidence in the stability of the government support rate made Abe believe that he could instantly become as efficient as Koizumi in imposing his will on veto players, even though he lacked Koizumi's experience and authority among the bureaucrats and LDP backbenchers. At the same time, excessive hastiness in the implementation of a right-wing policy agenda alienated Abe from a large part of the electorate. Numerous scandals with cabinet members and the missing pension records issue further shattered Abe's image as a credible leader. After the upper house election defeat in July 2007, voices of discontent in the LDP increased to the point that Abe had no choice but to step down from office. Paradoxically, this bitter lesson paved the way to Abe's long tenure after returning to power in 2012.

Notes

1. *Amakudari* ("descent from heaven") meant the tradition of employing retired bureaucrats on executive posts by public institutions and private companies.
2. In 1976, Tanaka was accused of taking bribes from US aerospace company, Lockheed Corporation, for arranging purchase of its aircraft by All Nippon Airways.
3. In 1988, it was revealed that the Recruit company had offered undisclosed stocks of its subsidiary, Cosmos, to many influential politicians, including Prime Minister Takeshita.
4. As a maverick, Koizumi did not enjoy much support in the LDP. Nevertheless, in the 2001 election, LDP executives decided to exceptionally increase the number of votes for each of the 47 prefectural party chapters from one to three and allow the holding of primaries among rank-and-file party members. Their aim was to show that the new LDP president would be elected by the ordinary Japanese, as opposed to Mori Yoshirō, who owed his prime ministership to a backstage agreement between intra-party factions. Thanks to a skilful electoral campaign, Koizumi unexpectedly won the primaries, which created pressure on lawmakers to switch their support to him. See Nakakita 2014: 208–211.
5. The Yasukuni Shrine in central Tokyo commemorates all the Japanese who died in the service of the emperor. As it also worships the souls of class-A war criminals, sentenced to death by the Tokyo Tribunal in 1948, since 1985, visits of Japanese prime ministers to the shrine have met with protests from China and South Korea.

References

Abiru, Rui (2016) *Sōri no Tanjō* [Birth of Prime Minister], Tokyo: Bungei Shunjū.
Angel, Robert C. (1988/1989) "Prime Ministerial Leadership in Japan: Recent Changes in Personal Style and Administrative Organization," *Pacific Affairs*, 61, 4: 583–602.
Asahi Shinbun (2007a) "Abe Shushō no Kongo, Yōsumi. San'insen Chokugo no Kinkyū Yoron Chōsa" [Future of Prime Minister Abe, Wait and See. Urgent Opinion Poll Right After the House of Councilors Election], August 2, morning edition, 3.
Asahi Shinbun (2007b) "Abe Shushō Jinin ni Jimin Shijisō mo Kibishii Me. 'Nattoku Dekinu' 61%. Asahi Shinbunsha Kinkyū Yoron Chōsa" [Also LDP Supporters' Harsh View on Prime Minister Abe's Resignation. 61% "Not Satisfied." Urgent Opinion Poll by Asahi Shinbun], September 14, morning edition, 3.
Asahi Shinbun Seijibu (1992) *Takeshita-ha Shihai* [Domination of the Takeshita Faction], Tokyo: Asahi Shimbunsha.
Barrett, Brendan F. D. & Therivel, Riki (1991) *Environmental Policy and Impact Assessment in Japan*, London and New York: Routledge.
Davis, Steven I (1996) *Leadership in Conflict. The Lessons of History*, Basingstoke and London: Palgrave Macmillan.

Eda, Kenji & Ryūzaki, Takashi (2002) *Shushō Kantei* [Prime Minister's Residence], Tokyo: Bungei Shunjū.

Fukunaga, Fumio (2004) *Sengo Nihon no Saisei – 1945-1965 Nen* [Regeneration of Postwar Japan – 1945-1965], Tokyo: Maruzen.

Furukawa, Teijirō (2015) *Watashi no Rirekisho* [My Curriculum Vitae], Tokyo: Nihon Keizai Shinbun Shuppansha.

Gaunder, Alisa (2007) *Political Reform in Japan. Leadership Looming Large*, London and New York: Routledge.

George Mulgan, Aurelia (2018) *The Abe Administration and the Rise of the Prime Ministerial Executive*, London and New York: Routledge.

Gotō, Motoo, Uchida, Kenzō & Ishikawa, Masumi (1994) *Sengo Hoshu Seiji no Kiseki* [The Path of Post-war Conservative Politics], part 2, Tokyo: Iwanami Shoten.

Gotōda, Masaharu (1989) *Naikaku Kanbō Chōkan* [Chief Cabinet Secretary], Tokyo: Kōdansha.

Hayao, Kenji (1993) *The Japanese Prime Minister and Public Policy*, Pittsburgh and London: University of Pittsburgh Press.

Honda, Masatoshi (2008) *Sōri no Yamekata* [Prime Minister's Way of Resigning], Tokyo: PHP Kenkyūjo.

Hoshi, Hiroshi (2014) *Kanbō Chōkan. Sokkin no Seijigaku* [Chief Cabinet Secretary. Politics of Aides], Tokyo: Asahi Shinbun Shuppan.

Iijima, Isao (2006) *Koizumi Kantei Hiroku* [Secret Records of the Koizumi Residence], Tokyo: Nihon Keizai Shinbunsha.

Iio, Jun (2008) *Nihon no Tōchi Kōzō* [Structure of Government in Japan], Tokyo: Chūō Kōron Shinsha.

Inoguchi, Takashi & Iwai, Tomoaki (1987) *"Zoku Giin" no Kenkyū* [A Study on "Parliamentary Tribes"], Tokyo: Nihon Keizai Shinbunsha.

Iseri, Hirofumi (1988) *Habatsu Saihensei. Jimintō Seiji no Omote to Ura* [Reorganization of Factions. Inside and Outside of LDP Politics], Tokyo: Chūō Kōronsha.

Ishibashi, Fumito (2019) *Abe "Ikkyō" no Himitsu* [The Secret of Abe's "Unilateral Strength"], Tokyo: Asuka Shinsha.

Ishihara, Nobuo, Mikuriya, Takashi & Watanabe, Akio (1997) *Shushō Kantei no Ketsudan. Naikaku Kanbō Fukuchōkan Ishihara nobuo no 2600 Nichi* [Decisions of the Prime Minister's Residence. 2600 Days of Deputy Chief Cabinet Secretary Ishihara Nobuo], Tokyo: Chūō Kōronsha.

Ishikawa, Masumi (2004) *Sengo Seiji Shi* [Postwar Political History], Tokyo: Iwanami Shoten.

Itō, Masaya (1985) *Nihon Saishō Retsuden 21 – Ikeda Hayato* [Biographies of Japanese Prime Ministers 21 – Ikeda Hayato], Tokyo: Jiji Tsūshinsha.

Iyasu, Tadashi (1983) *Seitō Habatsu no Shakaigaku. Taishū Minshusei no Nihonteki Tenkai* [Sociology of Party Factions. Japanese Evolution of Popular Democracy System], Kyoto: Sekai Shisōsha.

Kabashima, Ikuo & Steel, Gill (2010) *Changing Politics in Japan*, Ithaca and London: Cornell University Press.

Kaifu, Toshiki (2010) *Seiji to Kane – Kaifu Toshiki Kaikoroku* [Politics and Money – Memoirs of Kaifu Toshiki], Tokyo: Shinchōsha.

Kishi, Nobusuke (1983) *Kishi Nobusuke Kaikoroku – Hoshu Gōdō to Anpo Kaitei* [Memoirs of Kishi Nobusuke – Conservative Merger and Revision of Security Treaty], Tokyo: Kōsaidō.

Kitaoka, Shin'ichi (2008) *Jimintō – Seikentō no 38 Nen* [LDP – 38 Years of the Ruling Party], Tokyo: Chūō Kōron Shinsha.

Kohno, Masaru (1997) *Japan's Postwar Party Politics*, Princeton: Princeton University Press.

Koizumi, Jun'ichirō & Tokoi, Ken'ichi (2018) *Ketsudan no Toki – Tomodachi Sakusen to Namida no Kikin* [Time of Decision – Operation Tomodachi and the Fund of Tears], Tokyo: Shūeisha.

Koizumi, Jun'ichirō (1996) *Kanryō Ōkoku Kaitai Ron* [Discourse on the Demolition of the Bureaucratic Kingdom], Tokyo: Kōbunsha.

Kokkai Binran (1975–2006) Tokyo: Nihon Seikei Shinbunsha.

Krauss, Ellis S. & Pekkanen, Robert J. (2011) *The Rise and Fall of Japan's LDP. Political Party Organizations as Historical Institutions*, Ithaca and London: Cornell University Press.

Kusano, Atsushi (2012) *Rekidai Shushō no Keizai Seisaku. Zen Dētā. Zōhoban* [Economic Policy of Successive Prime Ministers. Full Data. Enlarged Edition], Tokyo: Kadokawa Shoten.

Makihara, Izuru (2009) "From a Clerk Room to Government Headquarters: The Cabinet Secretariat and its 'Rotation System' in Transition, 1997-2007," in Roland Czada & Kenji Hirashima (eds), *Germany and Japan after 1989. Reform Pressures and Political System Dynamics*, Tōkyō Daigaku Shakai Kagaku Kenkyūjo Kenkyū Shirīzu, 33, Tokyo: Tōkyō Daigaku Shakai Kagaku Kenkyūjo, 55–73.

Makihara, Izuru (2018) *Kuzureru Seiji o Tatenaosu. 21 Seiki no Nihon Gyōsei Kaikaku Ron*, [Reorganizing the Crumbling Politics. Discourse on Administrative Reform in the 21st Century Japan], Tokyo: Kōdansha.

Matoba, Junzō (2013) *Sono Toki, Nihon ga Ugoku. Watashi ga Mita Seiji no Uragawa* [At That Time, Japan Moves. The Other Side of Politics That I Saw], Tokyo: Kairyūsha.

Ministry of Internal Affairs and Communications (2019) "Naikakuhō" [Cabinet Law], January 16, 1947, revised April 26, 2019, https://elaws.e-gov.go.jp/search/elawsSearch/elaws_search/lsg0500/detail?lawId=322AC0000000005 (accessed May 25, 2020).

Morita, Minoru (1993) *Seikai Tairan. Jimintō Kaitai Shintō Sōsei* [Great Rebellion of the World of Politics. Disorganization of the LDP and Creation of New Parties], Tokyo: Tōyō Keizai Shinpōsha.

Nakakita, Kōji (2014) *Jimintō Seiji no Hen'yō* [Transformation of the LDP Politics], Tokyo: NHK Shuppan.

Nakakita, Kōji (2019) *Ji-Kō Seiken to wa Nanika? Renritsu ni Miru Tsuyosa no Shōtai* [What Is the LDP–Kōmeitō Government? True Image of the Strength Visible in the Coalition], Tokyo: Chikoma Shobō.

Nakasone, Yasuhiro (1991) *Yasuhiro Nakasone: The Statesman as CEO. From Overcoming the Agony of Defeat to the Japan in the World*, Tokyo: Yasuhiro Nakasone Office.

Nakasone, Yasuhiro (2004) *Nihon no Sōri Gaku* [Study on Japanese Prime Ministers], Tokyo: PHP Kenkyūjo.

52 Prime ministerial leadership in Japan

Nakasone, Yasuhiro (2007) Watashi no Rirekisho [My Curriculum Vitae], in Kishi Nobusuke et al., *Watashi no Rirekisho. Hoshu Seiken no Ninaite* [My Curriculum Vitae. Bearers of the Conservative Government], Tokyo: Nihon Keizai Shimbun Shuppansha, 461–574.

Nakasone, Yasuhiro (2010) *Hoshu no Yuigon* [Conservative Testament], Tokyo: Kadokawa Shoten.

Narai, Shigeo (1988) *Saishō – Nakasone Yasuhiro* [Prime Minister – Nakasone Yasuhiro], Tokyo: Taishū Nihonsha.

Neary, Ian (2002) *The State and Politics in Japan*, Cambridge: Polity Press.

Ochi, Takao (2015) "Party Politics and Leadership Change in Japan: The Prime Ministerial Relay," in Sahashi Ryo & James Gannon (eds), *Looking for Leadership: The Dilemma of Political Leadership in Japan*, Tokyo and New York: Japan Center for International Exchange, 83–107.

Ōno, Banboku (1962) *Ōno Banboku Kaisōroku* [Memoirs of Ōno Banboku], Tokyo: Kōbundō.

Ōsaka, Iwao (2014) *Nihon Seiji to Media* [Japanese Politics and Media], Tokyo: Chūō Kōron Shinsha.

Pharr, Susan (1986) "Japan in 1985: The Nakasone Era Peaks," *Asian Survey*, 26, 1: 54–65.

Satō, Seizaburō & Matsuzaki, Tetsuhisa (1986) *Jimintō Seiken* [LDP Government], Tokyo: Chūō Kōronsha.

Satō, Takumi (2008) *Yoron to seron – Nihonteki Min'i no Keifugaku* [Public Opinion and Popular Sentiments – Genealogy of Public Opinion in Japan], Tokyo: Shinchōsha.

Senda, Hisashi (1987) *Satō Naikaku Kaisō* [Memoirs of the Satō Government], Tokyo: Chūō Kōronsha.

Shindō, Muneyuki (2012) *Seiji Shudō. Kanryōsei o Toinaosu* [Politician-Led Government. Reexamination of the Bureaucratic System], Tokyo: Chikuma Shobō.

Shinoda, Tomohito (2000) *Leading Japan. The Role of the Prime Minister*, Westport: Praeger Publishers.

Shinoda, Tomohito (2007) *Koizumi Diplomacy. Japan's Kantei Approach to Foreign and Defense Affairs*, Seattle and London: University of Washington Press.

Shinoda, Tomohito (2013) *Contemporary Japanese Politics. Institutional Changes and Power Shifts*, New York: Columbia University Press.

Stockwin, J. A. A. (2008) *Governing Japan. Divided Politics in a Resurgent Economy*, Malden–Oxford–Carlton: Blackwell Publishing.

Sugawara, Taku (2009) *Yoron no Kyokkai – Naze Jimintō wa Taihai Shita no ka* [Distortion of Public Opinion – Why was the LDP Defeated?], Tokyo: Kōbunsha.

Takenaka, Harukata (2010) *Sangiin towa Nanika. 1947-2010* [What is the House of Councilors? 1947-2010], Tokyo: Chūō Kōron Shinsha.

Takenaka, Heizō (2006) *Kōzō Kaikaku no Shinjitsu. Takenaka Heizō Daijin Nisshi* [Truth about Structural Reform. Minister Takenaka Heizō's Diary], Tokyo: Nihon Keizai Shinbun Shuppansha.

Tsuchiya, Shigeru (2000) *Jimintō Habatsu Kōbōshi* [History of Rise and Fall of LDP Factions], Tokyo: Kadensha.

Uchida, Kenzō (1969) *Sengo Nihon no Hoshu Seiji* [Conservative Politics of Post-war Japan], Tokyo: Iwanami Shoten.

Uchida, Kenzō (1983) *Habatsu. Seiken Kōsō no Omote to Ura* [Factions. Inside and Outside of Struggle for Power], Tokyo: Kōdansha.

Uchiyama, Yū (2007) *Koizumi Seiken* [Koizumi Government], Tokyo: Chūō Kōron Shinsha.

Uji, Toshihiko (1983) *Suzuki Seiken 863 Nichi* [863 Days of the Suzuki Administration], Tokyo: Gyōsei Mondai Kenkyūjo.

Van Wolferen, Karel G. (1986/1987) "The Japan Problem," *Foreign Affairs*, 65, 2: 288–303.

Weber, Max (1968) *On Charisma and Institution Building*, S. N. Eisenstadt (ed.), Chicago and London: The University of Chicago Press.

Woodall, Brian (2014) *Growing Democracy in Japan: The Parliamentary Cabinet System Since 1868*, Lexington: The University Press of Kentucky.

Yasuoka, Okiharu (2008) *Seiji Shudō no Jidai* [The Era of Political Leadership], Tokyo: Chūō Kōron Shinsha.

Yomiuri Shinbun Seijibu (2006) *Gaikō o Kenka ni Shita Otoko. Koizumi Gaikō 2000 nichi no Shinjitsu* [The Man Who Made Diplomacy a Quarrel. The Truth about 2000 Days of Koizumi's Diplomacy], Tokyo: Shinchōsha.

Yomiuri Shinbun Seijibu (2008) *Shinkū Kokkai. Fukuda "Hyōryū Seiken" no Shinsō* [Void Diet. The Truth about Fukuda's "Drifting Administration"], Tokyo: Shinchōsha.

Yomiuri Shinbun Seijibu (2009) *Jimin Hōkai no 300 Nichi* [300 Days of Collapse of the Liberal Democrats], Tokyo: Shinchōsha.

Yomiuri Shinbun Seijibu (2010) *Minshutō. Meisō to Uragiri no 300 Nichi* [The Democratic Party of Japan. 300 Days of Straying and Betrayal], Tokyo: Shinchōsha.

Yomiuri Shinbun Yoron Chōsabu (2009) "Koizumi Naikaku Ikō no 10 Nen Shi" [History of 10 Years Since Koizumi Cabinet], in Tanaka Aiji, Kōno Masaru, Hino Airō, Iida Takeshi, & Yomiuri Shinbun Yoron Chōsabu (eds.), *2009 nen, Naze Seiken Kōtai Datta no ka* [2009, Why Did Alternation of Power Occur?], Tokyo: Keisō Shobō, 153–175.

Yomiuri Shinbunsha Yoron Chōsabu (ed.) (2002) *Nihon no Yoron* [Japanese Public Opinion], Tokyo: Kōbundō.

Yoshida, Shigeru (1998) *Kaisō 10 Nen* [Memoirs of 10 Years], part 1, Tokyo: Chūō Kōronsha.

Yuasa, Hiroshi (1986) *Kokkai "Giin Zoku" – Jimintō "Seichō" to Kasumigaseki* ["Parliamentary Tribes" – Kasumigaseki and the LDP "PARC"], Tokyo: Kyōikusha.

Zakowski, Karol (2015) *Decision-Making Reform in Japan: The DPJ's Failed Attempt at a Politician-Led Government*, London and New York: Routledge.

Zakowski, Karol (2019) "Strategic Use of Early Elections in Japan: Comparison of the Koizumi and Abe Cabinets," *Athenaeum. Polish Political Science Studies*, 63, 3: 78–91.

2 Remaining in power

Abe's efficiency in remaining in power for a longer period of time can be explained by the fact that he was the first LDP leader ever, and only the second prime minister since Yoshida Shigeru, to return to his post after an interval. He used his five years on the sideline of Japanese politics wisely to ponder the reasons for his defeat and reconsider policy priorities. In order to maximize his leadership, under his second administration, Abe consistently avoided the errors that had caused prime ministers' failures in the past and emulated the strategies that had ensured their successes.

Learning from his predecessors as well as from his own failure in 2006–2007, under his second administration, Abe put emphasis on stabilizing his position as the prime minister before launching institutional reforms. He managed to maintain intra-party harmony by means of the relatively high popularity of the government and inter-factional balancing techniques. Having learned from his disastrous prime ministership in 2006–2007, from 2012, Abe continually paid considerable attention to social moods. Instead of immediately imposing his right-wing initiatives in a top-down fashion, he chose to realize them gradually and instead focused on economic policy. His high popularity quelled the voices of discontent against his leadership in the LDP.

Abe was well aware that a long-lasting government was a necessary prerequisite for durable policy success. As indicated by his entourage, Abe's ultimate goal was to reorient the popular mood to the right. According to Abiru (2016: 55), a *Sankei Shinbun* journalist who boasted strong connections with Abe, ever since his first administration, Abe had dreamed about a Japan ruled for a full ten years by truly conservative politicians. As he admitted, only then would the bureaucrats understand they could not succeed in their careers unless they accepted right-wing ideals. Stabilization of the conservative way of thinking among the ruling elites, in turn, was to guarantee the absorption of nationalist ideals by the whole society. As such, the prolonged government and the gradual institutional reforms orchestrated by Abe can be treated as a part of his master plan to implement an ambitious policy agenda in foreign, security, and educational fields.

Polishing the policy agenda

Abe's main policy slogan under his first administration ("breaking out of the post-war regime") put little emphasis on economic matters, focusing instead on the problems of security policy and education. During the electoral campaign for the LDP presidency in September 2006, Abe based his policy agenda on four pillars: revision of the Constitution, legalization of the right to collective self-defense, budget cuts and an economic growth strategy, as well as redressing income disparities (Hoshi 2006: 70–71). Abe's policy priorities were reflected in his bestseller, *Towards a Beautiful Country*, published in 2006. While the first five chapters explained Abe's conservative convictions and his foreign policy agenda, the remaining two focused on domestic policies, such as the social security system and education reforms. On the last pages, Abe (2006: 222–228) noticed the problem of a growing income disparity and proposed the concept of "a society able to renew challenges" (*sai-charenji kanō-na shakai*). Nevertheless, the economic and social issues remained under-discussed in comparison with the comprehensive discourse on security and diplomatic matters.

Learning from his earlier failure, in 2012, Abe based his electoral campaign on a new strategy of overcoming economic stagnation. The new edition of his bestseller, entitled *Towards a New Country*, symbolized this change. The majority of the newly added chapter was devoted to the identification of the main causes of Japan's economic stagnation, such as deflation, expensive yen, and insufficient usage of the labor force potential in provincial regions. In order to redress this situation, he proposed an acceleration of economic growth by strengthening policy coordination with the Bank of Japan (BOJ), promoting innovative technology, participating in free trade agreements, and launching new public works projects in the countryside. According to Abe, Japan should follow its own version of capitalism, based on moral principles rather than greed. Only after having presented his vision of economic policy did Abe (2013: 236–254) remind readers that he never changed his earlier convictions and that LDP's electoral slogan "Restore Japan" (*Nihon o torimodosu*), in fact, meant a restoration of Japan from the post-war regime. This reversal of accents indicated that Abe was aware that before proceeding to the realization of his right-wing agenda he had to gain credentials in the economic field.

The "three arrows" of Abenomics, as Abe's economic policy was baptized by the media, consisted of monetary easing, expansive fiscal policy, and structural reforms to encourage private sector investments. This policy agenda sufficed to inspire the ordinary Japanese during the first two years of the second Abe administration, but afterward, the confidence in the efficacy of Abenomics waned. In order to remain credible in the eyes of the electorate, Abe periodically renewed the contents of Abenomics and supplemented it with additional catchy slogans. As stressed by Maeda (2018: 144–145), Abe was a master of buoying his approval rate through policies that were difficult to disagree with. Such valence issues included promotion of economic growth, postponement of a VAT hike, women's empowerment, and local revitalization.

Being aware that an excessive pursuit of neoliberal policy under the Koizumi administration resulted in an increase in the income gap, which in turn contributed to LDP's defeat in the 2009 election, Abe paid attention to satisfying the needs of low-income households. Before dissolving the House of Representatives in November 2014, he focused in particular on redressing the disparities between big cities and countryside regions. After all, the LDP owed its good electoral results to its strong position in provincial constituencies. Ishiba Shigeru, who in September 2014 became the first minister for overcoming population decline and vitalizing local economies, stated that his task was to answer the concerns that the economic prosperity brought by Abenomics was not sufficiently felt by the ordinary Japanese. He boasted that, in order to decrease regional disparities, he managed to partly move some of the central administration institutions outside of Tokyo: Agency for Cultural Affairs to Kyoto, Consumer Affairs Agency to Tokushima, and Ministry of Internal Affairs and Communications Statistics Bureau to Wakayama (Ishiba 2017: 12–166). In addition, the Abe administration expanded the systems of premium gift coupons for the purchase of articles in provincial regions as well as the hometown tax, enabling big city dwellers to contribute part of their income and residence tax to countryside areas. Both systems were also aimed at stimulating domestic consumption, as the local authorities that received the hometown tax often offered agricultural products of the value amounting to one-third of the donation to donors (Katayama 2016: 194–200). As such, vitalization of local economies can be treated as a regional-level version of Abenomics.

It was a necessity to renew the policy agenda again after Abe's re-election as LDP president in September 2015. In order to efface the negative impression caused by the forced passage of security bills in the Diet, the prime minister announced the second iteration of Abenomics based on the new catchy slogan of "dynamic engagement of all citizens" (*ichi oku sōkatsuyaku*). The new policy focused on the social dimensions of the economic growth strategy, such as the enhancement of childcare and elderly care systems. Just as in the case of the minister for overcoming population decline and vitalizing local economies, Abe established a new ministerial post for this task, which was assumed by Katō Katsunobu who had already been charged with the issues of women's empowerment and gender equality (Mori 2019: 21–23). In subsequent years, the Kantei attached much importance to the problems of overwork and "employment ice age generation" that graduated from universities during the economic stagnation of the 1990s and remained stuck in irregular jobs.

Not all of Abe's policies were popular, but the Kantei worked hard to at least assuage public criticism or reorient public interest to a different topic. For example, at the beginning of the second Abe administration, a

Remaining in power 57

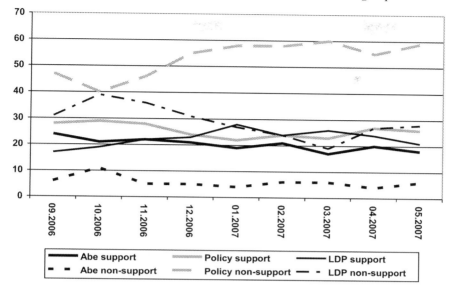

Figure 2.1 Reasons for support or non-support of the first Abe administration.
Source: Compiled by the author, based on *Asahi Shinbun*.

lot of mainstream media sympathized with the agricultural lobby's struggle against Japan's accession to the TPP. Nevertheless, Abe gradually redirected the interest of the media to the revolutionary reform of Japan Agricultural Cooperatives. Special Adviser to the Cabinet Taniguchi Tomohiko (2018: 167–168) compared this situation to a strategy of a winner who is able to set the battlefield.

The opinion polls confirm that the Abe cabinet to a great extent owed high public support to a popular policy agenda. As seen in Figure 2.1, under the first Abe administration, only 20%–30% of the supporters of the cabinet cited the government's policy agenda, while about 20% declared their sympathy toward Abe and the same number their support for the LDP as the main reasons behind their decision. Criticism toward the government's policy, in turn, was declared by as many as 47% of respondents as the reason why they did not support the Abe cabinet. However, under the second Abe administration, the evaluation of governmental policy agenda improved considerably. As shown in Figure 2.2, a few months after Abe's return to the post of the prime minister, almost 60% of those who supported the government cited the policy agenda, while only about 10% stressed their sympathy toward Abe, and about 20% their support for the LDP as reasons for their decision. Until mid-2016, support for the policy agenda remained at a decent level of approximately 40%, and afterward, it fell to the levels comparable with the first Abe administration. This trend indicates that it was the policy agenda that helped Abe to maintain high popularity in the first four years in office.

58 *Remaining in power*

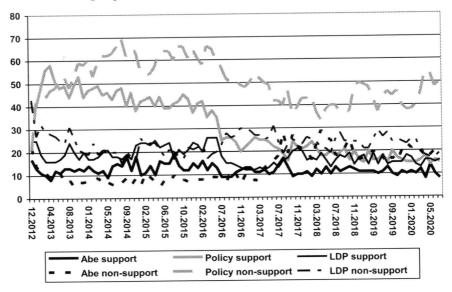

Figure 2.2 Reasons for support or non-support of the second Abe administration.
Source: Compiled by the author, based on *Asahi Shinbun*.

Maintaining the high popularity of the cabinet

In contrast to his first administration, Abe swiftly reacted to any negative shifts in the cabinet support rate. He did not protect the ministers involved in scandals, improved his media strategy, strengthened governmental control over state-owned media, and directed popular attention to the policy arena he felt strong in.

Unlike the situation in 2006, during the 2012 LDP presidential election campaign, Abe was not the favorite. According to an *Asahi Shinbun* (2012a: 5) opinion poll from the beginning of September 2012, 23% of respondents indicated Ishiba Shigeru, 19% Ishihara Nobuteru, and only 13% Abe Shinzō (7% Tanigaki Sadakazu, 4% Machimura Nobutaka, and 2% Hayashi Yoshimasa) as the most suitable leader of the LDP. At that time, Japanese voters still declared higher support for the DPJ (16%) than the LDP (15%). The mood started gradually changing after Abe's election as LDP president. According to an opinion poll conducted by *Asahi Shinbun* (2012b: 3), at the beginning of the parliamentary session in October 2012, Abe superseded Prime Minister Noda (39%–34%) as a politician worthy to chair the government, and the percentage of LDP supporters exceeded that of DPJ's (21%–14%). Nevertheless, 54% of respondents still did not place high hopes in the LDP under Abe's leadership. This ambiguity indicated that the growing popularity of the LDP resulted from the weakness of the Noda administration rather than enthusiastic support for Abe. The *Asahi Shinbun* (2012c: 4) opinion poll conducted immediately after the LDP's landslide victory in December 2012 confirmed this observation. Only 7% of respondents thought that support for the LDP was the main reason for the electoral result, while 81% claimed that disappointment with the DPJ government was decisive. While 57% were glad of the alternation of power (and 16% were not), 43% observed it was not good that the ruling coalition seized two-thirds of seats in the House of Representatives (35% thought otherwise). Totally, 51% of respondents placed hopeful expectations in the new prime minister. Being aware of the fact that he owed the electoral victory to the weakness of the DPJ administration, Abe had to invest much energy into maintaining the high popularity of his cabinet.

While Abe did not possess a charisma comparable to Nakasone's or Koizumi's, he skillfully shaped his media image as an energetic leader. He changed his suit to a slimmer version and raised his forelock to look more virile. Compared to his first term in office, Abe increased the number of appearances on television. At the same time, he intensively used social media to bypass the mainstream media and reprehend them for any comments critical of the government (Ōsaka 2014: 347). He was able to become more active in the media as a result of overcoming ulcerative colitis – a painful disease that caused severe diarrhea and had been one of the reasons for his resignation in 2007. Abe owed his better health condition to the discovery of a medicine that enabled him to almost completely eliminate the symptoms of this illness (Taniguchi 2018: 71–76).

Knowing that he was not as skillful as Koizumi in responding with witty remarks to reporters, Abe did not revive the tradition of answering questions from journalists when walking into the Prime Minister's Residence (so-called "hanging onto sources" – *burasagari shuzai*), which had been abandoned under the DPJ administration. Instead, he started dining frequently with the executive officers of friendly media corporations, such as *Yomiuri Shinbun*, Fuji TV, *Sankei Shinbun*, or Nippon TV, while keeping at bay *Asahi Shinbun* and TBS, which remained the most critical of his policy agenda. Abe did not respect the unwritten tradition of regular rotation between different television channels when giving exclusive interviews, and he preferred live broadcasts in order to exclude the possibility of reporters distorting his words (Sunagawa 2016: 112–125).

To maintain the positive image of the government, Abe gradually strengthened control over the state media. The new members of the Board of Governors of public television channel NHK, nominated by the Diet at the end of 2013, shared the prime minister's policy agenda. A lot of them belonged to such organizations as Shiki no Kai – a group of businesspeople and scholars sympathizing with Abe. The Board of Governors elected Momii Katsuto as NHK president, a conservative businessperson who kept programming in line with the government's policy. Also, the ruling party disciplined the media. In November 2014, LDP authorities summoned representatives of the biggest media corporations to lecture them about the necessity to maintain impartiality in commenting on the campaign to the

House of Representatives election. As a result, mainstream television channels drastically reduced the time devoted to information on the election, especially in "wide shows" that combined news with entertainment. Fearing repercussions, some channels abruptly changed their program so as to invite only politicians as commentators (Sunagawa 2016: 125–155). In April 2015, in turn, NHK and TV Asahi executives had to explain themselves before the LDP Research Commission on Information and Communications Technology for having staged programs critical of the government (George Mulgan 2017: 19).

According to Reporters Without Borders (2016), the pressure was exerted both on public and private media corporations. As a result, presenters and journalists who wanted to maintain objectivity, such as Kuniya Hiroko from NHK, Kishii Shigetaka from TBS, or Furutachi Ichirō from TV Asahi, were dismissed or forced to resign. The pressure was applied by Abe's closest entourage and cabinet members. For example, in February 2016, Minister of Internal Affairs and Communications, Takaichi Sanae, stirred a controversy when she expressed her opinion that broadcasters who aired "biased political reports" should be shut down. She referred to article 76 of the Radio Law, which allowed her to issue closure orders. Reporters Without Borders (2017) indicated "growing self-censorship within the leading media groups," increased difficulties of journalists to fulfill "their role as democracy's watchdogs," and harassment of reporters "by government officials, who do not hide their hostility towards the media." As a result of these developments, Japan's position in the Press Freedom Index dropped from 22 in 2012 to 72 in 2017.

On the other hand, not to give to the media a reason to criticize the government, Abe paid the uttermost attention to swiftly remove from his cabinet any politicians involved in scandals. In October 2014, he forced the resignation of Minister of Justice, Matsushima Midori, and Minister of Economy, Trade and Industry, Obuchi Yūko, immediately after the press reported misuse of their electoral funds. The prime minister did not waver even when sacrificing his closest associates if they were implicated in scandals. In January 2016, he accepted the resignation of Minister of State for Economic and Fiscal Policy, Amari Akira, who was a major decision maker behind the implementation of Abenomics. Amari stepped down from office due to allegations over accepting undisclosed money and gifts from a construction company. Perhaps the swiftest was Abe's reaction to an unfortunate remark by Minister of Reconstruction for Disaster-hit Regions, Imamura Masahiro, who, in April 2017, expressed his satisfaction with the fact that the Great East Japan Earthquake had struck in the Tōhoku region instead of Tokyo. On the following day, he was forced to resign. Abe made the only exception for his close protégé, Minister of Defense, Inada Tomomi. Despite numerous controversies, such as abusing her post to solicit electoral support, she survived in office for about one year until she was forced to resign in July 2017 due to allegations over hiding SDF logs on a peacekeeping operation in South Sudan.[1] It seems that the detrimental effect of Inada's scandals on the government support rate reminded Abe how dangerous it was to protect his friends at all costs, which perhaps prompted him to nominate more of his political opponents than protégés during the cabinet reshuffle of August 2017 (Carlson & Reed 2018: 112–116).

The most serious scandals, involving the prime minister himself, emerged in the first half of 2017. In February 2017, *Asahi Shinbun* reported that the prime minister's wife, Abe Akie, could be implicated in the government selling a parcel of land in the Osaka Prefecture at a reduced price to private school Moritomo Gakuen. She was not only a friend of the school head's wife but also served as an honorary principal of the institution. Moreover, the planned elementary school was to be named after Abe Shinzō and represent the ultraconservative ideals shared by the prime minister. It turned out that Moritomo Gakuen managed to purchase the land worth 956 million yen for a mere 134 million yen. While the authorities claimed that the reduced price resulted from the cost of disposal of the industrial waste that was found on the plot, it became evident that the school had received preferential treatment. Abe and his wife denied having played any role in the scandal and the prime minister even declared he would step down from office if his direct involvement was proved. The Osaka government eventually cancelled the permit for the opening of the school, which forced Moritomo Gakuen to return the land. Under pressure from the opposition parties, the school's Director Kagoike Yasunori was summoned to the Diet session to deliver a sworn testimony. He claimed that he had received a donation of 1 million yen from the prime minister through his wife and that he had asked Abe Akie to contact the Ministry of Finance (MOF) about an extension of the land's lease. The prime minister and his wife refuted his testimony. The opposition politicians kept accusing Abe of involvement in the scandal, though they lacked any solid proof (Carlson & Reed 2018: 117–121).

When it seemed that Abe had managed to overcome the crisis related to the Moritomo Gakuen problem by dissolving the House of Representatives and leading the LDP to electoral victory in October 2017, new facts were revealed about the scandal. In March 2018, the media reported that the MOF had falsified the documents regarding the Moritomo Gakuen issue. In the same month, one of the bureaucrats involved in the forgery committed suicide (Toshikawa 2019: 216). It turned out that as many as 38 civil servants participated in modifying the disclosed documents in 300 sections so as to delete any mention of the prime minister and his wife's involvement in the land sale process. As a result, National Tax Administration Agency Director-General Sagawa Nobuhisa, who had ordered the forgery, stepped down from office. While Prime Minister Abe and Minister of Finance Asō Tarō denied any knowledge of the falsification of the documents, opposition politicians called on them to resign. If not of direct involvement, the prime minister was accused of *sontaku*, which meant creating a system in which subordinates tried to preemptively fulfill the will of their superiors without being given any formal orders. To make things worse, in April 2018, Finance Administrative Vice-Minister Fukuda Jun'ichi resigned due to allegations over sexual harassment of a female journalist who had questioned him about the Moritomo Gakuen scandal. Eventually, in May 2018, the Osaka District Public Prosecutor's Office decided not to indict any MOF bureaucrats for the forgery of the documents (Mori 2019: 14–121).

In May 2017, another similar wrongdoing was reported by the media. *Asahi Shinbun* published documents leaked from the Ministry of Education, Culture, Sports, Science and Technology which indicated that officials from the Kantei had put pressure on the ministry to allow the Kake Gakuen school to establish a veterinary faculty in Ehime Prefecture. It was highly unusual, as the government had refused such applications for decades claiming that there was no need for another school of this kind. The faculty was to be founded within the framework of National Strategic Special Zones created as a part of the "third arrow" of Abenomics. Abe was implicated in the scandal when it turned out that he was an old friend of the school's head, Kake Kōtarō, and regularly played golf with him. After an initial denial, the government admitted that the leaked documents were authentic. Nevertheless, Abe continued claiming that he had no knowledge of the preferential treatment of Kake Gakuen. Under pressure from the opposition parties, former Ministry of Education Administrative Vice-Minister, Maekawa Kihei, was summoned to give unsworn testimony in July 2017. According to him, the government had reformulated the requirements to make Kake Gakuen win the bid for the faculty over another university (Carlson & Reed 2018: 121–123). Maekawa claimed that, in September 2016, he had been summoned to the Kantei by Special Adviser to the Prime Minister Izumi Hiroto, who instructed him to proceed quickly with the Kake Gakuen case. According to Maekawa, Izumi was to state that he was saying on behalf of the prime minister what Abe could not order directly. Izumi confirmed that the meeting had taken place, but he testified that he did not remember ever saying these words (Mori 2019: 68).

As shown by Figure 2.3, the Abe cabinet support rate did not drop excessively throughout his whole term in office. Immediately after returning as prime minister, Abe's rating was rather moderate. The opinion polls published by major newspapers at the end of December 2012 reported that the cabinet support rate was lower than at the beginning of the first Abe administration: 65% according to *Yomiuri Shinbun* (2012: 1) (70% in 2006), 52% according to *Mainichi Shinbun* (2012: 1) (67% in 2006), and 59% according to *Asahi Shinbun* (2012d: 5) (63% in 2006). Moreover, according to *Asahi Shinbun* (2012d: 5), only 17% of respondents indicated their affinity to Abe as the reason for supporting the government, while 25% stressed their affinity to the LDP, and 39% declared their support for the cabinet's policy.

The phenomenon of Abe's popularity did not lie in record-high cabinet support levels, but rather in their exceptional stability. According to *Asahi Shinbun* opinion polls, only four times did the number of respondents who

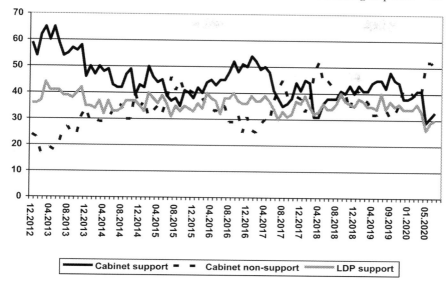

Figure 2.3 Cabinet and LDP support rates under the second Abe administration.
Source: Compiled by the author, based on *Asahi Shinbun*.

declared a lack of support for the government exceed the number of the cabinet's supporters: during deliberations in the Diet over the controversial security bills in the summer of 2015, after the emergence of the Moritomo Gakuen and Kake Gakuen scandals in mid-2017, following the disclosure of manipulation of documents by the MOF in March 2018, and after the outbreak of the coronavirus pandemic in the spring of 2020. As seen in Figure 2.2, due to the scandals, the amount of those who declared opposition to Abe (in comparison with a lack of affinity with the ruling party or the policy of the cabinet) permanently rose from about 10% to approximately 20%. Nevertheless, Figure 2.3 shows that the strategy of waiting out the popular criticism paid off and Abe managed to improve the government's popularity before it dropped below the alarming level of 30% in 2015, 2017, and 2018. The sudden drop in cabinet support level after Abe's decision not to introduce radical measures against the coronavirus pandemic in 2020 seemed to follow a similar pattern.[2] Yet, forced to postpone Tokyo Olympics until 2021, and faced with reemergence of ulcerative colitis, Abe announced his resignation on August 28, 2020.

In addition, every year a temporary decrease in cabinet support rate was visible during the Diet sessions when it was easier for the opposition politicians to publicly criticize the government. Exceptionally, in 2016, Abe's popularity kept increasing throughout the entire year, which can be linked with the destabilization of international politics. The North Korean missile crises and election of Donald Trump as US president helped to draw public attention to Japan's foreign and security policies that seemed to be a strong point of the Abe administration (Makihara 2018: 59). Moreover, as stressed by Maeda (2018: 135–136), based on Kyodo opinion polls, once Abe's economic credentials wore off, people kept supporting him simply because they were convinced no other politician would perform better as prime minister. Regardless of the reasons for the cabinet's high support rate, Abe's popularity among the public became instrumental in stabilizing his control over the LDP.

Assuaging factional struggles

Abe was equally skillful in neutralizing potential contenders for leadership in the ruling party. Because the LDP had been formed as a result of a gradual merger of smaller conservative parties, which eventually ended in 1955, it more closely resembled a loose alliance of groups led by charismatic leaders than a coherent party. The electoral system based on single non-transferable vote and middle-sized constituencies additionally fueled factionalism, as it forced LDP candidates to compete against each other in the same constituency (Ishikawa & Hirose 1989: 125–169). The interests of faction members and their bosses were complementary. While the former acquired electoral funds and recommendations for party and governmental posts from faction leaders, the latter counted on the votes of their followers during LDP presidential elections (Satō & Matsuzaki 1986: 56–66).

Over the decades of LDP's unceasing reign, factions became highly institutionalized. They boasted their own secretariats, published their own magazines, and even wrote their own statutes (Iseri 1988: 33–35; Stockwin 1989: 168). It became a custom for all factions to hold plenary meetings on Thursdays at noon, which prevented overlapping membership. Faction executives, whose decisions were almost automatically authorized during the factional get-togethers, remained the most influential politicians (Ishikawa & Hirose 1989: 212–214). As pointed out by Curtis (1988: 88), "From the beginning the role of LDP factions was to decide who the party's leaders would be, not what their policies should be." Nevertheless, constant rivalry between the prime minister and anti-mainstream faction leaders severely constrained his/her ability to rule in a top-down manner (Wang 2001: 332–333; Kong 2003: 139; Katō 1980: 3; Lee 2006: 123–124).

Factions were considerably weakened after the electoral reform of 1994, and this process continued under the Abe administration. Such previously powerful intra-party groups as Heisei Kenkyūkai and Kōchikai became much smaller than before the 1990s due to a loss of popularity among parliamentarians or splits. Even Seiwa Seisaku Kenkyūkai, which became the biggest faction, suffered from weak leadership. On the other hand, the number of unaffiliated LDP lawmakers rose dramatically.

Heisei Kenkyūkai (often abbreviated to Heiseikai) originated from the group that was led by such influential prime ministers as Satō Eisaku (1964–1972), Tanaka Kakuei (1972–1974), Takeshita Noboru (1987–1989),

Hashimoto Ryūtarō (1996–1998), and Obuchi Keizō (1998–2000). In the second half of the 1990s, it seemed that this biggest faction had managed to regain its dominant position, which had been endangered by the secession of about 50 of its members led by Hata Tsutomu and Ozawa Ichirō in 1992. Since 2000, however, none of Heiseikai leaders had become LDP president. As the faction used to gather many members of the construction and postal tribes, it was severely weakened by Prime Minister Koizumi who cut budget expenses on public works projects and decided to privatize Japan Post. In addition, a lot of its prominent members, such as Ishiba Shigeru, Kosaka Kenji, and Itō Tatsuya, defected from the faction after the loss of power by the LDP in 2009. Tsushima Yūji, Heiseikai chair in 2005–2009, and his successor Nukaga Fukushirō did not even run once in an LDP presidential election. Pressed by faction members from the House of Councilors, in March 2018, Nukaga was forced to pass the leader's position to Takeshita Noboru's younger brother, Takeshita Wataru. The weakening of Heiseikai was symbolized by the fact that the faction gradually decreased its office space, and the number of its administrative staff dropped from five to two persons (Nakakita 2017: 3–5).

Just like Heiseikai, Kōchikai traditionally belonged to the so-called "conservative mainstream" that was formed by Prime Minister Yoshida Shigeru (1946–1947, 1948–1954). During the Cold War, Kōchikai guarded the Yoshida doctrine that was based on a pro-American posture, focus on economic development, and reluctance to revise the pacifist Article 9 of the Constitution. It boasted such prime ministers as Ikeda Hayato (1960–1964), Ōhira Masayoshi (1978–1980), Suzuki Zenkō (1980–1982), and Miyazawa Kiichi (1991–1993). Nevertheless, Kōchikai's influence in the LDP had weakened since the mid-1990s. Interestingly, the only two LDP leaders who never became heads of government, Kōno Yōhei (1993–1995) and Tanigaki Sadakazu (2009–2012), belonged to this group. The main reason for Kōchikai's weakness was a series of defections. Kōno Yōhei left the group together with more than ten other politicians as soon as Miyazawa Kiichi ceded leadership to Katō Kōichi in 1998. Moreover, at the turn of 2000–2001, a majority of members of the faction rebelled against Katō as a result of his failed attempt at supporting a motion of no confidence against the Mori cabinet. Both the secessionists, led by Horiuchi Mitsuo (since 2005 by Koga Makoto), and those who remained loyal to Katō (who was succeeded by Ozato Sadatoshi in 2002 and subsequently by Tanigaki Sadakazu in 2005) claimed they were the rightful line of Kōchikai (Zakowski 2011: 179–205). The two factions reunited in 2008, but internal resentments persisted. Kōchikai once more split when Koga refused to support Tanigaki in the LDP presidential race in 2012. The Tanigaki group, composed of only about 10 members, established a faction called Yūrinkai. As Koga retired, in turn, Kōchikai leadership was passed to Kishida Fumio who served as foreign minister in the Abe cabinet from 2012 to 2017. Just like Heiseikai, Kōchikai had to severely limit its office space and reduce the number of staff (Nakakita 2017: 6–8).

By contrast, the last of the traditional "big three" LDP factions managed to improve its position vis-à-vis the other intra-party groups. Seiwa Seisaku Kenkyūkai (often abbreviated to Seiwakai) originated from the faction led by Prime Ministers Kishi Nobusuke (1957–1960) and Fukuda Takeo (1976–1978). The faction traditionally gathered numerous right-wing politicians who eagerly supported the remilitarization of Japan and opposed the Yoshida doctrine. What is important, a vast majority of LDP presidents in recent years – Mori Yoshirō (2000–2001), Koizumi Jun'ichirō (2001–2006), Abe Shinzō (2006–2007 and 2012–2020), and Fukuda Yasuo (2007–2008) – were members of Seiwakai. Under these circumstances, it is easy to understand why this group managed to significantly increase its number of members and has remained the largest faction since the first Abe administration. On the other hand, Seiwakai's dominant position in the ruling party did not necessarily translate into political influence for its bosses. Machimura Nobutaka, who took over leadership from Mori Yoshirō in 2006, ran in an LDP presidential election only once – in 2012 – when he was defeated by Abe Shinzō from his own group. It may even be considered that Seiwakai, which since 2014 has been officially headed by Hosoda Hiroyuki, has been in reality "owned" by Prime Minister Abe – grandson of the faction's founder Kishi and son of Abe Shintarō, Seiwakai's leader from 1986 to 1991. In addition, solidarity among Seiwakai members has weakened just as in other factions. After the loss of power by the LDP in 2009, the group was abandoned by such prominent politicians as Koike Yuriko, Takaichi Sanae, Yamamoto Ichita, and Nakagawa Hidenao. Moreover, Koizumi Jun'ichirō's son, Koizumi Shinjirō, who quickly gained considerable popularity, decided not to be affiliated with any group (Nakakita 2017: 8–11). Abe Shinzō himself frequently demonstrated his loose loyalty toward factional leadership. For example, in 2010, he opposed Machimura's and Mori's decision to support Tanigawa Shūzen in an election for the post of LDP House of Councilors Caucus chair and backed Nakasone Hirofumi instead (*Mainichi Shinbun* 2010). In 2012, in turn, despite the persuasion by Mori, Abe decided to run in the LDP presidential election, thus challenging Machimura. Eventually, the solidarity of the faction was maintained, as Machimura suffered from health problems during the campaign and appealed to his supporters to vote for Abe in the second round (Yomiuri Shinbun Seijibu 2013: 18–32).

Among the newer factions, Shikōkai, established through a fusion of Ikōkai and Banchō Seisaku Kenkyūjo in July 2017, had the greatest influence. The former group originated from Taiyūkai that was formed in 1999 by Kōno Yōhei who had defected from Kōchikai. While Kōno was a moderate, dovish lawmaker, Asō Tarō, who, in 2006, created Ikōkai on the basis of Taiyūkai members, was known as a more hawkish, right-wing politician. Banchō Seisaku Kenkyūjo, in turn, had a much longer history. It was established by Miki Takeo in 1956 and hosted many politicians of pacifist leaning. Its successive leaders were Kōmoto Toshio and Kōmura Masahiko.

Respecting the rule of political neutrality, when Kōmura became LDP vice-president in September 2012, he ceded leadership to Ōshima Tadamori. Once Ōshima was chosen as House of Representatives speaker in April 2015, he, in turn, followed the tradition of suspending his party affiliation, which paved the way for Santō Akiko – the first woman faction boss in LDP's history – to assume the leadership of Banchō Seisaku Kenkyūjo (Kōmura 2017: 123). Thanks to the merger, Shikōkai became the second largest group in the LDP. Its leader, former Prime Minister Asō Tarō, assumed the influential post of vice-premier and minister of finance in the Abe cabinet and was considered one of the closest associates of the head of government.

The other, smaller factions were led by Nikai Toshihiro (Shisuikai), Ishihara Nobuteru (Kinmirai Seiji Kenkyūkai), and Ishiba Shigeru (Suigetsukai). Suigetsukai, especially, has been considered as a potential alternative to Abe's rule. It was formed by a group of unaffiliated LDP lawmakers (Muhabatsu Renrakukai) after Abe's election for the second term in a row as LDP president in September 2015. Ishiba Shigeru, who had been defeated by Abe in the 2012 election, frequently expressed his intention to once more run for election. As he emphasized, Suigetsukai constituted the only LDP faction that was completely new, as all the other groups stemmed from splits and mergers of the factions that had been formed in the wake of the party's establishment more than half a century earlier (Suigetsukai 2015). Nevertheless, Ishiba's political convictions did not differ much from Abe's. As a former defense minister, he specialized in security policy and was known as a supporter of remilitarization and revision of the Constitution.

The general trend of weakening of the factions was symbolized by the increase in the number of unaffiliated LDP lawmakers. It was first visible after the 2005 election when a great majority of "Koizumi's children" remained loyal directly toward the prime minister and did not join any intra-party group. This process was supported by the LDP authorities who organized special information-sharing meetings and paid an exclusive allowance to unaffiliated LDP members of parliament. Over time, however, a lot of them formed interpersonal relations with different faction bosses. The ratio of unaffiliated lawmakers once more increased after the loss of power by the LDP in 2009. As the LDP became an opposition party, factions could no longer provide any assistance in gaining governmental posts and their fundraising power also weakened. The 2012 election resulted in a further increase in the number of unaffiliated LDP lawmakers because many of the first-time members of parliament were given an official party nomination through open recruitment rather than factional connections. As displayed in Figure 2.4, while 32 lawmakers did not belong to any faction in 2009, their number rose to 136 in 2013, which was more than the two largest factions combined together. While the formation of the Ishiba group in 2015 caused a reduction in the percentage of unaffiliated LDP lawmakers from over 30% to approximately 20%, it was still much higher than before 2005 (traditionally they constituted less than 10%). It also became a custom that all LDP

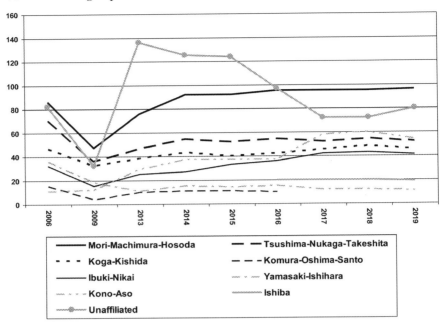

Figure 2.4 Evolution of the number of LDP faction members in 2006–2019.
Source: Compiled by the author, based on *Kokkai Binran* (2006–2019).

high-ranking officials, such as president, vice-president, secretary-general, or Policy Research Council and General Council chairs suspend their factional memberships while they remain in office (Nakakita 2017: 11–13).

As the fundraising, electoral support, and post-distribution functions of LDP factions weakened tremendously, intra-party groups became much looser organizations. The practice of distributing part of electoral funds from LDP authorities to individual lawmakers through factional structures was definitively ended in 2010. Factional affiliation still gave some benefits, especially to younger lawmakers, in such fields as training in political skills, gaining access to a personal network of more experienced statespersons, or acquiring additional financial support. For that reason, Thursday noon meetings of intra-party groups were continued, though they started serving as places for sharing information on the government's initiatives rather than for making strategic decisions. It is symptomatic that some factions, such as Kōchikai or Shisuikai, abandoned the practice of holding regular meetings of their high-ranking officials before the Thursday get-togethers as there was no longer any need for consultation in a small group of factional executives on important state matters. Each faction still had the right to nominate one LDP deputy secretary-general or Policy Research Council vice-chair, but politicians who served in these posts started acting more as deputies of their institutional bosses than as factional representatives, as they had done in the past. In fact, while the bottom-up role of factions as groups that transmitted backbenchers' voices to party authorities waned, their top-down function gained in prominence. Meetings of secretaries-general of each faction (*jimu sōchō kaigi*) were held every two months, but they served as forums for sharing information and strengthening party solidarity rather than venues for advance coordination on controversial policy decisions (Nakakita 2017: 24–45). As pointed out by LDP lawmaker Murakami Seiichirō, the new function of inter-factional meetings contrasted with their previous role of ensuring that party policy would not head in the wrong direction (interview by the author, Tokyo, October 17, 2019).

Although factions had been criticized for a lack of transparency, political corruption, and promotion of backstage politics, according to many commentators they also epitomized intra-party democracy. As the LDP was composed of both liberal and conservative wings, factional bosses representing the former and the latter groups were alternately elected as party leaders, thus renewing the party image. This "logic of the pendulum" (*furiko no ronri*) created an impression of an "artificial alternation of power" (*gijiteki seiken kōtai*), which helped the LDP to remain in power for decades (Iyasu 1983: 173; Kong 2003: 139; Kitaoka 2008: 11; Kusano 2008: 7–9). According to LDP lawmaker Murakami Seiichirō (2016: 84–135), strong factions ensured the ideological diversity of the old LDP, encouraged the free exchange of opinions even by younger parliamentarians, provided a place where lawmakers learned politics from their older colleagues, and constrained abuses of power by the prime minister. Concentration of power in the hands of party authorities, in turn, resulted in a decrease in the professionalism of politicians who instead of statecraft started focusing on maintaining good relations with the LDP president. The trauma of the 2005 election accelerated this process. Remembering the fate of the lawmakers who had opposed the privatization of Japan Post, LDP politicians started even less frequently questioning the policy of party authorities. However, the mechanism of "logic of the pendulum" waned over time not only due to the general weakening of factions, but also due to a relative increase in the number of right-wing politicians in the LDP (Nakano 2015). These processes facilitated such politicians as Abe, who never formally became a faction boss, to acquire backing from supra-factional policy groups in the LDP.

While Abe originated from the faction founded by his grandfather Kishi Nobusuke, he boasted his strongest connections with lawmakers who shared his nationalist convictions, regardless of their factional affiliations. In 1997, he participated in the creation of the Young Diet Member's Group to Consider Japan's Future and History Education (Nihon no Zento to Rekishi Kyōiku o Kangaeru Wakate Giin no Kai). This group of 87 right-wing politicians demanded re-examination of Japanese history textbooks in order to eliminate all "anti-Japanese" descriptions (Nihon no Zento to Rekishi Kyōiku o Kangaeru Wakate Giin no Kai 1997: 3). At that time, Abe served as Director of the LDP Youth Division (Seinen Kyoku), which facilitated him in establishing interpersonal ties with the politicians of his generation, such as Kishida Fumio, Noda Seiko, Nemoto Takumi, Hamada Yasukazu, Hayashi Yoshimasa, and Yamamoto Ichita (Tokoi 2014: 162–172). In 1998, together with Nemoto Takumi, Ishihara Nobuteru, and Shiozaki Yasuhisa, Abe created an informal group named NAIS after the initials of their family names. The four politicians frequently met to discuss joint policy ideas regardless of their different factional affiliations. In June 2006, 94 LDP lawmakers who supported Abe's candidature for the LDP presidential post established the Parliamentary League to Renew Challenges (Sai-Charenji Shien Giin Renmei) led by Yamamoto Yūji. It was a supra-factional group with members from the Mori (29), Niwa/Koga (9), Ibuki (9), and Tsushima (6) groups (Hoshi 2006: 28–54). After stepping down from office in 2007, Abe sympathized with the Truly Conservative Policy Research Association (Shin Hoshu Seisaku Kenkyūkai) that was formed by Nakagawa Shōichi to promote the candidature of Asō Tarō – a politician whose hawkish stance resembled Abe's – against dovish Prime Minister Fukuda Yasuo. When Nakagawa committed suicide after losing his parliamentary seat in 2009, Abe agreed to lead this group, which in 2010 changed its name to Creation "Japan" (Sōsei "Nippon"). Conservative politicians from Abe's entourage, such as Takaichi Sanae, Inada Tomomi, and Shimomura Hakubun, opposed liberal policies, for instance giving voting rights in local elections to foreign residents or allowing the retention of maiden names by wives after marriage.

Abe owed his election as LDP president in September 2012 to support both from supra-factional right-wing groups and faction bosses. Initially, it seemed that Tanigaki Sadakazu, who had been the leader of the opposition during three years of the DPJ administration, possessed the greatest chance to be re-elected. Nevertheless, two weeks before the voting, Tanigaki decided to withdraw from the race, citing as a reason the necessity of maintaining the unity of LDP authorities. He was, thus, referring to the fact that LDP Secretary-General Ishihara Nobuteru had announced his plan to run. As a son of the popular Tokyo Governor Ishihara Shintarō, Ishihara Nobuteru seemed to boast strong support both among the LDP rank-and-file party members and lawmakers. However, as he showed disloyalty toward Tanigaki, his chances abruptly weakened. Instead, former LDP Policy Research Council Chair Ishiba Shigeru became the new favorite. Ishiba was the most popular among rank-and-file party members, but he lacked strong factional support. A lot of lawmakers held a grudge against him, as in the 1990s, he had defected from the LDP. However, initially Abe's candidacy did not meet with a warm welcome either. The memory of the failure of the first Abe cabinet was still fresh. On September 5, 2012, Abe established the New Economic Growth Strategy Workshop (Shin Keizai Seichō Senryaku Benkyōkai), a policy group aimed at drawing to him supporters based on the appeal for monetary easing and overcoming deflation.

Against the initial projections that the group would attract 61 members, only 47 lawmakers (29 from the lower and 18 from the upper house) participated in the first meeting. Moreover, some of them declared their support for Ishiba. The situation started changing after Tanigaki's withdrawal from the race. Two faction leaders, Asō Tarō and Kōmura Masahiko, who had planned to vote for Tanigaki, switched their support to Abe. The other candidates, Seiwakai leader Machimura Nobutaka and Hayashi Yoshimasa from the Koga faction, did not count in the race – the former due to health problems, and the latter due to young age and insufficient recognizability. In the first round of the election on September 26, 2012, Ishiba won, receiving 199 votes, and Abe was second with 141 votes. While Ishiba gained a majority among rank-and-file party members (165 out of 300 votes), he won only 34 votes from lawmakers, less than Abe's 54. As none of the candidates achieved an absolute majority, the final decision belonged to the parliamentarians alone. In the second round, Abe defeated Ishiba by 108 to 89 votes, probably thanks to additional support from the members of the Machimura and Nukaga factions who, in the first round, had voted for Machimura and Ishihara, respectively. It was the first time since 1956 that the candidate who was second in the first round managed to win the final vote (Yomiuri Shinbun Seijibu 2013: 14–35).

After returning to the post of LDP leader, Abe skillfully pacified potential opponents through intra-party balancing techniques. In 2012, he entrusted the post of LDP secretary-general to Ishiba Shigeru, his main competitor in the LDP presidential election, and the prestigious post of minister of justice to Tanigaki Sadakazu, the previous LDP leader. From 2014 to 2016, in turn, Ishiba agreed to serve as minister for overcoming population decline and vitalizing local economies, while Tanigaki replaced him as LDP secretary-general (Nikai Toshihiro assumed this post after Tanigaki's bicycle accident in 2016). Before the 2015 LDP presidential election, almost all faction bosses had been neutralized in a similar way by nominations to high-ranking governmental or party posts. Asō Tarō served as vice-premier, Kishida Fumio as foreign minister, Kōmura Masahiko (former leader of Banchō Seisaku Kenkyūjo) as LDP vice-president, Hosoda Hiroyuki as LDP executive acting secretary-general, Nikai Toshihiro as LDP General Council chair, and Motegi Toshimitsu (Heiseikai vice-leader) as LDP Election Strategy Committee chair (Nakakita 2017: 90–91).

High levels of popular support for the government contributed to Abe's easy re-election as LDP president for a second consecutive term in September 2015. Abe's position was so strong that he was the only candidate. It was the first LDP presidential election without voting since 2001.[3] Although a popular woman politician, Noda Seiko, expressed her desire to challenge Abe, she was not even able to run due to a lack of the required support from 20 LDP lawmakers. One of the few LDP lawmakers who voiced strong opposition against Abe, Murakami Seiichirō, accused the prime minister of ordering LDP authorities to apply pressure on parliamentarians not to let Noda gather the sufficient number of signatures under her candidature. In an election, Abe would probably have had to face criticism over the legalization of collective self-defense, which was deemed unconstitutional by a majority of constitutionalists. Murakami (2016: 34–36) called the avoidance of an election a betrayal of rank-and-file party members who were thus deprived of an opportunity to vote.

In September 2018, Abe was finally challenged by Ishiba Shigeru, but he defeated him easily in the first round by a ratio of 553 to 254. Contrary to the situation in 2012, Abe gained more votes than Ishiba not only among LDP lawmakers (329–73) but also among rank-and-file party members (55.4% – 224 points to 44.6% – 181 points). Nevertheless, taking into account the strength of the Abe Kantei, Ishiba's result was above expectations. While most faction bosses declared their support for the prime minister, some of the Takeshita faction members voted for Ishiba. In addition, the popular son of Prime Minister Koizumi, Koizumi Shinjirō, revealed he had voted for Ishiba and appealed for respect for different points of view in the party. The fact that Abe only won by a small margin among rank-and-file party members, in turn, reflected the popular resentment to the Moritomo and Kake Gauen scandals (Minami & Iwao 2018: 2).

Just like Prime Minister Koizumi, Abe denied faction bosses' interference in the distribution of cabinet portfolios. Still, as admitted by Hayashi Yoshimasa who had served as minister of agriculture and minister of education under the second Abe administration, the prime minister to some extent respected factional recommendations (interview by the author, Tokyo, October 16, 2019). As many as four ministers who assumed office in December 2012 originated from the Kishida faction, which was traditionally considered a dovish group in terms of foreign policy and approach to history issues. It seems that through such favorable treatment Abe wanted to dissuade Kōchikai members from defying the government (George Mulgan 2018: 57). Nevertheless, after having strengthened his position in the party, the prime minister felt confident enough to change the "carrot" into a "stick." During the second major government reshuffle, in October 2016, Abe rewarded his supporters by increasing the representation of the Hosoda faction from two to four cabinet members, while isolating Kishida Fumio, one of the potential contenders for the prime ministership, as the only minister from Kōchikai (Mark 2016: 122). During the cabinet reshuffle in September 2019, in turn, the Ishiba faction was deprived of its only ministerial post, probably in retaliation for having defied Abe in the 2018 LDP presidential election. At the same time, the number of ministers unaffiliated with any faction rose from 2 to 6, which symbolized the waning influence of intra-party groups on the distribution of cabinet portfolios (Kihara 2019: 4).

In fact, even when Abe selected representatives of different factions for his cabinet, he most often handpicked those who shared his ideological stance. As many as nine cabinet members in 2012 belonged to the ultraconservative policy group Creation "Japan" (Abiru 2016: 125). Wider conservative movements were also strongly represented in the government. As many as 63% of ministers in 2012 and almost 80% in 2014 belonged to the Japan Conference Parliamentary Discussion Group (Nippon Kaigi Kokkai Giin Kondankai), the political branch of the Japan Conference (Nippon Kaigi). In 2016, in turn, 17 cabinet members belonged to the Shintō Politics League (Shintō Seiji Renmei), which was affiliated with the Association of Shintō Shrines (Jinja Honchō) (Aoki 2016: 50–126).

Moreover, consideration was given to the need to maintain inter-factional balance in the allocation of sub-ministerial posts in the government. However, Abe no longer automatically distributed posts of vice-ministers and parliamentary vice-ministers by faction. In fact, from the cabinet reshuffle in October 2015, the coordination of sub-ministerial nominations passed from the LDP secretary-general to the chief cabinet secretary (CCS). This change symbolized the growing superiority of the Kantei over the ruling party. In the past, the prime ministers had to rely on factional recommendations during the sub-ministerial nomination process not only due to the strength of intra-party groups but also because the Kantei lacked a better method for judging who was suitable for which post. However, when Abe was LDP secretary-general in 2004, he presided over the Party Reform Promotion Investigation Committee (Tō Kaikaku Kenshō Suishin Iinkai) that prepared a list of proposals for institutional changes in the LDP. One of the results of this initiative was the introduction of a questionnaire, through which all low- and mid-ranking LDP House of Representatives members gained the possibility of expressing their expectations regarding the party, government, or parliamentary committee positions they aspired to. This innovation provided the Kantei with data helpful in gaining greater control over the distribution of hundreds of posts over the heads of factional bosses (Nakakita 2017: 74–77).

The prime minister gained a freer hand also in party post nominations. Factional recommendations were still respected for the positions of deputy secretary-general, Policy Research Council vice-chair, or Diet Affairs Committee vice-chair. Moreover, the LDP secretary-general still had influence over the distribution of portfolios in parliamentary committees. In addition, the representative bodies of LDP lawmakers in the House of Councilors, traditionally controlled by the three biggest factions, enjoyed relative independence in choosing candidates for a number of party and sub-ministerial posts as well as two or three cabinet positions. Nevertheless, inter-factional balance was no longer a decisive factor in selecting the highest-ranking party officials. For example, after returning to power in 2012, Abe made the highly unusual decision of entrusting all three of the most important party posts to politicians unaffiliated with any faction – Secretary-General Ishiba Shigeru, General Council Chair Noda Seiko, and Policy Research Council Chair Takaichi Sanae (Nakakita 2017: 63–79).

Keeping the coalition partner in check

While Abe managed to put the LDP under his direct control, he had only a limited influence on their coalition partner, Kōmeitō. Despite a landslide victory in the 2012 election, the LDP needed this party's institutional assistance in electoral campaigns, as well as the votes of its lawmakers to ensure a majority in the House of Councilors.

Kōmeitō was established in 1964 as the political branch of the largest new religion in Japan, Sōka Gakkai (Value-Creation Society).[4] Kōmeitō's political program was based on pacifism, promotion of human rights, decentralization, protection of the natural environment, and representation of the interests of low-income households and small businesses, as well as opposition to narrow nationalism. Its policy platform declared "humanism that assigns the highest importance to life, living and the right to survival, and has as its primary objective the pursuit of happiness for both the individual and for humankind" (Kōmeitō 1998).

Kōmeitō was in a government for the first time from 1993 to 1994, as a part of a wide coalition that ousted the LDP from power. In 1994, Kōmeitō merged with small conservative parties, establishing the New Frontier Party (NFP, Shinshintō), which, however, was dissolved after only three years. As an element of political struggle against the NFP, after the sarin gas attack in the Tokyo Metro by the Aum Shinrikyō cult in 1995, the LDP vehemently criticized the lack of transparency of religious sects, including Sōka Gakkai. At that time, Abe Shinzō, who was a young parliamentarian, became a member of the Association Pondering Article 20 of the Constitution (Kenpō 20 Jō o Kangaeru Kai) that criticized Kōmeitō's ties with Sōka Gakkai as a violation of the rule of the separation of state and religion (Sataka 2016: 16–29).

The beginning of an alliance with Kōmeitō dates back to 1999, when, due to abandonment of the ruling coalition by the JSP, Prime Minister Obuchi Keizō sought a new coalition partner. He first signed an agreement with Ozawa Ichirō's Liberal Party (LP, Jiyūtō), which, in turn, invited Kōmeitō to the coalition. The LDP–Kōmeitō alliance survived Ozawa's return to the opposition in 2000. Abe respected this strategic partnership. In his speech at the Kōmeitō Congress in September 2006, he stressed that both his grandfather Kishi Nobusuke and father Abe Shintarō had maintained friendly relations with Kōmeitō politicians. The media reported that in the same month he even paid a courtesy visit to Sōka Gakkai leader Ikeda Daisaku (Sataka 2016: 3–29).

Over time, the LDP became increasingly dependent on electoral cooperation with Kōmeitō. Sōka Gakkai leaders asked their followers to vote for LDP candidates in most single-seat districts (79.6% in 2012, 91.5% in 2014, and 96% in 2017), while, in exchange, the LDP lent some of its electorates to Kōmeitō in the proportional representation. Such barter was possible only due to the fact that both parties boasted disciplined electorates belonging either to Sōka Gakkai or to individual LDP lawmakers' groups of support (*kōenkai*). In addition, the two electorates were largely complementary – the former recruited from the low and middle classes in the cities, while the latter inhabited mainly countryside regions (Nakakita 2019: 308–335). What is important, Sōka Gakkai provided a motivated electoral staff that effectively filled the gap after the weakening of LDP's traditional support groups, such as postal employees. Before the July 2013 upper house election, Abe strengthened electoral cooperation with Kōmeitō even further. In exchange for Kōmeitō's full support in single-seat constituencies, the LDP agreed to recommend several Kōmeitō candidates in multimember districts, even though they competed with LDP incumbents (Yomiuri Shinbun Seijibu 2013: 118–121). While the symbiosis with Kōmeitō alienated the LDP from the followers of new religions different than Sōka Gakkai, it paid off well. According to estimations by Nakakita (2019: 326–327), without the support from Kōmeitō, it would have been difficult for the LDP to gain a majority of seats in the 2017 lower house election.

The alliance with the LDP proved beneficial for Kōmeitō as well. While the LDP's coalition partner traditionally nominated only one cabinet member, usually it was the head of one of the influential ministries, such as the Ministry of Land, Infrastructure, Transport and Tourism, that administered public works. Kōmeitō ensured influence on the decision-making process through the Ruling Parties Policymakers' Council (Yotō Seisaku Sekininsha Kaigi) and the Government-Ruling Parties Liaison Council (Seifu-Yotō Renraku Kaigi). The former organ was composed of high party officials such as Policy Research Council chairs – five from the LDP and four from Kōmeitō – who gathered twice per week to summarize the results of advance screening of all bill projects. The latter, in turn, was composed of the prime minister, major cabinet members, and the highest officials of both parties who gathered once per month to exchange opinions on crucial policies and parliamentary strategies (Nakakita 2019: 269–281). Through these organs, Kōmeitō occasionally imposed welfare policies on the LDP. For instance, in 2009, under pressure from Kōmeitō, the Asō government introduced a special benefit of at least 12,000 yen for all Japanese, aimed at stimulating domestic consumption during the world financial crisis. The initiative encountered resistance from neoliberal LDP lawmakers led by former Prime Minister Koizumi Jun'ichirō. Kōmeitō's policy of protecting the interests of low-income families also incited divisions in the LDP under the Abe administration. In exchange for concessions in this field, Abe counted on his coalition partner's flexibility regarding such right-wing initiatives as constitutional revision.

The LDP–Kōmeitō coalition agreement, signed in December 2012, encompassed eight points: (1) recovery from the destruction caused by the Great East Japan Earthquake, (2) economic policy, (3) social security and tax reform, (4) energy policy, (5) reinvigoration of education, (6) foreign and security policy, (7) Constitution, as well as (8) political and administrative reforms. In the first three points, both sides promised to increase budget spending for public works projects, overcome deflation through specifying a 2% inflation target and conducting large-scale monetary easing, implement a growth policy based on relaxing regulations in the spheres of energy, environment, and medical services, as well as to take into account the interest of low-income taxpayers when increasing VAT. In the fourth point, Abe Shinzō and Kōmeitō leader Yamaguchi Natsuo agreed to strive for decreasing dependence on nuclear energy, promote renewable energy sources, and ensure the safety of nuclear power plants before their reopening. The fifth point stipulated revision of the system of Education Boards and a search for funds for free infant education. In the sixth point, both sides promised to strengthen the alliance with the US, while building relations based on trust with the neighboring countries, ensure a sufficient defense budget to protect Japan's territory, and promote liberalization of trade. The most controversial, seventh, point stipulated holding discussions on the revision of the Constitution, while the last point contained the plans for reducing the number of seats in the lower house, lawmakers' expenses and the personnel cost of public employees, as well as the introduction of a new administrative system based on big provinces (Liberal Democratic Party 2012).

One of the most visible policy differences between the LDP and Kōmeitō was the stance on remilitarization and Constitution revision. While Kōmeitō promoted pacifism and agreed only to small changes to Article 9 of the Constitution, Abe was an eager promoter of a complete revision of the Constitution. As a result, this point was only vaguely touched upon in the coalition agreement. On the other hand, Abenomics was largely consistent with Kōmeitō's policy goals. In other spheres both sides met in the middle. Kōmeitō protected the interest of low-income taxpayers and families raising children, while the LDP inserted into the agreement an increase in defense expenditure, liberalization of trade, and education system revision. Kōmeitō put emphasis on the promotion of renewable energy sources, Abe on reopening nuclear power plants.

In subsequent years, both sides made only slight changes to the coalition agreement. Following the House of Representatives election in December 2014, the two parties put more emphasis on economic recovery in provincial regions and the empowerment of women, which reflected the evolution of Abenomics. In addition, the LDP and Kōmeitō agreed to pursue an "active peace diplomacy" (*sekkyokuteki heiwa gaikō*) to contribute to peace and stability in the world (Kōmeitō 2014). In the coalition agreement signed after the October 2017 House of Representatives election, the first point was devoted to expressing the need for strong diplomacy against the North Korean threat, following a series of missile and atomic bomb tests conducted by that country. Additional attention was paid to employment policy, especially to solving the problems of overworking and unequal salaries for the same work. Particular emphasis was also put on a resolution of the problem of an aging society through increasing funds spent on child and elderly care. What is important, the last point of the agreement stipulated not only holding discussions on constitutional revision, but also making efforts to achieve consensus on that matter (Kōmeitō 2017).

In order to strengthen his bargaining position vis-à-vis Kōmeitō, Abe sought partial policy cooperation with conservative opposition parties. In particular, he approached the Japan Restoration Association (JRA, Nippon Ishin no Kai) and Your Party (YP, Minna no Tō), which, to a great extent, shared his ambition to revise the Constitution. At the end of 2013, Abe agreed to conduct negotiations with these two parties on the bills establishing the NSC and introducing the system of specially designated secrets. Interestingly, the Kantei occasionally played the role of mediator between the ruling coalition partner and the opposition. CCS Suga Yoshihide boasted particularly strong connections with Sōka Gakkai Vice-Chairperson Satō Hiroshi. On behalf of Satō, before the December 2014 House of Representatives election, Suga struck a backstage deal with JRA leader Hashimoto Tōru. In exchange for convincing Kōmeitō Osaka City Council members to support the plan to hold a referendum on the establishment of Osaka Metropolis, Hashimoto agreed not to field a candidate in the Kansai sixth constituency, thus increasing the electoral chances of the Kōmeitō politician. Paradoxically, while Kōmeitō's Osaka structures obeyed, due to dissatisfaction with this pressure, regional Sōka Gakkai members largely voted against the Osaka Metropolis idea in the referendum held in May 2015, which contributed to the rejection of this plan and the weakening of the JRA. As the support for conservative opposition parties started waning due to internal splits from 2015, Abe's bargaining position vis-à-vis Kōmeitō once more weakened (Nakano 2016: 50–57). While in the July 2016 upper house election the LDP secured half of the seats, thus theoretically eliminating the need for a coalition partner, it remained largely dependent on electoral support from Kōmeitō and Sōka Gakkai.

Despite the fact that Kōmeitō's policy agenda resembled more the agenda of the DPJ than the LDP, the party remained in the ruling coalition. On the one hand, Kōmeitō acted as a player slowing down and assuaging Abe's right-wing initiatives, but on the other hand, Kōmeitō's pacifism was bent to its limits under the pressure from the LDP. The two parties formed a "marriage of convenience" that was cemented by mutually beneficial electoral cooperation. As a pragmatic politician, Abe respected this uneasy alliance and did not resist accepting some Kōmeitō demands, in particular those concerning welfare state policy, while occasionally trying to play the opposition parties off against the LDP's coalition partner.

Ensuring electoral superiority over the opposition parties

Unlike during his first administration, after returning to power Abe did not rush his right-wing initiatives. As the LDP–Kōmeitō coalition initially did not possess a majority of votes in the House of Councilors, the electoral strategy for the upper house election became a priority of the new

78 *Remaining in power*

government. In subsequent elections, Abe strategically chose the moment of dissolution of the lower house to maximize the LDP's performance. The strength of Prime Minister Abe resulted also from a propitious position vis-à-vis opposition parties. The scale of the DPJ's failure in reforming Japan after the change of power in 2009 discouraged voters from trying to find an alternative to the LDP's rule. In addition, a wave of defections from the DPJ and creation of new parties before the 2012 election contributed to fragmentation of the opposition. Due to the disappearance of a clear "second pole" on the Japanese political scene, the mixed electoral system based mainly on single-seat constituencies worked in favor of the LDP.

Figure 2.5 illustrates the changes in the number of seats of the three largest parties after the House of Representatives elections in the post-war period. What is interesting, as a result of LDP's electoral victories under the Abe leadership, the dominant party outperformed the largest opposition party [DPJ in 2012 and 2014, and Constitutional Democratic Party of Japan (CDPJ) in 2017] by record-high levels (237, 218, and 227 seats respectively). Only one other time, under the Nakasone cabinet in 1986, did the number of seats gained by the LDP exceed the number of seats won by its main contender (JSP) by more than 200 (215). This data shows that never before

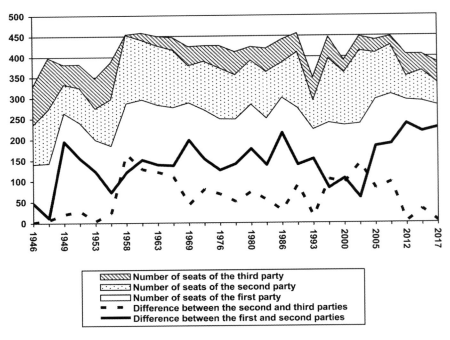

Figure 2.5 Difference in the sizes of the first, second, and third parties in the House of Representatives.

Source: Compiled by the author, based on many sources.

under the current constitutional system was the Japanese political arena to the same extent deprived of a viable "second pole" able to challenge the LDP's domination. The record-low differences in the number of seats won by the second and third parties (three in 2012, 32 in 2014, and four in 2017), in turn, illustrate the growing fragmentation of the opposition. Since the creation of the LDP in 1955, only in 1986 (29) and 1993 (15) was this gap comparably narrow. The main beneficiary of these tendencies was the LDP and its leader Abe. As noted by LDP lawmaker Hayashi Yoshimasa, the never-ending series of electoral victories became the crucial factor that decided about the strength of the Kantei (interview by the author, Tokyo, October 16, 2019).

In December 2012, Abe led the LDP to his first House of Representatives election victory. The LDP gained 294 seats, 175 more than in 2009, while the DPJ suffered a crushing defeat, reducing the number of its seats from 308, won three years earlier, to merely 57. LDP's coalition partner Kōmeitō gained 31 seats, 10 more than in 2009. The newly founded JRA performed very well, winning 54 seats, and thus becoming the third largest power in the Diet. While the LDP's victory was unquestionable, it resulted more from the fragmentation of the opposition than enthusiastic support from voters. In fact, in proportional representation, the LDP gained only a slightly higher percentage of votes than three years earlier (27.62% instead of 26.73%). After hearing the election result, Abe modestly admitted that LDP's victory was the fruit of "the three years of disorder under the DPJ government," and it did not mean that the voters had become fully confident in the LDP. As he stressed, "the battle was just beginning" (Yomiuri Shinbun Seijibu 2013: 87–88).

The JRA had been established only one month before the parliamentary election by Osaka Mayor Hashimoto Tōru, leader of the Osaka Restoration Association (Ōsaka Ishin no Kai), and Tokyo Governor Ishihara Shintarō, leader of the Sunrise Party (Taiyō no Tō). The JRA performed best in the Osaka region. Hashimoto's main goal was to reorganize Osaka into special wards within the Osaka Metropolis, similar to Tokyo. Interestingly, only a few months before the LDP presidential election in September 2012, Hashimoto tried to persuade Abe to leave the LDP and become the leader of the new party that he was planning to establish. At that time, such senior LDP politicians as Mori Yoshirō and Koga Makoto did not exclude the possibility of forming a grand coalition with the DPJ instead of putting pressure on Prime Minister Noda to call an early election. Abe decisively opposed this scenario, pointing to ideological differences with the DPJ. In terms of the policy agenda, Abe was much closer to the JRA than to the DPJ. For example, he lauded Hashimoto for the plan to punish school teachers who participated in political activities. Abe rejected the proposal of aligning with the popular Osaka mayor only after the LDP clearly rejected the possibility of forming a grand coalition with the DPJ (Abiru 2016: 157–160). Under these circumstances, it is not surprising that after becoming the prime minister, Abe perceived the JRA as a potential ally in the Diet.

80 *Remaining in power*

Following the crushing electoral defeat, Prime Minister Noda Yoshihiko resigned from the post of DPJ leader, and Kaieda Banri was chosen in his place. The new party authorities were unable to improve the image of the DPJ after the disastrous three years in power. Composed of both nationalist politicians and former Socialists, the largest opposition party could not offer a viable alternative to Abe's policy agenda. On the one hand, it was difficult for the DPJ to deny the initial positive effects of Abenomics, and on the other hand, each response to Abe's plans for constitutional revision exposed the DPJ's policy incoherence. The DPJ tried to hinder the legislative process by using its control over the upper house. As the opposition parties refused to immediately vote on the new division of single-seat districts in April 2013, the government had to wait 60 days until it was able to use its majority of two-thirds of votes in the lower house to pass this important bill in June 2013. On June 26, 2013, the opposition parties passed a censure motion against Prime Minister Abe and rejected four bills submitted by the government, but this gesture had only a symbolic significance due to the regaining of a majority in the House of Councilors by the ruling coalition one month later (Yomiuri Shinbun Seijibu 2013: 147–148).

Abe paid the utmost attention to polishing strategy for the upper house election in July 2013. To prevent dilution of votes (so-called *tomodaore* – falling together), in most multimember districts he fielded single candidates. The opposition parties, in turn, failed to create a common front against the LDP. Instead, four upper house members left the DPJ. Some of them felt they would perform better without party affiliation, while the others protested against the DPJ policy line steering overly to the left under the Kaieda leadership. Meanwhile, the JRA sought cooperation with the YP, but negotiations ended in failure due to JRA leader Hashimoto Tōru's controversial statement on "comfort women."[5] As a result of these developments, the election ended in another landslide victory for the ruling coalition. The LDP gained 65 seats, 28 more than six years earlier, when electoral defeat had forced Abe to step down from office. Also, Kōmeitō performed well, winning 11 seats, two more than in 2007. In total, the LDP possessed 115 and Kōmeitō 20 seats, which ensured the coalition a majority of votes in the 242-member house. The DPJ's total number of seats was reduced from 59 to 27. The election put an end to the "twisted Diet," thus removing a serious constraint on Abe's leadership.

Fragmentation of the opposition parties continued. In December 2013, Eda Kenji led 13 lawmakers out of the YP and created the Unity Party (UP, Yui no Tō). In May 2014, the Ishihara group defected from the JRA, disagreeing on a potential merger with the UP on the grounds that the UP supported maintenance of the pacifist Constitution. In August 2014, Ishihara's followers, led by Hiranuma Takeo, created the Party for Future Generations (PFG, Jisedai no Tō), renamed Party Cherishing Japanese Heart (Nippon no Kokoro o Taisetsu ni Suru Seitō) in December 2015, shortened to the Japanese Heart (Nippon no Kokoro) in February 2017. In September 2014, in turn, the JRA merged with the UP, creating the Japan Innovation Party (JIP, Ishin no Tō).

In the House of Representatives election in December 2014, the LDP won 291 seats. It was two seats fewer than before dissolution, but as the total number of seats was lowered from 480 to 475, it could be said that the ruling party performed even better than in 2012. Moreover, LDP's coalition partner Kōmeitō managed to increase the number of seats from 31 to 35. While the main opposition party, DPJ, also increased its number of seats (from 62 to 73), it was far too little to endanger the dominant position of the LDP. The JIP won 41 seats, losing one mandate. A considerable part of the electorate critical of the government voted for the Japanese Communist Party (JCP, Nihon Kyōsantō), which got 21 seats, much more than the 8 seats two years earlier. The LDP profited from a low voter turnout of only 52.63%, which resulted both from the apathy of the electorate and from the fact that the election was held in December (Mark 2016: 30–31).

After the electoral defeat, Kaieda Banri, who lost his parliamentary seat, resigned as DPJ leader and was replaced by Okada Katsuya. In May 2015, inhabitants of Osaka rejected the JIP's plan to create the Osaka Metropolis, which prompted Eda Kenji to step down from the post of party leader, which was assumed by Matsuno Yorihisa. While Matsuno leaned toward cooperation with other opposition parties, the policy agenda of the original founders of the JIP was closer to Abe's stance (Mark 2016: 110). In October 2015, Hashimoto Tōru and Osaka Governor Matsui Ichirō left the JIP, forming Initiatives from Osaka (Ōsaka Ishin no Kai). In March 2016, the DPJ merged with the JIP and the Vision of Reform (Kaikaku Kesshū no Kai) that had earlier split from the JIP, creating the Democratic Party (DP, Minshintō – in direct translation, Democratic Progressive Party). The new party based its political program on opposition to the revision of the pacifist Constitution. In order to challenge the LDP's domination, the DP agreed with the JCP, SDP, and People's Life Party (PLP, Seikatsu no Tō) not to endorse competing candidates in the upper house election single-seat districts and to sign a policy agreement based on the abolition of the security bills (Nakakita 2019: 351–352).

Despite the opposition's electoral agreement, the ruling coalition performed well in the election to the House of Councilors in July 2016. The LDP managed to win 56 seats (6 more than in 2010) and Kōmeitō 14 seats (5 more), which, together with the seats that were not up for election, gave the ruling coalition 146 seats in the 242-member house. In addition, the LDP alone secured 121 seats, thus approaching the majority necessary to govern alone. The total number of seats of the DP, in turn, decreased from 49 to only 14. Instead, more conservative opposition parties gained prominence, such as the Osaka Restoration Association that acquired an additional five seats (Pekkanen & Reed 2018: 20). As a result, not only did the ruling coalition maintain control over the upper house, but potentially it could also more easily secure two-thirds of votes in case of an attempt at constitutional revision. What contributed to the failure of the electoral cooperation by the four opposition parties was the fact that they avoided endorsing competing candidates only in single-seat districts and that the conservative opposition parties did not participate in the anti-LDP alliance (Nakakita 2019: 352–353).

Taking responsibility for the electoral defeat, Okada Katsuya stated he would not seek re-election as DP leader. In September 2016, Murata Renhō was elected in his place. As a woman and a half-Chinese, she seemed to have a chance to appeal to the liberal electorate. She entrusted the post of DP secretary-general to former Prime Minister Noda Yoshihiko, whose experience was to supplement her youthful zeal. However, it was not the DP that put up a real challenge to LDP's domination. The series of Abe's electoral victories was shaken by regional elections in Tokyo. Following Governor Masuzoe Yōichi's resignation in June 2016, Koike Yuriko from the LDP decided to run independently for the post of Tokyo governor, thus defying the ruling coalition's official candidate Masuda Hiroya. Not only did she defeat him (44.5% to 27.4%) in the July 2016 election, but she also established the Tokyoites First Association (Tomin Fāsuto no Kai) that achieved a landslide victory in the election to the Tokyo Metropolitan Assembly in July 2017, winning 55 seats in comparison with LDP's 23 (Pekkanen & Reed 2018: 21). Furthermore, in October 2016, Koike opened the Academy of Hope (Kibō no Juku) – a post-graduate school to educate potential candidates not only for a regional but also for a new, national-level party that she planned to establish. While the LDP was never strongest in big cities, such an initiative could endanger the dominant position of the ruling party. Koike based her political program on the slogans of representing the interests of metropolitan citizens, wise spending, and disclosure of information. She addressed the problems of big city dwellers, such as the insufficient number of nursery schools or slow pace of women's empowerment. As Koike wanted to rationalize wasteful budget spending, she reduced her own salary by half, and City Council members' by 20%. To increase the transparency of her office, she promised to improve access to public documents (Koike 2017: 6–162). Thanks to these moves, she gained much popularity not only in Tokyo but also nationwide.

Koike's ambitions prompted Abe to dissolve the House of Representatives on September 28, 2017. The prime minister probably hoped to conduct a "preemptive strike" before the Tokyo governor's plans to go national ripened. In addition, he wanted to exploit the fact that, after a North Korean missile test over Japanese territory at the beginning of September 2017, the media temporarily focused on security issues instead of the Moritomo and Kake Gakuen scandals. Due to revision of the electoral system for the lower house in July 2017, the number of single-seat districts was reduced from 295 to 289, and the number of proportional representation seats from 180 to 176. The sudden dissolution of the Diet caused an acceleration of party realignment. At the end of September 2017, Koike established the Party of Hope (PH, Kibō no Tō) and invited those opposition politicians who shared her views to join. As a result, DP leader Maehara Seiji decided to disband the DP House of Representatives caucus. Nevertheless, due to ideological differences, not all DP lawmakers were allowed to join the PH, as they did not share Koike's right-wing leaning. Instead, moderate politicians who opposed revision of the Constitution formed the CDPJ (Rikken Minshutō) led by Edano Yukio (Scheiner, Smith, & Thies 2018: 29–32).

Despite a strong challenge from the opposition parties who criticized Abe for the Moritomo and Kake Gakuen scandals, the LDP performed very well in the October 2017 election. It won 281 seats, only ten short of the 2014 result, in the smaller, 265-member house. Kōmeitō reduced its number of seats from 35 to 29. Surprisingly, the CDPJ (54 seats) outperformed the PH (50 seats) (Scheiner, Smith, & Thies 2018: 33–34). The electoral result of the new parties was severely damaged by the fact that they remained divided, and only to a minimal extent agreed not to field competing candidates (Nakakita 2019: 356–357). Taking responsibility for the not as good as expected result, Koike resigned as PH co-leader in November 2017, leaving this post to former DP politician Tamaki Yūichirō. In May 2018, the PH merged with the remnants of the DP, mainly from the House of Councilors, creating the Democratic Party For the People (DPP, Kokumin Minshutō). In April 2019, Ozawa Ichirō's LP joined the DPP, but the CDPJ still remained the largest opposition party.

The House of Councilors election in July 2019 ended in the LDP's sixth victory at the national level in a row under Abe's leadership. The LDP won 57 seats, 8 fewer than six years earlier, while Kōmeitō won 14 seats, 3 more than in 2013. In total, the ruling coalition reduced its number of seats from 146 to 141 in comparison with the 2016 election, in the 245-member house (three new seats were added in big city districts). While this result ensured the ruling coalition a majority of votes in the House of Councilors, it made the task of securing the two-thirds of votes necessary to revise the Constitution more difficult.

The continued fragmentation of the opposition, which remained divided especially over the stance toward constitutional revision, worked in favor of the LDP. Contrary to the LDP and Kōmeitō, whose electorates were largely complementary, the opposition parties were supported mainly by unaffiliated voters from big cities, which made their electoral cooperation much harder. Abe skillfully timed the moments of dissolution of the House of Representatives to keep the other parties unprepared for snap elections. His ability to ensure a stable majority in both houses greatly facilitated the decision-making process. After the elimination of the "twisted Diet," the opposition parties' efforts to prolong legislative procedures were limited to attempts at disturbing the work of commissions or plenary sessions through filibuster techniques or blocking the rostrum. Under these conditions, Abe focused on more ambitious goals, such as achieving a single majority for the LDP in the upper house or gaining the two-thirds of seats necessary for constitutional revision.

Conclusion

In order to remain in power for a longer period of time, Prime Minister Abe used a wide array of political tactics and strategies. He based his policy agenda on Abenomics while postponing more controversial goals, cautiously selected cabinet members to avoid politicians who were involved in scandals, and strengthened state control over the media. The high popularity of the cabinet enhanced Abe's position in the ruling party, which, in turn, helped him to quell voices of discontent among backbenchers. Thanks to the weakening of factions, reliance on supra-factional support from lawmakers who shared his ideological stance, and the strategic nomination of his potential rivals to high positions in the government and the party, Abe managed to easily ensure his re-election as LDP president. The prime minister's political flexibility enabled him to stabilize the coalition with Kōmeitō and keep the opposition parties at bay. The continued fragmentation of the opposition parties, coupled with the tactical choice of the moment of the House of Representatives' dissolution, ensured successive electoral victories that facilitated the maintenance of a top-down leadership style. While Abe, to a great extent, owed the stability of his administration to popular resentment against the DPJ after the failure of the Hatoyama, Kan, and Noda governments, he proved skillful in fully exploiting the propitious political conditions.

Abe invested extensive political capital in remaining in office, but his real aim was to implement profound reforms in the vein of his right-wing convictions. His prolonged term in office, in turn, created stable institutional conditions for reforming decision-making patterns in the government and the ruling party in an evolutionary way.

Notes

1. The logs concerned a situation in July 2016 when, due to fighting, Japan evacuated its embassy personnel from South Sudan. They contained the word "combat," which implied that the SDF were sent to a peacekeeping operation in a combat area although it was prohibited by law.
2. Severe acute respiratory syndrome coronavirus 2 (SARS-CoV-2), which was first identified in Wuhan, China in December 2019, gradually spread all over the world. To limit negative influence of the pandemic on the Japanese economy, Prime Minister Abe announced the national state of emergency relatively late, in mid-April 2020. Such a sluggish response met with criticism from Tokyo Governor Koike Yuriko and contributed to a rapid decrease in the government support rate.
3. However, the situation in 2015 was very different from 2001. In 2001, Prime Minister Koizumi had assumed office only four months before the regular election as a result of Mori Yoshirō's resignation, so his re-election seemed a formality.
4. Sōka Gakkai was established in 1930 by Makiguchi Tsunesaburō as an organization affiliated with the Buddhist Nichiren Shōshū sect. Makiguchi was sentenced for refusing to worship Shintō deities and died in prison in 1944.

In the post-war era, Sōka Gakkai rapidly expanded, filling the spiritual vacuum after abandonment by the government of the status of Shintō as a state religion.
5. "Comfort women" were sexual slaves recruited by the Japanese Imperial Army mainly on the Korean Peninsula during the Second World War. In May 2013, Hashimoto said that the system of "comfort stations" had been necessary to provide relaxation to the soldiers, which met with criticism from the media. See Yomiuri Shinbun Seijibu (2013: 118–131).

References

Abe, Shinzō (2006) *Utsukushii Kuni e* [Towards a Beautiful Country], Tokyo: Bungei Shunjū.
Abe, Shinzō (2013) *Atarashii Kuni e. Utsukushii Kuni e. Kanzenban* [Towards a New Country. Towards a Beautiful Country. Complete Edition], Tokyo: Bungei Shunjū.
Abiru, Rui (2016) *Sōri no Tanjō* [Birth of a Prime Minister], Tokyo: Bungei Shunjū.
Aoki, Osamu (2016) *Nippon Kaigi no Shōtai* [True Character of Japan Conference], Tokyo: Heibonsha.
Asahi Shinbun (2012a) "Asahi Shinbunsha Yoron Chōsa. Shitsumon to Kaitō" [Opinion Poll by *Asahi Shinbun*. Questions and Answers], September 11, morning edition, 5.
Asahi Shinbun (2012b) "Genpatsu Zero '30 Nandai yori Mae ni' 36%, Sonzoku Shiji wa 31%. Asahi Shinbunsha Yoron Chōsa" [36% Support Zero Nuclear Power "Before the 2030s," 31% Want Continuance. Opinion Poll by *Asahi Shinbun*], October 3, morning edition, 3.
Asahi Shinbun (2012c) "Asahi Shinbunsha Yoron Chōsa. Shitsumon to Kaitō" [Opinion Poll by Asahi Shinbun. Questions and Answers], December 19, morning edition, 4.
Asahi Shinbun (2012d) "Asahi Shinbunsha Yoron Chōsa. Shitsumon to Kaitō" [Opinion Poll by Asahi Shinbun. Questions and Answers], December 28, morning edition, 5.
Carlson, Matthew M. & Reed, Steven R. (2018) "Scandals During the Abe Administrations," in Robert J. Pekkanen, Steven R. Reed, Ethan Scheiner & Daniel M. Smith (eds.), *Japan Decides 2017. The Japanese General Election*, Cham: Palgrave Macmillan, 109–126.
Curtis, Gerald L. (1988) *Japanese Way of Politics*, New York: Columbia University Press.
George Mulgan, Aurelia (2017) "Media Muzzling under the Abe Administration," in Jeff Kingston (ed.), *Press Freedom in Contemporary Japan*, London and New York: Routledge, 17–29.
George Mulgan, Aurelia (2018) *The Abe Administration and the Rise of the Prime Ministerial Executive*, London and New York: Routledge.
Hoshi, Hiroshi (2006) *Abe Seiken no Nihon* [Japan under the Abe Government], Tokyo: Asahi Shinbunsha.
Iseri, Hirofumi (1988) *Habatsu Saihensei. Jimintō Seiji no Omote to Ura* [Reorganization of Factions. Inside and Outside of the LDP Politics], Tokyo: Chūō Kōronsha.

Ishiba, Shigeru (2017) *Nihon Rettō Sōsei Ron. Chihō wa Kokka no Kibō Nari* [Discourse on Revitalization of Japanese Archipelago. Regions as the Hope of the Country], Tokyo: Shinchōsha.

Ishikawa, Masumi & Hirose, Michisada (1989) *Jimintō – Chōki Shihai no Kōzō* [LDP – Structure of Long-Term Supremacy], Tokyo: Iwanami Shoten.

Iyasu, Tadashi (1983) *Seitō Habatsu no Shakaigaku. Taishū Minshusei no Nihonteki Tenkai* [Sociology of Political Factions. Japanese Development of Mass Democracy System], Kyoto: Sekai Shisōsha.

Katayama, Yoshihiro (2016) "Misshon Machigai no 'Chihō Sōsei'" [Mistaken Mission of "Regional Revitalization"], in Nakano Kōichi (ed.), *Tettei Kenshō. Abe Seiji* [Comprehensive Examination. Abe Politics], Tokyo: Iwanami Shoten, 194–202.

Katō, Hirohisa (1980) "Kenryoku Tōsō no Uchimaku – Jimintō Habatsu no Kōbōshi" [The Inside of Struggle for Power – Rise and Fall of LDP Factions], in Watanabe Tsuneo (ed.), *Nagatachō Kenbunroku* [Nagatachō Guide], Tokyo: Tōyō Keizai Shinpōsha, 87–114.

Kihara, Tamiyuki (2019) "Shuryū Habatsu Anjo, Gaman no Ishiba-ha. Muhabatsu Kakuryō Fue, Suga-Shi Sonzaikan. Naikaku Kaizō" [Relief of Mainstream Factions, Patience of the Ishiba Faction. Increase in Unaffiliated Cabinet Members, Presence of Mr. Suga. Cabinet Reshuffle], *Asahi Shinbun*, September 13, morning edition, 4.

Kitaoka, Shin'ichi (2008) *Jimintō – Seikentō no 38 nen* [LDP – 38 Years of the Ruling Party], Tokyo: Chūō Kōron Shinsha.

Koike, Yuriko (ed.) (2017). *Kibō no Seiji. Tomin Fāsuto no Kai Kōgiroku* [Politics of Hope. Lectures of the Metropolitan Citizens First Association], Tokyo: Chūō Kōron Shinsha.

Kokkai Binran (2006–2019) Tokyo: Nihon Seikei Shinbunsha.

Kōmeitō (1998) "Platform" (approved on December 5, 1994, partly revised on October 24). Online. Available: https://www.komei.or.jp/en/about/platform.html (accessed July 19, 2019).

Kōmeitō (2014) "Jimin–Kōmei Renritsu Seiken Gōi (Zenbun)" [LDP–Kōmeitō Ruling Coalition Agreement (Full Text)] (December 16). Online. Available: https://www.komei.or.jp/news/detail/20141216_15770 (accessed July 17, 2019).

Kōmeitō (2017) "Ji–Kō ga Renritsu Seiken Gōi" [The Ruling Coalition Agreement by the LDP and Kōmeitō] (October 24). Online. Available: https://www.komei.or.jp/news/detail/20171024_26095 (accessed July 17, 2019).

Kōmura, Masahiko (2017) *Furiko o Mannaka ni. Watashi no Rirekisho* [Pendulum to the Center. My Curriculum Vitae], Tokyo: Nihon Keizai Shinbun Shuppansha.

Kong, Uisik (2003) *Ilbon Hyeondae Jeongchi-ui Ihae* [Understanding of Contemporary Japanese Politics], Busan: Sejong Chulpansa.

Kusano, Atsushi (2008) *Seiken Kōtai no Hōsoku* [Rules of Alternation of Power], Tokyo: Kadokawa Shoten.

Lee, Kiwan (2006) *Ilbon-ui Jeondang-gwa Jeondang Jeongchi* [Japanese Parties and Party Politics], Seoul: Doseo Chulpan Maebong.

Liberal Democratic Party (2012) "Jiyū Minshutō – Kōmeitō Renritsu Seiken Gōi" [Liberal Democratic Party – Kōmeitō Ruling Coalition Agreement] (December 25). Online. Available: https://www.jimin.jp/policy/policy_topics/pdf/pdf083.pdf (accessed July 17, 2019).

Maeda, Yukio (2018) "Public Opinion and the Abe Cabinet: Alternating Valence and Position Issues," in Robert J. Pekkanen, Steven R. Reed, Ethan Scheiner & Daniel M. Smith (eds.), *Japan Decides 2017. The Japanese General Election*, Cham: Palgrave Macmillan, 127–147.

Mainichi Shinbun (2010) "Jimintō: San'in Kaichō ni Nakasone-shi. Tokuhyō Dōsū de Chūsen, Habatsu Rengō ni Shōri" [LDP: Mr. Nakasone for upper house chair. Drawing due to equal number of votes, victory over alliance of factions], August 12, Tokyo morning edition. Online. Available: http://mainichi.jp/select/seiji/news/20100812ddm005010030000c.html (accessed August 12, 2018).

Mainichi Shinbun (2012) "Mainichi Shinbun Yoron Chōsa: Abe Naikaku Shiji 52%, 'Seikatsu Kawaranu' 62%" [Opinion Poll by *Mainichi Shinbun*: 52% Support for the Abe Cabinet, 62% "Without Change of Level of Life"], December 28, Tokyo morning edition, 1.

Makihara, Izuru (2018) *Kuzureru Seiji o Tatenaosu. 21 Seiki no Nihon Gyōsei Kaikaku Ron* [Reorganizing the Crumbling Politics. Discourse on Administrative Reform in the 21st Century Japan], Tokyo: Kōdansha.

Mark, Craig (2016) *The Abe Restoration. Contemporary Japanese Politics and Reformation*, Lanham–Boulder–New York–London: Lexington Books.

Minami, Akira & Iwao, Masahiro (2018) "Shushō, Kuzureta 'Asshō.' Jimin Sōsaisen" [The Prime Minister, Failed "Overwhelming Victory." LDP Presidential Election], *Asahi Shinbun*, September 21, morning edition, 2.

Mori, Isao (2019) *Kantei Kanryō. Abe Ikkyō o Sasaeta Sokkin Seiji no Tsumi* [The Residence's Bureaucracy. The Sin of Aides' Politics that Supported Abe's Unilateral Strength], Tokyo: Bungei Shunjū.

Murakami, Seiichirō (2016) *Jimintō Hitori Ryōshikiha* [One Member of the LDP Faction of Common Sense], Tokyo: Kōdansha.

Nakakita, Kōji (2017) *Jimintō – Ikkyō no Jitsuzō* [LDP – Real Image of Unilateral Strength], Tokyo: Chūō Kōron Shinsha.

Nakakita, Kōji (2019) *Ji-Kō Seiken to wa Nanika? Renritsu ni Miru Tsuyosa no Shōtai* [What Is the LDP–Kōmeitō Government? True Image of the Strength Visible in the Coalition], Tokyo: Chikoma Shobō.

Nakano, Jun (2016) "'Kōmei Kirai' no Shushō ga Tsuyomeru Kōmei Izon. Kantei to Kōmeitō, Sōka Gakkai o meguru Kihon Kōzu" [Dependence on Kōmeitō Strengthened by a Prime Minister Who "Hates Kōmeitō." Basic Connections Between the Kantei, Kōmeitō and Sōka Gakkai], in Nakano Kōichi (ed.), *Tettei Kenshō. Abe Seiji* [Comprehensive Examination. Abe Politics], Tokyo: Iwanami Shoten, 48–61.

Nakano, Kōichi (2015) *Ukeika Suru Nihon Seiji* [Right-Wing Trend in Japanese Politics], Tokyo: Iwanami Shoten.

Nihon no Zento to Rekishi Kyōiku o Kangaeru Wakate Giin no Kai (ed.) (1997) *Rekishi Kyōkasho e no Gimon* [Doubts over History Textbooks], Tokyo: Nihon no Zento to Rekishi Kyōiku o Kangaeru Wakate Giin no Kai.

Ōsaka, Iwao (2014) *Nihon Seiji to Media* [Japanese Politics and Media], Tokyo: Chūō Kōron Shinsha.

Pekkanen, Robert J. & Reed, Steven R. (2018) "Japanese Politics Between 2014 and 2017: The Search for an Opposition Party in the Age of Abe," in Robert J. Pekkanen, Steven R. Reed, Ethan Scheiner and Daniel M. Smith (eds.), *Japan Decides 2017. The Japanese General Election*, Cham: Palgrave Macmillan, 15–28.

Reporters Without Borders (2016) "RSF Concerned About Declining Media Freedom in Japan" (April 11). Online. Available: https://rsf.org/en/news/rsf-concerned-about-declining-media-freedom-japan (accessed January 24, 2020).

Reporters Without Borders (2017) "The Threat from Shinzo Abe." Online. Available: https://rsf.org/en/japan (accessed May 5, 2017).

Sataka, Makoto (2016) *Jimintō to Sōka Gakkai* [The LDP and Sōka Gakkai], Tokyo: Shūeisha.

Satō, Seizaburō & Matsuzaki, Tetsuhisa (1986) *Jimintō Seiken* [LDP Government], Tokyo: Chūō Kōronsha.

Scheiner, Ethan, Smith, Daniel M. & Thies, Michael F. (2018) "The 2017 Election Results: An Earthquake, a Typhoon, and Another Landslide," in Robert J. Pekkanen, Steven R. Reed, Ethan Scheiner & Daniel M. Smith (eds.), *Japan Decides 2017. The Japanese General Election*, Cham: Palgrave Macmillan, 29–50.

Stockwin, J. A. A. (1989) "Factionalism in Japanese Political Parties," *Japan Forum*, 1, 2: 161–171.

Suigetsukai (2015) "Go Aisatsu" [Greeting]. Online. Available: http://www.suigetsukai.org/policy/ (accessed July 21, 2020).

Sunagawa, Hiroyoshi (2016) *Abe Kantei to Terebi* [The Abe Residence and Television], Tokyo: Shūeisha.

Taniguchi, Tomohiko (2018) *Abe Shinzō no Shinjitsu* [Truth About Abe Shinzō], Tokyo: Gokū Shuppan.

Tokoi, Ken'ichi (2014) *Daremo Kakanakatta Jimintō Sōri no Tōryūmon "Seinen Kyoku" no Kenkyū* [Unwritten Study on "Youth Division," LDP Gateway to Prime Ministerial Post], Tokyo: Shinchōsha.

Toshikawa, Takao (2019) *Seiji no Riarizumu. Abe Seiken no Yukue* [Political Realism. Whereabouts of the Abe Administration], Tokyo: Kadensha.

Wang, Zhensuo (2001) *Zhanhou Riben Zhengdang Zhengzhi* [Post-war Party Politics in Japan], Beijing: Renmin Chubanshe.

Yomiuri Shinbun (2012) "Abe Naikaku Shiji 65%, Keiki 'Kaifuku Dekiru' 48%, Honsha Kinkyū Chōsa" [65% Support for the Abe Cabinet, 48%: Boom "Can Be Restored," Urgent Opinion Poll by Our Company], December 28, Tokyo morning edition, 1.

Yomiuri Shinbun Seijibu (2013) *Abe Shinzō. Gyakuten Fukkatsu no 300 Nichi* [Abe Shinzō. 300 Days of Reversal and Restoration], Tokyo: Shinchōsha.

Zakowski, Karol (2011) "Kōchikai of the Japanese Liberal Democratic Party and Its Evolution After the Cold War," *The Korean Journal of International Studies*, 9, 2: 179–205.

3 Reforming governmental institutions

While Prime Minister Abe did not conduct a full-scale overhaul of governmental organs, he implemented gradual institutional changes, especially in the Cabinet Secretariat. The reforms were introduced incrementally, taking into account the limited capacities of legislative procedures to sustain a large number of revolutionary changes at one time. In the case of unofficial decision-making patterns, the Kantei took advantage of the high level of discretion in interpretation or enforcement of rules, for example, by regularizing daily meetings between the prime minister and his closest entourage, entrusting additional responsibilities to almost all ministers, and modifying the role played by the Administrative Vice-Ministers' Council. The Abe administration established only a few major formal institutions, such as the Cabinet Bureau of Personnel Affairs, and the NSC, but each of them was pinpointed to either bypass the preexisting organs or change the balance of power between the prime minister and the bureaucrats, whose veto powers were declining over time.

Bureaucrats as veto players

The power of the bureaucrats dates back to the Meiji Restoration of 1868. Civil servants not only led the industrialization and modernization of Japan, but they also influenced the everyday lives of all Japanese, especially following the passage of the National Mobilization Law in 1938. While after Japan's surrender in 1945, the US occupation authorities purged from public office the great majority of lawmakers, they relied extensively on bureaucratic knowledge, which further enhanced the position of civil servants (Inoguchi 1983: 142–171; Kerbo & McKinstry 1995: 86). In addition, in the post-war period, a lot of high-ranking bureaucrats decided to run in parliamentary elections, thus filling the gap that appeared after the purge of politicians. Until the 1980s, a majority of post-war heads of government, including Prime Minister Abe's grandfather Kishi Nobusuke and great uncle Satō Eisaku, were former bureaucrats. As a result, interdependence between the politicians and the civil servants remained one of the main characteristics of the Japanese political system.

Individualism was not highly valued among the bureaucrats. Civil servants of each ministry acted as a collective protecting their own interests, which resulted in strong sectionalism. As pointed out by Shindō (2019: 45–71), while the bureaucratic system was based on a strict hierarchy, the law did not clearly define the responsibilities for each post. Individualism was further weakened by the fact that only civil servants ranked bureau directors-general and above received separate offices, while division directors worked together with their subordinates in large rooms. This system improved the flow of information, but it also prevented the conceiving of radical solutions to problems. Each ministry relied on a round-robin (*ringi*) system in everyday decision making. Policy proposals were drafted by low or mid-level bureaucrats, approved by their immediate superiors, and eventually authorized by bureau directors-general and administrative vice-ministers. This mechanism blurred the responsibility for decisions, as succeeding officials collectively put their seals under the circular letters (Murakawa 1994: 11; Iio 2008: 52–54). Moreover, the tradition of round-robin strengthened risk aversion and attachment to the *status quo* among the bureaucrats. After all, not only did the relatively low-ranking bureaucrats who initiated the decision-making process not feel competent enough to make any alterations in the hitherto accepted policies of the ministry, but also proposals were usually watered down to please all of the involved parties (Nishimura 2002: 254).

The bureaucrats' power resulted from their specialist knowledge, experience in policymaking, and their right to interpret the law. It was common for governmental and ministerial ordinances to shape the actual meaning of ambiguous regulations (Nakano 2010: 35–39). Although the Supreme Court had the authority to interpret the Constitution, in reality, it was the bureaucrats from the Cabinet Legislation Bureau who performed this task (Iio 2008: 61–62). Furthermore, through administrative guidance, separate ministries issued directives, requests, warnings, and even detailed suggestions to private organizations and individuals (Kerbo & McKinstry 1995: 89). In addition, bureaucrats led the secretariats of numerous advisory councils (*shingikai*) established in separate ministries, thus influencing the selection of their members, choice of topics for discussion, as well as drafting proceedings and reports. The number of such councils was reduced from 210 to 105 when the administrative reforms entered into force in 2001, but rose again to 134 by 2014 (Nonaka & Aoki 2016: 12–36).

By protecting the interests of the industry sectors under their jurisdiction, civil servants catered for their own careers. The status of elite bureaucrats was dependent on the year they were recruited to the ministry. According to the seniority rule, usually only one civil servant of the same age in the ministry could become administrative vice-minister. Not to be subdued under him, all of his same-age colleagues retired early, and it was up to the ministry to find workplaces for them. Theoretically, former bureaucrats had to gain permission from the National Personnel Authority to be employed by private companies. In reality, however, retired civil servants circumvented this obstacle by proceeding to the private sector after having served for some time in executive posts in various public institutions administered by each ministry (Murakawa 1994: 75). This practice, which was called "descent from heaven" (*amakudari*), stirred many controversies. Employment of former bureaucrats was beneficial for private corporations, as former civil servants contributed not only with their experience, but also with their connections with their colleagues who remained in the ministries. As many public institutions were maintained only to provide executive posts for the retired civil servants, *amakudari* became one of the main sources of wasteful budget spending (Igarashi 2011: 43).

The Japanese bureaucrats' position was strengthened by the fact that ministers rarely interfered in the personnel affairs of their administrative staff. This practice was largely based on tradition rather than law. In order to ensure their political neutrality, public officials were guaranteed their status. They could not be dismissed, suspended, or demoted against their will unless specified otherwise by law. Theoretically, the Public Employees Law contained numerous exemptions from this rule. The bureaucrats could be deposed from office or demoted if they obstructed their duties, lacked qualifications for their job, underperformed, or even if their post was liquidated due to administrative reforms or budgetary constraints (Tanaka 2019: 127–128). Nevertheless, the politicians usually did not want to antagonize their administrative staff and simply authorized the personnel decisions made by the bureaucrats (Shinoda 2000: 7; Iio 2008: 40–42). The ministers who tried to exert their personnel management rights, in turn, often had to face criticism not only from the media, but also from the Kantei. The best example was Foreign Minister Tanaka Makiko's attempt at replacing high-ranking civil servants in her entourage as a part of an anti-corruption campaign in her ministry. The bureaucrats sabotaged Tanaka's efforts by leaking to the media information on confidential conversations between her and foreign politicians, which compromised her lack of experience in international affairs. As a result, Prime Minister Koizumi dismissed Tanaka from office in January 2002 (Yakushiji 2003: 87–103).

The career path of Japanese bureaucrats was unofficially divided into elite and non-elite tracks.[1] Both followed a fixed pattern according to seniority, but while the elite civil servants experienced different kinds of tasks and were trained as generalists, their non-elite colleagues gained narrow skills in specific policy fields. The top post for non-elite bureaucrats was usually division director (*kachō*), while elite bureaucrats competed for the offices of bureau directors-general (*kyokuchō*) and administrative vice-ministers (*jimujikan*). Theoretically, until the change of law in 2007, promotion to a higher post was decided through competitive exams. In reality, however, such exams were conducted only in 1950 and abandoned ever since. Instead, high-ranking bureaucrats were chosen through selection based on skills, which was allowed by law only as an extraordinary measure (Tanaka 2019: 130–133). Ambitious civil servants, who wanted to succeed in their careers, tended to avoid risky initiatives and instead focused on establishing personal connections in the ministry and with the politicians who were influential in their policy field (Nishimura 2002: 174–175). Those who reached the post of administrative vice-ministers were commonly considered as the real decision makers behind their political superiors. Deputy chief cabinet secretaries (CCSs), in turn, were positioned at the top of the bureaucratic hierarchy and acted as policy coordinators between the ministries, as well as between the Kantei and Kasumigaseki (metonym for Japanese bureaucracy).

While administrative vice-ministers were real experts in their policy field, the politically nominated ministers often lacked sufficient knowledge of the business of their ministry. Cabinet portfolios were distributed as rewards for gaining electoral votes rather than for the policymaking skills of individual politicians. Over the years, a typical career path for Liberal Democratic Party (LDP) lawmakers was standardized according to the seniority rule. While first-term parliamentarians could only become members of a parliamentary committee or a policy division in the LDP Policy Research Council, sixth-termers expected a ministerial post (Inoguchi & Iwai 1987: 121). Ministers who lacked specialist knowledge were easily manipulated by their administrative staff.

According to common knowledge, the Ministry of Finance (MOF) was the most powerful ministry of all. Its position resulted from its control over the budget compilation process. After the preparation of initial budget proposals by separate ministries, the MOF established a ceiling for expenditures. The budget compilation was characterized by incrementalism. Instead of conducting a thorough examination of old projects, current expenditures automatically became the basis for the next year's budget (Campbell 1980: 63). Such attachment to the *status quo* resulted in wasteful spending and an increasing budget deficit. To cope with this problem, a minus ceiling was introduced in the 1980s – all ministries were ordered to uniformly cut expenses, without conducting a comprehensive screening regarding the suitability of separate programs (Muramatsu 1994: 146). An important source of the MOF's power was its jurisdiction over the National Tax Agency. The mere threat of conducting a tax audit in the legislative office of a parliamentarian could be used to dissuade her/him from challenging the MOF's privileges (Takahashi 2011: 126–128). In addition, through the administrative guidance of private banks, and authority over the Japan Development Bank and the BOJ, the MOF shaped the loan policy toward separate industries and corporations (Kerbo & McKinstry 1995: 89). Due to numerous corruption scandals, the MOF became one of the main targets of popular criticism in the 1990s. As a result of the administrative reforms that entered into force in 2001, the MOF lost control over the Financial Services Agency, which came under the jurisdiction of the Cabinet Office (Tanaka 2019: 23–39).

MOF's main rival was the METI. Since the period of Japan's economic miracle in the 1950s and 1960s, METI (until 2001, MITI) bureaucrats boasted the role of overseers of economic growth. Through administrative guidance, they established development paths for big businesses and whole industry sectors (Kerbo & McKinstry 1995: 89). As stressed by Makihara (2018: 116–118), contrary to the MOF or the ministries that originated from the pre-war Ministry of Home Affairs, METI hosted a lot of reform-minded bureaucrats. This peculiarity of METI resulted from the fact that it had to actively adapt Japan to abrupt changes in the global economy. In the 1970s, METI led a reorganization of energy policy after the oil crisis, and in the 1980s and 1990s, it dealt with trade frictions with the US. As a result, METI officials were less inclined to defend the *status quo* than most of their counterparts in other ministries. As explained by a mid-ranking METI bureaucrat, an atmosphere of free discussion was usually respected in the ministry (interview by the author, Tokyo, October 17, 2019). Tanaka (2019: 74–75) claims that METI's tendency to overwrite old plans with new ones ideally fitted the Kantei's need for renewing the policy agenda on an annual basis. However, while such short-term orientation was instrumental in attracting popular support, METI bureaucrats were less skilful in following up on their own projects. As pointed out by Koga (2017: 117–118), when he worked in METI, it remained a common practice to draft policy proposals for realization in two years, even though the budget had not yet been decided for the following year. As there was fierce competition between different bureaus for implementation of novel policies, METI officials tended to refurbish old projects under catchy new names. According to Koga, such a ministerial culture generated budgetary costs without producing substantial economic gains.

The professional knowledge, experience in policymaking, high self-esteem, fixed career path, as well as the nexus with political and business elites lay at the foundation of the peculiar ethos of the Japanese civil service. While the administrative reforms of the 1990s weakened the bureaucrats' position vis-à-vis the Kantei, the bureaucrats remained a major veto player in the government. Nevertheless, the civil service was not a monolith. The prime minister could take advantage of the contradictory interests and rivalry between separate ministries, such as MOF and METI, in pursuing his/her ambitious policy agenda.

Daily meetings of prime minister's closest staff

One of the things that Prime Minister Abe learnt during his first administration was that selection of incompetent people as his closest subordinates and lack of effective communication between them may impede the normal functioning of the whole government. As a result, in 2012, he treated skills and knowledge, not only friendship, as criteria for choosing the politicians and bureaucrats to serve in the Kantei and the Cabinet Secretariat. Most significantly, Abe ensured swift exchange of information within his closest entourage by holding daily meetings of his most trusted staff.

One of the reasons for the deficient decision-making process under the first Abe administration was the personal composition of the Kantei and the Cabinet Secretariat. CCS Shiozaki Yasuhisa was Abe's good friend, but he lacked the experience and coordination skills required for that office (Ishibashi 2019: 127). In addition, former MOF bureaucrat Matoba Junzō, who assumed the post of administrative deputy CCS, had retired from central administration a decade earlier, which meant that he did not possess sufficient knowledge of the governmental structures after the implementation of administrative reforms. As a result, he was unable to make proper use of the coordination network of administrative vice-ministers who were one generation younger than him. What is more, Prime Minister's Executive Secretary Inoue Yoshiyuki, as a non-elite bureaucrat, could not take full advantage of the team of prime minister's administrative secretaries (Makihara 2018: 151–152). The selection of the wrong people for the three crucial posts in the Kantei and the Cabinet Secretariat led to organizational disorder, problems with communication, and even personal animosities among the prime minister's direct subordinates.

Not to let various figures from his closest entourage compete with each other for implementation of their individual initiatives, Abe started meeting on a daily basis with the key members of his staff. The group of core decision-makers in the Kantei was composed of four politicians: prime minister, CCS and two political deputy CCSs, as well as two bureaucrats: administrative deputy CCS and prime minister's executive (senior) secretary. These unofficial meetings (so-called *sei fuku kanbō chōkan kaigi*) took place every morning on the fifth floor of the Kantei building. Although they usually lasted only 10 or 15 minutes, they became instrumental in sharing information on current matters and avoiding any misunderstandings between the prime minister and his direct subordinates. As such, the daily meetings enabled better policy coordination both on routine tasks and long-term policies (Tazaki 2014: 26–33).

Abe carefully selected his closest staff. It was CCS Suga Yoshihide who became a pivot linking the efforts of the whole cabinet. Suga had attracted Abe's attention under the Koizumi administration, when he promoted the imposition of economic sanctions against North Korea. It was Suga who, in 2004, prepared the bills that prohibited the North Korean ship Man Gyong Bong from visiting Japanese ports and that halted all trade and financial transactions with that country. As Abe wholeheartedly supported a hardline policy toward Pyongyang to force Kim Jong-il to a final resolution of the abduction problem, both politicians quickly started a mutually fruitful cooperation.[2] This close relationship explains why, under the first Abe administration, Suga, despite being only a fourth-term parliamentarian, was entrusted with the responsible post of the minister of internal affairs and communications (Mori 2016: 187–189). However, it is mainly Suga's posture after Abe's resignation in 2007 that decided about his promotion to CCS. Suga was one of the few politicians who maintained a close relationship with

Abe in 2007–2012. Most significantly, it was Suga who played a crucial role in convincing Abe to once again run in the LDP presidential election and who actively engaged in his electoral campaign (Yamaguchi 2017: 111–118).

The posts of political deputy CCS were assumed by fourth-term House of Representatives lawmaker Katō Katsunobu and third-term member of the House of Councilors Sekō Hiroshige. Under the first Abe administration, Katō had served as Cabinet Office parliamentary vice-minister, and Sekō as prime minister's special adviser. Every Monday morning, Katō and Sekō held regular meetings with their direct superior Suga, during which they analyzed public opinion polls and often discussed current issues with media specialists (Tazaki 2014: 33–34). In October 2015, Katō was replaced with Hagiuda Kōichi, who, in turn, ceded the post of political deputy CCS to Nishimura Yasutoshi in August 2017. Sekō held his post the longest – until August 2016, when he was replaced by Nogami Kōtarō. In fact, it was Sekō who advised Abe to hold daily meetings of his closest staff in the Kantei during the tea break. He thus wanted to avoid the disorder of Abe's first administration. The tradition of daily meetings was continued even after Sekō left the Kantei, when he became minister of economy, trade, and industry (Taniguchi 2018: 148–150). After the government reshuffle in September 2019, posts of political deputy CCSs were assumed by Nishimura Akihiro and Okada Naoki, both belonging to the Hosoda faction (only Katō was a member of the Takeshita group).

Respecting tradition, the post of administrative deputy CCS was entrusted to Sugita Kazuhiro, a former bureaucrat from one of the institutions originating from the pre-war Ministry of Home Affairs – the National Police Agency. As a Deputy CCS for Crisis Management, Sugita had cooperated with Abe over the North Korean problem under the Koizumi administration, when Abe served as deputy CCS. Together with Director of Cabinet Intelligence, Kitamura Shigeru, another former National Police Agency official, Sugita provided Abe with information useful in managing the government. In particular, it was Sugita and Kitamura who persuaded the prime minister of the necessity to pass the Bill on Protection of Specially Designated Secrets together with the establishment of the NSC, which was a long-cherished goal of the Police bureaucrats (Mori 2019: 95–110). In addition, the close relationship between Sugita and the two Assistant CCSs, Furuya Kazuyuki in charge of domestic, and Kanehara Nobukatsu in charge of international affairs, was instrumental in transmitting the decisions reached at the daily meetings of the prime minister's closest entourage to a wider group of Kantei bureaucrats (George Mulgan 2018: 40–41). Kōno Tarō noted that, when he had served as the minister of state for disaster management in 2015–2016, he was impressed with Sugita's coordination skills (interview by the author, Tokyo, October 20, 2016). During the Kumamoto Earthquake in April 2016, Sugita called the representatives of all ministries to his office, gave them concrete instructions on disaster-relief activities, and supervised their implementation.

The last of the attendees of the daily meetings was Prime Minister's Executive Secretary Imai Takaya. Imai had served as prime minister's administrative secretary under the first Abe government. Enjoying Abe's trust, he acted not only as a gatekeeper to the prime minister who prepared the head of government's daily schedule, but also as an adviser who exerted influence on personnel affairs and policy matters. At the end of each day, Imai held get-togethers with all the prime minister's administrative secretaries, during which he coordinated current issues and sometimes transmitted to the staff decisions made during the prime minister's closest entourage's meetings (Tazaki 2014: 57–58). As a former METI Policy Planning and Coordination Division director and nephew of former Japan Business Federation Chairperson Imai Takashi, Imai Takaya boasted good connections with business circles and was particularly interested in economic policy, such as implementation of Abenomics, postponement of the consumption tax hike, and the reopening of nuclear power plants (Mori 2019: 18–38).

Imai's influence extended even to foreign policy making. For instance, the prime minister's executive secretary together with Special Adviser to the Cabinet Taniguchi Tomohiko co-authored the prime minister's address to the US Congress in April 2015 and the Abe Statement issued in mid-August 2015 to commemorate the 70th anniversary of the end of Second World War. Both documents represented a balanced approach that displayed repentance for war atrocities while avoiding direct apologies (Yomiuri Shinbun Seijibu 2015: 150–157). In addition, Imai established his own informal diplomatic channels with Chinese and Russian officials, which sometimes led to frictions between the Kantei and the MOFA. For example, in May 2017, he changed the contents of a letter from Abe to President Xi Jinping that was entrusted to LDP Secretary-General Nikai Toshihiro so as to express interest in cooperation with the Chinese Belt and Road Initiative.[3] As this interference was done without sufficient consultation with the MOFA, it presumably met with dissatisfaction from National Security Adviser Yachi Shōtarō (Mori 2019: 37–65). The broad fields of interest of Imai attest to the fact that his role greatly exceeded the functions of a mere secretary.

It is worth mentioning that Abe's administrative secretaries were experienced bureaucrats as well. Two of them (Suzuki Hiroshi from MOFA and Nakae Motoya from MOF) had already served as secretaries when Abe was CCS in the Koizumi cabinet and one of them (Yanase Tadao from METI) had been administrative secretary to Prime Minister Asō Tarō. It was very unusual to choose a secretary who had served in a different administration, which indicated that Abe valued skills as highly as loyalty when selecting his staff (Tazaki 2014: 58).

As outlined above, the group of Abe's closest subordinates was composed of his trusted associates, who, at the same time, boasted suitable experience to fulfill their functions. In particular, CCS Suga Yoshihide shouldered the most difficult task of micromanaging contacts with all ministries and the ruling parties, thus enabling the prime minister to focus on establishing the broader direction of state policy. At the same time, Abe relied on Sugita's and Imai's Kasumigaseki know-how to coordinate various issues with the bureaucrats in a top-down manner.

Chief cabinet secretary and the Cabinet Secretariat

From the beginning of his second administration, Abe relied on the CCS as the main policy coordinator. Suga Yoshihide exceeded the role of other influential CCSs in the past, such as Gotōda Masaharu in the Nakasone cabinet or Fukuda Yasuo under the Koizumi administration. He not only served as a pivot for policy coordination between various ministries and between the government and the ruling party, but also took charge of screening the nominations for high-ranking bureaucratic posts thanks to his control over the newly established Cabinet Bureau of Personnel Affairs.

Suga's traits of character made him an ideal candidate for the function of CCS. Unlike numerous LDP parliamentarians who had inherited the profession of politician from their parents, Suga was a self-made man. He was born the son of a farmer in the provincial Akita Prefecture. Only thanks to his hard work did he graduate from university, become a secretary to a lawmaker, work as a Yokohama City councilor, and, in 1996, get elected to the House of Representatives. During his early political career, Suga managed to build a dense network of personal connections with local politicians and businesspeople in the Kanagawa Prefecture (Mori 2016: 44–131, 282–285).

Perhaps thanks to the strong basis of electoral support in his constituency, after proceeding to central politics Suga behaved very flexibly in terms of political loyalty. In 1998, he defied his factional boss Obuchi Keizō and supported Kajiyama Seiroku in the LDP presidential race. In 2000, in turn, Suga backed Kōchikai leader Katō Kōichi in his attempt at overthrowing the Mori government and violated party rules by absenting himself from the voting on a no-confidence motion. Yet, against Kōchikai's decision to support Fukuda Yasuo, in 2007, he promoted the candidature of Asō Tarō for the post of LDP president. Suga eventually left Kōchikai in 2009, when he defied his factional boss Tanigaki Sadakazu by supporting Kōno Tarō against Tanigaki in another LDP presidential race. As we can see, he belonged to the new generation of LDP politicians who did not attach much importance to factional ties nor place loyalty in one person (Makihara 2016: 86).

Suga exhibited extensive skills of policy coordination. He lauded the bureaucrats for their professionalism and wide knowledge. According to Suga, the role of a politician was to motivate ministerial officials to overcome sectionalism and use their potential for realizing national interests. It is through close cooperation with, and listening to the advice of, his administrative staff that Suga, as the minister of internal affairs and communications, managed to implement such bold policy initiatives as the introduction of the hometown tax that allowed urban inhabitants to contribute part of their income and residence taxes to rural areas. Yet, Suga's abilities of interpersonal communication and policy coordination did not come at the expense of top-down leadership skills or a reform-minded attitude. In his book, he stressed that in order to make the bureaucrats work hard for implementation of the policy set up by their superior, the politician had to first clearly state that she/he would take full responsibility for her/his initiative (Suga 2012: 2–22).

Despite his respect toward the civil servants, Suga did not avoid confrontation whenever he encountered resistance from veto players. For example, regardless of concerns from the bureaucrats and accusations about interference in media freedom, as the minister of internal affairs and communications, he ordered the national broadcaster NHK to prepare the transmission of a shortwave message to the abducted Japanese who were potentially living in North Korea. In addition, to the displeasure of high-ranking officials in the ministry, he challenged the petrified system of promotion by ordering the nomination of non-elite bureaucrats to the posts of bureau director-general. Even when he served as METI parliamentary vice-minister from 2003 to 2004, he did not avoid confrontation with public servants who strongly opposed his initiative of reducing highway fees (Suga 2012: 56–154).

Suga's hard-working style became legendary after he assumed the office of CCS. He woke up every day at 4 am and devoted two hours to reading all the significant newspapers and magazines. Thanks to his broad knowledge of current issues, he could professionally conduct two press conferences per day, one in the morning and one in the evening. His daily schedule was packed with meetings and appointments until late evening. According to Special Adviser to the Cabinet Taniguchi Tomohiko (2018: 157–159), Suga did not rest even on the weekends, when he often acted as an arbiter in policy disputes between various officials.

Just like the prime minister, CCS Suga carefully selected experienced bureaucrats as his staff. Although it was a rule that CCS' secretaries changed every two years, Suga entrusted three of these posts to the bureaucrats from MOF, MOFA, and the National Police Agency who had already served under previous administrations (Tazaki 2014: 58). CCS' powers were strengthened by institutional changes in the Cabinet Secretariat. Contrary to the rigid structure of separate ministries, the organizational framework of the Cabinet Secretariat was flexible, with numerous strategy offices (*senryaku shitsu*), countermeasure offices (*taisaku shitsu*), secretariats (*jimukyoku*), policy offices (*seisaku shitsu*), and promotion offices (*suishin shitsu*) established temporarily to deal with various policy initiatives. In addition, while the number of the Cabinet Secretariat's staff was limited by a special regulation, the prime minister could easily increase it as a temporary measure (Kawato 2015: 162). As a result, the number of civil servants in the Cabinet Secretariat grew from circa 800 persons in 2012 to more than 1000 in 2015. The new staff were dispatched in particular to the National Security Secretariat and the Cabinet Bureau of Personnel Affairs (Makihara 2016: 81). The fact that both of these crucial new institutions were placed

Reforming governmental institutions 99

under the Cabinet Secretariat reflected the role of this organ as the main coordinating body of the executive branch. In addition, to provide sufficient administrative backing to the new advisory councils established under the cabinet, the number of bureaucrats seconded to the Cabinet Secretariat while preserving their affiliations with home ministries was increased from 539 in 2001 to 1905 in 2014 (Tanaka 2019: 96). As shown in Figure 3.1, at the

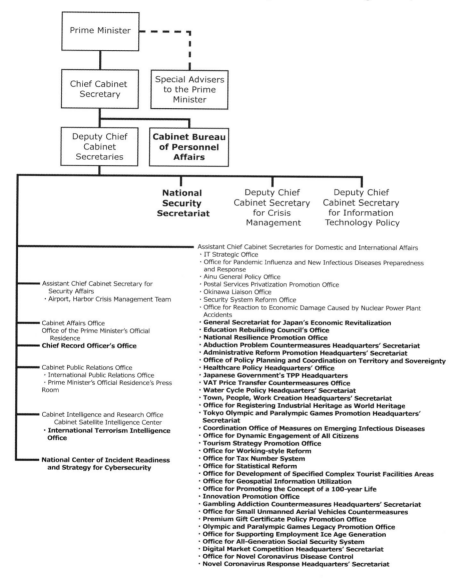

Figure 3.1 The Cabinet Secretariat's structure as of March 31, 2020.

Source: Compiled by the author, based on: Cabinet Secretariat (2020).

beginning of 2020, as many as 39 offices or secretariats existed under the assistant CCSs for domestic and international affairs, and 32 of them were established during the second Abe administration.

Suga's coordination skills and the coherent team under his command enabled the Cabinet Secretariat to change the logic of the decision-making process not only on the crucial initiatives promoted by the Kantei, but also on routine issues. As pointed out by Mikuriya (2015: 52–53), under Suga's leadership, the Cabinet Secretariat became a much busier place with secretaries and assistants constantly entering or leaving the building. Instructed by the CCS, the Cabinet Secretariat staff established numerous small teams to deal with distinct problems. Instead of letting the bureaucrats conduct lengthy inter-ministerial coordination on daily issues, the Cabinet Secretariat largely took the initiative in this field. Thanks to this new approach, the Kantei was able to impose the general direction for policy negotiations on ministry employees, thus creating an impression of the effectiveness and swiftness of the decision-making process.

Cabinet meetings and the Administrative Vice-Ministers' Council

Abe did not implement any revolutionary changes to the formal structure of the cabinet. After returning to power in December 2012, he not only continued the traditional pattern of cabinet meetings, but also decided not to experiment too extensively with the format of the Administrative Vice-Ministers' Council that had been subject to numerous changes under the DPJ government. Over time, however, evolution of the proceedings of both organs reflected the strengthened position of the Kantei.

As was mentioned in Chapter 1, until 2009, the Administrative Vice-Ministers' Council had gathered twice a week – on Mondays and Thursdays – to establish a schedule for cabinet meetings on Tuesdays and Fridays. Only the policies that had been agreed upon by the bureaucrats from all the ministries involved were submitted for cabinet approval. Under his first administration in 2006–2007, Abe Shinzō became the first prime minister who ever broke this unwritten principle and forcefully authorized a decision on limitation of *amakudari* without the Administrative Vice-Ministers' Council's prior consent. The DPJ government (2009–2012) initially abolished and eventually reestablished the Council in a diluted form (as Liaison Council of All Ministries, Kakufushō Renraku Kaigi).

After regaining power, Prime Minister Abe initially envisaged reestablishment of the Council in its traditional form, but, eventually, it was decided that such a move would expose the government to criticism over a revival of bureaucratic power. The organ was renamed the Administrative Vice-Ministers' Liaison Council (Jikan Renraku Kaigi) and institutionalized to gather once a week on Fridays – after, instead of prior to, cabinet meetings. As a result, its role was modified from prior authorization of policies to discussion on the ways of implementing cabinet decisions (Asakura 2016: 226).

As such, the Council was turned into a body that transmitted governmental policies to ministerial level in a top-down fashion. What further undermined the function of the Council as a venue for authorizing decisions for the cabinet's approval was the fact that its head, Administrative Deputy CCS Sugita Kazuhiro, lacked experience as an administrative vice-minister (Makihara 2018: 64). Rather than seeking consensus between the Council members, Sugita coordinated implementation of the policies decided upon by the Kantei. He also used the Council to keep an eye on the internal situation in separate ministries. In November 2016, a representative of the Imperial Household Agency was added as a member, which reflected the need to coordinate the preparation of a special law allowing the emperor to abdicate after the expression by Akihito of his intention to resign (*Asahi Shinbun* 2016: 4).

Just like the administrative vice-ministers' meetings, the cabinet meetings were preserved in a form similar to the one that had existed during the DPJ government. As admitted by Hayashi Yoshimasa, who had been minister of agriculture and minister of education under the second Abe administration, instead of serving as a forum for discussion on policies, the cabinet meetings constituted a place for final authorization of cabinet decisions the contents of which had been negotiated through prior coordination within the government and between the ruling parties (interview by the author, Tokyo, October 16, 2019). Kōno Tarō, in turn, who had served in the Abe cabinet as the minister of state for disaster management, minister of foreign affairs, and minister of defense, pointed out that even during the discussion time (*kakuryō kondankai*) held immediately after each cabinet meeting, there was barely any discussion, as a deputy CCS only read out various documents (interview by the author, Tokyo, October 20, 2016). While the cabinet meetings had been traditionally treated as get-togethers to sign documents, under previous administrations, at least the discussion time had been more vivid with ministers expressing their opinions on different topics.

In April 2014, CCS Suga decided to disclose cabinet proceedings within three weeks of each meeting. It was a continuation of a reform initiated under the DPJ government (Makihara 2018: 176). Until that point, no official records of the proceedings of this important decision-making venue had even existed. The disclosure of proceedings was probably aimed at diluting popular opposition against the Bill on Protection of Specially Designated Secrets. Nevertheless, it also indirectly strengthened the powers of the Cabinet Secretariat, which was charged with preparing the records. It seems that disclosure of proceedings exerted pressure on separate ministers to display constraint in opposing their superior during cabinet meetings. As such, the meetings themselves became even more petrified, thus leaving more room for the prime minister and the CCS to use their discretionary powers (Makihara 2016: 97–101). As seen in Figure 3.2, not only did an average cabinet meeting last about 11–12 minutes, but the duration also decreased over time. In addition, the percentage of meetings held in

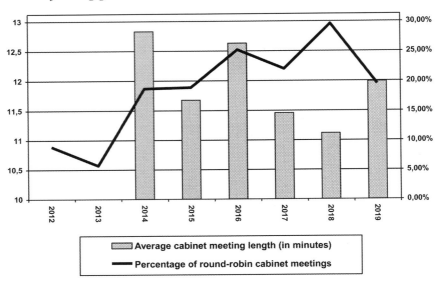

Figure 3.2 Average cabinet meeting duration and percentage of round-robin cabinet meetings.

Source: Compiled by the author, based on data from: Prime Minister of Japan and His Cabinet (2020a).

round-robin format, without actual get-togethers, increased from 1/20th in 2013 to 1/5th in 2019. This trend indicates that the Abe cabinet devoted less and less time to discussion.

On the one hand, the cabinet meetings and the Administrative Vice-Ministers' Liaison Council were continued in a format similar to that under the previous administrations. On the other hand, however, the significance of both bodies decreased. Instead of the ritualized cabinet meetings, real decisions were made during the unofficial get-togethers between Abe and his direct entourage in the Kantei.

Political appointees in the government

The traditional role of political appointees in the government was redefined under the second Abe administration. Instead of serving as spokespersons and representatives of the interests of their ministries, the ministers became agents of the Kantei whose careers depended on the loyal execution of the prime minister's policy agenda. The political appointees' new function was symbolized by seemingly minor institutional changes that enhanced the Kantei leadership.

In order to ensure the long-term policy orientation of the government, Prime Minister Abe initially refrained from frequent cabinet reshuffles. The first government reshuffle took place in September 2014, which is almost two years after its formation. As such, it was the longest-serving cabinet in post-war

Japan. Furthermore, Abe reappointed key cabinet members (such as Vice-Premier and Minister of Finance Asō Tarō, CCS Suga Yoshihide, and, until August 2017, Foreign Minister Kishida Fumio) for several terms. This practice enabled some ministers to gain extensive experience in their legislative fields, necessary for efficient implementation of government policies. In addition, as stressed by Mikuriya, Abe created a system of "senior ministers" whom he charged with distinct policy initiatives. This narrow group of his most trusted associates included Amari Akira, who, until January 2016, served as the minister of state for economic and fiscal policy. Amari's experience as a former minister of economy, trade and industry became instrumental in implementing Abenomics and promoting liberalization of trade (Mikuriya 2015: 47).

Abe used extensively the ministers of state for special missions to charge them with the numerous policies of his comprehensive agenda. The maximum number of ministers had been increased from 17 to 18 after the establishment of the Reconstruction Agency by the DPJ government in 2012. In 2015, Abe added one more minister of state for special missions to charge her/him with preparation for the Tokyo Olympic and Paralympic Games in 2020, thus increasing the total number of ministers to 19. As indicated by Shindō (2019: 170–171), this change strengthened the Kantei's control over the cabinet, as the ministers of state for special missions relied on the Cabinet Office staff in the realization of their tasks.

In addition, Abe entrusted supplementary responsibilities to almost all the cabinet members. As seen in Figure 3.3, since the entry into force of administrative reforms in 2001, the number of ministers charged with

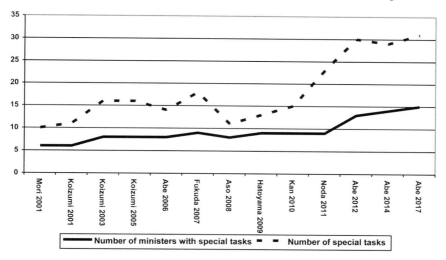

Figure 3.3 Number of special tasks and ministers therewith in the Japanese government after the administrative reform.

Source: Compiled by the author, based on the list of ministers from: Prime Minister's Office of Japan (2020).

special tasks has been gradually growing from 6 under the Mori administration, through 9 under the DPJ government, up to 13 when Abe returned to power in 2012, and 15 following the 2017 parliamentary election. In parallel, the number of ministers' special tasks increased abruptly from 23 under Noda to about 30 under the second Abe administration. After the government reshuffle in September 2019, only the ministers of justice, foreign affairs, agriculture, and defense were left exclusively with their original tasks (see Table 3.1). The number of responsibilities of each minister of state for special missions, in turn, oscillated between three and six.[4] As Kawato (2015: 167) stressed, entrusting additional tasks to almost all ministers turned them into assistants of the head of government. Furthermore, as the special tasks were usually administered by various units in the Cabinet Secretariat, the CCS indirectly gained a leverage over the cabinet members. Symbolically, all ministers became responsible for implementation of the tasks imposed on them by the Kantei rather than for representing the interests of their ministries.

The revision of the National Public Service Law in May 2014 changed the responsibilities of the prime minister's special advisers (*naikaku sōri daijin hosakan*). Previously, they had been charged only with advising and providing their opinion on important policies to the head of government. Article 22 of the new law broadened their functions to assisting the prime minister in planning basic strategic policies and other selected important policies, as instructed by the head of government (Cabinet Secretariat 2014a: 44). The reform actually made the responsibilities of special advisers more consistent with the original Japanese name of the post (*hosakan* means aide, not adviser). A separate cabinet decision from May 2014, in turn, clarified that special advisers were responsible directly to the head of government. As such, they were excluded from the chain of command in the Cabinet Secretariat, though they could be ordered to assist the CCS and his deputies in specific tasks (Cabinet Secretariat 2014b). In addition, the bill on the creation of the NSC stipulated that one special adviser would be charged with security issues.

Under his first administration in 2006, Abe had nominated as many as five prime minister's special advisers: Koike Yuriko in charge of security matters, Nakayama Kyōko in charge of abductions by North Korean spies, Yamatani Eriko in charge of education reform, Sekō Hiroshige in charge of public relations, and Nemoto Takumi in charge of economic and financial issues. As they were all politicians with high ambitions, they competed for access to the prime minister and quickly came into conflict between each other and with CCS Shiozaki Yasuhisa and Prime Minister's Executive Secretary Inoue Yoshiyuki (Uesugi 2011: 72–189). Nemoto (2015: 372–453) stressed that he received only one secretary as administrative staff and had to form a special taskforce of ministerial employees and private-sector specialists by himself. According to him, the greatest difficulty was policy coordination with ministers of the involved legislative fields who did not

Table 3.1 Composition of the Abe Cabinet, except for the ministers of state for special missions, in September 2019.

Minister	Main function	Additional tasks
As Tarō	Deputy Prime Minister Minister of Finance	Minister of State for Financial Services Minister in charge of Overcoming Deflation
Suga Yoshihide	Chief cabinet secretary	Minister in charge of Mitigating the Impact of US Forces in Okinawa Minister in charge of the Abductions Issue
Takaichi Sanae	Minister for Internal Affairs and Communications	Minister of State for the Social Security and Tax Number System
Mori Masako	Minister of Justice	-
Motegi Toshimitsu	Minister for Foreign Affairs	-
Hagiuda Kōichi	Minister of Education, Culture, Sports, Science and Technology	Minister in charge of Education Rebuilding
Katō Katsunobu	Minister of Health, Labor and Welfare	Minister for Working-style Reform
Etō Taku	Minister of Agriculture, Forestry and Fisheries	-
Kajiyama Hiroshi	Minister of Economy, Trade and Industry	Minister in charge of Industrial Competitiveness Minister in charge of International Exposition Minister for Economic Cooperation with Russia Minister in charge of the Response to the Economic Impact caused by the Nuclear Accident Minister of State for the Nuclear Damage Compensation and Decommissioning Facilitation Corporation
Akaba Kazuyoshi	Minister of Land, Infrastructure, Transport and Tourism	Minister in charge of Water Cycle Policy
Koizumi Shinjirō	Minister of the Environment	Minister of State for Nuclear Emergency Preparedness
Kōno Tarō	Minister of Defense	-

Source: Compiled by the author, based on Prime Minister of Japan and His Cabinet (2019).

necessarily feel that prime minister's special advisers were entitled to conduct any reforms. On the other hand, the greatest merit was the fact that special advisers could act behind the scenes without having to answer to Diet interpellations. Itō (2010: 86), who had been special adviser to Prime Minister Fukuda, suggested that, in turn, the excessive saturation of Abe's Kantei with politicians worked as a centrifugal force that weakened the prime minister's leadership.

In December 2012, Abe nominated three special advisers – former Ministry of Health, Labor and Welfare Vice-Minister Etō Seiichi (in charge of important matters of national administration), first-term House of Councilors member, former Ministry of Internal Affairs and Communications bureaucrat Isozaki Yōsuke (in charge of security policy and the electoral system), and former METI bureaucrat Hasegawa Eiichi (in charge of policy planning). In January 2013, one more person was appointed to this post – former Ministry of Land, Infrastructure, Transport and Tourism bureaucrat Izumi Hiroto (in charge of regional reconstruction and revival as well as development strategy regarding health matters). Only one of the special advisers, Etō, was a high-profile politician, and Abe's trusted associate. Thanks to that, the prime minister avoided a situation similar to his first administration, when special advisers competed one against another to implement their individual policy initiatives. In addition, by relying on former bureaucrats, Abe used their know-how to gain leverage over their home ministries.

At the same time, new posts of minister's assistants (*daijin hosakan*) were introduced. The revision of the National Public Service Law enabled the nomination of up to six minister's assistants in the Cabinet Office and one minister's assistant for each ministry. Their obligation was to help the minister in planning specific policies according to her/his instructions (Cabinet Secretariat 2014a). Similarly to prime minister's special advisers, minister's assistants were excluded from the chain of command in the ministry and answered directly to the minister, not to his deputies (Cabinet Secretariat 2014b). While CCS Suga appealed for the nomination of experts from the private sector to these posts, in some cases, they were assigned to mid-ranking politicians. For example, Minister for Overcoming Population Decline and Vitalizing Local Economy, Ishiba Shigeru, employed former Minister of State for Financial Services, Itō Tatsuya, Minister for Reconstruction, Takeshita Wataru, selected former Vice-Minister for Reconstruction, Tani Kōichi, Minister of State for Economic and Fiscal Policy, Amari Akira, chose LDP House of Representatives member, Fukuda Muneyuki, and Minister of Education Culture, Sports, Science and Technology, Shimomura Hakubun, entrusted this post, surprisingly, to Suzuki Kan, who had been education vice-minister under the DPJ administration. Minister's assistants to some extent reduced the workload of the ministers, thus strengthening political control over bureaucrats in respective ministries (Makihara 2016: 107–109).

Nevertheless, the abovementioned institutional changes did not fundamentally change the balance of power between political appointees and their administrative staff. In fact, as pointed out by Makihara (2016: 79), Prime Minister Abe used the fact that the "three political officials" (ministers, vice-ministers, and parliamentary vice-ministers) in separate ministries were still largely dependent on bureaucratic guidance to bolster his control over individual ministers. Thanks to the new institutional tools for exerting pressure on high-ranking civil servants, the Kantei simply gained the ability to influence the direction of bureaucratic guidance over the heads of ministers. According to Makihara (2018: 79–80), from 2016, such a situation started causing a serious distortion of the chain of command. Contrary to the DPJ administration that had tried to empower the "three political officials," under the Abe cabinet, the prime minister's secretaries transmitted orders to high-ranking bureaucrats in separate ministries over the heads of ministers, vice-ministers, and parliamentary vice-ministers. While such practices were instrumental in controlling the government, they also disturbed the transparency of the decision-making process, thus leading to such incidents as the forgery of documents related to the Moritomo Gakuen case by MOF officials without the knowledge of Minister of Finance Asō Tarō.

CCS Suga's strong position in the government enabled him to discipline other high-ranking politicians. For instance, in December 2013, he reprimanded Minister of State for Consumer Affairs and Food Safety Mori Masako for a statement that the contents of negotiations on TPP accession would be treated as a "special secret." Suga's power extended even to the activities of the politicians who were theoretically higher in the cabinet hierarchy. For example, in July 2013, the CCS put pressure on Vice-Premier Asō Tarō to force him to retract his controversial statement that Japan should learn from Nazi Germany how to revise the constitution (Shimizu 2014: 38). Analogically, in February 2014, he strongly reprimanded Prime Minister's Special Adviser Etō Seiichi for his comment that Japan was disappointed with the White House's negative reaction to Abe's visit to the Yasukuni Shrine in December 2013 (Makihara 2016: 89).

Criticizing the DPJ's failure in imposing political leadership on the bureaucrats, ministers from the LDP generally tried to build a relationship of trust with their administrative staff. For example, Minister for Reconstruction Nemoto Takumi (2015: 18–334) emphasized that yelling at the bureaucrats was counter-productive in persuading them to cooperate. According to him, the greatest mistake of DPJ politicians was the fact that they overfocused on details while neglecting a holistic approach to policy problems. Instead, Nemoto tried to overcome ministerial sectionalism by creating special taskforces composed of bureau directors-general from the ministries involved in separate policies. He stressed that ministers had to be able to indicate a general direction for policy deliberations, let the bureaucrats elaborate proposals based on their extensive knowledge, and take full

108 *Reforming governmental institutions*

responsibility for final decisions. That way, he argued, ties of trust were built between the politicians and their administrative staff.

As George Mulgan (2018: 89) pointed out, the strengthening of the Kantei did not necessarily translate into more powerful ministers, as "policymaking authority has shifted from the party to the prime ministerial executive rather than to the prime minister and cabinet." Apart from skills, Abe highly valued loyalty when selecting ministers, and he entrusted numerous additional tasks to cabinet members to make sure they would follow the Kantei's instructions. The political nominees in the prime minister's closest entourage were expected to actively promote the head of government's policy agenda. The prime minister's special advisers proved instrumental in enhancing the coordination capabilities of the Cabinet Secretariat, while the newly established posts of minister's assistants provided policymaking backing to individual ministers and to the Cabinet Office.

Cabinet Bureau of Personnel Affairs

Perhaps the most significant new source of power for the prime minister and the CCS were their prerogatives in nominating high-ranking bureaucrats. The Kantei had been entitled to interfere in bureaucratic appointments even before the second Abe administration. Since 1949, all nominations for the posts above bureau director-general had to be authorized by the cabinet. In reality, however, politicians rarely tried to change ministerial recommendations that were adopted during administrative vice-ministers' meetings and automatically submitted for the cabinet's approval. It does not mean that there were no attempts at changing the *status quo*. Prime Minister Hashimoto Ryūtarō (1996–1998), especially, tried to overhaul the civil service system as a part of his wide-scale administrative reforms. In 1997, Kajiyama Seiroku, CCS in the Hashimoto government, established the Personnel Examination Council (Jinji Kentō Kaigi), composed of the CCS and three deputy CCSs. The role of the new organ was to screen ministerial recommendations for all posts above the rank of bureau director-general before submitting them for approval during cabinet meetings. At the same time, the rank of such personnel decisions was raised from "understanding" (*ryōkai*) to "approval" (*shōnin*). While the new system theoretically facilitated political interference in the nomination process, in reality, the Personnel Examination Council quickly turned into yet another meaningless body that almost automatically authorized decisions made at the administrative level (Asakura 2016: 160–161, 207–208, 233).

In order to fundamentally change the balance of power between the bureaucrats and the politicians, during his first administration, Prime Minister Abe created an advisory council that prepared a draft of civil service reform. Its report, published under the Fukuda administration, recommended the creation of the Cabinet Agency of Personnel Affairs (Naikaku Jinji Chō) and centralization of personnel management under its jurisdiction. While Minister of State for Financial Services and Administrative Reform Watanabe Yoshimi stressed the necessity for full realization of the recommendations, these plans encountered strong opposition from the bureaucracy and CCS Machimura Nobutaka, who claimed that the new agency should become only an advisory organ. The bill project that was submitted to the Diet tried to find a compromise between the two stances by putting personnel assessment under the jurisdiction of both the new body and individual ministers. Nevertheless, as in July 2007, the ruling coalition had lost its majority in the upper house, the government had to further modify the law to please the largest opposition party. Under DPJ pressure, the new agency was downgraded to the status of a bureau, uniform management of fresh employees was abandoned, and bureaucrats were not prohibited contact with lawmakers. Civil Service Reform Basic Law was eventually passed in June 2008, but it needed additional legislation to be implemented. As there were still controversies over detailed competences of the Cabinet Bureau of Personnel Affairs and to what extent the new body would take over the functions fulfilled by the previously existing organs, it took a lot of time to draft detailed legislation (Tanaka 2019: 139–143). The Asō cabinet (2008–2009) and the DPJ administration (2009–2012) were unable to pass the bill due to disturbances caused by the alternation of power in 2009 and almost unceasing state of "twisted Diet." The second Abe cabinet managed to proceed to realization of plans from the 2008 law only after having regained a majority of seats in the House of Councilors in the July 2013 election.

The Bill Concerning Reform of National Public Service System was adopted as a cabinet decision in November 2013 and passed by the Diet in March 2014. The Cabinet Bureau of Personnel Affairs (Naikaku Jinji Kyoku) was eventually established at the end of May 2014. The new organ took over some functions of the Administrative Management Bureau (Gyōsei Kanri Kyoku) and the Personnel and Pension Bureau (Jinji Onkyū Kyoku) from the Ministry of Internal Affairs and Communications (Mori 2019: 187–189). Initially, it was planned that the post of Bureau director-general would be assumed by administrative deputy CCS Sugita Kazuhiro, but, eventually, CCS Suga selected one of his political deputies, Katō Katsunobu, for this responsible function. This decision symbolized the new system of political supervision over the bureaucrats (Asakura 2016: 234–237). In October 2015, Katō was replaced with his successor as Political Deputy CCS, Hagiuda Kōichi, and only in August 2017 was Sugita nominated as Cabinet Bureau of Personnel Affairs head. The last change was probably caused by the fact that Hagiuda was criticized by the opposition parties as one of the Kantei representatives who put pressure on the Ministry of Education, Culture, Sports, Science and Technology in the Kake Gakuen scandal (*Asahi Shinbun* 2017: 4).

The new organ enabled the strategic promotion of all executive officials (*kanbushoku*) starting from the rank of section heads (*buchō*), including administrative vice-ministers (*jimu jikan*) and bureau directors-general (*kyokuchō*). It remained the role of each minister and his/her administrative staff to draft the initial personnel assessment of candidates. What differed from the old system was the fact that all recommendations were subsequently thoroughly screened by the CCS who prepared a list of candidates based on the consistency of their qualifications with the government's overall policy. The "appointment and dismissal consultations" (*ninmen kyōgi*) were limited to the prime minister, the CCS, and individual ministers. Even the Cabinet Bureau of Personnel Affairs chair did not directly participate in the consultations, as his/her role was limited to the administrative supervision of the selection process. The Personnel Examination Council was held on the same day as "appointment and dismissal consultations," and all nominations were subsequently accepted as cabinet decisions. As such, the ministers could nominate executive bureaucrats only after authorization by the prime minister and the CCS (Mori 2019: 190–193).

In addition, the new bill clarified the rules for demoting high-ranking civil servants in cases where their achievements were inferior to those of officials in similar posts, there were reasons to believe that another person would work more efficiently in that post, and there was no post of similar rank to which to transfer the concerned official (Cabinet Secretariat 2014a). After the passage of the bill, the number of administrative posts distributed in a top-down manner was raised from 200 to more than 600 (Makihara 2016: 105; Mori 2019: 188). The new rules enabled the Kantei to flexibly select the promising, reform-minded civil servants at relatively early stages of their careers. At the same time, the Abe administration avoided overly antagonizing the bureaucrats and maintained the relative independence of the National Personnel Authority (Jinjiin) – an organ in charge of such matters as salaries, recruitment examinations, and labor standards in the civil service (Makihara 2016: 88–89). The Cabinet Bureau of Personnel Affairs was simply added as a new layer to the old system.

Abe had relied on trusted civil servants who shared his policy vision during his first administration. For example, Foreign Administrative Vice-Minister, Yachi Shōtarō, and another high-ranking MOFA bureaucrat, Kanehara Nobukatsu, were the main figures behind the concept of "value-based diplomacy" that was intensively promoted in 2006–2007. They were both employed by the prime minister after returning to power – Yachi as national security adviser and Kanehara as assistant CCS. However, such strategic use of bureaucrats had been limited to a narrow group of Abe's most loyal administrative staff and almost exclusively to the spheres of foreign and security affairs.

By contrast, under his second administration Abe took full advantage of the Cabinet Bureau of Personnel Affairs to overcome opposition to his policy initiatives by the bureaucrats. CCS Suga used the new rules to reward those civil servants who remained loyal toward the Kantei. In 2015, a number of former prime minister's administrative secretaries were nominated as bureau chiefs in their home ministries. For example, Yanase Tadao assumed the prestigious post of director-general of the Economic and Industrial Policy Bureau in METI, which was usually assigned to officials who had already served as heads of other bureaus. Similarly, Yamada Makiko became the director-general of Global ICT Strategy Bureau in the Ministry of Internal Affairs and Communications (Makihara 2016: 106–107). Abe used his nomination power to reward the initiatives that were in line with his agenda and strategy. For instance, without respecting the traditional career ladder in MOFA, in 2015, he promoted Kōzuki Toyohisa to the post of ambassador in Russia. Kōzuki had probably impressed Abe when, as MOFA European Affairs Bureau director-general, he proposed the introduction of only mild sanctions against Moscow after the annexation of Crimea by Russia in 2014. As a result, Japan, on the one hand, remained loyal toward its American ally, while, on the other hand, maintained an open door for negotiations over the Northern Territories (South Kuril Islands) dispute, which were a key diplomatic initiative of the Abe cabinet (Mori 2019: 217–218). Some nominations were decided upon against the ministerial recommendations. For example, in 2016, the Kantei entrusted the post of justice administrative vice-minister to Kurokawa Hiromu, who was considered a bureaucrat closely cooperating with CCS Suga, while rejecting the candidature of Hayashi Makoto. In 2018, the government once more disregarded the opinion of the ministry by allowing Kurokawa to remain in office and sending Hayashi to the Nagoya High Public Prosecutor's Office. Such intervention in the Ministry of Justice, which was traditionally expected to be isolated from politics, met with criticism from the media (Mori 2019: 163–180).

The press reported that CCS Suga did not waver from punishing those bureaucrats whose convictions differed from the policy of the government or who simply were deemed not sufficiently loyal toward the Kantei. For example, in 2015, Suga dismissed the Ministry of Internal Affairs and Communications Local Tax Bureau director-general who had opposed the introduction of the hometown tax under the first Abe administration. In 2017, in turn, it was widely commented that Ministry of Land, Infrastructure, Transport and Tourism Civil Aviation Bureau director-general, who had failed to clearly deny political intervention in the Moritomo Gakuen scandal, was dismissed from office, while MOF Financial Bureau director-general, who denied any involvement of the prime minister and his wife in the purchase of land by the school, was promoted to the post of National Tax Agency head (Tanaka 2019: 147).

The new rules facilitated the implementation of some of Abe's key policies, such as the empowerment of women. Under pressure from the Kantei, the number of women in administrative executive posts in all ministries rose from 16 in 2013 to 23 in 2014, and 30 in 2015 (Makihara 2016: 105–107). In order to promote the reform of the Central Union of Agricultural Cooperatives (JA Zenchū), in 2016, the Kantei appointed Okuhara Masaaki, a reform-minded bureaucrat in the Ministry of Agriculture, Forestry and Fisheries (MAFF), as agriculture administrative vice-minister (George Mulgan 2018: 46–48). Some revolutionary nominations were decided upon under pressure from individual politicians in the government. For example, under recommendation from Vice-Minister and later Minister of Agriculture, Forestry and Fisheries, Saitō Ken, who was a former METI bureaucrat, from 2016, Food Industry Affairs Bureau directors-general originated from METI. Such a nomination pattern helped the government to overcome the MAFF's opposition to Japan's accession to the TPP (Taniguchi 2018: 165).

Thanks to the Kasumigaseki know-how, provided by reform-minded bureaucrats in his closest entourage, Abe was skillful in playing one ministry off against another. This *divide et impera* approach was particularly visible toward the most powerful ministry, the MOF. It was not a coincidence that many of Abe's closest subordinates, such as Prime Minister's Executive Secretary Imai Takaya, Special Adviser to the Prime Minister Hasegawa Eiichi, and CCS's Secretary Kadomatsu Takashi, originated from METI (Shimizu 2014: 22). As a lot of Abe's initiatives, e.g. Abenomics and the reopening of nuclear power plants, were in line with METI policy, the prime minister eagerly relied on the expertise of METI staff. To some extent, such an attitude was also a reaction to the fact that METI had been treated coldly by the DPJ administration. DPJ politicians had not only focused on labor and environmental issues that were problematic for METI, but they also established the Nuclear Regulation Authority that weakened METI's control over the nuclear power plants after the Fukushima crisis (Makihara 2018: 193–194). Under these circumstances, it is not surprising that METI placed high expectations in Abe and established strong connections with the prime minister from the very beginning of his second administration.

Nevertheless, extensive interference by the Kantei in bureaucratic nominations had some detrimental effects. As Makihara pointed out, the establishment of the Cabinet Bureau of Personnel Affairs led to excessive subordination of ministerial officials to the will of the Kantei. As a result, instead of offering professional advice to the politicians, the bureaucrats started paying attention not to express opinions that could endanger their careers. What is even more dangerous, as exemplified by the forgery of documents concerning the Moritomo Gakuen issue by the MOF, some officials went as far as covering up evidence of scandals that involved their superiors. On the other hand, the nominations that ignored the opinion of ministry officials and the excessive collusion by high-ranking bureaucrats with the Kantei often caused dissatisfaction and internal frictions in ministries. It seems that the leak of documents concerning the Moritomo Gakuen scandal from the Kinki Local Finance Bureau and the testimonies by former Ministry of Education, Culture, Sports, Science and Technology Administrative Vice-Minister, Maekawa Kihei, regarding the Kake Gakuen issue were the results of the bureaucrats' frustration over the prime minister's policy. By surrounding himself with a narrow group of high-ranking officials ready to protect the Kantei at all costs, Abe decreased the transparency of the decision-making process (Makihara 2018: 56–209).

As Tanaka (2019: 149–161) indicated, the bureaucrats adapted to the creation of the Cabinet Bureau of Personnel Affairs by consulting the head of the Bureau on tentative lists of candidates in spring, several months before the yearly announcement of nominations in the summer. The Kantei arbitrarily imposed its own candidates in only 20% of cases, but it sufficed for the civil servants to act as "yes-men" of the government. In general, the rules of seniority and almost annual exchange of high-ranking bureaucrats were still respected, which put into question the Abe administration's intention to improve the quality of public officials. As a side-effect of centralization of power, in turn, the number of decisions made in a top-down manner increased also at the bureaucratic level – for instance, the functions previously fulfilled by special advisers to division directors (*kachō hosakan*) started being fulfilled by division directors (*kachō*) themselves. To some extent, these changes undermined the ethos and prestige of the bureaucracy, which was reflected in a decreasing number of graduates of top universities who aimed at becoming civil servants.

The Cabinet Bureau of Personnel Affairs enabled the strategic nomination of high-ranking bureaucrats, but the new institution showed its full potential in changing the balance of power between the Kantei and the bureaucrats only under a stable and long-lasting administration. Thanks to a prolonged term in office, Abe could promote to executive posts in ministries those public servants whose efficiency he had experienced when they served in the Kantei or the Cabinet Secretariat. Gradually, such nomination patterns influenced the ethos of the bureaucrats, placing their loyalty in the prime minister and the CCS rather than in their home ministries.

National Security Council

While the Cabinet Bureau of Personnel Affairs allowed Abe to strengthen control over the bureaucrats, the NSC (Kokka Anzen Hoshō Kaigi) enabled him to play a more important role in security and foreign policy making. The oldest post-war predecessor of the NSC had been the National Defense Council (Kokubō Kaigi) established in 1956. It was composed of five members (the prime minister, foreign minister, minister of the treasury, Japan Defense Agency director-general, and Economic Planning Agency director-general) and focused on maintaining civil control over the army through drafting basic policies on national defense (*kokubō no kihon hōshin*) as well as national defense program guidelines (*bōei keikaku no taikō*). Between 1980 and 2004, the Comprehensive Security Ministerial Council (Sōgō Anzen Hoshō Kankei Kakuryō Kaigi) had additionally existed to deal with a wider spectrum of security issues. It was chaired by the CCS and composed of eight other members (the same four ministers as in the National Defense Council, plus ministers of agriculture, international trade and industry, and transport, as well as the Science and Technology Agency director-general). As part of the reconstruction of the Cabinet Secretariat under the Nakasone administration in 1986, the National Defense Council was replaced with the Security Council (Anzen Hoshō Kaigi) and enlarged to seven members (the previous ones plus the CCS and the head of the National Public Safety Commission). In addition to the original functions, the new organ could be used to deal with serious emergency situations (Chijiwa 2015: 19–118).

The Great Hanshin Earthquake in Kōbe and the sarin subway attack by the Aum Shinrikyō sect in Tokyo in 1995 exposed the need to strengthen Japan's security institutions. As a result, the post of deputy CCS for crisis management (*naikaku kiki kanrikan*) was established in 1998. The new official was to deal with crisis situations other than those related to national defense, such as large-scale natural disasters, ship or airplane accidents, terrorist attacks, and operations to rescue Japanese citizens abroad. The administrative reforms that entered into effect in 2001, in turn, introduced the post of assistant CCS for security affairs (*anzen hoshō tantō kanbō fukuchōkanho*) who provided administrative backing to the deputy CCS for crisis management. As a result of the changes implemented in 2003 and 2006, in turn, the Security Council was enlarged to nine members (the prime minister, CCS, ministers of foreign affairs, defense, finance, internal affairs and communications, economy, trade and industry, land, infrastructure and tourism, as well as the National Public Safety Commission head) and additionally charged with dealing with other important issues related to national defense, specified at the head of government's discretion (Chijiwa 2015: 120–159).

Abe had tried to establish the NSC under his first administration. It seems that he conceived this concept in July 2006, when as CCS under the Koizumi cabinet, he communicated with the US on the reaction to the North Korean missile tests. Impressed by the coordination abilities of Assistant to the US President for National Security Affairs, Stephen J. Hadley, Abe became convinced of the necessity of establishing a Japanese version of the US NSC and making its head a counterpart to Hadley and his successors. After becoming the prime minister, Abe entrusted national security issues to one of his special advisers, Koike Yuriko, who also became the deputy chair of the Council on Strengthening the Functions of the Kantei Regarding National Security (Kokka Anzen Hoshō ni kan suru Kantei Kinō Kyōka Kaigi). The advisory body came to a conclusion that, over the years, the Security Council's meetings had become largely ritualized and limited to ensuring funds for the realization of national defense program guidelines and basic policies on national defense. As such, it was not a suitable organ for drafting long-term national strategies. In February 2007, the advisory council issued a report that became the foundation for a bill project on the creation of the NSC, which was submitted to the Diet in April 2007 (Chijiwa 2015: 162–188). In the same month, former US Deputy Secretary of State, Richard L. Armitage, and former US Assistant Secretary of Defense for

International Security Affairs, Joseph S. Nye, published a report for the Center for Strategic and International Studies, in which they recommended that Japan "continue to strengthen its national security institutions and bureaucratic infrastructure to facilitate the most effective decision making possible" (Armitage & Nye 2007: 21). It seemed that Japan experts in the US supported the creation of the NSC by Tokyo, but eventually the law was not passed due to Abe's premature resignation.

When Abe regained power in 2012, he quickly returned to the idea of establishing the NSC, which was included in the LDP electoral manifesto. Taking into account the diplomatic crisis with China caused by the nationalization of the Senkaku/Diaoyu Islands by the Noda cabinet in September 2012, it is understandable that security issues were treated seriously during both LDP presidential and parliamentary electoral campaigns. The fact that Abe entrusted the post of minister for strengthening national security to CCS Suga, and charged one of the special advisers to the prime minister (Isozaki Yōsuke) with preparation of the NSC's legal framework, indicated that the creation of this organ was treated as one of the priorities of the government. The Algerian crisis in January 2013, in turn, gave an ideal argument for acceleration of work in this field.[5] In February 2013, the Experts' Council for Establishment of the NSC (Kokka Anzen Hoshō Kaigi no Sōsetsu ni kan suru Yūshikisha Kaigi) was established in the Kantei. It was chaired by the prime minister and composed of scholars and officials from MOFA and MOD. Interestingly, the advisory organ did not even issue a report, as during its fifth meeting in May 2013, it simply entrusted the final decision to the prime minister. The law project on the creation of the new body was prepared by a special unit in the Cabinet Secretariat and submitted to the Diet in June 2013. The bill was passed by both houses in November 2013, after minor modifications made to please the DPJ (Chijiwa 2015: 205–206).

In its core version, the Council was composed of the prime minister as chairperson, the CCS, as well as ministers of foreign affairs and defense. The four members were to meet regularly to discuss basic policies and important issues on foreign and security matters. In line with the layering strategy, the previously existing, less institutionalized Security Council was preserved. It was additionally composed of the minister of finance, minister of internal affairs and communications, minister of land, infrastructure, transport and tourism, minister of economy, trade and industry, National Public Safety Commission chair, and vice-premier (in case someone was appointed to this post). The nine ministers' meeting was to be held irregularly to discuss in a broader context: (1) basic policies on national defense, (2) national defense program guidelines, (3) plans of coordinating industrial activities related to defense guidelines, (4) basic policies on reaction to armed attack, (5) important issues related to response to armed attack, (6) reaction to situations in areas surrounding Japan, (7) peacekeeping operations by the SDF, as well as (8) other important issues related to national defense and national security. Furthermore, the bill created the possibility of holding NSC meetings with participation of the CCS and any ministers relevant to the nature of the emergency situation in question. The prime minister could also request attendance as observers of the deputy CCS, special adviser to the prime minister on national security, chief of staff, and other officials. In order to provide expert knowledge to the members, a Situation Management Specialist Committee (Jitai Taisho Senmon Iinkai) was founded. It was chaired by the CCS and composed of high-ranking bureaucrats from the relevant ministries (Prime Minister of Japan and His Cabinet 2013).

The biggest difference between the plans for establishing the NSC in 2007 and the final version of the bill from 2013 was the status of the national security adviser. According to the 2007 draft, the person in this post was to be responsible directly to the prime minister, and the National Security Secretariat (Kokka Anzen Hoshō Kyoku) chaired by her/him was to be established outside of the Cabinet Secretariat. A heated debate took place on whether it would be more suitable to entrust such an important office to a politician, a bureaucrat, or a private-sector specialist. The 2013 bill, in turn, integrated the National Security Secretariat into the institutional structure of the Cabinet Secretariat. Instead of a high-profile politician, the post of secretary-general was entrusted to an experienced bureaucrat. As such, it was expected that the national security adviser would deal with administrative matters and inter-ministerial communication (Sunohara 2014: 136–142). Abe prepared this office specifically for his close adviser, former Foreign Administrative Vice-Minister Yachi Shōtarō, who, at the same time, served as the special adviser to the cabinet in charge of national security (*kokka anzen hoshō tantō naikaku tokubetsu komon*). In September 2019, Yachi was replaced by former Director of Cabinet Intelligence, Kitamura Shigeru.

Establishment of the NSC created a necessity to clarify the division of responsibilities between the National Security Secretariat head, special adviser to the prime minister on national security, and deputy CCS for crisis management. On the one hand, the bill stipulated that one of the special advisers to the prime minister should be permanently responsible for national security. On the other hand, instead of the special adviser, it was the National Security Secretariat head who represented the NSC externally and became a counterpart to the assistant to the US president for national security affairs. The National Security Secretariat secretary-general was ranked equally to the deputy CCS for crisis management (see Figure 3.1). Seamless cooperation between the two officials was to be ensured by the fact that two assistant CCSs, including the one responsible for security affairs, became National Security Secretariat vice-chairs (Chijiwa 2015: 215–231).

The National Security Secretariat was established in January 2014. Its approximately 70 staff originated mainly from the MOD, MOFA, and National Police Agency. The Secretariat was divided into six divisions. Three of them were responsible for general coordination, strategic planning, and information, while the other three were charged with drafting policies toward America and Europe, Northeast Asia and Russia, as well as the Middle East and Africa (Chijiwa 2015: 225). In the MOD, the Bureau of Operational Policy was abolished and its functions were taken over by the SDF Joint Staff Office, which symbolized the weakening of civilian control over the SDF. Moreover, SDF personnel quickly started accounting for one third of the National Security Secretariat's staff (Mark 2016: 67, 109). As the National Security Secretariat was created within the Cabinet Secretariat, it significantly strengthened CCS Suga's information-gathering abilities, which enabled him to conduct inter-ministerial coordination even more effectively.

In mid-December 2013, the NSC published the first National Security Strategy. The document called the NSC "the control tower" that would enable the government to "implement national security policies in a more strategic and structured manner through a whole-government approach," as well as to evaluate them regularly and revise if necessary (Cabinet Secretariat 2013b). The Strategy specified the principles upheld by Japan, such as "freedom, democracy, respect for fundamental human rights and the rule of law," "Open and Stable Seas," "Three Non-Nuclear Principles," support for economic growth and democratization in developing countries, and compliance with the UN Charter (Cabinet Secretariat 2013b). Most importantly, the document introduced the concept of "Proactive Contribution to Peace" (*sekkyokuteki heiwashugi*) that became a cornerstone of the Abe administration's foreign and security policies. Japan was to continue the position of a "peace-loving nation" while more actively participating in international cooperation for stability and peace in the region and the world. The Strategy clarified three national security objectives: (1) strengthening Japan's deterrence capabilities and minimizing damage done by external threats, (2) improving the security environment in the Asia-Pacific region through enhancing cooperation with the US ally and other partners, as well as (3) improving the global security environment through strengthening the international order founded on universal values and through proactive diplomacy in settlement of disputes. The document indicated many risks and challenges for Japan's security, such as provocative actions by North Korea and the rapid rise of China's power. To deal with them, it proposed numerous measures, including reinforcement of maritime surveillance capabilities; a review of land ownership in areas near national borders, such as remote islands; participation in anti-piracy and anti-terrorist operations; enhancement of cyber security and intelligence capabilities; strengthening of cooperation with the US, the Republic of Korea, Australia, ASEAN countries and India; promotion of disarmament and non-proliferation of nuclear weapons; and strategic utilization of Official Development Assistance (ODA) (Cabinet Secretariat 2013b).

The NSC's aim was both to formulate long-term defense guidelines and to enhance Japan's abilities in response to threats to national security in crisis situations. The new governmental body greatly facilitated inter-ministerial coordination on security and foreign affairs, thus strengthening the prime

118 *Reforming governmental institutions*

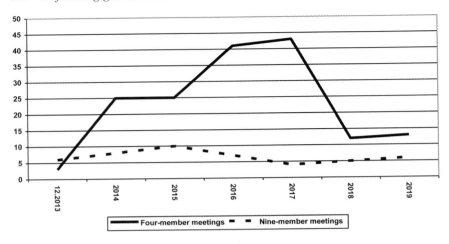

Figure 3.4 Number of National Security Council meetings in four-member and nine-member formats.

Source: Compiled by the author, based on data from: Prime Minister of Japan and His Cabinet (2020b).

minister's direct control over these important legislative fields. As depicted in Figure 3.4, only in December 2013 did the NSC meet more frequently in a nine- than four-member format, which resulted from the necessity of acknowledging the rules of proceedings and drafting the National Security Strategy. In 2014 and 2015, the four-member meetings were held approximately twice per month and devoted mainly to situations in East Asia, the Middle East, and Ukraine after the annexation of Crimea by Russia. In 2016 and 2017, the number of meetings almost doubled, mainly due to the intensification of North Korea's missile and nuclear tests. However, after a sudden détente between Pyongyang and Washington, symbolized by the Donald Trump–Kim Jong-un summit in Singapore in June 2018, the frequency of meetings dropped to little more than once per month. At the same time, the nine-member meetings were held only to discuss the most important decisions, such as national defense program guidelines, the specially designated secrets law, relaxation of the three principles on transfer of defense equipment and technology,[6] and security-related bills that re-interpreted Article 9 of the Constitution.[7]

Together with the establishment of the NSC, the Diet passed the Bill on Protection of Specially Designated Secrets. The aim of the law was to prepare the ground for intelligence cooperation between Japan's NSC and its US and UK counterparts. Indeed, the Obama administration kept insisting that Tokyo should tighten up the rules for dealing with sensitive data (Stockwin & Ampiah 2017: 141). The bill potentially improved cabinet members' control over the bureaucrats, who in the past had presumably leaked confidential data to the press to discredit their political superiors. It introduced a penalty of a maximum of ten years of imprisonment for public officials and five years for other persons for intentionally disclosing any information designated as "special secret." In case of an unintentional disclosure by negligence, the punishments were lowered to two (or a fine of up to 500,000 yen) and one year (or fine of up to 300,000 yen), respectively. The bill obliged the government to submit to the Diet and issue publicly, on an annual basis, a report on the enactment of the law, as well as to establish an independent body that would review the act's implementation (Cabinet Secretariat 2013a).

In order to create the standards for designating "special secrets," the Council for Protection of Information (Jōhō Hozen Shimon Kaigi) was established in January 2014. The new advisory organ was composed of non-governmental experts such as journalists, scholars, and lawyers, and chaired by *Yomiuri Shinbun* Editor-in-Chief Watanabe Tsuneo. Nevertheless, it seems that the Council met only once and it was its secretariat that prepared the standards, only occasionally consulting individual Council members. The criteria for designating "special secrets" were announced in July 2014. They encompassed 55 points that focused mainly on security and foreign policies. In addition, in order to ensure parliamentary surveillance over designation of "special secrets", Information Oversight Audit Committees (Jōhō Kanshi Shinsakai) were established in both houses of the Diet. However, it was the Cabinet Secretariat and the Cabinet Office that grasped control over designating "special secrets." For this purpose, the Cabinet Committee for Protection and Oversight (Naikaku Hozen Kanshi Iinkai), chaired by the CCS, was established in the former institution, and the Information Security Oversight Division (Jōhō Hozen Kansatsu Shitsu), led by the independent chief record officer (*dokuritsu kōbunsho kanrikan*), in the latter body (Makihara 2016: 93–94). As indicated by Shindō (2019: 132), the Kantei's control over information remained firm, as the lawmakers who became members of the Information Oversight Audit Committees had access only to the list of "specially designated secrets," not to their contents, and, thus, could not judge whether information was classified correctly or not.

Establishment of the NSC facilitated Abe in centralizing foreign policy making under the Kantei. To some extent, this process was implemented at the expense of foreign ministers. Kishida Fumio, Kōno Tarō, and Motegi Toshimitsu, despite being influential politicians, failed to formulate as ambitious policy initiatives as some of their predecessors, e.g. Asō Tarō, who had announced the concept of the "Arc of Freedom and Prosperity" under the first administration.[8] Instead, it was the prime minister himself who conceived, with the help of his direct entourage, succeeding security and foreign policy concepts, such as "Proactive Contribution to Peace" or "Asia's Democratic Security Diamond."[9] While the prime minister's complete domination in security and foreign policy making had been possible even before the creation of the NSC, the new organ provided the head of government with additional institutional backing to centralize decision-making in these important policy fields.

Council on Economic and Fiscal Policy and other advisory bodies

Apart from the newly established Cabinet Bureau of Personnel Affairs and the NSC, Abe took advantage of other advisory organs under the cabinet. Just like Nakasone and Koizumi, he extensively relied on *ad hoc* policy councils. It was the CEFP (Keizai Zaisei Shimon Kaigi) that initially had the strongest legal foundation as a tool for top-down decision making, but Abe freely chose separate councils to address different aspects of his comprehensive policy agenda, without heeding their legal underpinning.

While the CEFP dealt with macroeconomic policy, Abe established the Headquarters for Japan's Economic Revitalization (Nihon Keizai Saisei Honbu) that focused on the microeconomic aspects of reforms. The former body operated in the Cabinet Office, while the latter was administered by the Cabinet Secretariat. Both organs were chaired by the prime minister, but it was Minister of State for Economic and Fiscal Policy, Amari Akira, who coordinated their work (Shimizu 2014: 21–22). The revived CEFP was not as powerful as under the Koizumi administration, which reflected differences between the policy agendas of both prime ministers. While Koizumi sided with the MOF to privatize the Japan Post and cut budget spending, Abe, on the contrary, counterbalanced the MOF with METI in order to reduce taxes and conduct an expansive fiscal policy. As a result, the CEFP, whose secretariat remained largely under the MOF's control, became less influential than the Headquarters for Japan's Economic Revitalization, which generally shared METI's stance.

The CEFP had been established as part of the administrative reforms that entered into force in 2001. It had been extensively used by Prime Minister Koizumi to lead structural reforms in a top-down manner. In 2009, the DPJ decided to suspend the Council's proceedings and instead created two new bodies to strengthen the prime minister's powers – the National Strategy Unit and the Government Revitalization Unit. However, due to the failure to pass the Bill Establishing Political Leadership, both organs lacked a legal basis and authority comparable to the CEFP. As the Council was never really abolished, it was easy for Abe to simply resume its proceedings. Nevertheless, the Council was not to be as powerful as during the Koizumi era. In fact, METI bureaucrats, who approached Abe before the LDP regained power, planned to use this body as a less important equivalent of the Headquarters for Japan's Economic Revitalization. Presumably, their aim was to grasp control over the Headquarters, while leaving the Council under the MOF's influence (Karube 2018: 11–12).

The Headquarters for Japan's Economic Revitalization, named after its LDP counterpart, was dubbed the "control tower" of reforms in the LDP electoral manifesto (under a different English translation – Japan Economic Revival Headquarters). According to a cabinet decision from December 26, 2012, the Headquarters, under coordination with the CEFP, was to play "a central role in comprehensive coordination, planning and policy making" on "taking necessary economic measures as well as realizing the growth strategy by the government as a whole, in order to break away from yen appreciation and deflation, and then to bring back strong economy" (Prime Minister of Japan and His Cabinet 2012). It was composed of Prime Minister Abe as the chief, Vice-Premier Asō Tarō as the acting chief, Minister in charge of Economic Revitalization and Economic and Fiscal Policy Amari Akira and CCS Suga Yoshihide as vice-chiefs, as well as all ministers as members. The administrative matters were to be handled by the Cabinet Secretariat under the auspices of the Cabinet Office (Prime Minister of Japan and His Cabinet 2012).

It was Deputy CCS Sugita Kazuhiro and Assistant CCS in charge of Domestic Affairs, Sasaki Toyonari, who, in consultation with Minister Amari, coordinated the selection of the administrative staff of the Headquarters for Japan's Economic Revitalization and the CEFP. Aware of the importance of these bodies, all ministries dispatched to them their most promising bureaucrats. Iizuka Atsushi from the MOF, as the most senior of them, was charged with the task of general coordination, while Akaishi Kōichi from METI oversaw the works of the Industrial Competitiveness Council (Sangyō Kyōsōryoku Kaigi) established within the Headquarters, and Tawa Hiroshi from the Cabinet Office supervised the CEFP proceedings. In order to ensure a smooth exchange of information, they decided to share one office room. Recruitment of the administrative staff was exceptionally swift. On December 27, 2012, Sasaki summoned representatives of all ministries and gave them only one day to select an exact number of bureaucrats of different ranks. In addition, Amari did not hesitate to instruct ministries which bureaucrats to dispatch to the new bodies (Karube 2018: 69–117).

At the beginning of his term in office, Abe used the CEFP as a forum for reviewing the progress in the BOJ's policy of monetary easing aimed at achieving a 2% inflation target. Subsequently, he entrusted to the Council the drafting of Basic Policies for Economic and Fiscal Management and Reform for FY 2014. Nevertheless, the CEFP failed to act as an organ imposing bold reforms. Out of consideration for the upcoming upper house election, the Basic Policies announced in June 2013 did not contain details of budgetary cuts. The proposals of restraining medical fees and local allocation tax, in turn, closely followed the policy of MOF bureaucrats who provided administrative assistance to the Council. Even these plans, however, were watered down due to opposition from LDP parliamentary tribes. Takenaka Heizō, who had served as minister of state for economic and fiscal policy under the Koizumi administration, appealed to CEFP private-sector members to display more courage in challenging the interests of veto players (Suezaki 2014: 7).

In order to reinvigorate discussions in the Council, Minister Amari promised to increase the number of administrative staff to private-sector members and seek better cooperation with the Industrial Competitiveness Council.

Indeed, in mid-January 2014, a Private-Sector Members Unit (Minkan Giin Shitsu) was established in the CEFP, with three new employees recruited from the private sector and three from the Cabinet Office. As stressed by Amari, the new body was to support private-sector experts in preparing groundbreaking policy proposals without pondering the vested interests of various ministries (*Asahi Shinbun* 2014a: 6). According to University of Tokyo Professor Itō Motoshige, who became a CEFP member in 2013, the reform strengthened the administrative backing of private-sector specialists, but Abe did not attach a similar importance to the CEFP as Koizumi had (interview by the author, Tokyo, October 18, 2019). While the prime minister occasionally dined with CEFP private-sector experts, he did not treat these meetings as a venue for establishing the general economic policy that would be later imposed on veto players. Instead, Abe preferred to rely on advice from various councils.

Apart from countermeasures against the ageing society and proposals of deregulation in National Strategic Special Zones, throughout 2014, discussions in CEFP focused on plans for corporate tax reduction. The Basic Policies for Economic and Fiscal Management and Reform for FY 2015, announced by the CEFP in June 2014, contained a plan of gradually decreasing corporate tax to less than 30%. Despite resistance from the MOF and the LDP Research Commission on the Tax System, the Kantei thus challenged an unwritten rule that the CEFP would not indicate the detailed framework of the tax system. As the prime minister established the general policy direction, MOF bureaucrats and LDP backbenchers had no choice but to focus on debating how to implement the reform and where to find financial resources for the tax reduction (*Asahi Shinbun* 2014b: 4). The reform was eventually imposed by the Kantei after LDP's victory in the lower house election of December 2014.

In subsequent years, the CEFP served Abe as an organ closely following the Kantei's policy. Under Amari's influence, the Basic Policies for Economic and Fiscal Management and Reform for FY 2016, issued by the CEFP in June 2015, failed to specify concrete expenditure targets to attain a primary balance in 2020. Instead of imposing budget cuts on the government, private-sector members simply agreed with the Kantei's optimistic prognoses of economic growth. This led to a paradoxical situation that the LDP Special Committee for Financial Reconstruction (Zaisei Saiken ni kan suru Tokumei Iinkai) chaired by Inada Tomomi, which should be less eager to cut budget expenses, demanded from the CEFP a clarification of expenditure limits (Narabe, Ikuta & Aihara 2015: 7). Three years later, in June 2018, the CEFP announced a new plan to postpone the date of attaining primary balance to 2025, and remove the social security system expenditure limit that had been introduced in 2015 under pressure from Inada and the MOF. This change indicated the weakening of the MOF's influence on the CEFP and the LDP (Kuribayashi, Sasai, Itō & Fukuma 2018: 9).

In parallel to the proceedings of the CEFP, economic growth strategy was discussed in the Headquarters for Japan's Economic Revitalization and its sub-organ, the Industrial Competitiveness Council. Initially, Abe planned to nominate Takenaka Heizō, who had been the main brain behind Koizumi's neoliberal reforms, as a CEFP member, but due to opposition from Vice-Premier Asō, he renounced this plan. Instead, Takenaka was employed in the Industrial Competitiveness Council. Takenaka's vision of reforms clashed with the policy agenda of Minister Amari. While Amari preferred a traditional, METI-like approach of promoting economic growth through administrative guidance, Takenaka supported far-going deregulation to stimulate private investments (Kujiraoka 2015: 4).

As shown in Figure 3.5, the number of meetings of both the CEFP and the Headquarters for Japan's Economic Revitalization was the highest at the beginning of their existence – the former was held approximately twice, and the latter once per month. From 2014 to 2016, the frequency of meetings of both bodies decreased, but they were still held regularly. Minister Amari's stepping down from office in January 2016, and a gradual waning in significance of Abenomics as a means to bolster electoral support, in turn, seemed to cause further marginalization of both advisory bodies. In particular, discussions in the Headquarters for Japan's Economic Revitalization lost importance to the point that, since 2015, its meetings have not exceeded the round-robin format. Hayashi Yoshimasa, who was twice a cabinet member under the second Abe administration, stated that as the general direction for economic policy was established by the Kantei,

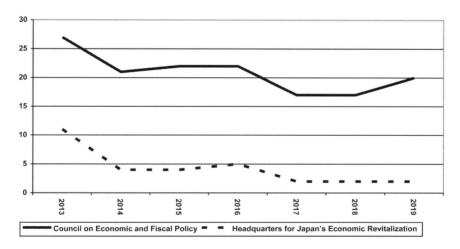

Figure 3.5 Number of meetings of the Council on Economic and Fiscal Policy and the Headquarters for Japan's Economic Revitalization under the second Abe administration.

Source: Compiled by the author, based on data from: Cabinet Office (2020), Prime Minister of Japan and His Cabinet (2020c).

there was no need for detailed discussion (interview by the author, Tokyo, October 16, 2019). The Industrial Competitiveness Council, in turn, was dissolved in 2016 and replaced with the Future Investment Council (Mirai Tōshi Kaigi) composed of a smaller number of private-sector members (Makihara 2018: 78).

What is important, among many advisory bodies established under the Abe cabinet, only a few, such as the National Strategic Special Zone Advisory Council (Kokka Senryaku Tokubetsu Kuiki Shimon Kaigi), were founded on the basis of a law passed in the Diet. Most of them had only weak legal underpinning in cabinet, prime minister's, CCS's, or ministers' decisions. As indicated by Tanaka (2019: 70–99), the multiplication of new advisory councils complicated the structure of the Cabinet Secretariat and the Cabinet Office to the point that the chain of command became unclear. All councils were provided administrative support from separate secretariats, established mainly under the two assistant CCSs in charge of domestic and international affairs. At the beginning of 2020, there were as many as 39 such secretariats. In parallel, the number of policy fields administered by the Cabinet Office increased from 63 in 2001 to 112 in 2015. As the responsibilities of separate councils often overlapped, it became difficult to divide jurisdiction areas of the Cabinet Secretariat and the Cabinet Office.

The government was aware of this problem. In January 2015, it issued a cabinet decision that admitted the need to simplify the organizational structure of advisory councils. Four of them (on postal privatization, social security system reform, nuclear energy regulatory reform, and legal training reform) were abolished, two (on intellectual property and ocean policy) were moved to the Cabinet Office, and four others (on treatment of chemical weapons, creation of provinces, vitalization of local economy, and space development strategy) were integrated and moved to the Cabinet Office. In addition, responsibility for some policy areas (e.g. on crime victims, consumer problems and food safety, information disclosure, suicide countermeasures, and drug abuse) was moved back from the Cabinet Office to separate ministries or agencies (Cabinet Secretariat 2015).

It cannot be excluded that Abe intentionally created a large number of advisory councils whose competences overlapped in order to become the ultimate arbiter in case of policy disputes between different bodies under his control. The composition of the councils reflected Abe's policy agenda. While the members of the organs related to economic policy were at least selected from among economists or businesspeople, the membership of other councils was connected with closeness to Abe's policy vision rather than expertise. For instance, only three out of 14 members of the Advisory Panel on Reconstruction of the Legal Basis for Security (Anzen Hoshō no Hōteki Kiban no Saikōchiku ni kan suru Kondankai) that paved the way toward the reinterpretation of Article 9 of the Constitution were professors of law, while others were recruited from among diplomats, security experts, or international relations and political science scholars.[10]

Takenaka Heizō lamented the fact that due to an excess of advisory bodies, it was difficult for their members to gain access to the prime minister (*Nihon Keizai Shinbun* 2016: 12). Moreover, as Makihara (2018: 79) pointed out, eventually Abe started to avoid holding too many council meetings in order to make decisions behind closed doors within a narrow group of his closest subordinates. Nonaka and Aoki (2016: 86–127) stressed that the long-term trend of increase in the number of politicians and private-sector experts as council members at the expense of civil servants was continued under the second Abe administration. Moreover, the Kantei did not leave much room for unrestrained discussion in policy councils. The first meeting usually started from a speech by the prime minister who clearly indicated his general intention and sometimes even specified the deadline for deliberations.

In fact, in some cases, the prime minister did not even wait for the reports of the councils before making decisions. For instance, in September 2017, the Kantei established the 100-Year Life Era Design Council (Jinsei 100 Nen Jidai Kōsō Kaigi) that was to elaborate a plan of reforms aimed at preparing Japan for the challenge of an aging society. One of the key components of the reform was a human resources development revolution. Nevertheless, without waiting for the Council's recommendations, the government announced it would use 2 trillion yen out of the new revenues gained after the increase in consumption tax to 10% for introducing free early childhood education. The main reason of speeding up the reform was the government's eagerness to include the new pledge in the LDP electoral manifesto after a sudden dissolution of the House of Representatives by Abe. Even following the electoral victory, the Kantei did not wait for the Council's report, and at the beginning of December 2017, it issued a New Economic Policy Package that specified the plans for free early childhood education and free higher education for students from households with exemptions from municipal residence tax. Only more than a week later did the Council publish its report that simply repeated the cabinet decision (Tanaka 2019: 76–77).

In addition to advisory bodies, Abe relied on the knowledge of individual specialists. Immediately after returning to power, he nominated as many as 11 experts as special advisers to the cabinet (*naikaku kanbō san'yo*). They included former Foreign Administrative Vice-Minister (later National Security Adviser) Yachi Shōtarō, former Finance Administrative Vice-Minister Tango Yasutake, and such economic "brains" as Professors Hamada Kōichi and Honda Etsurō (Shimizu 2014: 21). Two of them – Koizumi's former Executive Secretary, Iijima Isao, and the author of Abe's foreign policy speeches, Taniguki Tomohiko – visited the Kantei on a daily basis, while the others participated only in the meetings of separate advisory councils (Taniguchi 2018: 10).

Multiplication of advisory councils in the Cabinet Office and their secretariats in the Cabinet Secretariat proved instrumental in taking control over the crucial policy initiatives by the Kantei. While most of the new organs had only weak legal underpinnings, the empowered prime ministerial executive successfully used them to establish the general direction of policies and entrust only their implementation to separate ministries. Abe thus circumvented the traditional bureaucratic procedures without wasting time and energy on reforming the rigid structures of the Japanese government.

Conclusion

In contrast to the DPJ's failed attempt at decision-making reform, the institutional changes under the second Abe administration were introduced gradually, over a longer period of time. Instead of completely overhauling the decision-making process, the prime minister and his entourage exploited the old system. Through layering, they supplemented preexisting institutions with new organs that significantly changed the balance of power between the Kantei and the bureaucrats. The NSC and its Secretariat enabled the prime minister to play a more active role in foreign and security policies, while the Cabinet Bureau of Personnel Affairs enhanced his competences regarding the distribution of high-ranking bureaucratic posts. The administrative backing for both new organs was provided by the Cabinet Secretariat, which reflected CCS Suga's crucial role in decision making. A top-down decision-making style and centralization of power in the Kantei was achieved at the expense of political neutrality of the bureaucrats whose careers now depended on their proximity to the prime minister and the CCS.

The Kantei and the government generally behaved as a monolith. Prime Minister Abe carefully selected his closest administrative staff and cabinet members. Thanks to daily meetings with CCS, two political CCSs, administrative CCS, and the prime minister's executive secretary, he made sure that his intentions were precisely transmitted to his entourage. At the same time, Abe entrusted implementation of his policy agenda to his subordinates, thus avoiding excessive micromanagement. CCS Suga focused on internal affairs, Prime Minister's Executive Secretary Imai on economic policy, and National Security Adviser Yachi on foreign and security matters. Instead of representing the interests of their ministries, all cabinet members were expected to pursue the policy goals imposed on them by the Kantei, which was symbolized by the fact that almost all of them were entrusted with additional tasks apart from their basic responsibilities. The cabinet meetings served as venue for automatic authorization of the decisions made by the prime minister, not as forum for discussion.

Numerous advisory bodies established under the cabinet proved instrumental in circumventing the traditional bureaucratic procedures. Thanks to the fact that the competences of various councils overlapped, Abe acted as an arbiter who chose policy proposals of one organ or another at his discretion. While METI bureaucrats or politicians and advisers who preferred achieving a high economic growth rate to maintaining budgetary balance dominated in the prime minister's entourage, depending on the situation and political interests, Abe could always resort to the advice from the MOF or such neoliberal economists as Takenaka Heizō. This system enabled the prime minister to act as a pivot linking various groups and occasionally playing one of them off against another.

Notes

1. After the reform of the ministry entry exam system in 2007, theoretically, also non-elite bureaucrats were allowed to assume executive posts. Nevertheless, in reality, the public officials who passed exams for general posts (*sōgō shoku*) were still treated as elite, and those who passed exams for regular posts (*ippan shoku*) as non-elite bureaucrats. See Shindō (2019: 36–41).
2. North Korean agents abducted a number of Japanese citizens in the 1970s and 1980s. In 2002, Pyongyang admitted there had been 13 abductions, and released the five surviving victims.
3. The Belt and Road Initiative was announced as One Belt One Road in 2013. Its aim was to establish a new silk route through extensive infrastructural investments from China to Europe.
4. For example, Etō Seiichi became responsible for promoting dynamic engagement of all citizens, territorial issues, Okinawa and Northern Territories affairs, consumer affairs and food safety, measures for declining birthrate, as well as ocean policy. See Prime Minister of Japan and His Cabinet (2019).
5. In mid-January 2013, Islamist terrorists linked with al-Qaeda took as hostages hundreds of people working at the Tigantourine gas facility near Algerian In Amenas, including the employees of the engineering company JGC Corp. from Yokohama. The terrorists demanded France withdraw its forces from operations against Islamists in Mali. Despite a rescue operation by Algerian forces, many hostages were killed, including ten Japanese citizens.
6. In April 2014, the Abe administration significantly relaxed the ban on arms exports that had been introduced half a century earlier. The new rules allowed defense equipment and technology transfer, provided it contributed to promotion of international cooperation, peace, or Japan's security. See Ministry of Foreign Affairs of Japan (2014).
7. Full list of NSC meetings available at Prime Minister of Japan and His Cabinet (2020b).
8. The Arc comprised the countries at the outer rim of Eurasia that experienced significant changes after the end of the Cold War. Based on value-oriented diplomacy, Japan was to promote democratization, rule of law, human rights, and free-market economy in that region. See Asō (2008).
9. The geopolitical diamond embraced Japan, India, Australia, and the US state of Hawaii. Cooperation of the four democratic countries was to counterbalance Chinese influence in the region. See Abe (2012).
10. See the list of members at The Advisory Panel on Reconstruction of the Legal Basis for Security (2014: 54–55).

References

Abe, Shinzō (2012) "Asia's Democratic Security Diamond," *Project Syndicate* (December 27). Online. Available: https://www.project-syndicate.org/commentary/a-strategic-alliance-for-japan-and-india-by-shinzo-abe?barrier=accesspaylog (accessed December 25, 2018).

128 Reforming governmental institutions

Armitage, Richard L. & Nye, Joseph S. (2007) "The U.S.–Japan Alliance. Getting Asia Right through 2020," Center for Strategic and International Studies Report (February). Online. Available: https://csis-prod.s3.amazonaws.com/s3fs-public/legacy_files/files/media/csis/pubs/070216_asia2020.pdf (accessed December 13, 2019).

Asahi Shinbun (2014a) "Keizai Shimon Kaigi, Minkan Teigen Kyōka. Naibu Soshiki Kyō Hossoku" [CEFP, Strengthening of Private-Sector Suggestions. Internal Organ Inaugurated Today], January 15, morning edition, 6.

Asahi Shinbun (2014b) "Hōjin Genzei, Zaigen Atomawashi. Kantei Shudō, Ketsuron o Yūsen" [Corporate Tax Reduction, Postponement of Financial Resources. The Kantei Leadership, Priority of Decision], June 13, morning edition, 4.

Asahi Shinbun (2016) "Kunaichō Jichō mo Shusseki. Jimujikan Kaigi, Raigetsu kara" [Participation by the Imperial Household Agency Deputy as well. Administrative Vice-Ministers' Council, Starting Next Month], October 25, morning edition, 4.

Asahi Shinbun (2017) "'Naikaku Jinji Kyokuchō' Kanryō Toppu ni Henkō, Hagiuda Zen Fukuchōkan kara" ["Cabinet Bureau of Personnel Affairs Head" Changed to Top Bureaucrat, from former Deputy CCS Hagiuda], August 4, morning edition, 4.

Asakura, Hideo (2016) *Kantei Shihai* [Kantei's Supremacy], Tokyo: East Press.

Asō, Tarō (2008) *Jiyū to Han'ei no Ko* [The Arc of Freedom and Prosperity], Tokyo: Gentōsha.

Cabinet Office (2020) "Keizai Zaisei Shimon Kaigi" [Council on Economic and Fiscal Policy]. Online. Available: https://www5.cao.go.jp/keizai-shimon/index.html (accessed February 3, 2020).

Cabinet Secretariat (2013a) "Tokutei Himitsu no Hogo ni Kan Suru Hōritsu" [Bill on Protection of Specially Designated Secrets] (December 9). Online. Available: http://www.cas.go.jp/jp/tokuteihimitsu/pdf/bessi_kaisetsu.pdf (accessed September 5, 2017).

Cabinet Secretariat (2013b) "National Security Strategy" (December 17). Online. Available: https://www.cas.go.jp/jp/siryou/131217anzenhoshou/nss-e.pdf (accessed December 15, 2019).

Cabinet Secretariat (2014a) "Kokka Kōmuin Hō-tō no Ichibu o Kaisei Suru Hōritsu no Gaiyō" [Outline of Bill Revising Part of Civil Service Law etc.]. Online. Available: http://www.cas.go.jp/jp/gaiyou/jimu/jinjikyoku/files/h26-22-1.pdf (accessed September 4, 2017).

Cabinet Secretariat (2014b) "Naikaku Sōri Daijin Hosakan oyobi Daijin Hosakan no Shokumu Suikō ni Kakawaru Kihan [Standards Regarding Execution of Duties of Prime Minister's Special Advisers and Minister's Assistants] (May 27). Online. Available: http://www.cas.go.jp/jp/siryou/pdf/20140530_daijinhosakan.pdf (accessed September 6, 2017).

Cabinet Secretariat (2015) "Naikaku Kanbō oyobi Naikakufu no Gyōmu no Minaoshi ni tsuite" [On Overhaul of Responsibilities of the Cabinet Secretariat and the Cabinet Office] (January 27). Online. Available: https://www.cas.go.jp/jp/seisaku/cs_minaoshi/pdf/kakugikettei_h270127.pdf (accessed December 9, 2019).

Cabinet Secretariat (2020) "Naikaku Kanbō Soshiki Zu" [Diagram of the Cabinet Secretariat's Structure] (March 31). Online. Available: https://www.cas.go.jp/jp/gaiyou/pdf/200331_sosikizu.pdf (accessed July 1, 2020).

Campbell, John Creighton (1980) *Contemporary Japanese Budget Politics*, Berkeley: University of California Press.

Chijiwa, Yasuaki (2015) *Kawariyuku Naikaku Anzen Hoshō Kikō. Nihonban NSC Seiritsu E No Michi* [Changing Cabinet Security Structures. The Path towards Establishment of the Japanese Version of the NSC], Tokyo: Hara Shobō.
George Mulgan, Aurelia (2018) *The Abe Administration and the Rise of the Prime Ministerial Executive*, London and New York: Routledge.
Igarashi, Akio (2011) *Nihon Seiji Ron* [Discourse on Japanese Politics], Tokyo: Iwanami Shoten.
Iio, Jun (2008) *Nihon no Tōchi Kōzō* [Structure of Government in Japan], Tokyo: Chūō Kōron Shinsha.
Inoguchi, Takashi & Iwai Tomoaki (1987) *"Zoku Giin" no Kenkyū* [A Study on "Parliamentary Tribes"], Tokyo: Nihon Keizai Shinbunsha.
Inoguchi, Takashi (1983) *Gendai Nihon Seiji Keizai no Kōzu*[Contemporary Japanese Political Economy: Government and Market], Tokyo: Tōyō Keizai Shinpōsha.
Ishibashi, Fumito (2019) *Abe "Ikkyō" no Himitsu* [The Secret of Abe's "Unilateral Strength"], Tokyo: Asuka Shinsha.
Itō, Tatsuya (2010) *Sōri Kantei no Shinjitsu. Ozawa Minshutō to no Tatakai* [Truth about Prime Minister's Residence. Struggle with Ozawa's DPJ], Tokyo: PHP Kenkyūjo.
Karube, Kensuke (2018) *Kanryōtachi no Abenomikusu. Igyō no Keizai Seisaku wa Ika ni Tukurareta ka* [Abenomics of the Bureaucrats. How was the Odd-looking Economic Policy Created], Tokyo: Iwanami Shoten.
Kawato, Sadafumi (2015) *Giin Naikakusei* [Parliamentary Government], Tokyo: Tōkyō Daigaku Shuppankai.
Kerbo, Harold R. & McKinstry, John A. (1995) *Who Rules Japan? The Inner Circles of Economic and Political Power*, Westport: Praeger.
Koga, Shigeaki (2017) *Kokka no Kyōbō* [State Collusion], Tokyo: Kadokawa.
Kujiraoka, Hitoshi (2015) "'Han Takenaka' no Arashi, Miuchi ni Uzumaku" ["Anti-Takenaka" Storm, Swirls Around], *Asahi Shinbun*, December 5, morning edition, 4.
Kuribayashi, Fumiko, Sasai, Tsuneo, Itō, Maiko & Fukuma, Daisuke (2018) "Shinrai Teika, Zaisei Saiken Kōtai mo" [Decline of Trust, Setback of Financial Reconstruction], *Asahi Shinbun*, June 7, morning edition, 9.
Makihara, Izuru (2016) *"Abe Ikkyō" no Nazo* [The Mystery of "Abe's Unilateral Strength"], Tokyo: Asahi Shinbun Shuppan.
Makihara, Izuru (2018) *Kuzureru Seiji o Tatenaosu. 21 Seiki no Nihon Gyōsei Kaikaku Ron* [Reorganizing the Crumbling Politics. Discourse on Administrative Reform in the 21st Century Japan], Tokyo: Kōdansha.
Mark, Craig (2016) *The Abe Restoration. Contemporary Japanese Politics and Reformation*, Lanham, Boulder, New York, London: Lexington Books.
Mikuriya, Takashi (2015) *Abe Seiken wa Hontō ni Tsuyoi noka. Banjaku yue ni Moroi Seiken Un'ei no Shōtai* [Is Abe Government Really Strong? True Face of Political Management Weak as a Stone], Tokyo: PHP Kenkyūjo.
Ministry of Foreign Affairs of Japan (2014) "The Three Principles on Transfer of Defense Equipment and Technology" (April 6). Online. Available: http://www.mofa.go.jp/fp/nsp/page1we_000083.html (accessed December 16, 2019).
Mori, Isao (2016) *Sōri no Kage. Suga Yoshihide no Shōtai* [Prime Minister's Shadow. The Truth About Suga Yoshihide], Tokyo: Shōgakka.

Mori, Isao (2019) *Kantei Kanryō. Abe Ikkyō o Sasaeta Sokkin Seiji no Tsumi* [The Residence's Bureaucracy. The Sin of Aides' Politics that Supported Abe's Unilateral Strength], Tokyo: Bungei Shunjū.

Murakawa, Ichirō (1994) *Nihon no Kanryō* [Japanese Bureaucrats], Tokyo: Maruzen.

Muramatsu, Michio (1994) *Nihon no Gyōsei* [Japanese Administration], Tokyo: Chūō Kōronsha.

Nakano, Masashi (2010) *Seiji Shudō wa Naze Shippai Suru noka?* [Why Does the Politician-led Government Fail?], Tokyo: Kōbunsha.

Narabe, Ken, Ikuta, Daisuke & Aihara, Ryō (2015) "Zaisei Kenzenka, Mienu Michisuji. Saishutsu Mokuhyō Shimesazu. Keizai Kaigi Kosshian" [Fiscal Consolidation, Invisible Path. Without Indication of Expenditure Reduction Target. CEFP's Outline Plan], *Asahi Shinbun*, June 11, morning edition, 7.

Nemoto, Takumi (2015) *Shin no Seiji Shudō. Fukkō Daijin 617 Nichi* [True Political Leadership. 617 Days as Minister for Reconstruction], Tokyo: Chūō Kōron Jigyō Shuppan.

Nihon Keizai Shinbun (2016) "Ranritsu, Abe Kaigi – Moto Keizai Zaiseishō Takenaka Heizō-shi, Shimon Kaigi o Shireitō-yaku ni" [Randomization, Abe's Councils – Former Minister for Economic and Fiscal Policy Takenaka Heizō, Advisory Councils as Command Tower], June 5, morning edition, 12.

Nishimura, Takeshi (2002) *Kasumigaseki Zankoku Monogatari. Samayoeru Kanryōtachi* [Cruel Tale of Kasumigaseki. Loitering Bureaucrats], Tokyo: Chūō Kōron Shinsha.

Nonaka, Naoto & Aoki, Haruka (2016) *Seisaku Kaigi to Tōron naki Kokkai. Kantei Shudō Taisei no Seiritsu to Kōtai Suru Jukugi* [Policy Councils and the Diet Without Debates. Deliberation on the Establishment and Demise of the Kantei Leadership System], Tokyo: Asahi Shinbun Shuppan.

Prime Minister of Japan and His Cabinet (2012) "Establishment of the Headquarters for Japan's Economic Revitalization" (December 26). Online. Available: https://japan.kantei.go.jp/96_abe/decisions/2012/1226saiseihonbu_e.html (accessed April 6, 2019).

Prime Minister of Japan and His Cabinet (2013) "Kokka Anzen Hoshō Kaigi Setchi Hō" [National Security Council Establishment Law] (December 4). Online. Available: http://www.kantei.go.jp/jp/singi/anzenhosyoukaigi/konkyo.html (accessed December 14, 2019).

Prime Minister of Japan and His Cabinet (2019) "List of Ministers" (September 11). Online. Available: https://japan.kantei.go.jp/98_abe/meibo/daijin/index_e.html (accessed January 20, 2020).

Prime Minister of Japan and His Cabinet (2020a) "Kakugi" [Cabinet Meetings]. Online. Available: https://www.kantei.go.jp/jp/kakugi/index.html (accessed February 1, 2020).

Prime Minister of Japan and His Cabinet (2020b) "Kokka Anzen Hoshō Kaigi Kaisai Jōkyō" [State of Meetings of the National Security Council]. Online. Available: https://www.kantei.go.jp/jp/singi/anzenhosyoukaigi/kaisai.html (accessed February 3, 2020).

Prime Minister of Japan and His Cabinet (2020c) "Nihon Keizai Saisei Honbun Kaisai Jōkyō" [State of Meetings of the Headquarters for Japan's Economic Revitalization]. Online. Available: https://www.kantei.go.jp/jp/singi/keizaisaisei/kaisai.html (accessed February 3, 2020).

Prime Minister's Office of Japan (2020) "Rekidai Naikaku" [Successive Cabinets]. Online. Available: https://www.kantei.go.jp/jp/rekidainaikaku/index.html (accessed February 3, 2020).

Shimizu, Katsuhiko (2014) *Abe Seiken no Wana. Tanjunka Sareru Seiji to Media* [Trap of the Abe Government. Simplifying the Politics and Media], Tokyo: Heibonsha.

Shindō, Muneyuki (2019) *Kanryōsei to Kōbunsho. Kaizan, Netsuzō, Sontaku no Haikei* [Bureaucratic System and Official Documents. Manipulation, Forgery, Sontaku], Tokyo: Chikuma Shobō.

Shinoda, Tomohito (2000) *Leading Japan. The Role of the Prime Minister*, Westport: Praeger Publishers.

Stockwin, Arthur & Ampiah, Kweku (2017) *Rethinking Japan. The Politics of Contested Nationalism*, Lanham–Boulder–New York–London: Lexington Books.

Suezaki, Takeshi (2014) "Chōsei to Hairyo, Namaru Teigen. Fukkatsu 1 Nen no Keizai Zaisei Shimon Kaigi" [Coordination and Consideration, Dull Proposals. The Council on Economic and Fiscal Policy 1 Year After Revival], *Asahi Shinbun*, January 9, morning edition, 7.

Suga, Yoshihide (2012) *Seijika no Kakugo – Kanryō o Ugokase* [Politician's Readiness – Make Bureaucrats Move], Tokyo: Bungei Shunjū Kikaku Shuppanbu.

Sunohara, Tsuyoshi (2014) *Nihonban NSC to wa Nanika* [What Is the Japanese Version of the NSC?], Tokyo: Shinchōsha.

Takahashi, Yōichi (2011) *Kangu no Kuni. Naze nihon dewa, Seijika ga Kanryō ni Kussuru noka* [The Country of Bureaucratic Folly. Why do the Politicians Yield to the Bureaucrats in Japan?], Tokyo: Shōdensha.

Tanaka, Hideaki (2019) *Kanryōtachi no Fuyu. Kasumigaseki Fukkatsu no Shohōsen* [Winter of the Bureaucrats. Prescription for Revival of Kasumigaseki], Tokyo: Shōgakkan.

Taniguchi, Tomohiko (2018) *Abe Shinzō no Shinjitsu* [Truth About Abe Shinzō], Tokyo: Gokū Shuppan.

Tazaki, Shirō (2014) *Abe Kantei no Shōtai* [The True Image of the Abe Kantei], Tokyo: Kōdansha.

The Advisory Panel on Reconstruction of the Legal Basis for Security (2014) "Report of the Advisory Panel on Reconstruction of the Legal Basis for Security" (May 15). Online. Available: https://www.kantei.go.jp/jp/singi/anzenhosyou2/dai7/houkoku_en.pdf (accessed July 23, 2019).

Uesugi, Takashi (2011) *Kantei Hōkai: Nihon Seiji Konmei no Nazo* [Collapse of the Kantei: The Puzzle of Confusion of Japanese Politics], Tokyo: Gentōsha.

Yakushiji, Katsuyuki (2003) *Gaimushō – Gaikō Kyōka e no Michi* [Ministry of Foreign Affairs – Path towards Strengthening Diplomacy], Tokyo: Iwanami Shoten.

Yamaguchi, Noriyuki (2017) *Sōri* [Prime Minister], Tokyo: Gentōsha.

Yomiuri Shinbun Seijibu (2015) *Abe Kantei vs. Shū Kinpei. Gekika Suru Nitchū Gaikō Sensō* [Abe's Residence vs. Xi Jinping. Intensifying Sino-Japanese Diplomatic War], Tokyo: Shinchōsha.

4 Reforming the LDP

The institutional changes in the government were supplemented with skillful strategies to pacify voices of discontent in the LDP. Abe chose not to conduct any significant reform of decision-making process in the ruling party. He generally respected the unwritten principles of unanimity in such bodies as the Policy Research Council and the General Council, but, at the same time, he rendered previously existing organs less influential thanks to the creative use of party rules. On the one hand, Abe bypassed the traditional channels for decision making through newly established bodies under his direct control, and, on the other hand, he put pressure on parliamentary tribes by playing one *zoku* off against another. In addition, to counterbalance the influence of senior backbenchers, he occasionally appealed to a large group of first-term lawmakers, who generally remained loyal toward the prime minister. As the cabinet support rate remained high, all these strategies sufficed to discipline Abe's opponents in the LDP.

LDP backbenchers as veto players

Until the 1990s, factional struggles in the LDP had forced the head of government to ceaselessly monitor the situation in the ruling party and maintain harmony through highly institutionalized power-balancing activities. Moreover, since the 1970s, the prime ministers had had to cope with a new kind of intra-party veto player. So-called parliamentary tribes acted in concert with the bureaucrats from separate ministries to promote the interests of distinct industry sectors. Under these circumstances, extensive consensus-seeking activities became a necessity to keep the ruling party in one piece.

As illustrated in Figure 4.1, the traditional decision-making process was conducted concurrently in the government and in the LDP. Both policy venues were treated as separate entities, connected only by the prime minister who, at the same time, served as LDP leader. Before submission to the Diet, all bill projects were subject to so-called "advance screening" (*jizen shinsa*) – they had to be authorized by the LDP Policy Research Council and the General Council. The bureaucrats, acting on behalf of their ministries and

Reforming the LDP 133

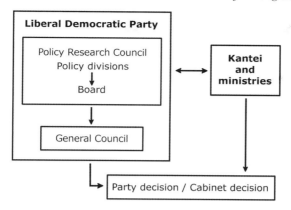

Figure 4.1 Traditional two-track decision-making process.
Source: Compiled by the author, based on many sources.

supervised by the Kantei, drafted initial versions of new laws, on which at an early stage they also consulted the influential members of the involved parliamentary tribes of the ruling party (Iio 2008: 84). This "two-track" nature of the decision-making process was sanctified by a political culture elaborated during the decades-long reign of the LDP.

Ruling party backbenchers rarely took advantage of their right to legislative initiative. Approximately two-thirds of law projects were drafted by the government, and the majority of the remaining one-third by opposition parties. While the adoption rate of government-sponsored bills was 85%, it remained at only 34% in case of the projects submitted by members of the House of Representatives, and 16% in case of those prepared by members of the House of Councilors (Kawato 2015: 135–137). Groups of lawmakers (20 in the lower, or 10 in the upper house) were allowed to submit their own bill proposals only after gaining permission from their party leadership. In 1952, the Liberal Party Secretary-General Masuda Kaneshichi asked the Diet not to accept any law projects that had not been accepted by party authorities, which became an unwritten rule. As a result, only those LDP lawmakers who had persuaded the secretary-general, as well as the General Council, Policy Research Council, and Diet Affairs Committee chairpersons, were able to sponsor bills (Kōno 2003: 75–76). Adding to that a weak administrative backing for Diet members, most LDP backbenchers preferred to rely on the bureaucrats to draft new laws by themselves.

While bill projects were prepared by the government, the ruling party was extensively consulted on their contents. The LDP Policy Research Council hosted policy divisions (*bukai*) responsible for separate legislative fields, research commissions (*chōsakai*) that formulated long-term general policies, special committees (*tokubetsu iinkai*) established to deal with different problems surpassing the competences of one ministry, as well as subcommittees (*shōiinkai*) and project teams (*purojekuto chīmu*), temporarily created within distinct policy divisions (Satō & Matsuzaki 1986: 85; Nakakita 2017: 94–95). Bureaucrats and private-sector experts were invited to the deliberations in these bodies to express their opinions on bill projects and answer questions from backbenchers. Various business sectors, social groups, and non-governmental organizations tried to influence the decision-making process through supportive Diet members. As the Policy Research Council respected an unwritten rule of unanimity, numerous backstage agreements were made to achieve a consensus (Yuasa 1986: 31–32). In case of differences of opinion among policy division members, a range of uncodified procedures was elaborated to maintain intra-party harmony. If, despite persuasion from the chairperson, faction bosses, and bureaucrats, bill opponents refused to yield, the decision was often entrusted to the policy division or research commission chair. In that case, the contents of the draft bill were usually diluted to satisfy all the interested parties. Those who conceded could count on repayment of the debt of gratitude on a different occasion (Iio 2008: 85–86). If a really important policy was widely opposed by LDP backbenchers, deliberations could be temporarily suspended, or the issue could be sent to a higher organ. All the decisions had to be authorized by the Policy Research Council Board (Seichō Shingikai) (Murakawa 2000: 171–175). This mature political culture made the decision making process time-consuming, but it also enabled preservation of intra-party unity, despite the existence of strong policy disagreements.

Each policy division hosted its own parliamentary tribe composed of politicians experienced in one legislative field. One of the most powerful *zoku* was the tax system tribe. The LDP Research Commission on the Tax System was led by a small group of senior politicians who served as Commission and sub-commission chairs or advisers. This inner circle of decision makers boasted the exclusive right to establish the annual tax system framework, based on policy coordination between various ministries and industry sectors. At the end of each year, Commission members assessed all tax proposals by marking them with a circle (*maru* – approval), a triangle (*sankaku – de facto* approval), or a cross (*batsu* – rejection). It was an unwritten rule that the Kantei and party authorities never interfered in the Commission's proceedings. Even Prime Minister Koizumi respected the independence of this body. As pointed out by Kidera (2017: 153–156), such a gentlemen's agreement was beneficial for both sides. As tax issues attracted the interest of many pressure groups and ordinary voters, the isolation of younger parliamentarians, whose position in their constituencies was weaker and who, thus, were more prone to external pressure, ensured the stability of the system. Veteran lawmakers gathered in the LDP Research Commission on the Tax System Board enjoyed extensive powers, while the Kantei could shed onto them the responsibility for management of this conflictual field of policymaking. As a side effect, the Commission's decisions were not always in line with the policy of the government.

After passing through the Policy Research Council Board, all bill projects were sent to the LDP General Council (Sōmukai) – a permanent organ that decided on daily issues in place of the Party Convention, the supreme body of the party, which convened once a year. In 1962, General Council Chairperson Akagi Munenori wrote a memo to Chief Cabinet Secretary (CCS), Ōhira Masayoshi, in which he requested the government to ask the General Council for authorization of all bill projects before their adoption by the cabinet and submission to the Diet (Krauss & Pekkanen 2011: 165). Ever since, it was this organ that had retained the right to approve all policies as "party decisions" (*tōgi kettei*). Although only General Council members, usually senior politicians, had the right to vote, all LDP lawmakers could attend meetings (Fukui 1969: 105). As a result, in the case of particularly controversial bills, the General Council served as a convenient forum for backbenchers to voice their objections. According to Article 41 of the LDP Constitution, the decisions of the General Council were "made by a simple majority of those present" (Liberal Democratic Party 2009). Similarly to other decision-making organs in the LDP, however, an unwritten rule of unanimity, coupled with additional codes of conduct, was respected. If one member's resistance against a bill was not shared by his/her colleagues in the General Council, the chairperson enabled the opponent to keep face, while gradually pushing the decision-making process forward. During the final voting, the member who objected simply left the room, so that he could explain to the represented pressure groups that the decision had been arbitrarily made in her/his absence (Ishikawa & Hirose 1989: 222). Adoption of the party decision by the General Council ended the process of advance screening and obliged all LDP lawmakers to vote for the authorized bill (Iio 2008: 87).

As LDP legislators had enough time to express their opinions on government-sponsored laws during deliberations in the party, they ceded most discussion time in the Diet to the opposition parties. The length of parliamentary sessions was greatly limited. In addition to regular sessions, held from January to June, extraordinary sessions were usually convoked from September to December. As it was very difficult to carry the legislative process over from one session to another, the ruling party remained under constant time pressure. Moreover, the Kantei had no direct control over scheduling of parliamentary committee meetings and plenary sessions. The speakers of both houses and parliamentary committee chairs enjoyed broad discretionary powers, such as sending bill projects to specific committees or shelving their proceedings. The schedule of deliberations was decided by the House of Representatives and the House of Councilors Steering Committees (Giin Un'ei Iinkai) (Takenaka 2013: 146–149). Unlike the UK government, the cabinet in Japan could neither impose the order in which bill projects were proceeded, nor even tie a bill with a vote of confidence, so as to discipline the backbenchers. Its role in the legislative process was limited to the legislative initiative and to answering Diet interpellations. As pointed out by Kawato (2015: 25–72), since the mid-1950s, the only way the government limited to some extent the Diet's independence was discouraging ruling party backbenchers from submitting lawmaker-sponsored bills. Nevertheless, this achievement was attained at the expense of vesting the right to authorize government-sponsored bills in LDP decision-making bodies.

Theoretically, before deliberations in the Diet, the process of advance screening had assuaged protests by LDP backbenchers against new laws. Nevertheless, the most controversial bills still occasionally encountered resistance from individual members of the ruling party. Opponents usually avoided severe punishment if they absented themselves from voting, but could be expelled from the party if they voted against government-sponsored laws. Without a whipping system similar to the UK, the LDP relied on less formal methods to discipline its members. In fact, opposing votes during most plenary sessions in the House of Representatives did not really matter.[1] Voting by acclamation applied whenever the representatives of all parliamentary caucuses agreed on a decision during the proceedings of the Steering Committee. Usually, this method was used for less important, procedural matters. In such cases, unanimity was assumed, even if individual lawmakers voiced an objection. When passing bill projects, voting by rising from one's seat remained the most common method. Also in this case, individual votes were rarely counted, and instead decisions of each party as a whole were respected.[2] Only adoption of the most important laws, such as international treaties or budgetary bills, necessitated voting through name cards. In such cases, whenever the ruling parties enjoyed only a minimal majority in the Diet, a revolt by a small group of lawmakers could counter the government's plans.[3]

Rather than disciplining LDP backbenchers, after submission of a bill project to the Diet, the ruling party focused on negotiations with the leaders of the opposition. As the Japanese public disliked excessive political quarrels, any "forced voting" (*kyōkō saiketsu*), conducted despite the demonstrative absence of opposition parties, could negatively impact the government support rate. In such cases, the government was accused of exercising "the tyranny of majority," which did not fit well with the preference for seeking consensus, inculcated in Japanese culture (Stockwin 2008: 161). It was the responsibility of the LDP Diet Affairs Committee (Kokkai Taisaku Iinkai) to assuage the stance of opposition politicians before the proceedings of the Steering Committee. The Diet affairs *zoku* maintained backstage channels to the opposition parties and negotiated which methods of resistance in the Diet would be tolerated (Ishikawa & Hirose 1989: 40–52; Murakawa 2000: 82–86). Such behind-the-scenes talks, often conducted in luxurious restaurants, usually sufficed to persuade the opposition politicians not to disturb the legislative process through filibuster techniques, door and rostrum blockade, or the "cow's walk tactic" (*gyūho senjutsu*). This last method meant walking extremely slow to the podium to vote by the use of name card. If voting took place at the end of the parliamentary session, the prolongation of proceedings could even lead to the rejection of a government-sponsored bill.[4]

The two-track decision-making system was based on a fragile balance of power between the Kantei and the LDP backbenchers. While the government initiated the legislative process, all bill projects were the fruits of compromise between various groups in the ruling party. Whenever the prime minister wanted to realize his policy ideas, he first had to initiate time-consuming negotiations with distinct parliamentary tribes. However, the electoral and administrative reforms of the 1990s disturbed the relationship between the Kantei and the backbenchers in favor of the former. Prime Minister Abe took full advantage of this change, while further weakening intra-party veto players through strategic personnel decisions and the creation of new policy venues in the ruling party.

Waning influence of parliamentary tribes

Abe exploited the waning impact of parliamentary tribes on the decision-making process. Pressure groups still exerted considerable influence on LDP backbenchers, but individual *zoku* were no longer able to effectively block decisions on matters of strategic importance for the cabinet. Just as in the case of bureaucrats, Abe used conflicts of interests among veto players to play one parliamentary tribe off against another. He also diluted the solidarity of separate *zoku* by offering important party and governmental posts to their members.

Similarly to factions, the process of weakening of parliamentary tribes started after the implementation of electoral reform in 1994. Under the old system, on average, three to five politicians from each district received seats in the House of Representatives, so representing the interests of one influential pressure group could provide a sufficient number of votes to be elected. In the newly established single-seat constituencies, however, only the strongest candidate could win. In order to approach multiple social groups, it became necessary even for politicians from rural districts to boast broad knowledge in all legislative fields. Responding to these changes, in May 1998, LDP Policy Research Council Chairperson, Yamasaki Taku, abolished formal membership of policy divisions. While previously LDP lawmakers had been allowed to actively participate in the proceedings of only two divisions of their choice (plus one division corresponding to the parliamentary committee they belonged to), they could now freely attend the meetings of any division they pleased. As a result, the borders between separate *zoku* started to blur. The broader the specialization of LDP lawmakers grew, the shallower their knowledge in single legislative fields became (Nishimura 2002: 178–183; Nakakita 2017: 121–122).

The long-term trend of the weakening of the traditional LDP support groups reduced the benefits of narrow specialization even further. As globalization pushed Japan toward liberalization of trade and privatization of inefficient state-owned companies, the dominant party could no longer win elections by appealing solely to its core electorate, such as farmers and postal employees. Moreover, under the DPJ government (2009–2012), some pressure groups previously loyal to the LDP, for example the Japan Trucking Association, Japan Dental Association, and Japan Medical Association, decided to remain neutral or switched their support to the new ruling coalition. The LDP regained the support of most of them after returning to power in 2012, but generally the trend of weakening of interest groups continued, which was also related to the rapid aging of the farming household population. This tendency was reflected in the composition of rank-and-file LDP members. While at the end of the 1990s, those belonging to professional groups constituted 65% of all LDP members, by 2015, this ratio had dropped to about 38% (Nakakita 2017: 196–215).

An important turning point in the evolution of parliamentary tribes was the disastrous electoral defeat of the LDP in 2009. Almost 200 LDP politicians lost their seats in the House of Representatives, which separated them from direct participation in state politics for more than three years. Deprived of access to reliable data on current policy projects, they could not develop their skills in the fields of their interests. Moreover, even those LDP lawmakers who survived the electoral "carnage" could no longer count on the same attention from the bureaucrats as in the time when the LDP remained in power. Only after the formation of the Abe government did the parliamentary tribes start making up for the period lost in opposition, but it took them some time to restore their former connections and absorb new knowledge (Nakakita 2017: 122).

The tax system *zoku*, composed exclusively of heavyweight politicians, was mostly spared from the decimation of the 2009 election. As a result, the LDP Research Commission on the Tax System remained one of the most powerful LDP organs. Initially, Abe respected the traditional decision-making patterns in this influential body. It was the party commission that prepared the general framework of the tax system every year, while its governmental counterpart simply confirmed these decisions (Nakakita 2017: 116). In fact, Abe abolished the governmental Research Commission on the Tax System composed of all vice-ministers, which had been created by the DPJ government, and he revived the previous version as a merely advisory council. Nevertheless, the prime minister's determination to implement his own version of tax reform quickly caused frictions between the Kantei and the tax system *zoku*.

At the end of January 2013, the LDP Research Commission on the Tax System prepared the general framework of the tax system for FY 2013. Out of consideration toward Kōmeitō, it contained plans for an increase in inheritance tax for the wealthiest and examination of the introduction of a reduced tax rate system for selected products at the time of the second stage of the VAT hike to 10%, scheduled for October 2015. Moreover, an intent to reduce corporate tax reflected the Abenomics policy. Most controversial, however, was the plan to revive earmarked funds for road improvement (*dōro tokutei zaigen*). The funds, based on fuel tax and auto purchase tax, devoted to the construction of new and maintenance of old roads, were a symbol of wasteful budget spending and had been abolished in 2009. The plan for their revival, promoted by the LDP road tribe, encountered strong opposition from the Kantei. During deliberations of the joint meeting of the LDP Policy Research Council Board and policy division chairs, lawmakers from the prime minister's entourage, such as Policy Research Council Acting Chairpersons Shiozaki Yasuhisa and Tanahashi Yasufumi, voiced their concerns that revival of the controversial fund would create the impression of excessive influence of parliamentary tribes on decision making. As a result, Policy Research Council Chairperson, Takaichi Sanae, postponed authorization of the tax system outline. Under pressure from party authorities, Research Commission on the Tax System Chairperson Noda Takeshi wrote a note explaining that the costs of maintaining roads would not necessarily be covered from an earmarked fund. The note was authorized as a party decision together with the general framework of the tax system (*Asahi Shinbun* 2013a: 2). This unusual intervention showed that while parliamentary tribes still boasted considerable influence in LDP decision-making bodies, central party authorities closely followed the Kantei's policy and were able to force even backbenchers as influential as Noda into concessions.

The prime minister did not intend to let the LDP Research Commission on the Tax System slow down or block his economic policy agenda. In June 2013, he ordered the Commission to accelerate discussion on a corporate tax reduction aimed at stimulating capital investments. The Commission had no choice but to start deliberations on the tax system for FY 2014 several months earlier than scheduled, but its members were hesitant to speed up the tax reduction (*Asahi Shinbun* 2013b: 4). Even more humiliating for the tax system *zoku* was the sudden announcement by Abe in September 2013 of his intention to abolish one year earlier than scheduled a special corporate tax for reconstruction of the regions ravaged by the Great East Japan Earthquake. The policy was prepared by Prime Minister's Secretary, Imai Takaya, in consultation with the MOF Tax Bureau Director-General, Tanaka Kazuho, who, under the first Abe administration, had served as the prime minister's administrative secretary. The final decision on this matter was made by Abe, Suga, Asō, and Amari (Kidera 2017: 167). The Kantei neglected policy coordination with heavyweight politicians in the LDP Research Commission on the Tax System. Only after a reprimand from such faction-boss-level backbenchers as Nukaga Fukushirō did Finance Minister Asō and Minister of State for Economic and Fiscal Policy Amari visit the Commission to explain the government's policy. Eventually, despite voices of discontent, the final decision was entrusted to Commission Chair Noda. In addition, the backbenchers felt indignant when on the same day they were informed of the governmental project of the Bill Concerning Reform of the National Public Service System. They blamed the Kantei not only for the fact that the details of such an important reform had not been sufficiently consulted with the party, but also for the fact that they were lectured by Minister in charge of Civil Service Reform, Inada Tomomi, who was only a third-term lawmaker (Watanabe 2013: 132).

It seemed that backbenchers were less afraid of challenging the government's policy whenever the Abe cabinet faced harsh criticism from the public. For instance, members of the LDP Research Commission on the Tax System announced the tax system outline for FY 2014 when the government was absorbed with the passage of the controversial Bill on Protection of Specially Designated Secrets. The outline from mid-December 2013 acknowledged corporate tax reduction for capital investments or research and development, but it did not allow a comprehensive decrease in corporate taxes nor their waiver in National Strategic Special Zones, whose creation was one of the key points of the "third arrow" of Abenomics (*Asahi Shinbun* 2013d: 4). As the LDP had regained power at the end of 2012, parliamentary tribes lacked time to influence the budget compilation for FY 2013. In December 2013, however, they intensified their activities. Under pressure from backbenchers, the government had to remove the policy of restraint in public works expenses from the preliminary budget draft. As stressed by an influential member of the construction tribe, LDP Disaster Resilient Japan General Research Commission (Kokudo Kyōjinka Sōgō Chōsakai) Chair, Nikai Toshihiro, it was improper to reduce expenditures for disaster prevention measures. Another pretext for increasing public works spending was a reference to expansive fiscal policy stipulated in the "second arrow" of Abenomics. The labor and welfare tribe, representing the interests of the Japan Medical Association, managed, in turn, to stop the government's plans to reduce health care fees. As a result, the budget project swelled to a record-high 95.9 trillion yen (*Asahi Shinbun* 2013e: 2).

In February 2014, LDP Research Commission on the Tax System Chair Noda announced that the Commission would issue a framework for the corporate tax rate for FY 2015 by June 2014. Such an early beginning of deliberations, which had usually been conducted at the end of the year, was an attempt to establish a basic direction for tax reform for the subsequent year before the publication of the Basic Policies for Economic and Fiscal Management and Reform by the CEFP, scheduled for June (*Asahi Shinbun* 2014b: 7). Noda's intention was probably not to let Abe repeat the situation from the previous year, when the Kantei had ordered the Commission to speed up work on lowering taxes in the middle of the year. Aware of the Commission's reluctance to acknowledge the corporate tax reduction, Abe and his entourage decided to appeal to less experienced Diet members, whose number increased significantly after LDP's electoral victory in 2012

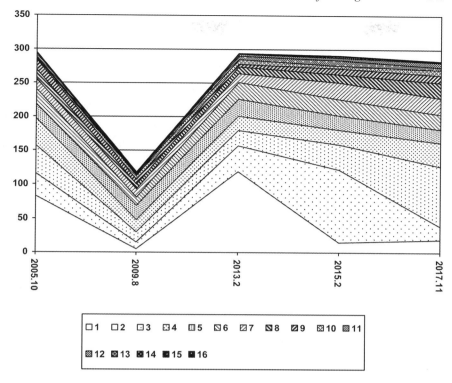

Figure 4.2 Number of LDP members of the House of Representatives according to the number of terms.

Source: Compiled by the author, based on *Kokkai Binran* (2005-2017).

(see Figure 4.2). On April 23, 2014, 87 lawmakers of up to four terms in the Diet established the Association to Consider the Tax System for the Next Generation (Jisedai no Zeisei o Kangaeru Kai). They criticized the exclusiveness and lack of transparency of the LDP Research Commission on the Tax System. The aim of the Association was to discuss the plan of corporate tax reduction from 35.64% to less than 30%, in order to make Japanese companies competitive against their counterparts in other Asian countries. The young lawmakers' initiative was inspired by CCS Suga Yoshihide and Takenaka Heizō who wanted to use the new group to apply pressure on senior politicians in the Commission not only in a top-down, but also in a bottom-up manner (Kujiraoka 2014: 4).

In subsequent years, the LDP Research Commission on the Tax System lost importance. Thanks to his strong position in the ruling party and electoral victory after the Diet dissolution in December 2014, Abe successfully forced the Commission to follow the Kantei's stance on the VAT hike postponement. When, in October 2015, Noda Takeshi refused to compromise on the reduced tax rate system, the prime minister simply replaced him with a less troublesome politician, Miyazawa Yōichi. As a former Minister of Economy, Trade and Industry, Miyazawa did not represent the interests of the tax system *zoku* alone. At the end of November 2015, he authorized the property tax reduction that was requested by the METI (Kidera 2017: 153). Admitting the growing importance of the Kantei, at the end of September 2016, the LDP Research Commission on the Tax System Board members decided to admit for membership former Minister of State for Economic and Fiscal Policy, Amari Akira. Their aim was to further strengthen ties with the prime minister's entourage (*Asahi Shinbun* 2016a: 4). In September 2019, Amari became the new Commission chair, which enhanced the Kantei's control over this body. Amari admitted he would prioritize a tax reform aimed at boosting economic growth, which contrasted with the stance of most members of the tax system *zoku* (Nishiyama & Okamura 2019: 4). Under his leadership, the new board became more willing to cooperate with the prime minister. Hayashi Yoshimasa, who became deputy chairperson of the LDP Research Commission on the Tax System in October 2015, admitted that the Commission remained only one of many sub-organs of the Policy Research Council and could not effectively oppose the party leader (interview by the author, Tokyo, October 16, 2019).

Over time, Prime Minister Abe gained greater leverage over parliamentary tribes than any of his predecessors. He used his enhanced position to infiltrate separate *zoku* with politicians from outside of the inner circles of distinct tribes. For instance, Abe made highly unusual decisions to nominate as chairs of the LDP Policy Research Council Agriculture and Forestry Policy Division politicians from urban constituencies – Saitō Ken in 2013 and Koizumi Shinjirō in 2015 – neither of whom belonged to the agricultural *zoku* (Nakakita 2017: 123). Analogically, he appointed Hayashi Yoshimasa, who was a member of the financial tribe, as agriculture minister in 2012. As noted by Hayashi, reliance on the prime minister's unwavering determination to reform the agriculture sector proved the most useful argument in applying pressure on the agricultural tribe (interview by the author, Tokyo, October 16, 2019).

One of the most difficult tasks for Abe was to quell voices of discontent in the LDP regarding Japan's accession to the TPP Agreement. TPP was a free-trade agreement that, as well as Japan, encompassed Australia, Brunei, Canada, Chile, Malaysia, Mexico, New Zealand, Peru, Singapore, Vietnam, and the US. Abe perceived this initiative not only as a way to promote exports of Japanese products, but also as a crucial element of the strategy of containing the rising China. The biggest line of discontent ran between the US and Japan. While Washington wanted to protect its automobile industry against Japanese cars, Tokyo insisted on partial maintenance of tariffs on agricultural products. TPP accession was promoted by the METI and MOFA, and opposed by the MAFF. As a lot of LDP lawmakers came from rural constituencies, they relied on support from the National Federation of Agricultural Cooperative Associations (Zennō) as well as its political body, the Central Union of Agricultural Cooperatives (JA Zenchū). Together with MAFF bureaucrats, the LDP agricultural tribe put pressure on the Kantei to reconsider joining TPP negotiations. In its 2012 electoral manifesto, the LDP declared opposition to participation in TPP talks if they were based on "removal of tariffs without sacred territories" (Liberal Democratic Party 2012: 12). The manifesto reflected the resolution of the LDP Research Commission on Comprehensive Agricultural Policy and Trade (Sōgō Nōsei Bōeki Chōsakai) from October 2011, which requested protection of five sensitive agricultural items: rice, beef and pork, dairy products, sugar, and starch. The Association Demanding Prompt Withdrawal from TPP Accession (TPP Sanka no Sokuji Tekkai o Motomeru Kai) gathered as many as 240 LDP lawmakers. While, after the announcement by Abe of Japan's participation in TPP talks in March 2013, the group displayed some flexibility and changed its name to the Association to Protect the National Interest During TPP Negotiations (TPP Kōshō ni Okeru Kokueki o Mamorinuku Kai), it still constituted the main obstacle against the Kantei's policy (Bochorodycz 2018: 210–211).

Aware of the strength of the agricultural tribe, Abe decided to first weaken its solidarity. At the beginning of 2013, he established the LDP Research Council for Regional Diplomatic and Economic Partnership (Gaikō, Keizai Renkei Chōsakai), later renamed Headquarters (Honbu). The organ was placed under Abe's direct jurisdiction and chaired by Etō Seishirō. Under the Headquarters, in turn, the Committee for TPP Measures (TPP Taisaku Iinkai) was founded. Surprisingly, Abe asked one of the influential members of the agricultural tribe, Nishikawa Kōya, to chair this organ. The prime minister probably remembered Nishikawa's behavior under the Koizumi administration, when after nomination to a vice-ministerial position he radically changed his stance from opposing to supporting the Japan Post privatization. This *similia similibus curantur* ("like is cured by like") tactic ended in success, as Nishikawa proved instrumental in assuaging the resistance of the agricultural tribe against the TPP. In September 2014, Abe rewarded him with the post of minister of agriculture, forestry and fisheries, though Nishikawa was forced to resign after only a few months due to a corruption scandal (Bochorodycz 2018: 211–212).

Interestingly, Nishikawa (2017: 48) himself admitted that his nomination was a part of Abe's strategy to "control *zoku* by the use of *zoku*" (*zoku o motte zoku o seisu*). Nishikawa closely cooperated with the Government Headquarters for TPP Measures (TPP Seifu Taisaku Honbu) and he engaged Association to Protect National Interest During TPP Negotiations Chair Moriyama Hiroshi in the negotiation process as the deputy chair of the LDP Committee for TPP Measures. As argued by Nishikawa (2017: 84–393), he believed that liberalization of trade would be a positive impetus for Japan's economy, which would translate into a revival of the agricultural sector as well. He boasted that thanks to his efforts, while other TPP member states agreed to eliminate almost 100% of tariffs, in the case of Japan the overall liberalization rate remained at 95%, and 82% for agricultural products. Despite his resignation from a ministerial post, in 2016, Nishikawa participated in the process of ratification of the TPP as the chair of the House of Representatives Special Committee on TPP. It was evident that Abe did not hesitate to reward politicians who cooperated on his policy agenda with lucrative positions.

Another strategy employed by Abe to overcome opposition from the agricultural tribe was taking advantage of the popularity of young, reform-minded politicians. In particular, LDP Policy Research Council Agriculture and Forestry Policy Division Chair Koizumi Shinjirō proved instrumental in calming the anxiety among farmers after the conclusion of TPP negotiations in October 2015. The highly popular son of Prime Minister Koizumi Jun'ichirō participated in 15 meetings in seven prefectures, during which he explained the contents and gravity of the agreement (Bochorodycz 2018: 212–213). While Koizumi did not fully agree with Abe on other policies, such as the reactivation of nuclear power plants, he was, thus, strategically used by the prime minister to promote the policies that both shared.

At the same time, the prime minister did not waver from eliminating the political influence of those pressure groups that hindered his policy agenda. During the World Economic Forum in Davos in January 2014, Abe emphasized that he was "willing to act like a drill bit; strong enough to break through the solid rock of vested interests" (Prime Minister of Japan and His Cabinet 2014). In fact, at the end of 2013, the Kantei decided to abolish in 2018 so-called *gentan*, which had been introduced in the 1970s. Under this system, farmers received subsidies upon the condition of reducing the acreage of rice paddies, which resulted in high rice prices. As *gentan* made the Japanese agricultural sector uncompetitive, its abolition was aimed at preparing farmers for the liberalization of trade. It was expected that discontinuation of farming by small-scale and part-time rice farmers would considerably reduce the number of JA Zenchū members (Terada 2016: 95–97). Abe also insisted on turning the Central Union of Agricultural Cooperatives into an incorporated association and abolishing its *de facto* monopoly on distributing state subsidies to the farmers. While the proposed changes were revolutionary, Abe displayed willingness to compromise with the agricultural tribe on the details of the reform. In the face of the Kantei's institutional strength, LDP lawmakers from rural constituencies quickly came to the conclusion that they would not be able to protect all the interests of JA Zenchū, but they at least managed to slow down and dilute the institutional changes. For example, the abolition of the *gentan* system was combined with the introduction of new subsidies for cultivating rice for flour making and as a feed crop, aimed at restricting the supply of rice as a staple food. Eventually, in November 2016, it was decided that the National Federation of Agricultural Cooperative Associations would be required to reform itself, rather than subjected to radical restrictions as had been proposed by the governmental Regulatory Reform Promotion Council (Honma & George Mulgan 2018: 128–144).

The strengthened Kantei centralized the decision-making process on drafting electoral manifestos, which further marginalized the role played by parliamentary tribes. For example, before the House of Representatives election in October 2017, the government decided to use part of the new revenues gained after an increase in consumption tax to 10% to introduce free early childhood education, which met with dissatisfaction from the labor and welfare *zoku*. LDP Health, Labor and Welfare Policy Division Chair, Hashimoto Gaku, criticized the fact that such an important policy change was included in the electoral manifesto despite his opposition and without sufficient consultation with the party. A lot of LDP lawmakers were surprised to hear about the new electoral pledge, especially taking into account the fact that until regaining power in 2012, the LDP had opposed the DPJ's ideas of introducing free education (Tanaka 2019: 78). The weakening of the labor and welfare tribe was reflected in the decrease in health care fees despite protests from LDP backbenchers and the Japan Medical Association. While the fees had been raised by 0.1% for FY 2014, in subsequent years, the Kantei did not hesitate to reduce them (by 0.84% in 2016, 1.19% in 2018, and 0.46% in 2020), though it conceded to a slight increase in the funds for medical personnel expenses (*Honkawa Data Tribune* 2020). Instead of paying heed to the vested interests of separate pressure groups, Abe put emphasis on limiting the burden for all Japanese in order to boost LDP's electoral performance. The waning influence of parliamentary tribes was not unnoticed by interest groups. As stressed by Mikuriya (2015: 108–109), the unilateral strength of the Kantei over the ruling party resulted in a decreased number of lobbyists visiting the LDP headquarters in Tokyo.

While Abe actively struggled with those parliamentary tribes that hindered his policy plans, he also took advantage of those whose policies were in line with his agenda. For instance, the nuclear energy lobby (so-called "nuclear village," *genshiryoku mura*) regained a strong position in the government after the DPJ was ousted from power in 2012. Abe abandoned the policy of gradually phasing out nuclear power plants, and authorized the reopening of the Sendai plant in August 2015 and the Takahama plant in January 2016. Analogically, the road and construction *zoku* managed to promote their interests thanks to large-scale infrastructure projects implemented within the framework of the "second arrow" of Abenomics. Both reconstruction after the Great East Japan Earthquake and holding the Tokyo Olympics in 2020 (later moved to 2021 due to the coronavirus pandemic) served as convenient pretexts to devote large funds to public works.

In addition, although Abe remained unyielding in pacifying those parliamentary tribes that challenged his policy agenda, he did not intend to make too many enemies among LDP backbenchers. The prime minister was ready even to curb the initiatives of his closest associates if he felt their realization would cost him too dearly. For instance, Abe did not support Minister of Health, Labor, and Welfare, Shiozaki Yasuhisa, in his efforts to completely prohibit indoor smoking in restaurants before the Tokyo Olympics. Shiozaki's initiative encountered strong opposition from the backbenchers related to the tobacco industry, including LDP Policy Research Council Chairperson, Motegi Toshimitsu, who was a former minister of economy, trade and industry. During a cabinet reshuffle in August 2017, Shiozaki was replaced with Katō Katsunobu, who, as a former MOF bureaucrat, proposed a less restrictive policy (Japan Tobacco remained one of *amakudari* targets for the MOF) (Koga 2017: 97–101). Eventually, an amendment to the Health Promotion Law, passed in July 2018, introduced a smoking ban only in the biggest restaurants.

The parliamentary tribes had been weakened before Abe's return to power, but the prime minister further eliminated LDP backbenchers' influence on decision-making. Although some *zoku* were still able to thrive, their successes depended on the conformity of their goals with the Kantei's agenda rather than on their ability to influence that agenda. The tribes that hindered Abe's plans, in turn, such as the agricultural and tax system *zoku*, were gradually pacified by the prime minister and his direct entourage. Abe's prolonged term in office excluded simple waiting out as a viable strategy for veto players to resist this gradual institutional change.

Extension of LDP president's term in office

Abe's policy agenda, especially such ambitious tasks as revision of the Constitution, required long-term planning. However, Japanese prime ministers have frequently changed. Short tenures of the heads of government, despite the almost ceaseless reign of the LDP, were a consequence of factional struggles in the ruling party. It was the search for intra-party balance through the creation of opportunities for all major faction bosses to assume the prime ministerial post that led to the reduction in the length of one tenure as LDP president from three to two years in 1977, as well as to the introduction of a limitation of time in office to two consecutive terms in 1980. The three-year-long tenure was restored under the Koizumi administration in 2002 (Nakakita 2017: 87). This change extended the maximum time in office from four to six years, but it still remained well below the standards of most Western democracies.

During the LDP presidential election in September 2012, it was Ishiba Shigeru who won the first round thanks to his popularity among rank-and-file party members. However, Abe managed to receive more votes in the second round, conducted only among LDP lawmakers. This distortion caused voices of discontent in the countryside, which led to the revision of party rules by the Party Convention in 2013, so as to take into account rank-and-file party members' votes also during the final round. The Party Convention in 2014 authorized further revision – an increase in the number of regional votes from 300 to the same number as LDP lawmakers had (Nakakita 2017: 88–89). All these changes theoretically reduced the role of backstage factional deals and made the individual candidate's image among the general public even more important.

Aware of Abe's ambition to remain in office until the Tokyo Olympic Games, in 2016, the prime minister's closest entourage intensified their efforts to amend LDP rules and extend the longest allowable tenure in the party president post from two to three consecutive three-year terms. Asked by LDP Secretary-General, Nikai Toshihiro, and his, deputy Shimomura Hakubun, LDP Vice-President, Kōmura Masahiko, assumed the post of chair of the Headquarters for the Party and Political System Reform (Tō–Seiji Seido Kaikaku Jikkō Honbu). The Headquarters discussed the allowable tenure length among the representatives of all factions. While such high-profile politicians as Kishida Fumio, who aimed for the prime ministerial position, were initially reluctant to concede, they were in no position to oppose. Kōmura (2017: 189–191) argued that even the term in office, not to mention the number of reelections, is rarely limited in parliamentary systems. After only three meetings, without much discussion, the Headquarters members entrusted the final decision to the LDP vice-president. At the end of October 2016, Kōmura proposed an increase in the allowable number of consecutive three-year-long terms to three. It is symptomatic that only 56 out of 414 LDP lawmakers participated in the Headquarters meeting, and Kōmura's decision was authorized after a mere 30 minutes of debate (Fujiwara 2016: 4).

The change in party rules was acknowledged unanimously by the LDP General Council at the beginning of November 2016. Although one member, Murakami Seiichirō, called into question the necessity for such a revision, he abstained from voting instead of overtly opposing. Even Ishiba Shigeru, considered as Abe's main rival in the LDP, did not use his membership of the LDP General Council to resist the change (*Asahi Shinbun* 2016b: 4). The new rules were formally approved by the LDP Convention in March 2017. The change allowed Prime Minister Abe to successfully run in the LDP presidential election in September 2018.

Just as the exceptional prolongation of Prime Minister Nakasone's tenure by one year in 1986, the extension of LDP president's longest allowable time in office to three consecutive three-year terms reflected the myth of invincibility of the incumbent leader. The speedy revision of party rules resulted from the unilateral strength of the Abe Kantei. Having pacified the main factions and parliamentary tribes, the prime minister created a system that discouraged potential opponents from resisting party authorities. Being unable to mobilize wider support against the change in party rules, even Abe's rivals had no choice but to reluctantly agree to the Kantei's initiative.

Changes in the competences of other LDP executives

While Abe did not conduct any major reform of the institutional structure of LDP authorities, he adapted, to some extent, the competences of LDP executives to better suit his political interests and serve the realization of his policy agenda.

According to Article 5 of the LDP Constitution, "The Vice-President shall assist the President and act on his behalf in the event the President is unable to perform his duties or in the event the President's seat becomes vacant" (Liberal Democratic Party 2009). The position of LDP vice-president was usually treated as an honorary post and often remained vacant. Boasting extensive experience as senior politicians, vice-presidents usually assisted LDP leaders in intra-party coordination. In 2012, Abe appointed Kōmura Masahiko to this office, expecting him to play a significant role in foreign policy making. As a former foreign minister in 1998–1999 and 2007–2008, as well as the chairperson of many parliamentary leagues for cooperation with different countries, such as China and Russia, Kōmura was well-suited to this task. After regaining power in December 2012, Kōmura remained LDP vice-president despite a proposal to become foreign minister. He emphasized that he wanted to focus on chosen issues deemed important by him or the prime minister from a freer position (Kōmura 2017: 169). According to Mikuriya (2015: 106–107), such a decision was a real Copernican Revolution. The fact that, instead of taking care of party affairs, Kōmura was expected to work hand in hand with the Kantei in foreign and security policy making, symbolized the lack of importance attached by the Abe administration to policy coordination with the LDP. Kōmura remained in office until October 2018, thus becoming the longest-serving vice-president in LDP's history.

While situated lower in the party hierarchy, LDP secretaries-general traditionally enjoyed broader prerogatives than vice-presidents. According to Article 8 of the LDP Constitution, their main function was to "assist the President in carrying out Party affairs" (Liberal Democratic Party 2009). As LDP leaders were usually overwhelmed with their responsibilities as prime ministers, secretaries-general normally enjoyed wide freedom in supervising party business. They had great influence on electoral strategies, administered party finances, coordinated contacts with other parties, decided about nominations for a number of party, but also parliamentary, posts, and were in charge of press conferences. The 1994 electoral reform strengthened the powers of LDP secretaries-general even further by enhancing their role in the appointment of official party candidates in single-seat constituencies and in the distribution of state subventions for political parties to individual lawmakers (Nakakita 2017: 81–83).

On the other hand, the weakening of factionalism reduced the role played by secretaries-general to some extent, as one of their unofficial functions was to coordinate conflicts of interests between intra-party groups. Moreover, in 1994, public relations were excluded from a secretary-general's prerogatives and put under the supervision of the Public Relations Headquarters chairperson (Kōhō Honbuchō) who was directly nominated by the LDP president. In addition, in 2007, Prime Minister Fukuda Yasuo decided to upgrade the post of Election Strategy General Bureau chair (Senkyo Taisaku Sōkyokuchō) to Election Strategy Committee chairperson (Senkyo Taisaku Iinchō) as one of the so-called four (previously three) party offices (tō yon yaku, previously tō san yaku). This decision was retracted when the LDP were in opposition from 2009 to 2012, but, after regaining power, Prime Minister Abe once more moved the Election Strategy Committee chairperson from under the LDP secretary-general's jurisdiction. All these changes relatively improved the LDP president's position vis-à-vis the secretary-general (Nakakita 2017: 84–86).

It is also highly probable that the last institutional reform was implemented because Abe wanted to limit the prerogatives of his potential rivals who assumed the secretary-general's post – Ishiba and Tanigaki. Abe did not consult Ishiba on nominations for governmental or party posts. Moreover, after the December 2012 parliamentary election victory, he eliminated from Ishiba's closest entourage his trusted associate, Acting Secretary-General Kamoshita Ichirō, whom he appointed as Diet Affairs Committee chairperson. At the same time, Abe replaced Suga Yoshihide, who became CCS, with former LDP General Council Chair, Hosoda Hiroyuki, as LDP executive acting secretary-general. Hosoda, as a member of the Machimura faction, from which Abe originated, closely followed the prime minister's instructions. As Ishiba was put outside of the inner circle of decision makers, the number of interest-seeking guests in the Secretary-General's Office decreased abruptly. Instead, pressure groups and politicians started seeking connections with Vice-Premier Asō Tarō or CCS Suga Yoshihide (Watanabe & Kanda 2013: 22).

Secretary-General Ishiba's relatively weak position in the LDP explains why he was unable to conduct any institutional reform in the ruling party. Ishiba admitted that he intended to inculcate the LDP with the political culture of the former Tanaka faction, to which he had belonged in the 1980s. Ishiba admired the efficiency of electoral campaigns conducted collectively by politicians and their secretaries from that intra-party group. In order to emulate this know-how, he proposed relocating the offices of all factions to the LDP headquarters, and turning electoral staff of each faction into regular LDP employees. Such a reform would enable the sharing of experience on electoral campaigns between all factions and better coordination of party electoral activities. Another of Ishiba's ideas was to devote one floor of the LDP headquarters to regional party organizations. Nevertheless, none of these ambitious plans was realized. Instead of creating a supra-factional electoral cooperation system, Ishiba barely managed to organize a course on electoral strategies for junior lawmakers. Instead of providing LDP regional structures with more office space, in turn, it took him several months to merely remove glass counter windows at the LDP headquarters reception desk, so that visitors would not feel distanced from the party central structures (Ishiba 2018: 156–164).

Abe's control over the party was further strengthened after an LDP executives reshuffle in September 2014. Not only was Ishiba replaced with Tanigaki Sadakazu, but also Ishiba's associates Kamoshita Ichirō and Hamada Yasukazu were deprived of the posts of secretary-general's special assistant and acting secretary-general, respectively. At the same time, General Council Chair Noda Seiko, who was deemed to be one of the potential rivals to Abe in the LDP presidential election, was replaced with Nikai Toshihiro. Policy Research Council Chair Takaichi Sanae, in turn, ceded her post to another woman politician from Abe's closest entourage, Inada Tomomi. Unlike Takaichi, who was not affiliated to any faction, Inada and the new Policy Research Council Executive Acting Chairperson, Shionoya Ryū, belonged to the largest LDP faction, the Machimura group, which enhanced their position vis-à-vis backbenchers. Another politician from Abe's closest entourage, former Minister of Economy, Trade and Industry Motegi Toshimitsu, was appointed as Election Strategy Committee Chairperson, while three protégés of CCS Suga – Yamaguchi Taimei, Kajiyama Hiroshi, and Sugawara Isshū – became his deputies (Ono & Hoshino 2014: 4).

In subsequent years, Abe maintained control over LDP executives. Most importantly, after Tanigaki's bicycle accident in July 2016, the post of LDP secretary-general was entrusted to Nikai Toshihiro, who became the main initiator of changing the party rules to extend the LDP president's term in office. In September 2019, Nikai became the longest-serving LDP secretary-general ever, which resulted both from his loyalty toward Abe and from his efficiency in pacifying intra-party opponents against the Kantei leadership. Other executive posts were distributed either among Abe's closest associates, such as Katō Katsunobu (General Council chair in 2018–2019), or to faction bosses, e.g. Hosoda Hiroyuki (General Council chair in 2016–2017), Takeshita Wataru (General Council chair in 2017–2018), and Kishida Fumio (Policy Research Council chair since 2017). By engaging influential backbenchers in party affairs, the prime minister mitigated their dissatisfaction with the fact that they had to wait longer than expected for the next chance to become LDP president.

Although the competences of high-ranking LDP officials remained almost unchanged, Abe exploited ambiguities in party rules to strengthen the position of those executives whose loyalty he was confident in, and to punish those whom he perceived as potential rivals. In particular, he strengthened the position of Vice-President Kōmura Masahiko, while not letting Secretary-General Ishiba Shigeru join the group of core decision makers or conduct any institutional reforms in the ruling party. Just like cabinet members, LDP executives were expected to follow the Kantei's policy agenda rather than come up with their own policy initiatives.

Circumvention of the preexisting LDP decision-making bodies

Abe generally did not implement any changes in the functioning of LDP decision-making bodies, such as the Policy Research Council or the General Council. Instead, he used his enhanced position as unquestioned LDP leader and a popular head of government to dilute the significance of the previously existing policy venues by infiltrating them with politicians from outside of the inner circles of parliamentary tribes. In addition, to some extent, he managed to circumvent the traditional policymaking organs through newly established bodies.

After the formation of the second Abe administration, the two-track decision-making structure was maintained. It was still necessary for all bill projects to gain concurrent authorization both at governmental and ruling party levels. Immediately after returning to power, Abe abolished LDP organs that had been created in opposition, such as the Shadow Cabinet and the Policy Council (Seisaku Kaigi, which replaced the Policy Research Council Board), and he restored the old ones (Nakakita 2017: 116). According to LDP lawmaker Hayashi Yoshimasa, Abe obeyed party rules more strictly than Koizumi (interview by the author, Tokyo, October 16, 2019). On the other hand, Abe displayed greater creativity in exploiting the ambiguities in party rules than his predecessors.

While respecting the traditional decision-making patterns, the prime minister partially moved the proceedings within the LDP on the most important decisions from the Policy Research Council policy divisions to bodies under the LDP president's direct control. He was entitled to do this according to Article 81 (previously Articles 79 and 80) of the LDP Constitution that stipulated: "If necessary The President, with the consent of the General Council, may establish special committees" (Liberal Democratic Party 2009). Importantly, Abe often appointed as chairpersons of these new policy venues politicians more experienced than even the head of the Policy Research Council. Despite the fact that decisions made by special committees had to be authorized by the Policy Research Council and the General Council, just like all other bill projects, it became easier for the Kantei to initiate and channel the decision-making process through the new organs. While there were at most 15 such bodies under the Koizumi administration, only 4 under the first Abe cabinet, 7 under Fukuda, and 8 under Asō's and Tanigaki's leaderships, at the beginning of the second Abe administration, their number quickly rose to 16, and it exceeded 20 in 2016 (Nakakita 2017: 117–118).

As illustrated by Figure 4.3, the bodies under the LDP president's direct control enabled partial circumvention of the preexisting LDP decision-making organs and changed the balance of power in advance screening in favor of the Kantei. Thanks to this layering strategy, Abe gained better supervision over the intra-party decision-making process at the expense of parliamentary tribes. Nakakita (2017: 118) stressed that the special committees greatly changed the function of advance screening. Instead of serving as

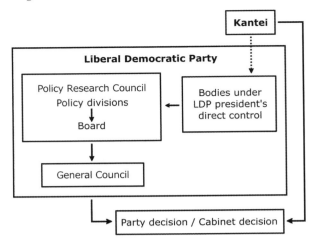

Figure 4.3 Two-track decision-making process under the Abe administration.
Source: Compiled by the author, based on many sources.

a forum for shaping intra-party consensus, deliberations were fossilized as a formality that simply legitimized the Kantei's decisions. Policy projects were imposed on the party together with a schedule that did not leave much room for making significant amendments. As George Mulgan (2018: 38) emphasized, the LDP's internal policymaking apparatus was thus successfully penetrated by the prime minister who now could "pursue his own policy initiatives through an internal party process in addition to executive channels."

The new bodies in the LDP covered all the crucial tasks of the Abe administration. For example, Abe relocated decision making in the ruling party on the controversial security bills from separate policy divisions to the newly established LDP Headquarters for Reconstruction of the Legal Basis for Security (Anzen Hoshō Hōsei Seibi Suishin Honbu) under his direct control. The LDP Headquarters for Japan's Economic Revitalization, in turn, was to support its governmental counterpart in elaborating the details of Abenomics. It was presided over by Abe's close associate, LDP Policy Research Council Chair Takaichi Sanae. In August 2018, there were 24 inter-sectional, topic-specific headquarters (*honbu*) or councils (*kaigi*). A lot of them were devoted to conducting important institutional changes, for instance, electoral, administrative, and educational reforms or constitutional revision, and often had similar names to their counterparts under the Kantei. Many of the new organs addressed difficult socio-economic problems and promoted different components of Abenomics, while some dealt with crucial foreign policy and security issues. Another group were the committees established for the promotion of Japan as the host of two prestigious international events: Tokyo Olympic and Paralympic Games in 2020, as well as Expo in Osaka in 2025 (Liberal Democratic Party 2018).

LDP backbenchers occasionally voiced their dissatisfaction with the fact that Abe made light of party decision-making bodies. For example, on January 21, 2014, the LDP General Council refused to authorize the governmental schedule for implementation of the economic growth strategy prepared by the Headquarters for Japan's Economic Revitalization that encompassed the passage of as many as 30 bills. According to General Council Chair, Noda Seiko, the government should have given more time for intra-party deliberations (the plan was submitted to the LDP on January 20). As she stressed, the two-track nature of decision-making ensured the high quality of laws and prevented abuses. Eventually, Minister of State for Economic and Fiscal Policy, Amari Akira, promised to improve policy coordination with the ruling party, and on January 24, the General Council authorized the government policy after minor changes (*Asahi Shinbun* 2014a: 4). Analogically, in March 2018, General Council members were dissatisfied with the fact that, despite differences of opinions among the participants of the Headquarters for the Promotion of Revision of the Constitution, the final decision on the project of constitutional reform was entrusted to Chairperson Hosoda Hiroyuki without sufficient discussion. Murakami Seiichirō criticized the lack of transparency in a hasty decision-making process based on formulating policy proposals consistent with the intentions of the Kantei alone (*Asahi Shinbun* 2018a: 4).

The Kantei not only put pressure on LDP decision-making bodies to speed up deliberations, but it also occasionally simplified intra-party procedures. For instance, voices of dissatisfaction among backbenchers appeared when, on August 19, 2013, the time for discussions on the outline of social security system reform was limited to a mere one and a half hours. Despite objections by individual LDP politicians, the members of the Special Committee on the Social Security System (Shakai Hoshō Seido Tokumei Iinkai) entrusted through acclamation the decision on the outline to the Committee Chairperson, Noda Takeshi, who confirmed support for the cabinet decision on that matter, scheduled for August 21. Intra-party procedures were greatly simplified, as in the past, the preliminary drafts of the most important bills had also been authorized by the Policy Research Council Board and the General Council. LDP General Council Chairperson, Noda Seiko, agreed to this simplification, stressing there was no need to discuss the government's proposal twice, as extensive deliberations on the final version of the bill project would suffice (*Asahi Shinbun* 2013c: 4). General Council member, Murakami Seiichirō, admitted that while the overall decision-making patterns under the Abe administration were maintained, discussion in the General Council lost importance (interview by the author, Tokyo, October 17, 2019).

Circumvention and simplification of party procedures was criticized by Abe's rivals in the LDP. For instance, Ishiba Shigeru (2018: 62–65) stressed that while, in the past, decisions on highly divisive issues had been made by prime ministers, they were always preceded by heated debates in the ruling party. By contrast, he lamented the fact that under the Abe administration, more and more policies were announced publicly without sufficient discussion with backbenchers. As an example, Ishiba cited the fact that he knew about the sudden change in the use of revenues from the VAT hike, announced before the October 2017 parliamentary election, when he was listening to the news on his car radio. Ishiba warned that while the Kantei's arbitrary decisions to some extent answered the popular demand for strong leadership, in fact, such behavior was in opposition to the spirit of a parliamentary cabinet system. After all, exhaustive consensus-seeking activities in the ruling party ensured better quality of new laws. Procedural short-cuts applied by the government, in turn, caused the risk that cabinet decisions would not reflect the interests and intentions of the people, which was detrimental for Japanese democracy.

Despite dissatisfaction with Abe's making light of party decision-making organs, most LDP lawmakers refrained from overtly criticizing the Kantei. The leader of the biggest faction, Hosoda Hiroyuki, admitted that such self-restraint was connected with the shock caused by the loss of power in 2009. The fear that intra-party struggles could endanger LDP's electoral performance prompted backbenchers to stand firmly behind the government (Mikuriya 2015: 112–113).

The situation changed only slightly after the post of LDP Policy Research Council chair was assumed by Kishida Fumio in September 2017. Kishida, considered as one of the potential successors of Abe as LDP president, put emphasis on reorganizing party structures to strengthen them against the Kantei. In October 2018, he decided that posts of Policy Research Council policy division chairs would be generally entrusted to four- or five-termers instead of three-termers. At the same time, Kishida announced a simplification of the overgrown structure of 130 research commissions and special committees. In addition, he persuaded Abe to reduce the number of bodies under the LDP president's direct control from 24 to 19. As a result, some of the policy venues whose competences overlapped with the competences of the Policy Research Council, such as the Headquarters for Japan's Economic Revitalization and the Strategic Council on Diplomacy, were abolished. Importantly, it was decided that the party leadership would refrain from establishing new bodies under the LDP president's direct control in the future (*Nihon Keizai Shinbun* 2018). As shown in Table 4.1, this policy led to a further reduction in the number of organs of this kind to 16 by January 2020. What is symptomatic, all of them were chaired by experienced politicians who had been ministers in respective policy fields. In addition, as many as six of them were faction bosses (Hosoda Hiroyuki and Nikai Toshihiro) or former faction bosses (Nukaga Fukushirō). Moreover, the bodies devoted to the most strategic points of the Kantei's policy agenda, such as the Headquarters for Promoting Administrative Reform or the Headquarters for the Promotion of Revision of the Constitution, were led by Abe's trusted associates.

Table 4.1 Special committees established directly under LDP president as of January 2020.

Name of decision-making organ	Chairperson
Headquarters for Promoting Administrative Reform	Shiozaki Yasuhisa
Headquarters for Party and Political System Reform Implementation	Noda Seiko
Headquarters for the Promotion of Revision of the Constitution	Hosoda Hiroyuki
Headquarters for Accelerating Reconstruction after the Great East Japan Earthquake	Nukaga Fukushirō
Headquarters for Electoral System Reform	Hosoda Hiroyuki
Headquarters for the Revitalization of Education	Hase Hiroshi
Headquarters for North Korean Abductions	Yamatani Eriko
Headquarters for the Action Committee for the Tokyo 2020 Olympic and Paralympic Games	Endō Toshiaki
Headquarters for Promoting Women's Active Participation	Inoguchi Kuniko
Headquarters for Overcoming Population Decline and Regional Revitalization	Kawamura Takeo
Headquarters for Promoting Dynamic Engagement of All Citizens	Kamikawa Yōko
Economic Strategy Headquarters for Building the Future Society based on AI	Shionoya Ryū
Headquarters for North Korea's Nuclear Tests	Nikai Toshihiro
Headquarters for Promoting the Establishment of a Disaster Resilient Japan	Nikai Toshihiro
Headquarters for the TPP, Japan-EU EPA, and the Japan-U.S. TAG	Moriyama Hiroshi
Bidding Headquarters for the EXPO 2025 Osaka	Nikai Toshihiro

Source: Compiled by the author, based on Liberal Democratic Party (2020).

Instead of openly challenging the preexisting party rules, Abe chose to exploit their ambiguities. He maintained discussions in various policy divisions of the Policy Research Council, while moving the decision-making process on the crucial initiatives of the government to separate organs under the LDP president's direct control. This layering strategy enabled the Kantei to push its controversial policy agenda ahead, while rendering the preexisting bodies devoid of meaning. Responding to dissatisfaction from backbenchers, the number of organs under the LDP president's direct control was reduced in 2018, but this change did little to alter the general trend of the atrophy of LDP decision-making bodies.

Enhancement of control over the legislative process

While the Abe administration did not implement any major reforms to parliament, the Kantei's control over the legislative process was enhanced through the establishment of special parliamentary committees, strict application of party discipline, and flexibility in scheduling Diet sessions. Just as in LDP decision-making organs, the Kantei quelled voices of discontent against Abe's top-down leadership style among LDP lawmakers.

The short length of parliamentary sessions and small number of parliamentary committees constituted a bottleneck in the legislative process. To overcome this obstacle, Abe streamlined deliberations in the Diet on the most controversial bills through special committees. As well as the 15 standing committees, extraordinary committees could be created for the duration of separate Diet sessions to deal with matters that exceeded one legislative field, such as consumer problems or rebuilding after the Great East Japan Earthquake. As most of them formulated long-term policies, they were usually re-established at the beginning of each session. The Abe administration used these bodies to bypass permanent committees, in which deliberations were subject to numerous institutional constraints, such as a lack of flexibility in scheduling meetings. For instance, in October 2013, a Special Committee for State Security (Kokka Anzen Hoshō ni kan suru Tokubetsu Iinkai) was established for only one extraordinary Diet session to prepare the passage of the law that founded the NSC. Similarly, the security bills that legalized collective self-defense were discussed in the Special Committee on Peace and Security System of Our Country and International Society (Waga Kuni oyobi Kokusai Shakai no Heiwa Anzen Hōsei ni kan suru Tokubetsu Iinkai), which existed for several months in mid-2015. Other initiatives of the Kantei that were dealt with by special committees included the TPP accession and the vitalization of local economies.[5]

Although many highly controversial government-sponsored bills were not sufficiently consulted with the ruling party, they encountered only minimal opposition from LDP lawmakers at the stage of discussions in the Diet. For example, Murakami Seiichirō was the only LDP parliamentarian who openly protested against the passage of the Bill on Protection of Specially Designated Secrets during deliberations of the LDP General Council and abstained from voting in the House of Representatives in December 2013. According to him, the bill excessively limited access to information by the people. Murakami (2016: 68–82) deplored the fact that such an important law was steamrolled through the Diet in only one and a half months without devoting sufficient time for discussion. He stressed that he had not been alone when Prime Minister Nakasone tried to pass a similar, anti-spy, law in 1987. At that time, Murakami belonged to a group of young parliamentarians who objected, together with Tanigaki Sadakazu and Ōshima Tadamori, which led to the withdrawal of the controversial bill. In 2013, both Tanigaki, as justice minister, and Ōshima went hand in hand with the government. According to Murakami, this symbolized the detrimental change in the LDP after the 1994 electoral reform, where free discussion was no longer welcome. For that reason, he dubbed the post-reform LDP a "Non-Liberal Democratic Party." At the same time, Murakami admitted that, theoretically, the possibility of free discussion in intra-party decision-making organs was maintained, but LDP lawmakers had become less eager to criticize the policy of the government out of fear that such behavior could endanger their careers (interview by the author, Tokyo, October 17, 2019).

Similarly to how he ignored unwritten rules in the LDP, Abe felt powerful enough to challenge the long-lasting, but uncodified parliamentary traditions. For instance, it was a custom to call an extraordinary Diet session every autumn, but Abe refused to hold a session in October 2015 despite a motion submitted by the opposition parties.[6] In September 2017, in turn, he called an extraordinary session only to dissolve the Diet. In both cases, Abe probably wanted to avoid difficult deliberations in the Budget Committee regarding the security laws and the Moritomo Gakuen scandal, respectively. After its parliamentary election victory in 2017, in turn, the LDP requested a reduction in the ratio of question time available for the opposition and ruling parties in the Diet from 8:2 to 5:5. The proposal met with protests from opposition politicians who stressed that the 8:2 ratio had been introduced under the DPJ government upon a demand from the LDP itself. Eventually, both sides settled on a 7:3 ratio. The Kantei insisted on increasing question time for LDP politicians, as ruling party backbenchers turned into loyal executioners of the prime minister's will. The subservient behavior of LDP backbenchers, for instance, first-term lawmaker Dōko Shigeru's lavish compliments toward Abe during question time in the House of Councilors Budget Committee in March 2017, was ridiculed on the Internet. Instead of focusing on policy questions, Dōko lauded the prime minister for the way he buttoned his jacket when standing before the podium (Osaki 2018). Another method of avoiding direct criticism from the opposition parties was decreasing the frequency of party leaders' policy debates (*tōshu tōron*). The year 2017 became the first year without even one such debate since the introduction of the question time system in 1999 (Hayasaka 2018: 105).

Abe's making light of Diet regulations met with dissatisfaction not only from opposition parties, but also from ruling party backbenchers. In June 2018, 31 junior LDP lawmakers led by Tachibana Keiichirō and Koizumi Shinjirō, gathered in the Council to Conceive Economy and Society After 2020 (2020 Nen Ikō no Keizai Shakai Kōsō Kaigi), submitted a petition to LDP Secretary-General Nikai Toshihiro. Concerned with a decrease in popular trust in the government due to the Moritomo and Kake Gakuen scandals, they demanded a redressing of the deficiencies of Kantei leadership, conduct of Diet reform, and convention of a special parliamentary committee to investigate the scandals (*Asahi Shinbun* 2018b: 4). Eventually, the group of young LDP lawmakers, together with representatives of opposition parties, formed the Council for Implementation of House of Representatives Reform "by the End of Heisei Era" ("Heisei no Uchi ni" Shūgiin Kaikaku Jitsugen Kaigi), that formulated less far-reaching proposals in July 2018. Most significantly, the supra-party group requested an increase in the frequency of party leaders' policy debates to one every two weeks and the restraining of each debate to a preset topic ("Heisei no Uchi ni" Shūgiin Kaikaku Jitsugen Kaigi 2018). Nevertheless, this recommendation was largely ignored by the LDP leadership.

Thanks to the Kantei's enhanced position vis-à-vis the ruling party, even without implementing any significant institutional changes in the Diet, the government managed to strengthen its control over LDP backbenchers' behavior during the legislative process. As expressing any opposition to cabinet-sponsored bills during deliberations in the parliament could negatively impact their political careers, LDP lawmakers acted as loyal executioners of Abe's policy agenda.

Conclusion

Prime Minister Abe did not have to implement too many institutional changes in the ruling party in order to enhance his position vis-à-vis the backbenchers. If read explicitly, the LDP Constitution already vested extensive powers in the party president, but they had been constrained due to numerous unwritten codes of conduct. As the strength of intra-party veto players – factions and parliamentary tribes – waned, Abe simply started using the preexisting institutional tools to his own advantage. Over time, he regularized the practice of ignoring some of the unwritten rules. While declaring maintenance of the two-track decision-making process, he greatly simplified the procedures in the ruling party and often neglected traditional consensus-seeking activities toward senior members of individual tribes. At the same time, by establishing numerous bodies under his direct control, Abe largely bypassed deliberations in the Policy Research Council on key policies of his government.

The Kantei leadership occasionally encountered resistance from parliamentary tribes. Abe clashed with the LDP Research Commission on the Tax System over the VAT hike postponement, reduced tax rate system, and corporate tax reduction. In order to overcome opposition from senior backbenchers, he relied on support from younger parliamentarians who eagerly embraced the idea of reducing taxes or postponing their increase. It was more difficult to pacify the agricultural tribe, as the TPP accession was unwelcome to farmers who constituted a powerful interest group. Also in this case, however, Abe played one group of backbenchers off against another. He fulfilled the ambitions for governmental posts of individual members of the agricultural tribe, such as Nishikawa Kōya, thus turning them into loyal promoters of the Kantei's policy agenda. In the face of the high cabinet support rate, veto players were unable to form a united front against the domination of the prime minister and his closest entourage.

Voices of discontent in the party were particularly weak regarding the policies that did not endanger the interests of any pressure group, such as the passage of the Bill on Protection of Specially Designated Secrets. The institutional strength of the Kantei was visible even in its enhanced control over the legislative process. Without conducting any serious reform of the Diet, the government channeled the most controversial bills through special parliamentary committees and flexibly shaped the schedule of parliamentary sessions. By refusing to hold extraordinary sessions, the Abe administration not only avoided the emergence of intra-party divisions, but also limited opportunities for the opposition parties to criticize the government. While the policy cohesion of the administrations of Abe's predecessors had been weakened by LDP factions and parliamentary tribes, Abe managed to mobilize party resources to the maximum to implement his policy initiatives.

Notes

1. In the House of Councilors, voting through pressing buttons was introduced in 1998.
2. As LDP lawmaker Kōno Tarō (2003: 86–97) admitted, his votes against the decision of his party authorities were simply ignored.
3. Such a situation happened in 1980, when anti-mainstream factions absented themselves from voting on a no-confidence motion against the Ōhira cabinet, which forced the prime minister to dissolve the Diet. In 2005, in turn, individual LDP lawmakers rebelled against the Japan Post privatization bill, but it still passed through the lower house to be rejected by the upper house.
4. Some "cow's walks" lasted many hours. Nevertheless, this tactic lost in popularity after television started transmitting Diet sessions. See Miyazawa, Mikuriya & Nakamura (2007: 211–214).
5. See the full list of House of Representatives committees at House of Representatives, Japan (2020).
6. The Constitution obliges the government to call a Diet session in case of a motion submitted by one-fourth of upper or lower house members, but as it does not specify when such session should be held, it is possible for the prime minister to simply wait until inauguration of the ordinary session that starts every January.

References

Asahi Shinbun (2013a) "Jimin, Dotanba no Konran. Dōro Tokutei Zaigen Fukkatsu, Shushō 'Kore wa Hidoi.' 13 Nendo Zeisei Taikai Kettei" [LDP, Last Minute Confusion. Revival of Earmarked Funds for Road Improvement, Prime Minister: "It's Terrible." Decision on FY2013 Tax System Outline], January 25, morning edition, 2.

Asahi Shinbun (2013b) "Setsubi Tōshi Genzei Itsu? Seiken 'Nennai,' Jimin wa Shinchō" [When Tax Reduction for Capital Investments? The Government "Until the End of the Year," the LDP Cautious], June 20, morning edition, 4.

Asahi Shinbun (2013c) "Seikō Tōtei. Jimin, Seisaku Kettei no Tōnai Tetsuzuki Shōryaku" [Government High, Party Low. The LDP, Omission of Intra-Party Policy Decision], August 20, morning edition, 4.

Asahi Shinbun (2013d) "Hōjinzei Zero Tokku, Dannen. Seifu, Rainen Ikō ni Saikentō" [Zero Corporate Tax Special Zones, Renunciation. The Government, Reexamination Next Year], December 11, morning edition, 4.

160 Reforming the LDP

Asahi Shinbun (2013e) "Kiritsu Naki Saishutsu Bōchō, Jiminryū Yosan, Zoku Giin ga Fukkatsu" [Expansion of Expenditures Without Discipline, LDP-like Budget, Revival of Parliamentary Tribes], December 25, morning edition, 2.

Asahi Shinbun (2014a) "Seichō Senryaku no Kōtei Kettei. Hyōgen Kae, Jimin to Chōsei" [Decision on Roadmap for Growth Strategy. Change of Expressions, Coordination with the LDP], January 25, morning edition, 4.

Asahi Shinbun (2014b) "Hōjin Zeiritsu Sage, 6 Gatsu ni Hōkōsei. Jimin Zeichō ga Hōshin" [Corporate Tax Reduction, Direction in June. Policy of the LDP Research Commission on the Tax System], February 8, morning edition, 7.

Asahi Shinbun (2016a) "Jimin Zeichō Kanbukai ni Amari-shi" [Mr. Amari to the LDP Research Commission on the Tax System Board], October 1, morning edition, 4.

Asahi Shinbun (2016b) "Sōsai '3 Ki 9 Nen,' Jimin Sōmukai Ryōshō" [President's "3 Terms 9, Years," Acknowledged by the LDP General Council], November 2, morning edition, 4.

Asahi Shinbun (2018a) "Kaiken An 'Ichinin' ni Jimin-nai kara Hihan. Tō Sōmukai" [Criticism from the Party on "Entrusting" Constitution Revision Draft. Party General Council], March 24, morning edition, 4.

Asahi Shinbun (2018b) "Koizumi Shi-ra Kokkai Kaikaku Teigen. Giwaku Tsuikyū wa 'Tokubetsu Chōsakai de.' Yosan'i wa 'Seisaku Hon'i de'" [Koizumi and Others Recommend a Diet Reform. Investigation on Scandal in a "Special Committee." Budget Committee "Policy-Based"], June 28, morning edition, 4.

Bochorodycz, Beata (2018) "Abe Cabinet and the TPP Negotiations on 'Trade Sensitivities,'" in Karol Zakowski, Beata Bochorodycz & Marcin Socha (eds), *Japan's Foreign Policy Making: Central Government Reforms, Decision-Making Processes, and Diplomacy*, Cham: Springer, 203–231.

Fujiwara, Shin'ichi (2016) "Jimin Sōsai Ninki '3 Ki 9 Nen' de Ketchaku. Yoron Ishiki, 'Museigen' Miokuri" [LDP President's Tenure Settled at "3 Terms 9, Years." Awareness of Public Opinion, Renunciation of "Limitless"], *Asahi Shinbun*, October 27, morning edition, 4.

Fukui, Haruhiro (1969) *Jiyū Minshutō to Seisaku Kettei* [Liberal Democratic Party and Policy Decisions], Tokyo: Fukumura Shuppan.

George Mulgan, Aurelia (2018) *The Abe Administration and the Rise of the Prime Ministerial Executive*, London and New York: Routledge.

Hayasaka, Yuki (2018) "Dai 196 Kai Kokkai ni okeru Tōshu Tōron. Tōgi Gaiyō to Un'ei no Kadai" [Party Leaders' Policy Debates in the 196th Diet. Tasks for Discussion Outline and Management], *Rippō to Chōsa*, 403: 100–108.

"Heisei no Uchi ni" Shūgiin Kaikaku Jitsugen Kaigi (2018) "Teigen" [Recommendation] (July). Online. Available: https://shinjiro.info/teigen.pdf (accessed April 22, 2020).

Honkawa Data Tribune (2020) "Shinryō Hōshū no Kaiteiritsu no Suii" [Change in Health Care Fee Revisions]. Online. Available: http://honkawa2.sakura.ne.jp/1933.html (accessed April 17, 2020).

Honma, Masayoshi & George Mulgan, Aurelia (2018) "Political Economy of Agricultural Reform in Japan under Abe's Administration," *Asian Economic Policy Review*, 13, 1: 128–144.

House of Representatives, Japan (2020) *Iinkai Nyūsu* [Committee News]. Online. Available: http://www.shugiin.go.jp/internet/itdb_rchome.nsf/html/rchome/IinkaiNews_m.htm (accessed May 11, 2020).

Iio, Jun (2008) *Nihon no Tōchi Kōzō* [Structure of Government in Japan], Tokyo: Chūō Kōron Shinsha.
Ishiba, Shigeru (2018) *Seisaku Shijōshugi* [Policy Supremacy], Tokyo: Shinchōsha.
Ishikawa, Masumi & Hirose, Michisada (1989) *Jimintō – Chōki Shihai no Kōzō* [LDP – Structure of Long-Term Supremacy], Tokyo: Iwanami Shoten.
Kawato, Sadafumi (2015) *Giin Naikakusei* [Parliamentary Government], Tokyo: Tōkyō Daigaku Shuppankai.
Kidera, Hajime (2017) "Shōhizei Zōzei. Shakai Hoshō to no Ittai Kaikaku" [Consumption Tax Increase. Joint Reform with the Social Security], in Takenaka Harukata (ed.), *Futatsu no Seiken Kōtai. Seisaku wa kawatta no ka* [Two Alternations of Power. Has the Policy Changed?], Tokyo: Keisō Shobō, 152–179.
Koga, Shigeaki (2017) *Kokka no Kyōbō* [State Collusion], Tokyo: Kadokawa.
Kokkai Binran (2005-2017) Tokyo: Nihon Seikei Shinbunsha.
Kōmura, Masahiko (2017) *Furiko o Mannaka ni. Watashi no Rirekisho* [Pendulum to the Center. My Curriculum Vitae], Tokyo: Nihon Keizai Shinbun Shuppansha.
Kōno, Tarō (2003) *Kōno Tarō no Kokkai Kōryaku Hon* [The Book about Capture of the Diet by Kōno Tarō], Tokyo: Eiji Shuppan.
Krauss, Ellis S. & Pekkanen, Robert J. (2011) *The Rise and Fall of Japan's LDP. Political Party Organizations as Historical Institutions*, Ithaca and London: Cornell University Press.
Kujiraoka, Hitoshi (2014) "Jimin, Hōjin Genzei de Wakate to Jūchin Gekitotsu? Shushō Ōendan to Tō Zeichō Hibana" [LDP, Young Lawmakers' Heavy Clash Over Corporate Tax Reduction? Spark Between the Prime Minister's Support Group and the Party Research Commission on the Tax System], *Asahi Shinbun*, April 24, morning edition, 4.
Liberal Democratic Party (2009) "LDP Constitution" (January 18). Online. Available: https://www.jimin.jp/english/about-ldp/constitution/index.html (accessed May 13, 2020).
Liberal Democratic Party (2012) "Nihon o Torimodosu" [Restore Japan]. Online. Available: https://jimin.jp-east-2.storage.api.nifcloud.com/pdf/seisaku_ichiban24.pdf?_ga=2.156227707.1712537556.1554297229-464335118.1554297229 (accessed April 3, 2019).
Liberal Democratic Party (2018) "Official English Translations for LDP Officials and Party Organs." Online. Available: https://www.jimin.jp/english/profile/english/ (accessed August 18, 2018).
Liberal Democratic Party (2020) "Sōsai, Soshiki Undō Honbu, Senkyo Taisaku Honbu ta" [President, Structure Activities Headquarters, Election Strategy Headquarters, etc.] (January 17). Online. Available: https://www.jimin.jp/member/officer/ (accessed April 22, 2020).
Mikuriya, Takashi (2015) *Abe Seiken wa Hontō ni Tsuyoi noka. Banjaku yue ni Moroi Seiken Un'ei no Shōtai* [Is the Abe Government Really Strong? True Face of Political Management Weak as a Stone], Tokyo: PHP Kenkyūjo.
Miyazawa, Kiichi, Mikuriya, Takashi & Nakamura, Takafusa (2007) *Kikigaki. Miyazawa Kiichi Kaikoroku* [Interview. Miyazawa Kiichi's Memoir], Tokyo: Iwanami Shoten.
Murakami, Seiichirō (2016) *Jimintō Hitori Ryōshikiha* [One Member of the LDP Faction of Common Sense], Tokyo: Kōdansha.
Murakawa, Ichirō (2000) *Seisaku Kettei Katei* [Policy Decision-Making Process], Tokyo: Shinzansha.

Nakakita, Kōji (2017) *Jimintō – Ikkyō no Jitsuzō* [LDP – Real Image of Unilateral Strength], Tokyo: Chūō Kōron Shinsha.

Nihon Keizai Shinbun (2018) "Jimin ga Seichō Kaikaku, Tō Shudō o Kyōchō. Chōsakai, Tokubetsu I o Saihen" [LDP Conducts Policy Research Council Reform, Stresses Party Leadership. Reconstruction of Research Commissions, Special Committees] (October 15). Online. Available: https://www.nikkei.com/article/DGXMZO36490280V11C18A0PP8000/ (accessed April 22, 2020).

Nishikawa, Kōya (2017) *TPP no Shinjitsu: Sōdaina Kyōtei o Matomeageta otokotachi* [Truth About the TPP: The Men Who Finalized the Grand Agreement], Tokyo: Kaitakusha.

Nishimura, Takeshi (2002) *Kasumigaseki Zankoku Monogatari. Samayoeru Kanryōtachi* [Cruel Tale of Kasumigaseki. Loitering Bureaucrats], Tokyo: Chūō Kōron Shinsha.

Nishiyama, Akihiro & Okamura, Natsuki (2019) "Amari Zeichō, Seichō o Jūshi. Keisan Hata, Zaimushō ni Keikaikan mo" [Amari's Research Commission on the Tax System, Focus on Growth. METI's Field and MOF's Vigilance], *Asahi Shinbun*, October 3, morning edition, 4.

Ono, Kōtarō & Hoshino, Norihisa (2014) "Jimin, Tō Jinji mo Kantei Shudō. Ishiba Jinmyaku Issō de Hakusha" [LDP, Kantei Leadership Also Regarding Party Personnel Affairs. Ishiba's Connections Wiped Out], *Asahi Shinbun*, September 10, morning edition, 4.

Osaki, Tomohiro (2018) "In Japan's Diet, Is There Such a Thing as too Much Time for Questions?" (February 26). Online. Available: https://www.japantimes.co.jp/news/2018/02/26/reference/ldp-pushes-reduce-time-abe-spends-opposition-scrutiny-diet/ (accessed May 4, 2020).

Prime Minister of Japan and His Cabinet (2014) "A New Vision from a New Japan, World Economic Forum 2014 Annual Meeting, Speech by Prime Minister Abe" (January 22). Online. Available: https://japan.kantei.go.jp/96_abe/statement/201401/22speech_e.html (accessed March 26, 2020).

Satō, Seizaburō & Matsuzaki, Tetsuhisa (1986) *Jimintō Seiken* [LDP Government], Tokyo: Chūō Kōronsha.

Stockwin, J. A. A. (2008) *Governing Japan. Divided Politics in a Resurgent Economy*, Malden–Oxford–Carlton: Blackwell Publishing.

Takenaka, Harukata (2013) "Minshutō Seiken to Nihon no Giin Naikakusei" [DPJ Government and Japan's Parliamentary System], in Iio Jun (ed.), *Seiken Kōtai to Seitō Seiji. Rekishi no Naka no Nihon Seiji 6* [Alternation of Power and Party Politics. Japanese Politics in History 6], Tokyo: Chūō Kōron Shinsha, 139–180.

Tanaka, Hideaki (2019) *Kanryōtachi no Fuyu. Kasumigaseki Fukkatsu no Shohōsen* [Winter of the Bureaucrats. Prescription for Revival of Kasumigaseki], Tokyo: Shōgakkan.

Terada, Takashi (2016) "Japan and Entanglement of Regional Integration in the Asia-Pacific: Combining Cutting-Edge and Traditional Agendas," in S. Basu Das & M. Kawai (eds), *Trade Regionalism in the Asia-Pacific. Developments and Future Challenges*, Singapore: ISEAS – Yusof Ishak Institute, 85–101.

Watanabe, Tetsuya & Kanda, Tomoko (2013) "Abe Jiki Shushō, Ki ga Tsukeba Hitori Kachi. 'Ishiba Kanjichō Muryokuka Sakusen' Shinkō. Nichigin Sōsai mo KO" [Next Prime Minister Abe, When You Realize It, One-Man Victory. Progress in "the Tactics of Neutralizing Secretary-General Ishiba." Also BOJ Governor Knocked Out], *Shūkan Asahi*, January 11, 22.

Watanabe, Tetsuya (2013) "TPP Jinji, Zeisei, Kōmuin Kaikaku... Abe Dokusai de Jimin wa Bakuhatsu Sunzen" [Personnel Decisons on TPP, Tax System, Public Service Reform... The LDP on the Verge of Explosion Due to Abe's Despotism], *Shūkan Asahi*, October 18, 132.

Yuasa, Hiroshi (1986) *Kokkai "Giin Zoku" – Jimintō "Seichō" to Kasumigaseki* ["Parliamentary Tribes" – Kasumigaseki and the LDP "PRC"], Tokyo: Kyōikusha.

5 Abenomics

Before returning to power in 2012, Abe Shinzō announced an economic policy based on monetary easing, expansive fiscal policy, and structural reforms to encourage private-sector investments. In order to implement Abenomics, he relied on a range of strategies and institutional solutions. Even before the 2012 parliamentary election, Abe founded the Liberal Democratic Party (LDP) Headquarters for Japan's Economic Revitalization, which took charge of polishing his economic policy agenda. After assuming prime ministerial office, he revived the CEFP that dealt with macroeconomic policy, established the Headquarters for Japan's Economic Revitalization that focused on microeconomic aspects of reforms, and created such new bodies as the National Strategic Special Zone Advisory Council that were devoted to more detailed initiatives. This chapter analyzes how Abe took advantage of his strong position in the ruling party and the government to impose his will on LDP backbenchers, bureaucrats, and the BOJ. The prime minister's policy-making strategy was less dependent on reform of official institutions than on changes in informal decision-making mechanisms. Most significantly, Abe paid much attention to exploiting inter-ministerial rivalry by playing the METI off against the MOF.

Interests behind the formulation of Abenomics

The announcement of Abenomics was surprising due to the fact that during his first prime ministership Abe had failed to announce a detailed economic policy agenda. In order to fully understand the process that led to the formulation of this bold initiative, one has to analyze the interests of the individual and institutional actors involved. Besides Abe and his direct political entourage, they included METI and MOF bureaucrats, BOJ, as well as Abe's economic advisers.

Stimulation of economic growth remained a priority for METI and the LDP commerce and industry parliamentary tribe. The generous welfare-state initiatives of the DPJ government, such as the introduction of child allowance, were not in line with the policy of that ministry. For that reason, METI bureaucrats perceived Abe's election as LDP leader in September 2012 as an opportunity for promoting their long-cherished goals. METI made use of the connections its high-ranking bureaucrats, such as Imai Takaya (who later became the prime minister's secretary) or Hasegawa Eiichi (who later assumed the post of special adviser to the prime minister), had with Abe. Moreover, it was the Director-General of METI Manufacturing Industries Bureau Sugawara Ikurō (who, in 2015, would be promoted to a vice-ministerial post), who actively promoted METI's policy vision, so that it was reflected in the LDP's electoral manifesto. As Japan was still ruled by the DPJ, METI Administrative Vice-Minister, Adachi Ken'yū, could not participate in this process, but he turned a blind eye to the activities of his subordinates. Most significantly, METI bureaucrats coined the idea of three policy packages that would later be baptized the "three arrows" of Abenomics. Originally, they included fiscal stimulation exceeding 10 trillion yen, growth policy based on private investment, and monetary easing (Karube 2018: 8–15).

The MOF together with the LDP financial parliamentary tribe remained the main opponent of METI's economic policy. Instead of promoting economic growth or fighting deflation, MOF's main goal was to restore a balanced government budget, either through cutting budget expenses or through increasing taxes. Former MOF bureaucrat Takahashi (2018: 90), who had served as cabinet counselor under the first Abe administration, claimed that his colleagues in the ministry did not overly rejoice in economic prosperity, as, thanks to their stable jobs and privileges, their relative social status was higher during the periods of economic recession. Unlike METI, the MOF, to a great extent, had cooperated with the DPJ government, particularly regarding the extensive screening of budgetary projects (*jigyō shiwake*) under the Hatoyama cabinet and consumption tax hike under the Noda administration (Zakowski 2015: 90–97, 175–185). Just like METI, the MOF boasted connections with Abe through individual former bureaucrats who had cooperated with the LDP leader when he was prime minister in 2006–2007. Nevertheless, some of them, such as Takahashi, were treated as outsiders by the ministry due to their pro-reform attitude. In addition, in early autumn 2012, the MOF was focused on convincing the LDP to pass the Special Bond Bill that authorized the issuance of government bonds up to 2015. For these reasons, the MOF started trying to influence Abe's economic policy later than METI (Karube 2018: 16–22).

Another institutional veto player against Abenomics was the BOJ. According to Article 3 of the BOJ Act from June 1997, the BOJ was endowed with "autonomy regarding currency and monetary control" (Japanese Law Translation 1997). The governor, deputy governors, and members of the BOJ Policy Board were appointed for five-year terms by the cabinet with the consent of both houses of the Diet. The governor and other BOJ officers could not be dismissed except for such rare situations as a ruling of the commencement of bankruptcy proceedings, punishment, sentence to imprisonment, or incapability of carrying out their duties due to physical or mental disorder (Japanese Law Translation 1997). Over the years, the BOJ management tended to underestimate the negative influence of deflation on the Japanese economy, interpreting a decrease in the level of average prices as a result of a boost in productivity caused by technological innovation. Only in 2001 did the BOJ start implementing an unconventional monetary policy by purchasing government securities in order to increase money supply. However, it was too late to overcome deflation through such intervention on a limited scale (Noguchi 2018: 34–36). Moreover, in March 2006, the BOJ abandoned the quantitative easing policy, which met with dissatisfaction from Abe who, at that time, served as the chief cabinet secretary (CCS) in the Koizumi government (Karube 2018: 27).

Prime Minister Abe's position on economic growth strategy had been much closer to METI's than MOF's and BOJ's long before returning to the post of LDP leader. Ever since his first term in office, Abe had sympathized with the commerce and industry parliamentary tribe. In 2006, he even appointed two leading representatives of that group (the so-called "line of rising tide," *ageshio rosen*) – Shiozaki Yoshihisa and Nakagawa Hidenao – as CCS and LDP secretary-general, respectively. For Abe, it was deregulation and creation of a favorable environment for private business that were to guarantee higher budget revenues, which could be used to achieve budget balance and finance the social security system (Shimizu 2014: 72–73).

After stepping down from office in 2007, Abe put much effort into gaining more knowledge on ways of reviving the Japanese economy. Invited by Yamamoto Kōzō, an LDP parliamentarian who promoted a reflation (overcoming deflation) policy, in 2011, Abe became chairperson of a supra-party parliamentary league, the Association Seeking Recovery Funds Without Tax Increase. The group proposed to cover the costs of reconstruction of the regions destroyed by the Great East Japan Earthquake through issuing bonds purchased by the BOJ instead of through a VAT hike (Noguchi 2018: 48). An equally important role was played by scholars who became Abe's economic advisers. Two professors especially – Hamada Kōichi and Honda Etsurō – were consulted by Abe. In spring and summer 2012, Honda, who was Abe's old acquaintance, visited the former prime minister many times, teaching him how monetary easing would contribute to yen depreciation, an increase in the value of stocks, improvement of the situation of Japanese businesses, increase in salaries, and, as a result, increase in average prices. Yale University Professor Hamada, in turn, had been the head of the Economic and Social Research Institute in the Cabinet Office, when Abe served as the deputy CCS under the Koizumi administration. Abe sought his advice on economic policy during the electoral campaign in autumn 2012. Just like Honda, Hamada belonged to the camp of strong supporters of reflation (Karube 2018: 25–30).

Under the influence of his political entourage, economic advisers, and METI, Abe formulated the basic principles of Abenomics. On November 15, 2012, one day after the announcement of his intention to dissolve the House of Representatives by Prime Minister Noda Yoshihiko, Abe stated that in order to achieve the inflation target it was necessary to conduct unlimited monetary easing (Karube 2018: 23–24). As opinion polls indicated that Abe would become the next prime minister, his mere words caused a sudden depreciation of the yen and increase in stock values on the Tokyo Stock Exchange. The media quickly baptized the main principles of the economic policy proposed by Abe – monetary easing, expansive fiscal policy, and structural reforms to encourage private sector investments – as the "three arrows" of Abenomics.

Abe's bold economic plans became the foundation of the LDP electoral manifesto. While the main electoral slogan was "restore Japan" (*Nihon o torimodosu*), it was "restore the economy" (*keizai o torimodosu*) that was formulated as action 1. The LDP promised to make the Headquarters for Japan's Economic Revitalization the "control tower" of reforms, shift from the policy of distributing shrinking budget funds to one of creation of wealth through economic growth, overcome deflation and the strong yen, and achieve a 3% nominal GDP growth rate. In order to realize these goals, the LDP planned to impose a 2% inflation target and "bold monetary easing" on the BOJ, without excluding the possibility of revising the BOJ Act. In addition, the LDP promised to pass a large-scale supplementary budget immediately after regaining power, remove unnecessary rules that hindered entrepreneurship, make Japanese industry more competitive in the world, decrease corporate tax, and promote liberalization of trade (Liberal Democratic Party 2012: 5–8).

Abenomics met with high popular support. According to an *Asahi Shinbun* (2012: 3) opinion poll from December 2012, it was the economic recovery and employment policy that attracted the greatest interest of respondents (35%), followed by VAT and the social security system (30%), nuclear power plants, and energy problems (17%), as well as constitutional revision, security, and foreign issues (12%). The economic policy was particularly important for LDP voters (46%). A similar opinion poll conducted by *Yomiuri Shinbun* (2012: 1) at the end of the same month indicated that 95% of respondents wanted Abe to prioritize economic policy and recovery after the Great East Japan Earthquake, followed by foreign and security policy (81%), as well as social security system and tax reform (74%). At the same time, 48% of respondents believed that Abe would be able to achieve economic recovery, while 39% remained skeptical.

LDP's electoral victory and the formation of the Abe cabinet in December 2012 signified that Abenomics had become one of the crucial policies of the new government. In his policy speech to the Diet in January 2013, Abe stated that he considered "prolonged deflation and the appreciation of the yen to be shaking from their very base the foundations of trust in society that 'those who work hard shall be rewarded'" (Prime Minister of Japan and His Cabinet 2013d). As stressed by the prime minister, "It will be impossible for us to break free of deflation and the appreciating yen by dealing with them in ways that are an extension of what we have done thus far" (Prime Minister of Japan and His Cabinet 2013d). For that reason, Abe declared his intention to "press forward with economic revival under the three prongs of bold monetary policy, flexible fiscal policy, and a growth strategy that encourages private sector investment" (Prime Minister of Japan and His Cabinet 2013d).

Abenomics was a well-timed initiative. Although it can be perceived as a set of policies proposed by the METI, it fitted Abe's convictions and was eagerly embraced by him in the electoral campaign. Having learned a bitter lesson under his first administration, Abe needed a policy agenda that would appeal to the voters. The popular support for the "three arrows" and the first signs of economic recovery fueled the decision-making process on implementation of the bold economic plans.

Decision-making bodies on Abenomics

The first decision-making bodies on Abenomics were established inside the LDP even before its victory in the parliamentary election. After returning to the post of LDP president, Abe created the LDP Headquarters for Japan's Economic Revitalization, whose first meeting took place on October 24, 2012. It was chaired by Abe, with his close associates LDP Policy Research Council Chair Amari Akira as deputy chair and Motegi Toshimitsu as secretary-general. METI bureaucrats used this body to exert influence on LDP's economic policy before the upcoming election. They particularly took advantage of their connection with Amari, who had served as the minister of economy, trade and industry from 2006 to 2008. However, it was Abe himself who put strong pressure on the Headquarters to include such bold policy goals as the 2% inflation target in its mid-term report from mid-November 2012 (Karube 2018: 10–41).

Immediately after the formation of the cabinet, Abe channeled decision making on Abenomics into two bodies under his direct control: the newly established governmental Headquarters for Japan's Economic Revitalization for microeconomic, and the revived CEFP for macroeconomic policy. Another important organ, the Industrial Competitiveness Council, was created based on a decision of the Headquarters for Japan's Economic Revitalization, on January 8, 2013. It was composed of the same members as the Headquarters, with Minister of Economy, Trade and Industry, Motegi Toshimitsu, as additional deputy chair, as well as private-sector experts as additional members. The Council's aim was to promote the strengthening of competitiveness and expansion into international markets of the Japanese industrial sector (Prime Minister of Japan and His Cabinet 2013a). During the first meeting of the Council on January 23, 2013, Abe emphasized that the new body's main task was to draft a sustainable growth strategy under the "third prong" of economic revival. The prime minister stressed that he planned "to take actions in rapid succession, without waiting for the strategy to be compiled" (Prime Minister of Japan and His Cabinet 2013c). Abe admitted: "I would like to restore a 'strong economy' and a 'strong Japan' with the public and private sectors working together. I would like to aim for being number one in the world" (Prime Minister of Japan and His Cabinet 2013c). The Council was abolished in September 2016, simultaneously with the establishment of its successor, the Future Investment Council. The new body continued to be administered mainly by the METI and still focused on microeconomic aspects of reforms. Nevertheless, its agenda was gradually broadened to include the social security system and VAT hike issues, as Abe preferred to discuss his most important plans outside of the CEFP, which remained under the MOF's influence (Ukishima 2019: 2).

Realization of the more detailed tasks of Abenomics was entrusted to separate decision-making bodies. Abe relied on a large number of councils under the Kantei's direct control, through which he partly circumvented the decision-making process on economic policy from separate ministries. The most important bodies included the Council for Regulatory Reform (Kisei Kaikaku Kaigi) created in January 2013 (in September 2016 replaced by the Regulatory Reform Promotion Council – Kisei Kaikaku Suishin Kaigi) and the Council for Science and Technology (Sōgō Kagaku Gijutsu Kaigi) that had been established as a part of administrative reforms in 2001. Every one or two weeks, former Finance Administrative Vice-Minister, Special Adviser to the Cabinet, Tango Yasutake, held meetings of the administrative staff of all the councils to ensure a swift exchange of information on their proceedings and coordinate the schedule of issuing their reports (Karube 2018: 125). In May 2014, the Council for Science and Technology was renamed the Council for Science, Technology and Innovation (Sōgō Kagaku Gijutsu Inobēshon Kaigi). Importantly, the new organ was charged with a Cross-ministerial Strategic Innovation Promotion Program, thus gaining the competence to plan the budget for scientific and technological innovation, which had been earlier managed mainly by the Ministry of Education, Culture, Sports, Science and Technology (Cabinet Office 2014).

Thanks to the abovementioned reforms, the Kantei became a real pivot for all the councils. The situation differed from the practice under the Koizumi administration, when the decision-making process had been channeled through the CEFP alone. Ōta Hiroko, who had served as the minister of state for economic and fiscal policy in the first Abe cabinet and was employed as a Council for Regulatory Reform member under his second administration, noted that while discussion topics in different councils sometimes overlapped, such situations resulted in synergy rather than turf battles (*Nikkei Purasuwan* 2013: 11). Owing to the highly efficient coordination of the council proceedings, the Kantei maintained control over the contents of the crucial documents issued by the CEFP (Basic Policies for Economic and Fiscal Management and Reform, so-called "Big-Boned Policy" – *Honebuto no Hōshin*), the Headquarters for Japan's Economic Revitalization and the Industrial Competitiveness Council (Japan Revitalization Strategy – *Nihon*

Saikō Senryaku), as well as the Council for Regulatory Reform (Regulatory Reform Implementation Schedule – *Kisei Kaikaku Jisshi Keikaku*). The documents were adopted as cabinet decisions every year in June, thus becoming the foundation for budget compilation and concrete economic policy measures (Nakakita 2017: 114–115).

Relying on METI, Abe frequently refurbished his economic policy agenda to offer new catchy slogans before every parliamentary election. Such an approach resulted in the creation of short-lived advisory bodies that were abolished as soon as the Kantei moved on to a new policy proposal. For instance, the Council in Support of Women who Shine (Kagayaku Josei Ōen Kaigi) convened only once in March 2014, and the People's Council for Dynamic Engagement of All Citizens (Ichi Oku Sōkatsuyaku Kokumin Kaigi) was summoned eight times between October 2015 and May 2016. Similarly, the Council for the Realization of Work Style Reform (Hatarakikata Kaikaku Jitsugen Kaigi), established in September 2016, held ten meetings and was dissolved after issuing an Action Plan for the Realization of Work Style Reform in March 2017 (Ukishima 2019: 2).

Similar councils were established in the ruling party. After the LDP regained power, the aim of the party Headquarters for Japan's Economic Revitalization became to support its governmental counterpart in elaborating the details of Abenomics. It was presided over by Abe's close associate, LDP Policy Research Council Chairperson, Takaichi Sanae. In addition, various inter-sectional, topic-specific headquarters (*honbu*) addressed difficult socio-economic problems and promoted various aspects of Abenomics. They included Headquarters for Promoting the Establishment of a Disaster Resilient Japan (Kokudo Kyōjinka Suishin Honbu), Headquarters for Promoting Women's Active Participation (Josei Katsuyaku Suishin Honbu), Headquarters for Overcoming Population Decline and Regional Revitalization (Chihō Sōsei Jikkō Tōgō Honbu), Headquarters for Promoting Dynamic Engagement of All Citizens (Ichi Oku Sōkatsuyaku Suishin Honbu), and Headquarters on Creation of Regional Vitality in Agriculture, Forestry, and Fisheries (Nōrin Suisan Gyō Chiiki no Katsuryoku Sōzō Honbu) (Liberal Democratic Party 2018). Placed under the LDP president's direct jurisdiction, these bodies proved instrumental in partly circumventing other decision-making organs in the ruling party.

In the proceedings on Abenomics, the prime minister relied on assistance from trusted top-class politicians in the government. Former Prime Minister Asō Tarō was reappointed as the vice-premier, minister of finance, and, concurrently, minister of state for financial services during all the cabinet reshuffles. While Asō, to some extent, represented the interests of the MOF, he also loyally implemented Abe's decisions. However, it is the Minister of State for Economic and Fiscal Policy, Amari Akira, who coordinated the work of the CEFP and the Headquarters for Japan's Economic Revitalization (Shimizu 2014: 21–22). Just like Asō, Amari was reappointed during cabinet reshuffles in September 2014, December 2014, and

October 2015, but he resigned due to a corruption scandal in January 2016. His successors were Ishihara Nobuteru (2016–2017), Motegi Toshimitsu (2017–2019), and Nishimura Yasutoshi (since 2019).

Each of the "three arrows" of Abenomics necessitated a different approach. The first arrow required putting effective pressure on the BOJ to conduct monetary easing; the second, ordering the MOF to increase budget expenses on infrastructural projects; and the third, overcoming opposition from different parliamentary tribes in the LDP. A dense network of newly established bodies in the government and the ruling party gave the prime minister the instruments to deal flexibly with various aspects of economic reforms.

Implementation of the "first arrow" of Abenomics

Realization of the goals specified in the "first arrow" of Abenomics only partly depended on the government. In order to succeed, the Kantei had to persuade the BOJ to cooperate – either through applying pressure on the incumbent Policy Board, or through replacing it with a new one.

Abe's statements from November 2012 on the necessity of introducing a 2% inflation target and the purchasing of bonds by the BOJ to cover infrastructural projects met with dissatisfaction from BOJ Governor Shirakawa Masaaki. Due to the independence of the BOJ, the government could not directly demand that this institution obey its instructions on monetary easing, but the LDP leader (and prime minister *in spe*) put pressure on Governor Shirakawa by hinting at the possibility of revising the BOJ Act. On December 18, 2012, two days after LDP's electoral victory, Abe met with Shirakawa, conveying to him his intention to sign a policy agreement with the BOJ that would contain a 2% inflation target – a one-percentage point increase from the 1% inflation target accepted by the BOJ in October 2012. The role of the mediator between the Kantei and the BOJ was shouldered by the MOF. Abe insisted that the BOJ should assume full responsibility for attaining the inflation target in a two-year period, thus stabilizing the employment rate. The BOJ, in turn, claimed that inflation was not only a monetary phenomenon, but that it required a structural approach that was outside of the BOJ's full control. On December 20, 2012, the BOJ Policy Board decided to increase the asset purchase program of treasury discount bills and Japanese government bonds by 10 trillion yen, but this move turned out to be insufficient to please the prime minister. Eventually, in mid-January 2013, Asō and Amari convinced Abe to abandon the two-year realization period for the sake of persuading the BOJ to specify the 2% inflation target (Karube 2018: 50–184).

On January 22, 2013, the government and the BOJ issued a Joint Statement on Overcoming Deflation and Achieving Sustainable Economic Growth. Both sides agreed to enhance policy coordination between them. The BOJ set "the price stability target at 2 percent in terms of the year-on-year rate of change in the consumer price index," under which it promised to "pursue monetary easing and aim to achieve this target at the earliest possible time" (Bank of Japan 2013a). The government, in turn, confirmed its intention to "flexibly manage macroeconomic policy but also formulate measures for strengthening competitiveness and growth potential of Japan's economy, and promote them strongly under the leadership of the Headquarters for Japan's Economic Revitalization" (Bank of Japan 2013a). In addition, it was clarified that the review of "the progress in the conduct of macroeconomic policies including monetary policy, the current condition and future prospects of prices in the context of the price stability target under those policies, economic and fiscal situation including employment conditions, and progress in economic structural reform" would be conducted by the CEFP (Bank of Japan 2013a). The document was the fruit of a compromise between the two sides. While Prime Minister Abe managed to impose the 2% inflation target on Governor Shirakawa, the BOJ avoided formulation of a clear deadline for achieving this task and diluted its own responsibility for the effects of monetary easing by hinting at the necessity of the government strengthening economic competitiveness. However, during the second CEFP meeting on the same day, Abe explained that he "would like to ask the Bank of Japan to take responsibility to make an effort for realizing this price stability goal" (Prime Minister of Japan and His Cabinet 2013b).

On February 5, 2013, Governor Shirakawa and his two deputies announced their intention to resign before the end of their terms in office, scheduled for April. As the ruling coalition did not possess a majority of seats in the House of Councilors, Abe had to persuade at least part of the opposition parties to support his candidates to these offices. In 2008, the DPJ had blocked similar nominations, claiming that the selection of the BOJ management from among former MOF bureaucrats would weaken the bank's independence. However, thanks to his international experience and management skills, former Finance Administrative Vice-Minister, Asian Development Bank President Kuroda Haruhiko's candidacy for the governorship did not arouse controversies similar to the candidacy of Gakushūin University Professor, Iwata Kikuo, for the deputy's post. As Iwata was considered overly radical by the critics of Abenomics, the search for a majority in the upper house was not easy. Eventually, the nomination of the new BOJ management was approved by the Diet in mid-March 2013, thanks to support from smaller opposition groups – JRA and YP (Shinoda 2013: 231–232).

As expected, Governor Kuroda was much more willing to cooperate with the government regarding anti-deflation policy than his predecessor. Deputy Governor Iwata even pledged he would resign if the 2% inflation target were not achieved within two years (though he later did not fulfill his vow).[1] On April 4, 2013, the BOJ Policy Board eventually decided it would "achieve the price stability target of 2 percent in terms of the year-on-year rate of change in the consumer price index (CPI) at the earliest possible time, with a time horizon of about two years" (Bank of Japan 2013b). In order to realize this goal, the BOJ announced its intention to double the monetary base up to 270 trillion yen by the end of 2014. The annual purchase of Japanese government bonds was to be increased by 50 trillion yen, that of the exchange-traded funds by 1 trillion yen, and of the Japan real estate investment trusts by 30 trillion yen (Bank of Japan 2013b).

The large-scale monetary easing policy was maintained in the following years, thus supporting the economic policy of the government and guaranteeing the continued depreciation of yen and increases in stock values on the Tokyo Stock Exchange. In October 2014, BOJ Policy Board members decided by five votes to four to accelerate purchases of Japanese government bonds to an annual pace of 80 trillion yen, buy longer-dated debt, and to triple the purchases of exchange-traded funds and real-estate investment trusts. The same number of Policy Board members authorized adoption of negative interest rates in January 2016. In September 2016, in turn, the bank resorted to quantitative and qualitative monetary easing with yield curve control, targeting both short-term and long-term policy interest rates. At the same time, the BOJ committed itself to expanding the monetary base until the year-on-year rate of increase in the consumer price index stayed above the 2% inflation target in a stable manner. Despite these measures, any attempts at persistently boosting inflation turned out to be futile. BOJ Deputy Governor Iwata (2018: 146–399) claimed that this failure resulted from the VAT hike and a massive drop in oil prices in 2014.

Thanks to the centralization of the decision-making process in the Kantei and the CEFP, as well as massive popular support for Abenomics, the prime minister, and his closest entourage effectively forced the BOJ to specify a 2% inflation target, even under the old management. Through the selection of Kuroda Haruhiko as the new governor, in turn, the Kantei ensured full BOJ conformity with governmental plans. Having charged the BOJ with the realization of the "first arrow" of Abenomics, the government could thus focus on planning implementation of the remaining two "arrows."

Implementation of the "second arrow" of Abenomics

In order to reinvigorate the Japanese economy, Abe planned to increase budget expenses for public works projects, which was consistent with the interests of the construction parliamentary tribe in the LDP. Faced with the Kantei's determination in pursuing an expansive fiscal policy, MOF bureaucrats were in no position to oppose.

Until the end of the 20th century, increased budget expenses for infrastructure projects had been LDP's traditional strategy for gaining votes in rural districts. While "pork barrel politics" was abandoned by Prime Minister Koizumi (2001–2006), under the first Abe cabinet (2006–2007), the LDP started reverting to the old practices. As such, the "second arrow" of Abenomics can be interpreted as a continuation of this trend. Also Finance Minister Asō Tarō was known as a supporter of an active fiscal policy, as symbolized by a large-scale supplementary budget that had been passed under his prime ministership, in the middle of the world financial crisis in 2009.

Knowing the LDP's intention, after the announcement of electoral results in December 2012, MOF bureaucrats started planning changes in FY2012 budget aimed at pleasing the new ruling party. As their main goal was to implement a VAT hike as scheduled, they probably did not want to antagonize the prime minister by overly opposing expansive fiscal policy. MOF bureaucrats gathered ideas on public works projects from individual ministries, such as repairs of tunnels and bridges, and disaster prevention construction plans that could be realized immediately, thus reinvigorating local businesses (Karube 2018: 116). In January 2013, the Abe cabinet drafted a supplementary budget of 13.1 trillion yen, which, at that time, was the largest in Japan's history aside from the one introduced by Asō after the bankruptcy of Lehman Brothers. More than 10 trillion yen of that amount was devoted to "emergency economic measures for the revitalization of the Japanese economy," in particular to infrastructure projects under the categories of "acceleration of reconstruction from the Great East Japan Earthquake disaster" (1.6 trillion yen), "advance disaster prevention" (2.2 trillion yen), and "regional economy activation reflecting local features including strengthening of the constitution of agriculture and acceleration of building areas comfortable for living" (579 billion yen) (Ministry of Finance 2013a). Additionally, new funds were to be spent on "growth potential strengthening through stimulating private investment" (1.8 trillion yen), "measures for SMEs, small-scale business operators, agriculture, forestry and fishery" (946 billion yen), "human resource development and employment measures" (266 billion yen), and establishment of a temporary grant for "regional economic vitalization and job creation" (1.4 trillion yen) (Ministry of Finance 2013a).

In addition, the budget for FY2013 allocated 5.29 trillion yen to public works, which meant an increase of 15.6% in comparison with the previous year. The Special Account for Reconstruction from the Great East Japan Earthquake, in turn, contained public works projects amounting to 879.3 billion yen. Total budget expenses amounted to 70.37 trillion yen, which was 2.9% more than in FY2012, although the bond dependency ratio fell from 47.6% to 46.3% (Ministry of Finance 2013b). The trend of increasing expenses for public works was maintained, though to a lesser extent, in the following years, which was related not only to disaster reconstruction measures, but also to the preparations for the Tokyo Olympic Games in 2020 (later postponed to 2021).

In June 2013, the CEFP issued Basic Policies for Economic and Fiscal Management and Reform that specified the aim to halve the primary deficit to GDP between FY2010 and FY2015 and achieve a surplus by FY2020. The government was to prioritize social infrastructure development projects "based on the degree of stimulative impact on private demand and cost effectiveness of investment" (Prime Minister of Japan and His Cabinet 2013e: 4). In subsequent years, the Abe cabinet periodically resorted to economic stimulus packages. For instance, the FY2014 supplementary budget, announced in December 2014, was to boost Japan's GDP after the first signs of economic stagnation since the introduction of Abenomics. Of the total 3.53 trillion yen, 1.74 trillion was devoted to disaster reconstruction and prevention projects, with the rest to support for households and businesses, as well as revitalization of local regions. The financial resources were secured by additional tax revenues and unspent funds from previous budgets (Ministry of Finance 2015). An even larger economic stimulus package of 4.52 trillion yen from August 2016 was covered mainly through construction bond issues. It was devoted to such aims as "support for building school facilities," development of "21st-century-type infrastructure," launch of a maglev fast train line, and "reconstruction from the Kumamoto Earthquake and the Great East Japan Earthquake" (Ministry of Finance 2016).

Expansive fiscal policy was elevated to a new level after the outbreak of the coronavirus pandemic at the beginning of 2020. In April 2020, Abe announced a stimulus package of 108 trillion yen, followed by an even larger one, amounting to 117 trillion yen, in the following month. These record-high funds were devoted to tax breaks, zero-interest loans, rent subsidies, and benefits for business owners and families who lost their incomes, as well as to additional salaries for medical staff (Pham & Wakatsuki 2020). Due to the extraordinary character of the pandemic, increased budget spending in 2020 cannot be interpreted solely as an element of Abenomics, but it fitted ideally with the economic policy agenda formulated by Abe in 2012.

While implementation of the "first arrow" of Abenomics required the prime minister to overcome pressure from the BOJ, the "second arrow" was welcomed by most veto players. In particular, construction and road parliamentary tribes in the ruling party used the "second arrow" to promote the old wasteful budget spending under a new name. Without finding allies in the LDP, the MOF, which remained the largest opponent of an expansive fiscal policy, was unable to reduce budget expenses on infrastructure projects.

Implementation of the "third arrow" of Abenomics

The "third arrow" of Abenomics remained the most vague and diversified one. It mixed incentives for entrepreneurs, such as corporate tax reduction and creation of special economic zones, with pressure on business circles to promote women's empowerment and increase salaries.

In order to encourage private sector investments, the Industrial Competitiveness Council gradually elaborated a set of policy proposals. Initially, Minister Amari pointed to health, energy, and next-generation infrastructure, as well as agriculture and tourism as four strategic fields. Private-sector Council members, however, insisted that instead of supporting distinct sectors, the government should improve the general environment for business (*Nihon Keizai Shinbun* 2013: 3). In June 2013, the cabinet approved the Japan Revitalization Strategy "Japan Is Back." Its aim was "to achieve a vibrant economy that will register over 2% labor productivity improvement in the medium to long term, and around 3% nominal gross domestic product (GDP) growth and around 2% real GDP growth, on average, over the next ten years" (Prime Minister of Japan and His Cabinet 2013f: 2). This goal was to be realized thanks to improving the competitiveness of Japanese companies through ensuring a stable economic environment, accelerating the efforts for the establishment of international economic partnerships, enabling low-cost energy supplies, and overhauling those regulations and institutions that inhibited investment. In addition, emphasis was put on developing human resources, in particular through promotion of active social participation by women. More detailed policies included the creation of National Strategic Special Zones, legalization of Internet sales of non-prescription drugs, liberalization of the electricity retail market, and promotion of such free trade agreements as the TPP. The government promised to implement the reforms "at unprecedented speed" and provide details of the planned measures by the end of August 2013 (Prime Minister of Japan and His Cabinet 2013f: 10–26).

During his speech at the New York Stock Exchange in September 2013, Abe deplored the fact that while Japanese businesspersons had symbolized the economic prowess of Japan in Oliver Stone's *Wall Street* movie from 1987, they were replaced by their Chinese counterparts in the 2010 sequel. Nevertheless, Abe expressed his hope that Japan could return to its former position after a long absence, just like investor Gordon Gekko, played by Michael Douglas. To achieve this aim, the prime minister called on US business circles to "buy" his Abenomics. At the same time, he promised to fire the next "arrow" of his growth strategy and "assertively push through a bold tax reduction in order to stimulate investment" immediately after returning to Japan (Prime Minister of Japan and His Cabinet 2013g). Indeed, in the same month, Abe suddenly announced his decision to abolish one year earlier than scheduled a special corporate tax for reconstruction of the regions destroyed by the Great East Japan Earthquake, and imposed his will on the MOF and the LDP Research Commission on the Tax System.[2]

Just as promised in the Japan Revitalization Strategy, most of the reforms were swiftly implemented. Abe baptized the extraordinary session of the Diet in autumn 2013, a "growth strategy parliament." The Bill on National Strategic Special Zones was approved as a cabinet decision on November 5, and passed in the Diet on December 7, 2013. As the National Strategic Special Zone Advisory Council was established on the basis of a law, not a mere cabinet decision, it had as strong a legal foundation as the CEFP. It was composed of the prime minister, as chair, as well as CCS, minister of internal affairs and communication, minister of state for fiscal and economic policy, and private-sector specialists. What is important, to avoid excessive pressure from bureaucrats, parliamentary tribes, and interest groups, the ministers in charge of the involved deregulation fields, such as health, employment, agriculture, and education, did not become Council members (Kiyoi 2013: 1). The Council started deliberations in January 2014 with the participation of former Minister of State for Economic and Fiscal Policy, Takenaka Heizō, who had been the main author of structural reforms during the Koizumi administration. Under Takenaka's guidance, the Council swiftly selected regions that were to lead deregulation efforts to attract private investment. In March 2014, the government announced six zones: Tokyo area, Kansai area, Niigata City, Yabu City in Hyōgo Prefecture, Fukuoka City, and Okinawa Prefecture. At the same time, deliberations started on the legalization of gambling resorts in specially designated places (Shimizu 2014: 66–68).

Liberalization of the electricity retail market was another policy specified in the new growth strategy. Efforts in this field had been initiated under the DPJ government, though they were not realized due to opposition from power plant trade unions. Similarly, a strong lobby of politicians who received electoral funds from energy providers existed in the LDP. Nevertheless, the political influence of the largest Japanese electricity utility holding company, Tokyo Electric Power Company, was significantly weakened after the Fukushima Daiichi Nuclear Power Plant disaster in 2011. While METI maintained behind-the-scenes connections with energy providers, who also provided lucrative *amakudari* posts, within the ministry, there existed a large group of bureaucrats who promoted liberalization of the electricity retail market in order to reduce the energy costs borne by Japanese industry. It was under their influence that Minister for Economy, Trade and Industry, Motegi Toshimitsu, expressed his will to continue the plans of reform initiated by the DPJ. While liberalization of the electricity retail market was not included in the LDP electoral manifesto in 2012, Abe and Amari embraced the new policy as a part of the "third arrow" of Abenomics. In addition, as the prime minister planned to overhaul the policy of abandoning nuclear power, liberalization of the electricity retail market would weaken the impression that he overly bent to the demands from electricity utility holding companies. In February 2013, METI announced a roadmap of electricity system reform that specified full liberalization of entry to electricity retail business by 2016 and legal unbundling of the electricity transmission and distribution sector by 2018–2020. Under pressure from Abe, this policy was authorized by the LDP Policy Research Council and approved as a cabinet decision in April 2013. While the Reform Program under the supplementary provisions of the Act for Partial Revision of the Electricity Business Act failed to be voted through during the ordinary Diet session, it was passed in November 2013, after the LDP and Kōmeitō coalition regained a majority of seats in the House of Councilors (Kamikawa 2017: 53–84).

Promotion of women's empowerment was another element of the "third arrow" of Abenomics. In June 2013, Deputy CCS Sugita Kazuhiro instructed representatives of all ministries at the Administrative Vice-Ministers' Liaison Council to actively nominate women to important bureaucratic posts. To give a good example, in November 2013, the Kantei selected Yamada Makiko from METI as the first female to serve as the prime minister's administrative secretary. At the same time, Deputy CCS Katō Katsunobu instructed all administrative vice-ministers to hire at least 30% of new bureaucrats from among women in 2015. In April 2014, in turn, Ichimiya Nahomi was appointed as the first female president of the National Personnel Authority. In parallel, the prime minister directly asked Japan Business Federation (Nippon Keidanren) Chairperson Yonekura Hiromasa, Japan Chamber of Commerce and Industry Chairperson Okamura Tadashi, and Japan Association of Corporate Executives Chairperson Hasegawa Yasuchika to encourage advancement of women to executive posts in Japanese business. In response, in April 2014, Nippon Keidanren prepared a special action plan for women's promotion. In addition, the Act on Promotion of Women's Participation and Advancement in the Workplace was passed by the Diet in August 2015. It imposed an obligation of collecting and disclosing data on rates of woman managers and newly hired woman employees, as well as devising action plans to improve gender equality in all governmental agencies, local government, and private-sector corporations, employing more than 300 people (Kakizaki 2015: 32–51).

The media pointed out that the planned reforms did not go as far as had been anticipated. Former METI official Koga (2017: 80–136) stressed that the growth strategy failed to sufficiently address such important issues as promotion of renewable energy sources. The "third arrow" of Abenomics only to a minimal degree endangered the privileges of the bureaucrats. In fact, due to the arbitrary decisions on where to establish new National Strategic Special Zones, or which investor to partially exempt from taxes, in some aspects, the reforms even strengthened bureaucratic guidance. For instance, the creation of casino resorts was subject to a number of new regulations. Moreover, numerous newly established, public-private funds served bureaucrats as convenient *amakudari* institutions. In addition, as shown by the Kake Gakuen scandal, centralization of the decision-making process on deregulation could be used by the Kantei to favor one legal person against another.

Some of the goals of the "third arrow" of Abenomics were not realized due to circumstances outside of Abe's control. Most importantly, the prime minister invested much effort in imposing on the LDP agricultural tribe ratification of the TPP treaty, which never entered into force in its original version due to a withdrawal from the agreement by the newly elected US President Donald Trump in January 2017. On the other hand, the Kantei succeeded in partially abolishing protectionism toward farmers and turning the Central Union of Agricultural Cooperatives into an incorporated association. It remains to be seen, however, if these reforms suffice to make Japanese agriculture more competitive in the world.

In many cases, the policies pursued within the "third arrow" of Abenomics were prepared by METI bureaucrats in cooperation with the Kantei. Taking into account METI's tendency to refurbish its policy agenda on an annual basis, this explains why many projects were used mostly to attract popular support and were not sufficiently followed up on. Such initiatives as the National Strategic Special Zones to some extent facilitated conducting businesses, though they were sometimes implemented at the expense of strengthening bureaucratic guidance and increasing room for arbitrary decisions by the prime minister and his direct entourage.

Evaluation of Abenomics and its new iteration

Abe positively self-evaluated the effects of his economic policy. In his policy speech to the Diet in January 2018, he stressed:

> Due to the five years of Abenomics, the Japanese economy has grown for seven consecutive fiscal quarters for the first time in 28 years. As a result of four consecutive years of wage increases, economic growth with strong private sector demand has been achieved and we are now steadily advancing down the path toward an exit from deflation. Before New Year's Day, nearly 90% of university graduates seeking employment had been offered jobs. This percentage is the highest ever in history. The overall ratio of active job openings to applicants for regular employees exceeds 1, and conversions to regular employees has been accelerated.
> (Prime Minister of Japan and His Cabinet 2018)

Similarly, BOJ officials positively evaluated the effects of Abenomics. For instance, BOJ Deputy Governor Iwata (2018: 395) claimed that the new economic policy contributed to a decrease in the number of suicides from 5219 in 2012 to 3522 in 2016.

Nevertheless, despite the initial credit of trust in Abenomics, the evaluation of Abe's economic policy by the public remained mixed. According to an opinion poll conducted by *Asahi Shinbun* (2014: 4) after the dissolution of the House of Representatives in November 2014, 30% of respondents claimed that Abenomics had succeeded, while 39% deemed it a failure. Moreover, as many as 65% thought that Abenomics did not translate into an increase in wages or improvement on the employment market (20% believed otherwise). The evaluation of the economic policy of the government had turned even worse by the July 2016 House of Councilors election. In May 2016, only 28% of respondents believed that Abenomics would lead to economic growth, while 50% remained skeptical about its efficiency (*Asahi Shinbun* 2016: 4). Analogically, according to an opinion poll conducted by *Tokyo Shinbun* (2017) before the lower house election in October 2017, 56% of respondents did not have (and 41% had) high expectations of Abenomics.

Some economists remained critical of Abe's policy. Yanbe (2016: 100–101) indicated that the average annual GDP growth rate during the first three years of the second Abe administration (0.6%) was much lower than during a period of similar length under the DPJ government (1.7%). Hattori (2017: 32–111) stressed that the failure of the monetary easing policy was symbolized by the fact that the BOJ endlessly postponed the deadline for attaining the 2% inflation target. The sudden weakening of the yen resulted in an increase in prices of imported food and other commodities, thus reducing household disposable income and internal consumption. According to Hattori, the decrease in the unemployment rate was caused more by the depopulation of Japan than by the economic policy of the government. In fact, Abenomics contributed to an increase in the number of part-time workers and a decrease in the number of regular employees, without raising labor productivity. Even Wakatabe (2015: 134–135), who lauded the reflation policy, noted that the implementation of the "third arrow" of Abenomics should be based on deregulation rather than on bureaucratic guidance by METI.

Only a few LDP lawmakers overtly criticized Abenomics. In June 2017, they created the Study Group on Financial, Fiscal, and Social Security Problems, led by Noda Takeshi. Approximately 40 parliamentarians who participated in the initiative put into doubt the effectiveness of the monetary easing policy. What is symptomatic, two potential contenders for the post of LDP president, Noda Seiko and Ishiba Shigeru, also attended the meeting (*Asahi Shinbun* 2017: 5). Murakami Seiichirō, who was one of the co-creators of the group, stressed that it was impossible to increase public debt infinitely (interview by the author, Tokyo, October 17, 2019).

The mixed evaluation of the results of Abenomics was probably one of the factors that prompted the prime minister to constantly add new elements to his policy agenda. After the re-election as the LDP president in September 2015, Abe announced "Abenomics 2.0," which focused on social issues. He formulated a "new three arrows" of expanding GDP to 600 trillion yen, "raising the birthrate to 1.8 children per woman," as well as "eliminating cases in which people have no choice but to leave their jobs to provide nursing care" (Prime Minister of Japan and His Cabinet 2015). The basic ideas of "Abenomics 2.0" were drafted by METI, but it is Prime Minister's Executive Secretary Imai Takaya who inserted detailed goals to the plan and coined the slogan of "dynamic engagement of all citizens" (Mori 2019: 21–23).

Realization of the new set of policies was entrusted to Cabinet Office Minister Katō Katsunobu and the newly established People's Council for Dynamic Engagement of All Citizens chaired by the prime minister and composed of all ministers and private-sector specialists. The Council issued "Japan's Plan for Dynamic Engagement of All Citizens," which was acknowledged as a cabinet decision in June 2016. The document proposed a set of policies to improve the working conditions of non-regular workers; redress the problem of long working hours; promote employment of the elderly; enhance the childcare and nursing care systems; support youths, families with multiple children, single-parent families, and marriages; create educational opportunities for schoolchildren who need special consideration; expand the scholarship system; improve the environment for three-generation families; extend healthy life expectancy; support activities of people with disabilities or fighting intractable diseases and cancer; facilitate innovations in robotics and artificial intelligence; overcome environmental and energy constraints through renewable energy sources; change sports into a growth industry; improve productivity in the service sector; and put more emphasis on tourism. In order to achieve these ambitious goals, the Plan formulated "Roadmap toward the Future of 10 Years from Now," which contained 43 detailed measures. Realization of the "new three arrows" was linked with already existing economic growth strategies, such as the National Strategic Special Zones (Prime Minister of Japan and His Cabinet 2016).

Abe's critics claimed that the "new three arrows" were launched to divert public attention from the fact that the original Abenomics had ended in failure. Hattori (2017: 16) indicated that some of its goals were nothing more than refurbished old targets. For instance, the 3% nominal GDP growth rate, stipulated in the 2013 Japan Revitalization Strategy, would suffice to expand GDP to 600 trillion yen by 2020 and beyond. Attaining the birthrate of 1.8 children per woman, in turn, was interpreted by some commentators as dangerous interference by the government in family planning, reminiscent of Imperial Japan (Kakizaki 2015: 52–61).

The addition of new elements to Abenomics was aimed both at adapting the government's policy to popular expectations and at camouflaging the fact that most of the goals of the original "three arrows" remained unachieved. Such multiplication of novel projects reflected the institutional culture of the METI, which ideally fitted the Kantei's need to constantly appeal to voters with catchy new slogans.

Conclusion

Abenomics was a policy that met with a warm reception from the Japanese electorate, thus facilitating Abe to maintain high popularity. For that reason, it is easy to understand why the prime minister devoted so much energy in pushing his economic policy agenda forward. However, in order to realize the "three arrows" of Abenomics, the head of government had to overcome opposition from such institutional veto players as the BOJ, MOF, and LDP financial parliamentary tribe. It is symptomatic that the prime minister achieved these ambitious goals without conducting profound institutional reforms, but rather by creatively using the instruments of power that already existed.

Thanks to full support from the METI and effective pressure on the MOF through the Headquarters for Japan's Economic Revitalization and the CEFP, Abe managed to force the BOJ to acknowledge the 2% inflation target and monetary easing policy, and the new BOJ governor fully cooperated with the government. Skillful coordination of the efforts of the newly established councils under the cabinet as well as the inter-sectional, topic-specific headquarters under the LDP president's direct jurisdiction, was equally instrumental in realizing the second and third "arrows" of Abenomics. Having grasped control over budget compilation, the Kantei imposed an increase in expenses for public works projects on the MOF. Analogically, supervision over the proceedings of the Industrial Competitiveness Council and the institutional strength of the Kantei contributed to swift implementation of decisions within the scope of the new growth strategy such as establishment of the National Strategic Special Zones. While playing METI off against the MOF, Abe gradually strengthened his domination in economic policy making and enhanced the Cabinet Secretariat's pivotal role in inter-ministerial coordination.

Notes

1. Iwata (2018: 10–12) claimed he merely said that resignation was an ultimate way of taking responsibility for not achieving policy aims, not that he promised to resign in such a case.
2. See details in Chapter 4.

References

Asahi Shinbun (2012) "Shūinsen de Mottomo Kanshin o Motta Seisaku, 'Keiki, Koyō' Saita 35%. Asahi Shinbunsha Yoron Chōsa" [Policy that Attracted Most Interest in House of Representatives Election "Economic Recovery, Employment" Highest 35%. Opinion Poll by Asahi Shinbunsha], December 19, morning edition, 3.

Asahi Shinbun (2014) "Abenomikusu 'Shippai' 39%, 'Seikō' wa 30%. Asahi Shinbunsha Yoron Chōsa" [Abenomics "Failure" 39%, "Success" 30%. Opinion Poll by Asahi Shinbunsha], November 21, morning edition, 4.

Asahi Shinbun (2016) "Asahi Shinbunsha Yoron Chōsa. Shitsumon to Kaitō" [Opinion Poll by Asahi Shinbunsha. Questions and Answers], May 24, morning edition, 4.

Asahi Shinbun (2017) "Datsu-Abenomikusu, Jimin 40 Nin. Ishiba, Noda-shi-ra Benkyōkai" [Anti-Abenomics, 40 Persons from LDP. Study Group with Ishiba, Noda], June 16, morning edition, 5.

Bank of Japan (2013a) "Joint Statement of the Government and the Bank of Japan on Overcoming Deflation and Achieving Sustainable Economic Growth" (January 22). Online. Available: https://www.boj.or.jp/en/announcements/release_2013/k130122c.pdf (accessed April 10, 2019).

Bank of Japan (2013b) "Introduction of the 'Quantitative and Qualitative Monetary Easing'" (April 4). Online. Available: https://www.boj.or.jp/en/announcements/release_2013/k130404a.pdf (April 12, 2019).

Cabinet Office (2014) "'Naikakufu Setchi Hō no Ichibu o Kaisei Suru Hōritsu' no Shikō ni tsuite" [About Enforcement of "Law to Revise a Part of the Cabinet Office Establishment Bill"]. Online. Available: https://www8.cao.go.jp/cstp/stsonota/settihou/settihou.html (accessed June 17, 2020).

Hattori, Shigeyuki (2017) *Itsuwari no Keizai Seisaku. Kakusa to Teitai no Abenomikusu* [False Economic Policy. Abenomics of Disparities and Stagnation], Tokyo: Iwanami Shoten.
Iwata, Kikuo (2018) *Nichigin Nikki. Go Nenkan no Defure to no Tatakai* [BOJ Diary. Five Years of Struggle with Deflation], Tokyo: Chikuma Shobō.
Japanese Law Translation (1997) "Bank of Japan Act," Act No. 89 (June 18). Online. Available: http://www.japaneselawtranslation.go.jp/law/detail/?vm=02&re=01&id=92&lvm=01 (accessed April 5, 2019).
Kakizaki, Meiji (2015) *Kenshō. Abeizumu. Taidō Suru Shin Kokkashugi* [Analysis. Abeism. Emerging New Statism], Tokyo: Iwanami Shoten.
Kamikawa, Ryūnoshin (2017) "Denryoku Shisutemu Kaikaku. Denryoku Jiyūka o meguru Seiji Katei" [Electricity System Reform. Political Process on Liberalization of Electricity Market], in Takenaka Harukata (ed.), *Futatsu no Seiken Kōtai. Seisaku wa Kawatta noka* [Two Alternations of Power. Has the Policy Changed?], Tokyo: Keisō Shobō, 53–84.
Karube, Kensuke (2018) *Kanryōtachi no Abenomikusu. Igyō no Keizai Seisaku wa Ika ni Tukurareta ka* [Abenomics of the Bureaucrats. How Was the Odd-looking Economic Policy Created], Tokyo: Iwanami Shoten.
Kiyoi, Satoshi (2013) "Tokku Shimon Kaigi Setchi e. Iryō, Koyō, Nōgyō Kisei Gawa Daijin Hazusu" [Towards Establishment of Special Zone Advisory Council. Medical Care, Employment, Agriculture Regulatory Side Ministers Removed], *Asahi Shinbun*, October 21, morning edition, 1.
Koga, Shigeaki (2017) *Kokka no Kyōbō* [State Collusion], Tokyo: Kadokawa.
Liberal Democratic Party (2012) "Nihon o Torimodosu" [Restore Japan]. Online. Available: https://jimin.jp-east-2.storage.api.nifcloud.com/pdf/seisaku_ichiban24.pdf?_ga=2.156227707.1712537556.1554297229-464335118.1554297229 (accessed April 3, 2019).
Liberal Democratic Party (2018) "Official English Translations for LDP Officials and Party Organs." Online. Available: https://www.jimin.jp/english/profile/english/ (accessed August 18, 2018).
Ministry of Finance (2013a) "Outline of the FY2012 Supplementary Budget" (January 15). Online. Available: https://www.mof.go.jp/english/budget/budget/fy2012/e20130204a.pdf (accessed April 12, 2019).
Ministry of Finance (2013b) "Highlights of the Budget for FY2013" (January 29). Online. Available: https://www.mof.go.jp/english/budget/budget/fy2013/01.pdf (accessed April 17, 2019).
Ministry of Finance (2015) "Outline of the Supplementary Budget for FY2014" (January 9). Online. Available: https://www.mof.go.jp/english/budget/budget/fy2014/03.pdf (accessed April 17, 2019).
Ministry of Finance (2016) "Outline of the Second Supplementary Budget for FY2016" (August 24). Online. Available: https://www.mof.go.jp/english/budget/budget/fy2016/05.pdf (accessed April 17, 2019).
Mori, Isao (2019) *Kantei Kanryō. Abe Ikkyō o Sasaeta Sokkin Seiji no Tsumi* [The Residence's Bureaucracy. The Sin of Aides' Politics that Supported Abe's Unilateral Strength], Tokyo: Bungei Shunjū.
Nakakita, Kōji (2017) *Jimintō – Ikkyō no Jitsuzō* [LDP – Real Image of Unilateral Strength], Tokyo: Chūō Kōron Shinsha.

Nihon Keizai Shinbun (2013) "Kisei Kaikaku, TPP Yōbō, Kyōsōryoku Kaigi de Minkan Giin, Seifu no Kajō Kan'yo Keikai" [Request for Regulatory Reform, TPP, Private-Sector Members Concerned with Excessive Government Interference at the Competitiveness Council], January 24, morning edition, 3.

Nikkei Purasuwan (2013) "Keizai Seisaku no Shireitō tte Doko? Kadai-goto ni Kaigi ga Rinritsu" [Where is the Command Tower of Economic Policy? Multiple Councils for Distinct Tasks], October 12, 11.

Noguchi, Asahi (2018) *Abenomikusu ga Kaeta Nihon Keizai* [Japanese Economic Changed by Abenomics], Tokyo: Chikuma Shobō.

Pham, Sherisse & Wakatsuki, Yoko (2020) "Japan's Economy Just Got Another $1 Trillion Shot in the Arm," CNN Business (May 27). Online. Available: https://edition.cnn.com/2020/05/27/economy/japan-economic-stimulus-coronavirus/index.html (accessed June 19, 2020).

Prime Minister of Japan and His Cabinet (2013a) "Sangyō Kyōsōryoku Kaigi no Kaisai ni tsuite" [On Holding of the Industrial Competitiveness Council] (January 8). Online. Available: https://www.kantei.go.jp/jp/singi/keizaisaisei/skkkaigi/konkyo.html (accessed April 9, 2019).

Prime Minister of Japan and His Cabinet (2013b) "Council on Economic and Fiscal Policy" (January 22). Online. Available: https://japan.kantei.go.jp/96_abe/actions/201301/22zaiseisimon_e.html (accessed April 11, 2019).

Prime Minister of Japan and His Cabinet (2013c) "Industrial Competitiveness Council" (January 23). Online. Available: https://japan.kantei.go.jp/96_abe/actions/201301/23sangyoukyousou_e.html (accessed April 9, 2019).

Prime Minister of Japan and His Cabinet (2013d) "Policy Speech by Prime Minister Shinzo Abe to the 183rd Session of the Diet" (January 28). Online. Available: https://japan.kantei.go.jp/96_abe/statement/201301/28syosin_e.html (accessed April 5, 2019).

Prime Minister of Japan and His Cabinet (2013e) "Basic Policies for Economic and Fiscal Management and Reform. Ending Deflation and Revitalizing the Economy (Summary)" (June 14). Online. Available: https://www5.cao.go.jp/keizai1/2013/20130614summary_02.pdf (accessed April 17, 2019).

Prime Minister of Japan and His Cabinet (2013f) "Japan Revitalization Strategy – Japan Is Back" (June 14). Online. Available: https://www.kantei.go.jp/jp/singi/keizaisaisei/pdf/en_saikou_jpn_hon.pdf (accessed April 13, 2019).

Prime Minister of Japan and His Cabinet (2013g) "Address by H.E. Mr. Shinzo Abe, Prime Minister of Japan, at the New York Stock Exchange" (September 25). Online. Available: https://japan.kantei.go.jp/96_abe/statement/201309/25nyse_e.html (accessed June 10, 2020).

Prime Minister of Japan and His Cabinet (2015) "Press Conference by Prime Minister Shinzo Abe" (October 7). Online. Available: https://japan.kantei.go.jp/97_abe/statement/201510/1213721_9930.html (April 15, 2019).

Prime Minister of Japan and His Cabinet (2016) "The Japan's Plan for Dynamic Engagement of All Citizens" (June 2). Online. Available: https://www.kantei.go.jp/jp/singi/ichiokusoukatsuyaku/pdf/plan2.pdf (accessed November 18, 2019).

Prime Minister of Japan and His Cabinet (2018) "Policy Speech by Prime Minister Shinzo Abe to the 196th Session of the Diet" (January 22). Online. Available: https://japan.kantei.go.jp/98_abe/statement/201801/_00002.html (accessed April 12, 2019).

Shimizu, Katsuhiko (2014) *Abe Seiken no Wana. Tanjunka Sareru Seiji to Media* [Trap of the Abe Government. Simplifying Politics and Media], Tokyo: Heibonsha.

Shinoda, Tomohito (2013) *Contemporary Japanese Politics: Institutional Changes and Power Shifts*, New York: Columbia University Press.

Takahashi, Yōichi (2018) *Zaimushō o Kaitai Seyo!* [Let's Dismantle the Ministry of Finance], Tokyo: Takarajimasha.

Tokyo Shinbun (2017) "Abenomikusu 'Kitai Sezu' 56%. Zenoku Yoron Chōsa" [56% "Without Expectations" of Abenomics. All-Country Opinion Poll] (October 1). Online. Available: https://www.tokyo-np.co.jp/senkyo/shuin2017/shuin_article/zen/CK2017100102000132.html (accessed April 12, 2019).

Ukishima, Tsubasa (2019) "Kantei Kaigi ga Utsusu Seisaku Yūsendo – Abe Seiken wa Keizai Jūshi" [Policy Priorities Reflected in the Kantei Councils: Abe Administration Focuses on Economy], *Nihon Keizai Shinbun*, March 8, evening edition, 2.

Wakatabe, Masazumi (2015) *Neo-Abenomikusu no Ronten. Rejīmu Chenji no Kantetsu de Nihon Keizai wa Fukkatsu Suru* [Points of Neo-Abenomics. Japanese Economy will be Revived Through Implementation of Regime Change], Tokyo: PHP Kenkyūjo.

Yanbe, Yukio (2016) Kurashi kara Mita Abenomikusu [Abenomics as Seen from Daily Lives], in Nakano Kōichi (ed.), *Tettei Kenshō. Abe Seiji* [Comprehensive Examination. Abe Politics], Tokyo: Iwanami Shoten, 97–106.

Yomiuri Shinbun (2012) "Abe Naikaku Shiji 65%. Keiki 'Kaifuku Dekiru' 48%. Honsha Kinkyū Chōsa" [Support for Abe Cabinet 65%. Economic Boom "Can Be Revived" 48%. Our Urgent Opinion Poll], December 28, Tokyo morning edition, 1.

Zakowski, Karol (2015) *Decision-Making Reform in Japan: The DPJ's Failed Attempt at a Politician-Led Government*, London and New York: Routledge.

6 Postponement of the VAT hike

Prime Minister Abe twice – in November 2014 and June 2016 – made decisions to postpone an increase in consumption tax. He did so against strong pressure from MOF bureaucrats and members of the LDP financial *zoku*. In 2014, the postponement of the VAT hike was used by Abe as a pretext for dissolving the lower house, but, in reality, the motives behind this move were more complex. The prime minister probably intended to challenge the opposition parties while they were still divided, and while the public still believed in the effectiveness of Abenomics. Analogically, a similar decision in 2016 was aimed at improving LDP's performance in the upper house election. Both electoral victories not only ensured the prolongation of the Abe cabinet, but they also significantly improved the Kantei's position vis-à-vis veto players.

The VAT hike as a political issue

The Japanese electorate has felt strong resentment against the consumption tax. The announcement of the plan of its introduction by Prime Minister Ōhira Masayoshi contributed to LDP's poor performance in the 1979 House of Representatives election. When 3% VAT was introduced in 1988, the furious voters punished the dominant party with its first defeat in the House of Councilors election one year later. Subsequent heads of government referred to a consumption tax increase as a way of limiting the budget deficit, but with little success. As soon as Prime Minister Hosokawa Morihiro declared his intention to introduce a "national welfare tax" that would *de facto* mean raising VAT to 7%, the popularity of his government suddenly declined, and he was forced to resign in 1994. In the same year, the Murayama cabinet decided to increase the consumption tax to 5%, which contributed to a massive drop in the electoral performance of the JSP in the 1996 House of Representatives election. After the tax reform was implemented by Murayama's successor, Prime Minister Hashimoto Ryūtarō in 1997, the LDP suffered a crashing defeat in the upper house election, which forced Hashimoto to resign in 1998. The VAT hike caused a sudden drop in domestic consumption, which exacerbated the economic recession in the era of the Asian crisis. Aware of the political risk connected with tax reform, Prime Minister Koizumi Jun'ichirō excluded the possibility of another hike under his long tenure from 2001 to 2006 (Takahashi 2019: 173–197). Less prudently, Prime Minister Kan Naoto mentioned the necessity to raise the consumption tax, which led to the DPJ's humiliating defeat in the House of Councilors election in 2010.

The bill on a VAT hike was eventually passed by the House of Representatives in June 2012 and by the House of Councilors in August 2012. The consumption tax increase was divided into two stages: to 8% (from 5%) in April 2014, and to 10% in October 2015. The new budget revenues were to be devoted to financing the social security system. The bill resulted from a compromise between the DPJ, the ruling party at that time, as well the LDP and Kōmeitō, whose agreement was necessary due to the governing coalition's lack of a majority in the upper house. In exchange, Prime Minister Noda Yoshihiko promised to dissolve the lower house, which paved the way for LDP's return to power. What is important, the VAT hike bill contained a clause, according to which a 3% nominal and 2% real economic growth rate was to be achieved to proceed with the reform. Despite being only a non-binding condition, the clause created a possibility for the prime minister to postpone the tax increase in case of sudden deterioration of the economic situation (Zakowski 2015: 175–185).

LDP heavyweight politicians were not unanimous regarding the VAT hike. The tax increase had been long promoted by the MOF, which perceived it as a tool for reducing a record-high public debt that exceeded 200% of Gross Domestic Product (GDP). On the other hand, the METI put achieving a high economic growth rate above maximizing tax revenues. Both ministries remained in close relationship with influential LDP politicians from the tax system and commerce/industry parliamentary tribes, respectively. The former group was content that the unpopular, yet inevitable, decision on raising consumption tax had been made by the DPJ instead of the LDP, and was determined to implement it as scheduled. The latter, by contrast, perceived the three-party agreement as an unnecessary burden that constrained the new government.

Ever since his first term in office, Abe Shinzō sympathized with the commerce and industry parliamentary tribe. His economic brain, reform-minded MOF bureaucrat, Takahashi Yōichi, claimed that the MOF was manipulating data to persuade the government to implement another VAT hike. According to Takahashi (2019: 24–66), the argument that a tax increase was necessary to reduce public debt was exaggerated, as Japan's economy remained in good condition, taking into account the sound balance between all state assets and debts. Instead of resorting to a VAT hike, he suggested that the government should reduce the debt through privatization of state-owned companies which existed only to provide well-paid jobs for retired bureaucrats. In 2006, Abe appointed two politicians who put boosting economic growth above a tax increase – Shiozaki Yasuhisa and Nakagawa Hidenao – as chief cabinet secretary (CCS) and LDP secretary-general, respectively. For Abe, it was deregulation and creation of a favorable environment for private business that were to guarantee higher budget revenues, which, in turn, could be used to finance the social security system (Shimizu 2014: 72–73). In addition, in his bestseller, *Towards Beautiful Japan*, published in 2006, Abe (2006: 192) stressed that covering all the costs of the social security system by the consumption tax would be unfair to older people who had paid annuities in the past and would have to bear the additional financial burden of raised prices. After returning to power, Abe once more had to balance the need for guaranteeing economic growth with ensuring stable tax revenues.

Authorization of the first stage of the VAT hike

The first stage of the VAT hike was planned for April 2014. As the LDP had voted for the tax increase along with the DPJ, the Abe cabinet generally leaned toward proceeding with the reform as scheduled. On the other hand, the prime minister did not exclude resorting to the economic growth clause in case of a deterioration of economic conditions.

In the 2012 electoral manifesto, the LDP confirmed that 10% VAT would serve the stabilization of finances and that the tax would not be devoted to any other ends than the social security system (Liberal Democratic Party 2012: 22). MOF bureaucrats warned that the VAT hike was an international pledge and that retraction of this policy would inevitably lead to a rise in the interest rates of Japanese bonds (Yamaguchi 2017: 133–134). BOJ Governor Kuroda Haruhiko shared this stance (Iwata 2018: 77–78). At the end of August 2013, the Council on Economic and Fiscal Policy (CEFP) conducted hearings on the consumption tax increase among 59 representatives of academia, big business, and NGOs. Opinions were divided, but Japan Business Federation Chairperson Yonekura Hiromasa and Japanese Trade Union Confederation (Rengō) President, Koga Nobuaki, approved the hike (*Asahi Shinbun* 2013a: 3). Another powerful group that insisted on fulfilling the electoral pledge were senior members of the LDP Research Commission on the Tax System. In September 2013, such faction-boss-level backbenchers as Machimura Nobutaka and Nukaga Fukushirō appealed to the members of their intra-party groups to proceed with the reform. As stressed by Commission Chair Noda Takeshi, before starting deliberations among a larger group of LDP lawmakers, it was important to establish the general direction for discussions (*Asahi Shinbun* 2013c: 4).

The appeal from faction leaders was aimed at disciplining first-term parliamentarians, who were exceptionally numerous after LDP's landslide victories in elections to both houses. Without strong *kōenkai* in their constituencies, the freshly elected lawmakers not only remained more sensitive to the voice of voters, but they also did not feel personally obliged to support the VAT hike, as they had not voted for it when the LDP was an opposition party (*Asahi Shinbun* 2013b: 7). In addition, the prime minister was advised to remain prudent on raising taxes by CCS Suga Yoshihide and Minister of State for Economic and Fiscal Policy, Amari Akira, as well as by Watanabe Tsuneo, editor-in-chief of *Yomiuri Shinbun* – an opinion-making newspaper that generally sympathized with Abe's policy agenda (Shimizu 2014: 73). The prime minister's most influential economic advisers, Professors Hamada Kōichi and Honda Etsurō, as well as BOJ Deputy Governor Iwata Kikuo, held similar opinions. They claimed that the hike could put the realization of the aims of Abenomics at risk. To mitigate the impact of tax reform on the Japanese economy, Hamada and Honda tried to persuade the prime minister to increase VAT by only 1% per year, but to no avail (Iwata 2018: 70–87).

While Abe leaned toward increasing the tax as scheduled, he took maximum advantage of the hike and traded it off to the MOF and the LDP Research Commission on the Tax System in exchange for their concession on corporate tax reduction. In September 2013, Abe ordered Commission Chair Noda Takeshi to examine measures aimed at assuaging the impact of the VAT hike on the Japanese economy. During the Commission meeting on September 9, 2013, LDP Policy Research Council Chair Takaichi Sanae and her deputy Shiozaki Yasuhisa acted as representatives of the Kantei, stressing the importance of reducing corporate tax by the end of the year (*Asahi Shinbun* 2013d: 4). On September 18, 2013, the prime minister suddenly communicated to Finance Minister Asō his intention to abolish, one year earlier than scheduled, a special corporate tax for reconstruction of the regions devastated by the Great East Japan Earthquake. Asō persuaded MOF bureaucrats to cooperate by warning them that the second stage of the VAT increase would be endangered in case of a negative impact of the first hike on the Japanese economy. Out of consideration for the finance minister, in turn, Abe agreed to insert the word "examination" into the announcement on corporate tax reduction, thus implying it was not a final decision. Without consultation with the senior members of the LDP Research Commission on the Tax System, not even with his former faction boss Machimura, Abe ordered Commission Chair Noda to start deliberations on the abolition of the reconstruction tax. While at the end of September 2013, the prime minister took part in the session of the UN General Assembly in New York, he entrusted pacification of the LDP Research Commission on the Tax System to CCS Suga Yoshihide, LDP Vice-President Kōmura Masahiko, and Prime Minister's Secretary Imai Takaya. Responding to voices of criticism from the members of the tax system parliamentary tribe, the Kantei implied that those Commission members who did not share the prime minister's policy agenda could be replaced (*Asahi Shinbun* 2013e: 1).

On October 1, 2013, Prime Minister Abe eventually confirmed that the first stage of the tax increase would proceed as scheduled. As he stressed, "There is no time to lose in securing financial resources to stabilize social security and rebuild the severe fiscal situation" (Prime Minister of Japan and His Cabinet 2013). Abe explained that the VAT hike was possible thanks to the signs of economic recovery: a more than 3% economic growth rate registered for two consecutive quarters, improvement in the ratio of job offers to job seekers, as well as increases in production, consumption, and capital investment. The prime minister reconfirmed that consumption tax revenues would be used exclusively for social security purposes. At the same time, to ease the burden on taxpayers, he promised special benefit measures, a 10,000 yen allowance to those with low incomes, as well as tax breaks for housing loans (Prime Minister of Japan and His Cabinet 2013).

In order to make the VAT hike more palatable to the public, Abe convinced Minister of Finance Asō to authorize a special supplementary budget for FY 2013, which included expenditures for public works projects, vitalization of small and medium-sized enterprises, as well as support for child-rearing and low-income earners. The bill on the stimulus package of 5.5 trillion yen was passed through the Diet in February 2014, two months before the first stage of the VAT hike (Shimizu 2014: 73–74). In December 2013, in turn, the LDP and Kōmeitō agreed to introduce a special reduced tax rate system for selected products together with increasing VAT to 10%. They intentionally did not clarify the date of the hike, which signified that the Kantei did not want to be bound by any declarations regarding the second stage of the tax increase (Okamura 2013: 2).

While the economic growth clause theoretically enabled Abe to postpone the first stage of the VAT hike, the political cost of such a decision would have been high. In the face of relatively good economic conditions, the prime minister leaned toward the stance of the MOF and the LDP Research Commission on the Tax System. Even so, Abe traded the VAT hike off to veto players for their concession on corporate tax reduction and a special supplementary budget, which indicated that he was concerned with the fact that the tax increase could negatively influence the implementation of Abenomics.

First VAT hike postponement in 2014

One year after the decision on the first stage of the VAT hike, the government was to judge whether to increase the tax to 10% in October 2015, as planned.[1] Abenomics prioritized achieving a high rate of GDP growth and overcoming deflation over balancing budget expenses, so the Kantei's policy agenda fitted the goals of METI rather than MOF. METI bureaucrats, in turn, were afraid that the Japanese economy had started stagnating after the first stage of the VAT hike. On the other hand, the CEFP leaned toward proceeding with the tax reform as scheduled. At the first meeting of the CEFP Policy Commentators Committee (Seisaku Komentēta Iinkai), composed of 61 businesspeople, in mid-September 2014, most members agreed that economic trends were positive and that confusion caused by postponement of the VAT increase would have a detrimental effect on the Japanese economy (*Asahi Shinbun* 2014a: 7).

LDP backbenchers remained divided over the VAT hike. Young parliamentarians continued to voice their concerns over the negative impact of tax increase on their electoral performance. In October 2014, 42 lawmakers of the ruling party belonging to the Association for the Success of Abenomics (Abenomikkusu o Seikō Saseru Kai) petitioned the prime minister to postpone the hike. The group was led by Yamamoto Kōzō, the same politician who had cooperated with Abe in the Association Seeking Recovery Funds Without Tax Increase. They invited to the meeting Prime Minister's Adviser, Honda Etsurō, who warned against detrimental effects of tax increase on Japanese economy. At the same time, supporters of the reform, gathered around such high-profile politicians from the LDP Research Commission on the Tax System as Noda Takeshi, Nukaga Fukushirō, and Kōmura Masahiko, organized a research meeting attended by more than 70 lawmakers. They argued that the three-party agreement from 2012 allowed tax increase postponement only in case of a crisis similar to the one started by the bankruptcy of Lehman Brothers in 2008 (Ono & Kujiraoka 2014: 2).

According to Yamaguchi Noriyuki (2017: 139–146), a high-profile TBS journalist who remained in close contact with Abe, the prime minister secretly started planning VAT hike delay in September 2014, when GDP growth data for April–June 2014 turned out to be far below expectations. In mid-October 2014, CCS Suga ordered the MOF to prepare a simulation of the budget for FY 2015, which did not take into account revenues from the increased tax. From that moment onward, MOF bureaucrats mobilized all their forces to dissuade the prime minister from postponing the VAT hike. They not only provided Suga with data that clearly indicated the merits of the reform and the demerits of a potential delay in its implementation, but also used CEOs of financial groups that remained under MOF's indirect influence to exert pressure on Abe in this regard. Yamaguchi (2017: 146–151) suspects that BOJ Governor Kuroda Haruhiko's surprising decision from October 31, 2014, to accelerate monetary easing was also related to the MOF's strategy. After all, Kuroda originated from that ministry and represented its interests. As such, the announcement of an intention to increase purchases of Japanese government bonds from an annual pace of 30 trillion yen to 80 trillion yen, to buy longer-dated debt, and to triple the purchases of real-estate investment trusts as well as exchange-traded funds, could have been aimed at improving the economic situation in Japan in the short term to the level that would make it more difficult for the prime minister to resort to the economic growth clause from the 2012 agreement.

Despite these efforts, the MOF could not change Japan's economic performance in past months. In November 2014, it became evident that Japan's GDP had contracted for the second quarter in a row. It was not insignificant that Abe eventually set his mind on a VAT hike postponement during the Asia-Pacific Economic Cooperation (APEC) summit in Beijing on November

10–11, 2014. As MOF bureaucrats had limited access to the prime minister abroad, in no way could they affect his final decision (Mikuriya 2015: 25–26). Immediately from Beijing, Abe went to the Japan–ASEAN Summit Meeting in Naypyidaw, Myanmar. Prime Minister's Executive Secretary Imai, who accompanied Abe, suddenly returned to Japan to communicate the prime minister's intention to MOF Budget Bureau Director-General Tanaka Kazuho. Tanaka reluctantly admitted the possibility of postponing the VAT hike on the condition of abolishing the economic growth clause. Imai transmitted the MOF's stance to Abe after rejoining him at the G20 summit in Brisbane (Mori 2019: 35–36).

Immediately after returning to Tokyo, Abe started consultations on the VAT hike postponement with influential LDP politicians. At the same time, he communicated his intentions to leaders of Kōmeitō – not only as a coalition partner, but also as one of the sides of the three-party agreement from 2012. MOF bureaucrats started even more vigorously lobbying against the VAT hike delay, but it was too late to change the prime minister's mind (Makihara 2016: 190–191). To ensure unanimity among cabinet members and LDP executives, before postponing the VAT hike, Abe had to first persuade two prominent members of the financial *zoku* – LDP Secretary-General Tanigaki Sadakazu (who, as the LDP president in 2012, had been one of the main authors of the agreement on the VAT hike bill), as well as, most importantly, Vice-Premier and Minister of Finance Asō Tarō. Tanigaki had publicly expressed his opinion that such a decision would cause the risk of losing the ability to cover the costs of the social security system. Asō, in turn, tried to convince Abe not to cite the consumption tax increase postponement as the direct reason for Diet dissolution. As reported by Yamaguchi (2017: 139–174), during the G20 summit in Brisbane on November 16, 2014, the minister of finance cited several arguments why Abe should not exclude the possibility of implementing the second stage of the VAT hike as scheduled. According to Asō, economic indicators for October would be much better than for previous months, Japanese companies had already taken into account the tax increase in their business plans, a VAT hike postponement could prompt some high-ranking MOF bureaucrats to resign from office, it was difficult to predict global economic conditions in the long term, and the VAT hike was consistent with the expectations of International Monetary Fund (IMF) Managing Director Christine Lagarde. All these arguments, including the last one, were in line with the MOF's stance. After all, thanks to the fact that numerous Japanese MOF bureaucrats traditionally assumed executive positions in the IMF, they were known for their ability to influence the policies of that institution.

On the other hand, the VAT hike postponement was promoted by CCS Suga Yoshihide. It is probable that Suga remembered the political cost of the consumption tax increase to 5%, which was borne by his political patron, CCS Kajiyama Seiroku, in 1997 (Iwasaki 2019: 32–33). In fact, Suga not only wanted to postpone the VAT hike, but also probably insisted that the government should not specify the date of the second stage of the tax increase, which met with decisive protests from the MOF (Iwasaki 2019: 117). Thanks to the empowered Kantei and the Cabinet Secretariat, Abe could ensure the unanimity of cabinet members and effectively play METI off against MOF. When the prime minister decided to delay the hike by one and a half years, none of the heavyweight LDP politicians overtly objected.

Under these circumstances, on November 18, 2014, Abe announced his intention to postpone the second stage of the consumption tax increase until April 2017. As he argued:

> A rise in the consumption tax rate is necessary in order for Japan to pass down to the next generation a social security system that is one of the best in the world and in order to enhance our support for child-rearing. (…) However, if raising the consumption tax causes the economy to falter, it will impart a major strain upon people's daily lives. And if, as a result, tax revenues do not increase despite raising the tax rate, then no benefits will derive from it.
> (Prime Minister of Japan and His Cabinet 2014)

At the same time, Abe ruled out the possibility of referring to the economic growth clause in the future. He declared "unambiguously" that there would "be no further postponements" and that the VAT hike in April 2017 would "be carried out without fail, without any provisos for decisions based on the economic climate" (Prime Minister of Japan and His Cabinet 2014).

What was less understandable to the public than the delay of the tax reform was the fact that, at the same time, Abe called an early election. After all, thanks to the economic growth clause, the prime minister could make such a decision at his discretion. As such, contrary to Koizumi, who dissolved the House of Representatives in 2005 to force passage of the Japan Post privatization bill, Abe was not compelled to this drastic move by opposition from any rebellious backbenchers. The prime minister stated that as "the tax system is very closely connected with people's daily lives," he needed "to listen to the people's voice" (Prime Minister of Japan and His Cabinet 2014). He further explained: "This is the 'Abenomics' dissolution (…) I'd like to ask the public whether my economics policies are wrong or right, or if there is any other choice" (Aoki 2014). In its electoral manifesto, the LDP stressed that the VAT hike delay was necessary not to waste the first signs of the economic recovery achieved by the new government (Liberal Democratic Party 2014: 6).

The prime minister selected for the main electoral campaign topic a decision, over which the public and political parties were not overly polarized. After all, the consumption tax increase had been unpopular ever since the introduction of VAT in 1988. According to an opinion poll conducted by *Asahi Shinbun* (2014b: 4), at the end of October 2014, 67% of respondents opposed the increase in consumption tax, while only 24%

194 *Postponement of the VAT hike*

supported the hike. Moreover, 71% claimed that it was not a good time to conduct the tax reform, and only 16% thought otherwise. Even more respondents, 84%, were strongly (27%) or moderately (57%) concerned that the VAT increase would have a detrimental impact on the economic situation. At the same time, 79% supported (and 14% did not) the introduction of a special reduced tax rate system for selected products. Still, according to an *Asahi Shinbun* (2014c: 4) opinion poll conducted immediately after the dissolution of the lower house, the respondents were not enthusiastic about the prime minister's decision. After postponement, the percentage of opponents of the VAT hike dropped to 49% (and of supporters rose to 39%), but 62% of respondents disagreed (and 18% agreed) on the need to call an early election. 65% were not satisfied (and 25% were satisfied) with the prime minister's explanation that the reason for the election was to gain the people's understanding on the tax increase delay. As the VAT hike remained unpopular, it was difficult for the opposition parties to criticize Abe for its postponement. The opposition focused on analyzing the seriousness of Japan's economic situation, without proposing alternatives to Abenomics (Noble 2016: 159–160). Pekkanen, Reed, and Scheiner (2016: 265–278) stressed that the prime minister employed a "bait-and-switch" strategy and framed election as a referendum on a much more convenient topic for him than constitutional revision or other controversial policies he pursued.

In addition, the prime minister took advantage of the snap election to renew the mandate for his government after its first scandals and failures. In October 2014, two woman cabinet members –Minister of Economy, Trade and Industry Obuchi Yūko and Justice Minister Matsushima Midori – stepped down from office due to accusations over misuse of political funds and violation of election campaign law, respectively (Aoki & Yoshida 2014). Moreover, similar problems were found with the electoral financing of Obuchi's successor, Miyazawa Yōichi, who, however, avoided removal from office.[2] Diet dissolution could also have been aimed at camouflaging the expected defeat of LDP's candidate in the Okinawa gubernatorial election. The incumbent, Nakaima Hirokazu, supported by the ruling party, was losing popularity after he agreed to Abe's plan of relocation of US Marine Corps Air Station Futenma to the coast of Henoko. In an election held on December 9, 2014, only five days before the national vote, he did indeed lose to Naha Mayor Onaga Takeshi, who opposed the construction of the Futenma replacement facility in the Okinawa Prefecture. Despite a minor decrease in government popularity because of these failures, Abe knew that the LDP could not lose a parliamentary election, due to the lack of a unified "second pole" on the Japanese political scene.

The parliamentary election of December 14, 2014 ended in a landslide victory for the LDP. As a result, Abe's leadership was enhanced even further, which enabled him to assuage any voices of discontent in the ruling party. The convocation of new House of Representatives became an opportunity for the prime minister to replace Speaker Ibuki Bunmei, who had disagreed with Abe over the need for dissolving the lower house, with Abe's former factional boss, Machimura Nobutaka (Makihara 2016: 201–208). Just like Koizumi after the postal election in 2005, Abe thus managed to solidify his support base in the LDP. The new coalition agreement with Kōmeitō clearly stated that VAT would be increased to 10% in April 2017, while promising the introduction of a reduced tax rate system for selected products (Kōmeitō 2014). This modification answered Kōmeitō's concerns about the impact of a VAT hike on low-income taxpayers.

Thanks to the renewal of his mandate, the prime minister felt strong enough to challenge a powerful veto player – the LDP Research Commission on the Tax System. This influential decision-making body that hosted a separate *zoku* generally represented the same stance on taxes as the MOF. It was chaired by a veteran LDP politician, Noda Takeshi, who boasted as many as 15 terms as a member of the House of Representatives. Theoretically, nothing changed in the official decision-making process – the governmental Research Commission on the Tax System simply authorized the yearly tax guidelines prepared by its party counterpart. However, despite its reputation as a largely independent organ, under the second Abe administration, the party Commission's decisions in reality closely followed the Kantei's instructions. The tax reform outline for FY 2015, prepared by the Commission, reflected Abe's intention to cut the corporate tax rate in order to make the second stage of the VAT hike more acceptable to Japanese business circles. Nevertheless, after the 2014 election, the Kantei felt legitimized to impose its own version of the tax reform outline that emphasized the need for attaining a high rate of economic growth, and thus left the corporate tax rate reduction while removing reference to the VAT hike (George Mulgan 2018: 69–70).

The members of the LDP Research Commission on the Tax System felt powerless in the face of the Kantei's institutional strength. When Abe called the early election, Noda criticized this move as a decision without any reasonable cause. The Kantei reciprocated by hinting that Noda could be not endorsed as an official LDP candidate, which sufficed to bring him back into line. The dissolution of the House of Representatives at the end of the year effectively disturbed the finalization of the tax system framework for FY 2015 by the Commission. After the electoral victory, Noda asked Abe for permission to extend discussions on the tax outline until January 2015, but the prime minister refused. As a result, negotiations between the LDP and the government took only five days. Under time pressure, the Commission accepted not only the Kantei's plan of corporate tax reduction by 2.51 percentage points in 2015 and 0.78 percentage point in 2016, but also the introduction of gift tax exemptions for marriage or child rearing, and expansion of the Nippon Individual Savings Account system aimed at encouraging people to save money for retirement with tax-exempt benefits (Ono & Ikejiri 2014: 2).

The decision on the VAT hike postponement reflected not only the deteriorating economic conditions in Japan, but also the institutional prowess of the Kantei. Abe felt strong enough to ignore the opinion of the MOF and the LDP Research Commission on the Tax System, and delay the tax increase. At the same time, he strategically used his decision as a convenient electoral topic, thus further enhancing his position against veto players.

Second VAT hike postponement in 2016

Despite the abolition of the economic growth clause, Abe repeated his decision to postpone the VAT hike in 2016. Once more, he strategically used the discourse on tax postponement to bolster the LDP's electoral chances and challenge the MOF at the same time.

At the end of 2015, the Kantei won another battle with the MOF and the LDP Research Commission on the Tax System. In order to weaken popular resentment against the VAT hike and please coalition partner Kōmeitō, Abe and Suga planned exemptions to the consumption tax increase for food products. The MOF, in turn, in September 2015 proposed the introduction of a refund system instead. The system would be highly inconvenient for consumers who would have to apply for the reimbursement of 2% of the value of selected products. It was prepared secretly by Research Commission on the Tax System Chairperson Noda Takeshi, Kōmeitō Vice-President Kitagawa Kazuo, and MOF Tax Bureau Director-General Satō Shun'ichi (*Asahi Shinbun* 2015: 3). Kōmeitō authorities seemed willing to compromise, but they encountered strong opposition from Sōka Gakkai. As a result, Kōmeitō leader Yamaguchi Natsuo hardened his stance. Without excluding the possibility of leaving the coalition, he decisively requested the introduction of a special reduced tax rate system together with the VAT hike. As Abe was determined to gain Sōka Gakkai's assistance in the upcoming Ginowan City mayoral election in Okinawa, he ceded to Kōmeitō's demands (Nakano 2016: 58).

In the MOF, even Administrative Vice-Minister Tanaka Kazuho, who owed his post to connections with Abe, opposed the Kantei's plans (Kidera 2017: 168–169). LDP Research Commission on the Tax System Chairperson, Noda Takeshi, who stressed the need for maintaining fiscal discipline, refused to comply with the Kantei's and Kōmeitō's demands. This time, in October 2015, Abe simply removed Noda from office and replaced him with former Minister of Economy, Trade and Industry, Miyazawa Yōichi. Although Miyazawa, just like Noda, was a member of the tax system *zoku*, he was much less experienced, and thus more vulnerable to pressure from the Kantei (Asakura 2016: 132–133). Instructed by the prime minister, Miyazawa agreed to introduce the special reduced tax rate system together with the VAT hike. He also excluded Noda, who remained in the LDP Research Commission on the Tax System as highest adviser, from the deliberations between the coalition partners on the details of the new system. The main role in the talks was played by the secretaries-general of both parties, Tanigaki Sadakazu and Inoue Yoshihisa. While the LDP tax system tribe tried to limit the reduced tax rate to fresh products, the Kantei decided to cede to Kōmeitō's demands and apply the exemption also to processed food. As a result, the reduced tax rate system was applied to all food products except for alcohol and dishes served in restaurants. In addition, the ruling coalition agreed to maintain the 8% rate for newspapers issued more than twice per week under subscription contracts. This decision was important for Kōmeitō, as Sōka Gakkai largely depended on the revenues from distribution of the newspaper *Seikyō Shinbun* among its members. In mid-December 2015, the reduced tax rate system was acknowledged by the LDP Research Commission on the Tax System within the tax system framework for FY 2016. It seemed that Abe had successfully pacified the main center of resistance in the ruling party against his plans for tax reform. Unlike Noda, Miyazawa not only did not oppose the reduced tax rate system, but he was also willing to extend it to the food served in restaurants. Eventually, it was Finance Minister Asō, not LDP backbenchers, who limited the extent of concessions to Kōmeitō by excluding dishes served in restaurants from the system (Sasagawa 2015: 4). Still, the Kantei was so eager to please Kōmeitō before the July 2016 upper house election that it agreed to introduce the reduced tax rate system without clearly indicating how it would be financed. In March 2016, the bill on that matter passed through both houses (Iwasaki 2019: 213–236).

Meanwhile, the prime minister and his closest entourage once more started seriously envisaging the possibility of postponing the VAT hike. Until the beginning of 2016, Abe had repeatedly stated that a second postponement would be theoretically possible only in case of an emergency situation comparable to the bankruptcy of Lehman Brothers in 2008 or Great East Japan Earthquake in 2011. However, during deliberations of the House of Representatives Budget Committee on February 19, 2016, he added a "large-scale contraction of the world economy" to these conditions (Asakura 2016: 24–25). One week later, CCS Suga explained during a press conference that "It's impossible to raise the consumption tax if such a hike is unlikely to lead to an increase in tax revenue" (*Mainichi Japan* 2016). On February 29, 2016, Abe further clarified that it would be impossible to raise the tax if the deflationary gap (a situation where demand is lower than supply), which was observed after the first stage of the VAT hike in April 2014, continued. At the same time, he denied that his intention was to politically exploit another freezing of the tax increase in order to call double elections in July 2016 (*Mainichi Japan* 2016).

It became even more evident that the Kantei was leaning toward another VAT hike postponement when on March 16, 2016, the government held the first Analysis Meeting on International Finance and Economy (Kokusai Kin'yū Keizai Bunseki Kaigō). The new forum became a place for exchange of opinions between economic experts and cabinet members. The first of the invited guests, Nobel Prize laureate, Columbia University Professor, Joseph Stiglitz, stressed that the economic situation, at that time, did not favor increasing VAT, as it would not contribute to increased demand. At a press conference after the meeting, Abe admitted that domestic consumption suffered after the previous VAT hike and that prospects for the world economy were not optimistic (Prime Minister of Japan and His Cabinet 2016a). Also, experts from Abe's closest entourage, such as Special Advisers to the Cabinet Honda Etsurō and Hamada Kōichi, suggested suspending the second stage of the tax increase. Honda even started mentioning that the 5% VAT rate should be restored (Asakura 2016: 111–112). The Kantei once more relied on support from junior lawmakers. During the meeting of the Association for the Success of Abenomics at the beginning of April 2016, most members claimed that the prospects for economic stagnation were as real as before the Lehman Brothers shock, and that the prime minister should postpone the hike, or even decrease the consumption tax (Iwasaki 2019: 256).

In mid-April 2016, a series of earthquakes caused considerable destruction in the Kumamoto Prefecture. About 50 people were killed and thousands were evacuated. The disaster caused rumors that the Kantei could cite the emergency situation as a reason to postpone the VAT hike. LDP Research Commission on the Tax System Chair Miyazawa opposed such a scenario by stressing that the social and economic impact of the Kumamoto Earthquake was far weaker than the trauma after the Great East Japan Earthquake (*Asahi Shinbun* 2016a: 4). The stance of some of the inner members of the Commission was only a little more nuanced. For example, LDP Vice-President Kōmura agreed that the economic slowdown was incomparable with the Lehman Brothers shock and that the Kumamoto disaster was smaller in scale than the earthquake from 2011, but he did not exclude the possibility that the combined effect of the two factors created new conditions for the Japanese economy (*Asahi Shinbun* 2016b: 4).

The second VAT hike postponement encountered opposition from Abe's closest associates. Just as in 2014, LDP Secretary-General Tanigaki insisted that the tax increase should be implemented as scheduled. He argued that as the economic growth clause had been abolished, any decision on delaying the VAT hike had to be authorized by the Diet (Iwasaki 2019: 256). Another heavyweight politician, Vice-Premier Asō, claimed that in order to delay the hike, it was necessary to dissolve the House of Representatives and gain popular approval in an election. LDP Policy Research Council Chair Inada Tomomi, who, at the same time, chaired the LDP Special Committee for Financial Reconstruction, in turn, argued that the tax increase was necessary to balance the budget. When Abe started planning another postponement, she tried to convince him that he should at least consider dividing the hike into two stages and increase VAT by 1% per year (Abiru 2016: 236–238).

What prompted Abe to delay the tax increase was data on domestic consumption for the first quarter of the year, announced in mid-May 2016, which turned out to be below expectations. On May 30, the prime minister conveyed his decision to postpone the VAT hike by two and a half years to LDP Vice-President Kōmura, General Council Chair Nikai, and Policy Research Council Chair Inada. Only Inada claimed that Abe should dissolve the lower house. Having no other choice, both LDP Secretary-General Tanigaki and Kōmeitō leader Yamaguchi acknowledged the prime minister's decision. In the LDP, only General Council member Murakami Seiichirō demonstratively protested against the imposition of the VAT hike delay by the Kantei. Not to let Abe exploit the tax increase postponement in an electoral campaign, the DP prepared their own bill project on a hike delay by two years, while criticizing the government for the failure of Abenomics. Nevertheless, a no-confidence motion submitted by four opposition parties was easily voted down by the ruling coalition in the Diet (Iwasaki 2019: 260–274).

Regardless of the stance of the MOF, LDP Research Commission on the Tax System, and some of the members of his closest entourage, on June 1, 2016, Abe officially announced his decision to delay the VAT hike until October 2019. After enumerating a list of the successes of Abenomics, such as elevating the ratio of job offers to job seekers to levels unseen for 24 years, achieving a high pace of wage increases, and attaining an all-time record job placement rate for university graduates, he stressed that prospects for the global economy, especially for such developing countries as China, were still not good. In this light, Abe claimed that a consumption tax increase would overtly curb domestic demand, thus endangering the economic achievements of his government. He emphasized that the additional two and a half years before raising VAT would be used to accelerate Abenomics in order to prepare the ground for achieving a primary balance surplus in FY 2020. At the same time, he underscored that he did not consider the risks for the global economy as comparable to the situation after the bankruptcy of Lehman Brothers, or the Kumamoto Earthquake as similar in scale with the Great East Japan Earthquake. As such, Abe admitted that the decision to once more postpone the VAT hike contradicted his previous pledge that there would be no further delays. Forestalling criticism, he said that he would ask Japanese voters for judgment on that matter during the upcoming House of Councilors election (Prime Minister of Japan and His Cabinet 2016b).

In fact, Abe once again strategically used the decision to postpone the VAT hike in order to improve LDP's electoral chances. For most voters, the welcome suspension of the unpopular tax increase was more important than their indignation at the violation of the promise on that matter. According to an *Asahi Shinbun* (2016c: 4) opinion poll from May 2016, 59% of respondents thought that the VAT hike should be postponed, while 29% supported its increase as previously planned. 79% were strongly (27%) or moderately (52%) concerned that the VAT hike would negatively influence the economic situation. The poll of the same newspaper conducted immediately after the announcement of the tax increase postponement indicated that 56% of respondents positively evaluated the prime minister's decision (34% did not). Only 28% were satisfied (58% were not satisfied) with the explanation that postponement was caused by increased risk to the world economy, but 53% thought that the violation of the previous electoral promise on the VAT hike was not a big issue (37% thought it was) (*Asahi Shinbun* 2016d: 1). Abe was also confident that the LDP would perform well in the upper house election for other reasons. At the end of May 2016, Japan hosted the G7 summit in Ise-Shima. As usual, presiding over such an international event gave much publicity to the Japanese prime minister. As opposition parties declared greater coordination of candidates than three years earlier, the decision to delay the VAT hike could tip the scales in favor of the LDP. Just as expected, the election to the House of Councilors on July 10, 2016 ended in a considerable victory for the ruling parties.

In fact, Abe tried to use the G7 summit to gain international recognition regarding the VAT hike postponement. During a press conference, he emphasized that the risks for the global economy had grown within the preceding year. To support this thesis, he cited declines in stock markets that "resulted in asset losses in excess of 1500 trillion yen worldwide in less than a year," a slowdown in emerging economies, a drop in "prices of commodity including crude oil, steel, and other raw materials and agricultural products," a drop in the rate of increase of investment, "expansion of non-performing loans and other issues in China," and the fact that "the global economic growth rate last year recorded its lowest level since the financial crisis after Lehman Brothers' collapse" (Ministry of Foreign Affairs 2016). The pessimistic economic data, aimed at justifying the VAT hike postponement, was prepared by the bureaucrats under instruction from Prime Minister's Secretary Imai Takaya and METI Administrative Vice-Minister Sugawara Ikurō. Nevertheless, these arguments surprised the leaders of the G7 countries, and British Prime Minister David Cameron disagreed that the world economy was experiencing risks comparable to the Lehman shock (Kidera 2017: 170–171).

It is also probable that Abe initially planned to dissolve the lower house just as in 2014 and call a double election. The biggest obstacle was the stance of Kōmeitō. For the LDP's coalition partner, last-minute double elections would have been particularly inconvenient. Sōka Gakkai usually needed at least half a year to fully mobilize its members to seek support also among unaffiliated voters. In addition, as Kōmeitō fielded candidates only in some districts, Sōka Gakkai members from the entire country focused their activities on these constituencies. In the case of double elections, the number of districts with Kōmeitō candidates would also double, which would require Sōka Gakkai's mobilization on too many fronts. Moreover, double elections would complicate the strategy of sharing the electorate in single-seat districts and proportional representation regions between Kōmeitō and the LDP. In order to persuade the coalition partner to concede, Abe presumably telephoned Sōka Gakkai President Harada Minoru and perhaps even gained some understanding on the dissolution (Nakano 2016: 58–59). Nevertheless, a series of earthquakes in the Kumamoto Prefecture in mid-April 2016 hindered the prime minister's plans. Due to serious damage to local buildings and disaster-relief activities, it would have been difficult to organize an election in that region. As a result, Abe abandoned the idea of Diet dissolution, and the postponement of the VAT hike was used as an electoral topic during the campaign for the upper house alone.

On August 24, 2016, the government officially issued a cabinet decision on the postponement of tax increase by two and a half years, which was acknowledged by both houses of the Diet the following month (Iwasaki 2019: 280–281). In subsequent years, Abe continued to exploit the VAT hike issue in electoral campaigns. In September 2017, he cited the change in the usage of consumption tax revenue to cover the costs of free early childhood education as one argument to dissolve the lower house. The LDP–Kōmeitō coalition agreement signed after the October 2017 House of Representatives election reconfirmed the creation of a special reduced tax rate system together with the VAT hike. Moreover, both sides stated that the income from the increased tax would be devoted to welfare measures (Kōmeitō 2017). It also seems that Abe envisaged postponing the VAT hike for a third time as a pretext for dissolving the lower house in spring 2019, but he renounced that idea due to the fact that such a decision would complicate the introduction of free early childhood education, promised two years earlier (Toshikawa 2019: 240–241). Eventually, consumption tax was raised to 10% as scheduled, in October 2019.

By postponing the VAT hike in 2016, Abe emulated his successful strategy from 2014. He used economic data provided by the METI to gain an argument for delaying tax reform. At the same time, Abe channeled the electoral campaign toward a topic convenient for the ruling coalition. While some resistance against the VAT hike postponement appeared in the ruling party, the MOF and LDP Research Commission on the Tax System were too weak to block the cabinet decision.

Conclusion

The three-party agreement from 2012 had been a considerable achievement for the MOF, and the bureaucrats from this ministry were determined to guard its implementation at all costs. In order to postpone the VAT hike, Abe had to rely on a whole array of political strategies. He exploited the weakening of the tax system parliamentary tribe in the LDP and counterbalanced the influence of MOF bureaucrats with their colleagues from the METI.

The most powerful tool used by the prime minister, however, was a reference to the "will of the people." It is the lower house election in 2014 and the upper house election in 2016 that gave Abe a powerful mandate to overhaul the previous decisions on the VAT hike. In both cases, the prime minister made the consumption tax increase postponement the main electoral topic. In 2014, he also strategically took advantage of the right to dissolve the House of Representatives to improve his position in the LDP and further his policy agenda. After LDP's landslide victories, it was impossible for veto players to continue overtly opposing the VAT hike delay.

Abe fully used the institutional strength of the Kantei to either circumvent or impose his will on the LDP Research Commission on the Tax System. Surrounded by administrative staff from METI and economic advisers who appealed for striving to achieve a high rate of economic growth rather than preserving budget balance, Abe overcame the MOF's opposition against VAT hike postponements. At the same time, the Kantei played junior lawmakers from the Association for the Success of Abenomics off against senior members of the tax system *zoku*. This skillful *divide et impera* approach made the prime minister a real power broker, able to push his policies forward without heeding to voices of discontent.

Notes

1. This section is partly based on the author's previous study: Zakowski (2019: 78–91).
2. Also, Minister of Defense Eto Akinori and Minister of the Environment Mochizuki Yoshio were involved in similar scandals, but they were disclosed after the 2014 election. See (Makihara 2016: 183).

References

Abe, Shinzō (2006) *Utsukushii Kuni e* [Towards a Beautiful Country], Tokyo: Bungei Shunjū.

Abiru, Rui (2016) *Sōri no Tanjō* [Birth of Prime Minister], Tokyo: Bungei Shunjū.

Aoki, Mizuho & Yoshida, Reiji (2014) "Two of Abe's Female Ministers Resign Over Separate Scandals," *The Japan Times* (October 20). Online. Available: https://www.japantimes.co.jp/news/2014/10/20/national/politics-diplomacy/two-of-abes-female-ministers-resign-over-separate-scandals/#.Wy_CYvl4mpo (accessed June 24, 2018).

Aoki, Mizuho (2014) "Abe Dissolves Lower House for Snap Election," *The Japan Times* (November 21). Online. Available: https://www.japantimes.co.jp/news/2014/11/21/national/politics-diplomacy/lower-house-dissolved-general-election/#.Wy5kyPl4mpo (accessed June 23, 2018).

Asahi Shinbun (2013a) "Shōhi Zōzei, 59 Nin Dō Kataru. 26-31 Nichi, Seifu Chōshu. Seiken no Dokudan, Hihan Kaihi Nerau" [VAT Hike, How Will 59 Persons Narrate. Governmental Hearings on 26-31. Government's Arbitrary Decision, Aiming at Evading Criticism], August 21, morning edition, 3.

Asahi Shinbun (2013b) "Shōhi Zōzei Hantai Ron, Jimin Zeichō ga Keikai. Tōnai Teatsuku Setsumei e [Debate Against VAT Hike, the LDP Research Commission on the Tax System Alerted. Towards Comprehensive Explanation in the Party], September 5, morning edition, 7.

Asahi Shinbun (2013c) "Habatsu Ryōshū, Zōzei e Kowadaka. Jimin Zeichō Kaigō Mae ni Kugi Sasu" [Faction Bosses, Loudly on Tax Hike. Nailing Before the LDP Research Commission on the Tax System Meeting], September 7, morning edition, 4.

Asahi Shinbun (2013d) "Jimin Zeichō, Karuku Naru. Zōzei Taisaku, Shushō ga Shudō" [LDP Research Commission on the Tax System, Made Light of. Tax Hike Measures, The Prime Minister Leads], September 12, morning edition, 4.

Asahi Shinbun (2013e) "Shōhizei 10%, Abe Shushō 'Hitsuyō Aru noka'" [VAT Hike 10%, Prime Minister Abe "Is It Necessary?"], October 2, morning edition, 1.

Asahi Shinbun (2014a) "Iin no Kahansū ga Keiki Dōkō 'Kaifuku.' Seisaku Komentētā I" [Majority of Members: Economic Trend "Recovery." Policy Commentators Committee], September 12, morning edition, 7.

Asahi Shinbun (2014b) "Asahi Shinbunsha Yoron Chōsa. Shitsumon to Kaitō" [Opinion Poll by Asahi Shinbun. Questions and Answers], November 11, morning edition, 4.

Asahi Shinbun (2014c) "Abenomikusu 'Shippai' 39%, 'Seikō' wa 30%, Asahi Shinbunsha Yoron Chōsa" [Abenomics "Failure" 39%, "Success" 30%, Opinion Poll by Asahi Shinbun], November 21, morning edition, 4.

Asahi Shinbun (2015) "2% Kanpu, Chūmon Zokuzoku. 'Tema Kakaru,' 'Kosuto Gimon.' Ji-Kō Kyōgi" [2% Refund, Continuous Orders. "It Takes Time," "Cost Question." LDP–Kōmeitō Consultation], September 11, morning edition, 3.

Asahi Shinbun (2016a) "Yotei Dōri no Zōzei Motomeru. Jimin Miyazawa Zeisei Chosakaichō" [Requesting Tax Hike as Scheduled. LDP Research Commission on the Tax System Chair Miyazawa], April 22, morning edition, 4.

Asahi Shinbun (2016b) "Kōmura-shi, Shōhi Zōzei Meguri Shisa" [Mr. Kōmura, Suggestion on VAT Hike], May 7, morning edition, 4.

Asahi Shinbun (2016c) "Asahi Shinbunsha Yoron Chōsa. Shitsumon to Kaitō" [Opinion Poll by Asahi Shinbun. Questions and Answers], May 24, morning edition, 4.

Asahi Shinbun (2016d) "Zōzei Enki 'Hyōka' 56%, Shushō Setsumei ni 'Nattoku' 28%, Asahi Shinbunsha Renzoku Yoron Chōsa" [Postponement of VAT Hike "Appraisal" 56%, "Satisfaction" with the Prime Minister's Explanation 28%, Continued Opinion Poll by Asahi Shinbun], June 6, morning edition, 1.

Asakura, Hideo (2016) *Kantei Shihai* [Kantei's Supremacy], Tokyo: East Press.

George Mulgan, Aurelia (2018) *The Abe Administration and the Rise of the Prime Ministerial Executive*, London and New York: Routledge.

Iwasaki, Takehisa (2019) *Shōhizei "Zōzei" no Seiji Katei* [Political Process of VAT "Increase"], Tokyo: Chūō Keizaisha.

Iwata, Kikuo (2018) *Nichigin Nikki. Go Nenkan no Defure to no Tatakai* [BOJ Diary. Five Years of Struggle with Deflation], Tokyo: Chikuma Shobō.

Kidera, Hajime (2017) "Shōhizei Zōzei. Shakai Hoshō to no Ittai Kaikaku" [Consumption Tax Increase. Joint Reform with the Social Security], in Takenaka Harukata (ed.), *Futatsu no Seiken Kōtai. Seisaku wa kawatta no ka* [Two Alternations of Power. Has the Policy Changed?], Tokyo: Keisō Shobō, 152–179.

Kōmeitō (2014) "Jimin–Kōmei Renritsu Seiken Gōi (Zenbun)" [LDP–Kōmeitō Ruling Coalition Agreement (Full Text)] (December 16). Online. Available: https://www.komei.or.jp/news/detail/20141216_15770 (accessed July 17, 2019).

Kōmeitō (2017) "Ji–Kō ga Renritsu Seiken Gōi" [The Ruling Coalition Agreement by the LDP and Kōmeitō] (October 24). Online. Available: https://www.komei.or.jp/news/detail/20171024_26095 (accessed July 17, 2019).

Liberal Democratic Party (2012) "Nihon o Torimodosu. Jūten Seisaku 2012 Jimintō" [Taking Back Japan. Important Policy Points 2012 LDP]. Online. Available: https://jimin.jp-east-2.os.cloud.nifty.com/pdf/seisaku_ichiban24.pdf?_ga=2.60292907.765409726.1535200690-920333633.1535200690 (accessed August 25, 2018).

Liberal Democratic Party (2014) "Keiki Kaifuku, Kono Michi Shika Nai. Jūten Seisaku Shū 2014 Jimintō" [Economic Recovery, There is No Other Way. List of Important Policy Points 2014 LDP]. Online. Available: https://jimin.jp-east-2.os.cloud.nifty.com/pdf/news/policy/126585_1.pdf?_ga=2.107469956.765409726.1535200690-920333633.1535200690 (accessed August 25, 2018).

Mainichi Japan (2016) "Speculation of Further Delay in Consumption Tax Hike Spreading" (March 1). Online. Available: https://mainichi.jp/english/articles/20160301/p2a/00m/0na/006000c (accessed August 20, 2018).

Makihara, Izuru (2016) *"Abe Ikkyō" no Nazo* [The Mystery of "Abe's Unilateral Strength"], Tokyo: Asahi Shinbun Shuppan.

Mikuriya, Takashi (2015) *Abe Seiken wa Hontō ni Tsuyoi noka. Banjaku yue ni Moroi Seiken Un'ei no Shōtai* [Is Abe Government Really Strong? True Face of Political Management Weak as a Stone], Tokyo: PHP Kenkyūjo.

Ministry of Foreign Affairs (2016) "Press Conference by Prime Minister Shinzo Abe, Chair of the G7 Ise-Shima Summit" (May 27). Online. Available: https://www.mofa.go.jp/ms/is_s/page4e_000465.html (accessed August 30, 2019).

Mori, Isao (2019) *Kantei Kanryō. Abe Ikkyō o Sasaeta Sokkin Seiji no Tsumi* [The Residence's Bureaucracy. The Sin of Aides' Politics that Supported Abe's Unilateral Strength], Tokyo: Bungei Shunjū.

Nakano, Jun (2016) "'Kōmei Kirai' no Shushō ga Tsuyomeru Kōmei Izon. Kantei to Kōmeitō, Sōka Gakkai o meguru Kihon Kōzu" [Dependence on Kōmeitō Strengthened by a Prime Minister Who "Hates Kōmeitō." Basic Connections Between the Kantei, Kōmeitō and Sōka Gakkai], in Nakano Kōichi (ed.), *Tettei Kenshō. Abe Seiji* [Comprehensive Examination. Abe Politics], Tokyo: Iwanami Shoten, 48–61.

Noble, Gregory W. (2016) "Abenomics in the 2014 Election: Showing the Money (Supply) and Little Else," in Robert J. Pekkanen, Steven R. Reed & Ethan Scheiner (eds.), *Japan Decides 2014. The Japanese General Election*, Basingstoke and New York: Palgrave Macmillan, 155–169.

Okamura, Natsuki (2013) "Rinen Naki Zeisei Taikō. Ji-Kō Heikōsen, Dakyō no Ketchaku. Jimi Zeichō, Tsugitsuki Zero Kaitō" [Tax System Outline Without Philosophy. LDP-Kōmeitō Parallel Line, Compromise Settlement. LDP Research Commission on the Tax System, Continuous Zero Answer], *Asahi Shinbun*, December 13, morning edition, 2.

Ono, Kōtarō & Ikejiri, Kazuo (2014) "Zeisei, 'Abe Shirushi' Zurari." Shūinsen Taishō de Shushō Pēsu, Kyōgi Jisshitsu Itsuka" [Research Commission on the Tax System, Only Abe's Seal. Prime Minister's Pace After House of Representatives Electoral Victory, Discussions in Realty in 5 Days], *Asahi Shinbun*, December 31, morning edition, 2.

Ono, Kōtarō & Kujiraoka, Hitoshi (2014) "Shōhizei 10%, Jimin nai de Kōbō. 42 Giin, Enki Teigen e Kaigō" [VAT 10%, Struggle in the LDP. 42 Lawmakers Meet to Suggest Postponement], *Asahi Shinbun*, October 23, morning edition, 2.

Pekkanen, Robert J., Reed, Steven R. & Scheiner, Ethan (2016) "Conclusion: Japan's Bait-and-Switch Election 2014," in Robert J. Pekkanen, Steven R. Reed & Ethan Scheiner (eds.), *Japan Decides 2014. The Japanese General Election*, Basingstoke and New York: Palgrave Macmillan, 265–278.

Prime Minister of Japan and His Cabinet (2013) "Press Conference by Prime Minister Shinzo Abe" (October 1). Online. Available: https://japan.kantei.go.jp/96_abe/statement/201310/01kaiken_e.html (accessed August 12, 2019).

Prime Minister of Japan and His Cabinet (2014) "Press Conference by Prime Minister Abe" (November 18). Online. Available: https://japan.kantei.go.jp/96_abe/statement/201411/1118kaiken.html (accessed August 23, 2018).

Prime Minister of Japan and His Cabinet (2016a) "Dai Ikkai Kokusai Kin'yū Keizai Bunseki Kaigō. Giji Yōshi" [First Analysis Meeting on International Finance and Economy. Proceedings outline] (March 16). Online. Available: https://www.kantei.go.jp/jp/singi/kokusaikinyu/dai1/gijisidai.pdf (accessed August 20, 2018).

Prime Minister of Japan and His Cabinet (2016b) "Press Conference by Prime Minister Shinzo Abe" (June 1). Online. Available: https://japan.kantei.go.jp/97_abe/statement/201606/1218234_11009.html (accessed August 24, 2018).

Sasagawa, Shōhei (2015) "Tanigaki-shi, Yaomote. Keigen Zeiritsu, Kantei ni Kanpai" [Mr. Tanigaki, Standing in the Breach. Reduced Tax Rate, Completely Defeated by the Kantei], *Asahi Shinbun*, December 16, morning edition, 4.

Shimizu, Katsuhiko (2014) *Abe Seiken no Wana. Tanjunka Sareru Seiji to Media* [Trap of the Abe Government. Simplifying the Politics and Media], Tokyo: Heibonsha.

Takahashi, Yōichi (2019) *"Shōhi Zōzei" wa Uso Bakari* ["VAT Hike" is Full of Lies], Tokyo: PHP Kenyūjo.

Toshikawa, Takao (2019) *Seiji no Riarizumu. Abe Seiken no Yukue* [Political Realism. Whereabouts of the Abe Administration], Tokyo: Kadensha.

Yamaguchi, Noriyuki (2017) *Sōri* [Prime Minister], Tokyo: Gentōsha.

Zakowski, Karol (2015) *Decision-Making Reform in Japan: The DPJ's Failed Attempt at a Politician-Led Government*, London and New York: Routledge.

Zakowski, Karol (2019) "Strategic Use of Early Elections in Japan: Comparison of the Koizumi and Abe Cabinets," *Athenaeum. Polish Political Science Studies*, 63, 3: 78–91.

7 Revision of interpretation of Article 9 of the Constitution

In July 2014, Prime Minister Abe issued a cabinet decision that changed the interpretation of Article 9 of the Constitution to allow Japan's participation in collective self-defense pacts. The new interpretation was reflected in a set of security laws passed by the Diet one year later. This revolutionary change can be treated as an important step toward Abe's long-cherished dream: revision of the Constitution itself. In order to achieve this difficult task, the prime minister was ready to antagonize the opposition parties and sacrifice some of his popularity. He used his strong position in the government to ignore the unwritten rules of bureaucratic nominations and play MOFA off against the Cabinet Legislation Bureau. At the same time, Abe agreed to some concessions to Kōmeitō and the Cabinet Legislation Bureau by accepting their stance on limitations on collective self-defense.

Political stances on revision and reinterpretation of Article 9

The Japanese Constitution was promulgated on November 3, 1946, and entered into effect on May 3, 1947. The American occupation authorities imposed on Japan Article 9 that stipulates as follows:

> Par. 1. Aspiring sincerely to an international peace based on justice and order, the Japanese people forever renounce war as a sovereign right of the nation and the threat or use of force as means of settling international disputes.
> Par. 2. In order to accomplish the aim of the preceding paragraph, land, sea, and air forces, as well as other war potential, will never be maintained. The right of belligerency of the state will not be recognized (Prime Minister of Japan and His Cabinet 1946).

If read literally, Article 9 prohibits Japan from possessing any military potential either for offensive or defensive purposes. However, after the outbreak of the Korean War in 1950, the US started putting pressure on Japan to assume more responsibility for its own security, and thus relieve part of the American forces which were needed on the Korean Peninsula. The Yoshida government agreed to establish the National Police Reserve (Keisatsu Yobitai) in 1950, the Coastal Safety Force (Kaijō Keibitai) in 1952, and the SDF (Jieitai) together with the Japan Defense Agency (Bōeichō) in 1954. At the same time, a new interpretation of the Constitution was coined that allowed Japan to defend itself in case of an armed attack on its territory, but prohibited participation in collective self-defense pacts. This interpretation was reconfirmed by the government's views in subsequent decades.[1] The SDF were not treated as a regular army and could not possess exclusively offensive weaponry, such as large aircraft carriers. As a result, realization of the 1960 US–Japan security treaty was subject to Japan's constitutional constraints. While Washington promised to protect Japan in case of an invasion of Japanese territory, Tokyo could reciprocate only by providing land for US military bases and sharing the costs of their maintenance.

From the beginning of its existence, the LDP emphasized the need to amend Article 9 in order to make the US–Japan alliance more equal. The LDP political platform from 1955 stressed the necessity of constitutional revision. Nevertheless, due to the fact that the revision required two-thirds of votes in both houses of the Diet and authorization in a national referendum, this task was never realized. During the Cold War, the JSP and other left-wing parties, which decisively opposed any changes to the Constitution, possessed enough parliamentary seats to block such attempts. In fact, the pacifist Constitution was convenient also to a large number of LDP politicians, especially those originating from the Yoshida faction, as it enabled Japan to focus on economic development instead of remilitarization.

The situation changed after the end of the Cold War. Not only did conservative politicians start to more boldly demand Japan turn into a "normal country" with a regular army, but also the Socialists weakened their resistance against such a move. Though the JSP still opposed remilitarization, when it formed the Murayama cabinet together with the LDP in 1994, it acknowledged the constitutionality of the SDF. Most Socialists participated in the formation of the DPJ in 1996. As this, the largest, opposition party was composed of both conservative and left-wing politicians, it was internally divided over the plans for constitutional revision. After the split of the DPJ in 2017, the CDPJ joined the SDP and the JCP in voicing strong opposition against the change of Article 9. Meanwhile, the LDP issued two drafts of a new Constitution in 2005 and 2012. The former version proposed establishing a Self-Defense Army (Jieigun) subordinate to the prime minister. The latter version went further by stipulating the creation of a National Defense Military (Kokubōgun). Moreover, the 2012 draft made renunciation of war from the first paragraph less categorical and added a new paragraph that obliged the state to defend its sovereignty and independence (Stockwin & Ampiah 2017: 127–128).

Abe Shinzō had been an eager supporter of Japan's participation in collective self-defense pacts and revision of the pacifist Constitution long before returning to the post of prime minister in December 2012. He stressed that overfocusing on economic development and neglecting revision of the Constitution in the post-war period deprived Japan of its spirit. As a counter-example, he pointed to West Germany which quickly revised the constitution imposed by the occupying powers and reestablished a regular army. Abe inherited his political *credo* from his grandfather, Prime Minister Kishi Nobusuke. In the bestseller *Towards a Beautiful Country*, Abe (2006: 23–24, 125–134) expressed his respect for Kishi, who, thanks to the revision of the security treaty in 1960, changed Japan's position in the alliance with the US from the one of "vassalage" to partnership. As stressed by Abe, however, the unilateral dumping of responsibility for protecting Japan on US forces still constrained both allies in building a bilateral relationship based on mutual trust. He noted that Article 51 of the UN Charter clearly treated both individual and collective self-defense as an inherent right of all independent states. According to Abe, due to the fact that the Japanese Constitution was promulgated after the Charter, Japan, in a natural way, was entitled to participate in collective self-defense pacts. He claimed that the official interpretation of Article 9, based on an assumption that Japan possessed the right of self-defense, but could not exercise it, was unprecedented in the international arena and should be overhauled. Not surprisingly, for many years, Abe was an active member of the cross-party Diet Members' Alliance for Promoting the Assessment of the Constitution (Kenpō Chōsa Suishin Giin Renmei) (Hughes 2015: 13).

In order to change the *status quo*, the prime minister had to cope with resistance by two kinds of veto players: influential LDP backbenchers who called for prudence in planning a revision of the Constitution, and bureaucrats from the Cabinet Legislation Bureau (Naikaku Hōsei Kyoku) who were *de facto* in charge of interpreting the Constitution. In addition, he had to persuade the LDP's coalition partner, Kōmeitō, to accept his stance. On the other hand, Abe's plans were in line with the policy of MOFA.

The opponents of constitutional revision in the LDP were gathered mainly in Kōchikai, the faction that felt the greatest attachment to the Yoshida doctrine (postponement of remilitarization to focus on economic development). For example, Miyazawa (1995: 58–59), prime minister from 1991 to 1993, warned that it was easy to exceed the limits of necessary self-defense. Kōno (2015: 184–187), LDP leader in 1993–1995 who originated from the former Miyazawa faction, stressed that the argument that legalization of collective self-defense would contribute to amelioration of relations with the US was misleading, as the Obama administration was more concerned with Abe's historical revisionism than the constraints imposed by the Japanese Constitution. Nevertheless, the liberal camp in the LDP gradually lost in importance. The main senior LDP politicians of moderate orientation, such as Kōno Yōhei, former Chief Cabinet Secretary (CCS) Katō Kōichi, and former LDP Secretary-General Koga Makoto, had already retired by the time Abe returned as prime minister. Lawmakers of the younger generation, in turn, felt less attachment to the pacifist Constitution.

It was more difficult to overcome the opposition of another veto player, the Cabinet Legislation Bureau. As the Supreme Court used to decline direct judgment in cases of highly political decisions of the government, it was the Cabinet Legislation Bureau that enjoyed considerable autonomy in stating whether bill proposals or cabinet decisions conformed with the Constitution or not. The status of this advisory organ was symbolized by the fact that its director-general attended cabinet meetings, though he/she did not have the right to vote. The officials of the Cabinet Legislation Bureau were tested legal specialists with at least 15 years of experience, dispatched by various ministries. The power of the organ derived from the fact that it issued "unified government interpretations" (*tōitsu kenkai*) that became the foundation of Japan's legal order (Samuels 2004). As such interpretations were usually formulated to answer parliamentarian interpellations, they also established a common understanding of law by the ruling coalition and the opposition parties (Makihara 2018: 122–123).

Once the official interpretation of Article 9 had been formulated in the 1950s, the bureaucrats from the Cabinet Legislation Bureau started consistently claiming that the exercise of the right to collective self-defense would violate the Constitution. The Cabinet Legislation Bureau's role attracted public attention immediately after the end of the Cold War. Despite pressure from the US, LDP politicians such as Secretary-General Ozawa Ichirō, and pro-American MOFA bureaucrats, Prime Minister Kaifu Toshiki was unable to actively assist the allied powers in Operation Desert Storm that liberated Kuwait from Iraqi occupation in 1991. It was due to the clear stance of the Cabinet Legislation Bureau director-general who claimed that sending the SDF abroad, even under the aegis of the UN and only in order to evacuate refugees or conduct minesweeping activities, would violate the Constitution (Samuels 2004).

Pursuing a pacifist policy, Kōmeitō also opposed excessive revision of Article 9 of the Constitution. It stressed that the Constitution should mainly limit the power of the state, not impose excessive constraints on the rights of the people. As such, instead of changing the text of the Constitution, Kōmeitō (2013) proposed adding to the Constitution new passages in order to better reflect the needs of new times. According to this approach, called *kaken* (from *kuwaeru* – "add," and *kenpō* – "constitution"), new rights related to protection of the natural environment, privacy, or regional authorities, should be taken into account during the revision process. As for Article 9, Kōmeitō supported maintenance of the renunciation of war, while acknowledging the necessity to hold a discussion on adding new regulations concerning the existence of the SDF and its contribution to international security.

On the other hand, at least since the Operation Desert Storm shock, MOFA bureaucrats were eager to allow collective self-defense in order to strengthen Japan's position in the UN and in alliance with the US. Instead of dispatching the military, Japan provided 13 billion USD to the coalition forces that liberated Kuwait in 1991, but this financial contribution was not sufficiently appreciated on the international scene. The shock caused by the lack of listing Japan in a thank-you letter published by Kuwait in mainstream Western newspapers facilitated the passage of a revolutionary bill that legalized Japan's participation in UN peacekeeping operations in 1992. Nevertheless, MOFA insisted that the interpretation of the Constitution should be modified even further to enable participation in collective self-defense pacts. In particular, the MOFA Treaties Bureau (Jōyaku Kyoku) bureaucrats insisted that international law, such as the UN Charter, should be treated as superior to domestic law (Asahi Shinbun Seijibu Shuzai Han 2015: 46–49).

When Japan provided rear support to the US Navy in the Indian Ocean during operations in Afghanistan in 2001 and dispatched the SDF to Iraq in 2004, the Koizumi administration skillfully avoided antagonizing the Cabinet Legislation Bureau. The interpretation of the Constitution was strained to its limits. Koizumi bypassed the prohibition of collective security by announcing an unqualified solidarity accompanied by "cooperative and supportive activities" with their US ally. As the prime minister did not openly challenge the authority of the Cabinet Legislation Bureau, the director-general of this body turned a blind eye to the two controversial decisions (Samuels 2004). From the very beginning of the Koizumi administration in April 2001, Abe together with an influential diplomat, former Ambassador to Thailand, Okazaki Hisahiko, kept trying to persuade the prime minister of the necessity of legalizing collective self-defense, but to no avail (Abiru 2016: 41–42).

Abe intended to legalize participation in collective self-defense pacts under his first administration. Knowing that the Cabinet Legislation Bureau could become an obstacle, in September 2006, he planned to make a political appointment of the head of that organ, but Director-General Sakata Masahiro persuaded the prime minister to respect the traditional career patterns in the Bureau (Makihara 2017: 254). As expected, Abe's intention to change the interpretation of Article 9 encountered strong resistance from the new Cabinet Legislation Bureau Director-General, Miyazaki Reiichi. When Miyazaki threatened he would resign if the prime minister proceeded with his plans, Administrative Deputy CCS Matoba Junzō advised Abe against rushing the controversial decision (Mizuno 2017: 137).

Nevertheless, the prime minister created the Advisory Panel on Reconstruction of the Legal Basis for Security (Anzen Hoshō no Hōteki Kiban no Saikōchiku ni kan suru Kondankai) that examined the possibility of changing the interpretation of Article 9. The Panel issued a report in June 2008, after Abe's resignation as the prime minister. The document indicated four situations which explained the necessity to allow collective self-defense: (1) protection of US naval vessels on the high seas, (2) interception of ballistic missiles aimed at US territory, (3) use of weapons by the SDF participating in international peacekeeping operations, and (4) logistics support for the operations of other countries that take part in international activities together with the SDF. The panel concluded that Article 9 should be reinterpreted without the need to revise the Constitution "in order to make it compatible with today's security environment and the common sense shared within the international community" (The Advisory Panel on Reconstruction of the Legal Basis for Security 2008: 17). At the same time, it recommended restrictions on Japan's activities within the four cases: stipulation of the scope and procedures by relevant laws, Diet approval of each overseas dispatch of the SDF, and establishment of basic security policies regarding participation in peacekeeping operations and cooperation with the US (The Advisory Panel on Reconstruction of the Legal Basis for Security 2008). Prime Minister Fukuda Yasuo, under whose administration the report was issued, was not interested in its implementation, and thus the task of legalization of collective self-defense disappeared from the policy agenda until the formation of the second Abe cabinet.

Pacification of the Cabinet Legislation Bureau

During his first term in office in 2006–2007, Abe managed to pass a bill that clarified the procedures for holding referenda on constitutional revision, upgraded the Japan Defense Agency to the MOD, and started research on the legalization of collective self-defense. Nevertheless, Abe's hastiness in implementing right-wing policies exposed him to criticism from the opposition parties, which contributed to LDP's defeat in the House of Councilors election in July 2007 and Abe's resignation two months later. The initial failure explains why, once Abe returned to the office, he did not immediately announce his intention to completely overhaul the Constitution. Instead, in January 2013, Abe proposed only a revision of Article 96 that stipulated the procedures for constitutional revision. The prime minister's plan was to lower the threshold in both houses of parliament from two thirds to an ordinary majority, while maintaining the requirement of holding a referendum. Nevertheless, this idea encountered strong opposition from public opinion and Kōmeitō, and was abandoned in May 2013 (Shiota 2016: 122–131).

Instead, the prime minister started preparing the ground for changing the interpretation of the Constitution, not the Constitution itself. Abe's closest entourage consulted Cabinet Legislation Bureau Director-General, Yamamoto Tsuneyuki, on the possibility of legalizing collective self-defense immediately after LDP's return to power in December 2012. Yamamoto reconfirmed that such an important policy change was not allowed without revision of the Constitution. On the other hand, he showed some flexibility by stressing that among the four situations indicated in the 2008 report of the Advisory Panel on Reconstruction of the Legal Basis for Security, only the interception of ballistic missiles aimed at US territory could not be handled under the framework of individual self-defense. Such an answer, however, did not satisfy the prime minister (Asahi Shinbun Seijibu Shuzai Han 2015: 39–41). Yamamoto defended the hitherto agreed interpretation of Article 9 during deliberations on revision of the SDF Law that allowed the SDF to evacuate Japanese citizens from conflict areas, submitted to the Diet in April 2013. As a result, the SDF was permitted to use weapons during such operations only in self-defense or to defend the evacuees (Mizuno 2017: 152–153).

Until the House of Councilors election in July 2013, Abe avoided touching upon overly controversial matters, such as constitutional revision, and instead focused on promoting Abenomics. The LDP electoral manifesto did not mention collective self-defense, but it promised the revision of the Japan–US security guidelines and the SDF Law, as well as drafting a Basic Law on Security aimed at protecting peace in Japan and stability in the region (Liberal Democratic Party 2013: 27). At the same time, behind the scenes, the Kantei prepared a plan for pacifying the Cabinet Legislation Bureau by the use of MOFA bureaucrats. It was a tradition that the director-general of the Bureau originated from one of the ministries related to internal affairs: Justice, Finance, International Trade and Industry, or Local Affairs, but Abe intended to ignore this unwritten rule. He managed to dispose of Yamamoto by offering him the prestigious post of justice of the Supreme Court. At the beginning of August 2013, only a few days after the ruling coalition regained a majority of seats in the upper house, the prime minister announced his decision to replace Yamamoto with former MOFA bureaucrat, Ambassador to France, Komatsu Ichirō (Asahi Shinbun Seijibu Shuzai Han 2015: 42–45). This decision almost coincided with Vice-Premier Asō's remark at the end of July 2014 that the LDP should learn how to revise the constitution from Nazi Germany (Shiota 2016: 53). These controversial words indicated that, after the electoral victory, the government felt much less constrained in plans to amend Article 9 or at least change its interpretation.

As expected, the new Cabinet Legislation Bureau director-general proved much more willing to overhaul the official interpretation of Article 9 than his predecessors. Under the first Abe administration, Komatsu had served as MOFA International Legal Affairs Bureau (previously Treaties Bureau) director-general and shared the prime minister's stance on the necessity of increasing Japan's contribution to the alliance with the US. On the other hand, in order to persuade the staff of the Cabinet Legislation Bureau to cooperate, Komatsu had to agree that the right of collective self-defense should be subject to some limitations, such as not exceeding the minimum extent necessary. During bureaucratic-level discussions, the Cabinet Legislation Bureau was represented by Komatsu and his deputy Yokobatake Yūsuke, the Kantei by Assistant CCSs Kanehara Nobukatsu from MOFA and Takamizawa Nobushige from the MOD, MOFA by International Legal Affairs Bureau Director-General Ishii Masafumi, and the MOD by Defense Policy Bureau Director-General Tokuchi Hideshi. Kanehara and Ishii wanted to broaden the spectrum of international activities of the SDF as much as possible by referring to the concept of collective security (*shūdanteki anzen hoshō*) that allowed use of force against countries recognized as aggressors by the UN. Yokobatake, in turn, tried to contain these ambitions in order to maintain the stability of Japan's legal system. Komatsu's role was to find a solution that satisfied both sides (Asahi Shinbun Seijibu Shuzai Han: 50–61).

In September 2013, Komatsu presented a draft of new conditions of self-defense to Abe. It was prepared by Yokobatake, based on the government's official stance from 1972, which stipulated that Japan was allowed to use force in situations that brought the danger of fundamentally overturning the people's right to life, freedom, and pursuing happiness. The prime minister was not enthusiastic about accepting these conditions, as he thought they put excessive constraints on the use of collective self-defense outside of the regions in Japan's direct vicinity. He eventually conceded to this solution after erasing the expression "fundamentally overturning" (*kontei kara kutsugaesareru*). During the proceedings of the House of Representatives Budget Committee in February 2014, Abe, for the first time, admitted that he did not intend to authorize an unrestricted use of collective self-defense (Asahi Shinbun Seijibu Shuzai Han: 62–64). Nevertheless, the exact meaning and scope of the "limited" collective self-defense was subject to further deliberations.

Deliberations in the advisory panel and the LDP

The preparation for the revision of the interpretation of the Constitution started even before the nomination of Komatsu as Cabinet Legislation Bureau director-general. As early as February 2013, the prime minister resumed the meetings of the Advisory Panel on Reconstruction of the Legal Basis for Security. In parallel, discussions were held in LDP decision-making bodies. Nevertheless, it was the Kantei that maintained control over the deliberations, both in the Panel and in the ruling party.

The Advisory Panel was composed of the same members as the one under Abe's first administration, with the addition of one person. It was chaired by former Administrative Vice-Minister of Foreign Affairs, International Tribunal for Law of the Sea President Yanai Shunji. It is symptomatic that Yanai had served as MOFA Treaties Bureau (International Legal Affairs Bureau) director-general, just as the three other bureaucrats in Abe's entourage who were heavily involved in the decision-making process on reinterpretation of the Constitution had: National Security Adviser Yachi Shōtarō, Assistant CCS Kanehara Nobukatsu, and Cabinet Legislation Bureau Director-General Komatsu Ichirō. The proceedings of the Panel were kept under strict control of the Cabinet Secretariat (Asahi Shinbun Seijibu Shuzai Han 2015: 136–139). In May 2014, Komatsu resigned due to health problems and controversial behavior when answering interpellations in the Diet. He was replaced by his deputy Yokobatake, which indicated a return to the traditional nomination patterns in the Cabinet Legislation Bureau.[2]

While Panel members naturally leaned toward the same conclusions as in 2008, LDP Vice-President Kōmura Masahiko sought a better legal foundation for the legalization of collective self-defense than reference to international law. Kōmura had been involved in discussions on the revision of interpretation of Article 9 since his participation in the proceedings of the LDP Constitution Research Committee (Kenpō Chōsakai) under the Tanigaki leadership. It was then that he started referring to the ruling on the so-called Sunagawa case as a foundation for reinterpretation of the Constitution. In 1959, the Supreme Court ruled on the legality of the presence of US military forces in Japan, stipulating that Japan possessed the right to self-defense and that cooperation with other countries in defense was equal to protecting one's own country. It is important that the ruling did not distinguish between the right of individual and collective self-defense. Moreover, the Supreme Court ruled that decisions on "highly political matters" in the security field should be left to the government (Hughes 2015: 44). Kōmura (2017: 174–181) claimed that, in this light, the Constitution did not prohibit collective self-defense as long as defense did not exceed the minimum extent necessary. Kōmura felt surprised that this reasoning was quickly accepted by Abe, who, in 2006, had insisted that interpretation of Article 9 should be changed without additional conditions.

After Abe had mentioned his intention to authorize collective self-defense in the Budget Committee in February 2014, voices of discontent appeared among liberal LDP backbenchers. Most controversial was the fact that the prime minister said he was the highest person in charge of interpreting the Constitution, as it was him, not the Cabinet Legislation Bureau director-general, who would be subject to the judgment of the people through an election (*Asahi Shinbun* 2014a: 4). In addition, members of the LDP General Council expressed their dissatisfaction with the fact that such an important policy change as legalization of collective self-defense had not been consulted with the ruling party. Under a proposal from the LDP Research Commission on the Tax System Chair Noda Takeshi, General Council Chairperson Noda Seiko decided to convene the LDP General Affairs Deliberative Council (Sōmu Kondankai). The meeting was usually convened to ensure free discussion on the most controversial decisions, and it was the first such situation since the privatization of Japan Post in 2005. During the Council's deliberations on March 17, 2014, Kōmura cited the ruling on the Sunagawa case to rebuff the accusations that legalization of collective self-defense violated the Constitution. This reasoning sufficed to persuade most LDP backbenchers to comply with Abe's policy agenda (Asahi Shinbun Seijibu Shuzai Han 2015: 105–107).

Nevertheless, one of the LDP General Council members, Murakami Seiichirō, continued voicing strong opposition against legalization of collective self-defense. He argued, as a graduate of the University of Tokyo Faculty of Law, that he understood that the ruling on the Sunagawa case did not allow collective self-defense (interview by the author, Tokyo,

October 17, 2019). As stressed by Murakami, the right to interpret the Constitution belonged to the Supreme Court, not to the prime minister or the government, and the decision on sending Japanese troops abroad, thus endangering their lives, should be authorized by the people in a referendum. Murakami emphasized that legalization of collective self-defense would open the way to changing interpretation of the Constitution after each alternation of power, which would undermine the principle of the separation of powers. He drew attention to the fact that the cabinet decision on reinterpretation of the Constitution cannot become a foundation for acts of higher status, such as the SDF Law. Murakami warned that such flexible treatment of the Constitution dangerously resembled the Enabling Act of 1933 that gave dictator-like powers to German Chancellor Adolf Hitler, without formally amending the Weimar Constitution. According to him, instead of remilitarizing Japan, Abe should invest more diplomatic efforts into building the ties of trust with other Asian countries. Murakami deplored the fact that the new electoral system of 1994 quelled intra-party democracy, as younger politicians were afraid to challenge the policy of LDP authorities so as not to lose their nomination as LDP candidates in subsequent elections, while more experienced lawmakers behaved similarly in order to gain governmental portfolios (Kumagai & Murakami 2014: 11–16). As admitted by Kōmura (2017: 181), LDP Secretary-General Ishiba warned that Murakami would not receive an official LDP nomination in the upcoming election, but this threat was not fulfilled after Ishiba's replacement by Tanigaki Sadakazu.

In order to allow discussion on the problem of reinterpretation of Article 9 among a broader group of LDP backbenchers, in March 2014, Abe established the LDP Headquarters for Reconstruction of the Legal Basis for Security under his direct control. The new organ was composed of 30 members, mainly chairs of the most important LDP bodies and former defense or foreign ministers. Apart from supporters of reinterpretation of Article 9, also skeptics, such as LDP House of Councilors Caucus Secretary-General Waki Masashi, became members (Miwa 2014: 4). Headquarters' Chair, LDP Secretary-General Ishiba Shigeru, however, admitted that legalization of collective self-defense was his political *credo*. He had been long involved in drafting the project of Basic Law on State Security (*Kokka Anzen Hoshō Kihon Hō*) in the LDP Policy Research Council Defense Policy Division. In his book on collective self-defense, published in 2014, Ishiba (2014: 6–186) stressed that it was unnatural that such an important aspect of administration as security policy was regulated by separate cabinet decisions or official views of the Cabinet Legislation Bureau, instead of a basic law. In Article 10 of the Basic Law on State Security draft, he proposed to allow self-defense in cases of an armed attack on a country remaining in a close relationship with Japan. Ishiba argued that Article 9 of the Constitution should be interpreted flexibly in light of the evolving international circumstances, analogically to the change in interpretation of Article 25 that defines "the minimum standards of wholesome and cultured living." As he pointed out, in the past, it used to be a rule that only households deprived of air conditioning could receive public assistance, but afterwards this limitation was removed. According to Ishiba, the Constitution did not prohibit self-defense in any form, as it only prohibited the use of force "as means of settling international disputes." He stressed that denial of the right to collective self-defense undermined Japan's credibility among Southeast Asian countries that would like Japan to constitute a counterbalance to the rising China. At the same time, Ishiba claimed that Beijing's concerns about a revival of Japanese militarism were groundless, as, depending on the situation, legalization of collective self-defense could also enable Japan to assist China in case of an armed attack on Chinese territory.

During the first meeting of the Headquarters on March 31, 2014, Kōmura once more referred to the ruling on the Sunagawa case to persuade the discontents. During the second meeting, on April 7, 2014, Ishiba delivered a comprehensive lecture on the legal aspects of collective self-defense, emphasizing that the interpretation of Article 9 had already been changed several times since the Yoshida administration. He added that as this issue had been discussed within the LDP since 2006, legalization of collective self-defense could not be treated as a decision imposed on the ruling party by the Kantei (Liberal Democratic Party 2014). During subsequent meetings, various security policy scholars were invited to the Headquarters, and, finally, the Advisory Panel on Reconstruction of the Legal Basis for Security Deputy Chair, International University of Japan President, Kitaoka Shin'ichi, explained to LDP lawmakers the results of the Panel's deliberations (Tamura 2014: 124–125).

The report of the Advisory Panel was issued on May 15, 2014. It was drafted by Kitaoka together with Assistant CCSs Kanehara Nobukatsu and Takamizawa Nobushige. As both Kanehara and Takamizawa in parallel served as National Security Secretariat vice-chairs, the report closely reflected the stance of the NSC. Unlike in 2008, the contents of the report were not a result of a free discussion among panel members, but were rather imposed by the Kantei in order to better reflect the results of initial negotiations with Kōmeitō. To keep the report secret, panel members received copies of it at the last moment. Despite these security measures, the text of the report leaked to the press and some members learned of the final version from newspapers (Asahi Shinbun Seijibu Shuzai Han 2015: 136–139, 207–209).

The report stressed that the security environment surrounding Japan had changed considerably even in comparison with the situation at the moment of publication of the previous report in 2008. The document indicated the spread of international terrorism and cyber-attacks, expansion of missile and nuclear weapon capabilities by North Korea, increased military spending by China and tensions in the East and South China Seas, strengthening of Japan–US and Japan–ASEAN security cooperation, as well as participation in new kinds of international activities, such as anti-piracy operations or large-scale natural disaster relief operations as the main new developments. For that reason, the panel did not limit examination to the four cases from the previous report and indicated six new situations that explained the necessity to allow collective self-defense: (1) contingency in areas neighboring Japan, such as repelling attacks against US vessels or ship inspections, (2) reaction to an armed attack against the US, (3) minesweeping in areas important for the navigation of Japanese ships, (4) participation in activities under the aegis of the UN in cases of an armed attack that significantly endangers the international order, (5) unauthorized sailing of submerged foreign submarines in the territorial waters of Japan, and (6) unlawful acts by armed groups against vessels or civilians in maritime areas or remote islands where the Japan Coast Guard cannot respond promptly (The Advisory Panel on Reconstruction of the Legal Basis for Security 2014: 1–21).

Referring to the ruling on the Sunagawa case to argue that the Supreme Court never prohibited collective self-defense, the report emphasized that:

> if a constitutional theory shown under a specific situation at some given point in time takes hold and security policies become inflexible under that theory despite significant changes of the security environment, there is a possibility that the security of the people could be compromised because of a constitutional argument. This goes against the very basis of constitutionalism, whereby the constitution is formulated by the people themselves, for the protection of the people with whom sovereign power resides. (The Advisory Panel on Reconstruction of the Legal Basis for Security 2014: 8)

In light of the Constitution Preamble and the UN Charter, the document concluded that the unconstitutionality of collective self-defense was groundless. The report reasoned that Article 9 prohibited "the threat or the use of force as means of settling international disputes to which Japan is a party," without prohibiting "the use of force for the purpose of self-defense, nor imposing any constitutional restrictions on activities that are consistent with international law" (The Advisory Panel on Reconstruction of the Legal Basis for Security 2014: 24). As such, the Panel recommended acknowledgement of the right of Japan to participate in operations aimed at repelling an attack against "a foreign country that is in a close relationship with Japan (…) by using force to the minimum extent necessary, having obtained an explicit request or consent of the country under attack, and thus to make a contribution to the maintenance and restoration of international peace and security even if Japan itself is not directly attacked" (The Advisory Panel on Reconstruction of the Legal Basis for Security 2014: 29–30).

Negotiations with Kōmeitō and public discourse on the revision

After the election in July 2013, the LDP, together with its coalition partner Kōmeitō, regained control over the House of Councilors, which greatly facilitated the decision-making process. Nevertheless, revision of the interpretation of Article 9 still posed a grave problem. Every cabinet decision required a signature from all ministers, including those from Kōmeitō. The coalition partner's support was even more important in voting through security bills in the upper house where the LDP alone did not have a majority. Taking into account the fact that Kōmeitō was strongly attached to pacifist ideals, it was unlikely that LDP's coalition partner would easily concede to Abe's plans.

Inside the religious group Sōka Gakkai, whose policy line Kōmeitō generally followed, the central leadership reluctantly agreed to initiate cautious talks on Constitution revision within the framework of *kaken*, but the Married Women Division (Fujinbu) was strongly opposed to any amendments. When, at the beginning of 2013, Abe started a discourse on modification of Article 96, Sōka Gakkai President Harada Minoru and Secretary-General Tanigawa Yoshiki were willing to compromise, but they encountered strong resistance from the Married Women Division. Eventually, Sōka Gakkai authorized Kōmeitō to start negotiations with Abe on constitutional revision, but only upon the condition that both paragraphs of Article 9 remained untouched (Nakano 2016: 52–54). At that time, the prime minister abandoned the plan of changing Article 96, but Sōka Gakkai's position translated into Kōmeitō's decisive resistance against any reinterpretation of Article 9.

In order to weaken Kōmeitō's stance, Abe sought temporary alliances with the opposition parties. In his policy speech to the Diet in January 2014, the prime minister stated that the government would "examine how to deal with the issues of the right of collective self-defense, collective security, and the like, taking into account the report prepared by the Advisory Panel on Reconstruction of the Legal Basis for Security" (Prime Minister of Japan and His Cabinet 2014a). At the same time, he said he would "conduct policy consultations flexibly and sincerely with 'responsible opposition parties' that aim to bring policies into being" (Prime Minister of Japan and His Cabinet 2014a). Abe thus hinted at the possibility of striking a deal on revision of Article 9 over the head of the coalition partner with such conservative parties as the JRA or YP. Aware of that risk, Kōmeitō leader Yamaguchi Natsuo, who, as a former defense parliamentary vice-minister, boasted wide knowledge on security issues, periodically stressed that realization of the Advisory Panel's report should be subject to negotiations within the ruling coalition (Asahi Shinbun Seijibu Shuzai Han 2015: 67–80).

Unofficial talks between both parties started at the beginning of March 2014 with the participation of Yamaguchi Natsuo, his deputy Kitagawa Kazuo, and Secretary-General Inoue Yoshihisa from Kōmeitō, as well as Kōmura Masahiko, Secretary-General Ishiba Shigeru, and former Japan

Defense Agency Director-General Nakatani Gen representing the LDP. This 3+3 formula was proposed by Ishiba, who, as a security policy expert, wanted to play a leading role in negotiations. While the LDP secretary-general eagerly supported legalization of collective self-defense, he disagreed with Abe on the form and the timing of the reform. Firstly, he claimed that interpretation of Article 9 should be changed by a Basic Law on State Security, not a mere cabinet decision. Secondly, Ishiba wanted to postpone this controversial decision for the sake of maintaining the coalition with Kōmeitō and ensuring a good performance of the LDP in the Okinawa gubernatorial election in November 2014 and local elections in spring 2015. Due to the lack of progress in negotiations in the 3+3 formula, eventually, the backstage talks were channeled through Kōmura and Kitagawa alone. Both party vice-leaders were lawyers, which facilitated discussion on the legal aspects of the reform. Ousted from the negotiations, in April 2014, Ishiba tried to convince Abe to at least remove the word "collective" from the text of the cabinet decision, but to no avail. Interestingly, the gap between the stances of the LDP and Kōmeitō narrowed thanks to the reference to the statement of Abe's grandfather, Prime Minister Kishi Nobusuke. In 1960, Kishi said that the Constitution prohibited the right to collective self-defense in the sense of Japanese forces protecting a foreign country, but he also added he did not believe that the right of collective self-defense entailed only such a situation (Asahi Shinbun Seijibu Shuzai Han 2015: 83–135). This statement opened the window for acknowledging Japan's right to collective self-defense while imposing severe limitations on its usage.

The official talks with Kōmeitō, which began in May 2014, were also entrusted by Abe to the LDP vice-president. The beginning of negotiations coincided with publication of the Report of the Advisory Panel on Reconstruction of the Legal Basis for Security. At a press conference on May 15, 2014, Abe stressed that two different views were presented in the report: the Constitution imposed no restrictions on Japan's participation in collective security measures, or that the right of collective self-defense was subject to constitutional limitations. The prime minister admitted that as the former "view does not make logical consistency with the Government's constitutional interpretation to date," it was not supported by the cabinet (Prime Minister of Japan and His Cabinet 2014b). This statement was a considerable concession to Kōmeitō.[3]

Still, the official negotiations between the coalition partners posed a considerable challenge. The first meeting of the Ruling Coalition Conference on Reconstruction of the Legal Basis for Security (Anzen Hoshō Hōsei Seibi ni kan suru Yotō Kyōgikai), composed of six members from the LDP and five from Kōmeitō, took place on May 20, 2014. Kōmeitō requested detailed examples of the situations that would require Japan to react by the use of collective self-defense. When the Kantei indicated 15 cases, Kōmeitō representatives deemed them either unrealistic or not exceeding the framework of individual self-defense. It seemed that Kōmeitō's strategy was to prolong the discussions through meticulous analysis of each case. In order to make progress in negotiations, Kōmura once more approached Kitagawa (Asahi Shinbun Seijibu Shuzai Han 2015: 149–160).

Meanwhile, Abe and his closest entourage started to lose patience. At a press conference during a visit to Brussels in June 2014, the prime minister said that while achieving an agreement within the ruling coalition was very important, the JRA and YP were showing understanding on the need of allowing collective self-defense. The strategy of playing the opposition parties off against Kōmeitō was supplemented with even more explicit threats toward the coalition partner. In the same month, Abe's adviser Iijima Isao mentioned during a lecture in Washington the possibility of re-examining whether relations between Kōmeitō and Sōka Gakkai did not violate the constitutional principle of separation of the state and religion. These statements were aimed at assuaging Kōmeitō's resistance (Nakano 2016: 54–55).

As admitted by Kōmura (2017: 183–187), it was nonetheless not an easy task to persuade Yamaguchi, who claimed it would be an over-interpretation to say that the ruling on the Sunagawa case allowed collective self-defense. Nevertheless, Kōmeitō vice-leader Kitagawa Kazuo seemed to be more willing to compromise, as he admitted that the ruling did not exclude the possibility of collective self-defense either. The coalition partners held as many as 25 official meetings in addition to the same number of backstage get-togethers between Kōmura and Kitagawa. Yamaguchi agreed to a reinterpretation of Article 9 upon the condition that the right to collective self-defense would be clearly linked with the previous stance of the government. In order to please the Kōmeitō leader, Kitagawa and Kōmura referred to the people's right to the pursuit of happiness stipulated in the Preamble of the Constitution and the official interpretation of Article 9 from 1972. Kōmura consulted on the details of this solution with the Cabinet Legislation Bureau and Assistant CCSs Kanehara and Takamizawa before gaining final authorization from Abe. The reference to the government's view from 1972 was consistent with the solution submitted to Abe by Komatsu and Yokobatake in September 2013. Nevertheless, this time, the prime minister agreed not to erase the expression "fundamentally overturning" (of the people's right to life, freedom, and pursuit of happiness) from the new conditions of collective self-defense. This concession paved the way to the final agreement between the coalition partners at the end of June 2014 (Asahi Shinbun Seijibu Shuzai Han 2015: 170–180).

Kōmeitō's reluctance to allow collective self-defense resulted from the fact that its electorate was opposed to revision of Article 9. Public opinion remained divided over the need to acknowledge Japan's right to collective self-defense. According to *Asahi Shinbun* (2014b: 3) opinion poll from June 2014, 56% of respondents were opposed to the change of interpretation of the Constitution, while 28% supported the prime minister's decision. Moreover, 67% claimed it was improper to amend the interpretation instead of the Constitution itself, 76% felt that the debate on the policy change was insufficient, and 65% disagreed with the need for Japan to use force within the UN collective security system. As a result, the cabinet support rate fell to 43%, 6 percentage points less than one month earlier. Abe, however, was aware that, thanks to its economic credentials, his administration was popular enough to trade a few points of support in exchange for the shift in interpretation of the Constitution.

Additionally, governmental plans did not seem to be clearly understood by a large part of society. According to an opinion poll published by *Yomiuri Shinbun* (2014: 1) at the beginning of June 2014, as many as 60% of respondents were willing to accept a "limited" collective self-defense, while 11% supported "full" collective self-defense, and only 24% did not feel the need for exercising any form of collective self-defense. Asked in more detail, 75% of respondents acknowledged the necessity for protection by Maritime SDF of US ships transporting Japanese refugees, 74% approved of Maritime SDF's participation in minesweeping operations, but only 44% would authorize intercepting missiles launched against American Guam or Hawaii. The confused public seemed to be willing to support only some of the types of operations envisaged by Abe, but they had insufficient knowledge on the gravity of the cabinet decision in question. The lack of clarity of the concept of a "limited" collective self-defense served the Kantei in assuaging popular concerns.

The agreement between the LDP and Kōmeitō was swiftly acknowledged by the LDP Security Research Commission (Anzen Hoshō Chōsakai), Policy Research Council Joint Conference of Diplomatic and Defense Policy Divisions (Gaikō Bukai Kokubō Bukai Gōdō Kaigi), Policy Research Council Board, and General Council (Tamura 2014: 125). While, in order to please Kōmeitō, Abe abandoned the plans for legalizing unrestricted collective self-defense, it was rather Kōmeitō that bent to LDP's demands, than *vice versa*. After all, reinterpretation of Article 9 undermined the pacifist credentials of Kōmeitō, thus straining the ties of this party with Sōka Gakkai.

Cabinet decision and new Japan–US defense cooperation guidelines

As Abe found it improper that, in the past, the official interpretation of the Constitution had been established through mere answers to Diet interpellations, he insisted that the new interpretation should be announced through a cabinet decision (Makihara 2017: 265). Eventually, on July 1, 2014, the cabinet issued a revolutionary Cabinet Decision on Development of Seamless Security Legislation to Ensure Japan's Survival and Protect Its People. The extraordinary cabinet meeting lasted a mere 23 minutes, and most of this time was devoted to an explanation of the contents of the decision by Deputy CCS Sekō Hiroshige. What is symptomatic, none of the ministers expressed his/her opinion during the discussion time (Prime Minister of Japan and His Cabinet 2014c).

Based on the report of the Advisory Panel on Reconstruction of the Legal Basis for Security and the policy agreement with Kōmeitō, it was announced that due to the changes in the international security environment, the Japanese government no longer considered a direct armed attack against Japan as a necessary prerequisite for the use of force. Instead, the Abe administration declared that "an armed attack against a foreign country that is in a close relationship with Japan," which "threatens Japan's survival and poses a clear danger to fundamentally overturn people's right to life, liberty and pursuit of happiness," would permit Japan to use force, if only "there is no other appropriate means available to repel the attack and ensure Japan's survival and protect its people" (Cabinet Secretariat 2014: 7–8). Kōmeitō did not manage to limit collective self-defense to Japan's allies, or just the US, but it persuaded Abe to narrow it down to states "in a close relationship" (*kinmitsu no kankei ni aru takoku*), not all "other states" (*takoku*), as had been proposed by the Kantei. Moreover, under LDP's coalition partner's pressure, the wording "fear" (*osore*) of threat was replaced with "clear danger" (*meihaku-na kiken*) (Hughes 2015: 53).

The use of force was still subject to three conditions: (1) the situation should pose a clear threat to Japan or fundamentally threaten the Japanese people's right to life, liberty, and pursuit of happiness; (2) it was the only way to repel the attack; and (3) it was limited to the minimum extent necessary (Hughes 2015: 52). Nevertheless, the new interpretation of the Constitution paved the way to permit the SDF to provide direct military assistance to US forces if they were assaulted in the vicinity of Japan, or to the soldiers of other countries participating together with Japan in peacekeeping operations. Moreover, it did not stipulate any geographical limitation to the application of collective self-defense. Due to consideration for Kōmeitō, the cabinet decision did not contain any reference to collective security, leaving some space for more detailed interpretation by the Cabinet Legislation Bureau (Asahi Shinbun Seijibu Shuzai Han 2015: 193–194). The Bureau, however, seemed to have been pacified by Abe. Asked by the National Security Secretariat for an opinion on the cabinet decision, the Bureau answered it did not have any, which symbolized its conformity with the Kantei's policy (Soeya 2016: 207–208).

At a press conference after issuing the cabinet decision, Abe stressed that the new interpretation of the Constitution was consistent with the previous stance of the government:

> There is a misunderstanding that Japan will become caught up in wars in order to defend foreign countries. In fact such a case is also entirely out of the question.
> The measures that the Constitution of Japan permits are only self-defense measures for the purpose of ensuring Japan's survival and protecting its people. Japan will continue not to engage in the use of force for the purpose of defending foreign countries. Rather, taking all

possible preparations will serve as a great deal of power that will thwart schemes to wage war on Japan. This is what we call deterrence. (Prime Minister of Japan and His Cabinet 2014d)

It quickly turned out, however, that Kōmeitō interpreted the three conditions slightly differently from the prime minister. As stressed by Kitagawa, they:

> limit the use of force to situations that pose a clear danger to the survival of Japan and the rights of its people due to an armed attack to Japan or a country with close ties with it. What "a clear danger" means here is a situation equivalent to an armed attack on Japan that poses a serious threat to the Japanese people. (...) The right of collective self-defense for the purpose of defending another country as provided for in Article 51 of the Charter of the United Nations is not allowed. (Kōmeitō 2015)

Moreover, Kitagawa emphasized that international activity of the SDF permitted by the security laws would not exceed the limits of logistical assistance to US forces engaged in defending Japan or to other countries involved in operations under a UN resolution. As such, Japan "would not be following after the US military everywhere as some critics say" (Kōmeitō 2015). Abe, however, leaned toward a broader definition of a "limited" collective self-defense. In particular, he claimed that under the new interpretation of Article 9, Japan was allowed to dispatch the SDF abroad for economic reasons, for instance, to ensure safety of oil supplies through minesweeping activities in the Strait of Hormuz (Klein 2016: 76).

Without waiting for the passage of security bills through the Diet, the Abe administration negotiated with Washington new Guidelines for Japan–US Defense Cooperation that were announced at the end of April 2015. They encompassed several fields of cooperation: (1) "strengthened alliance coordination," (2) "seamlessly ensuring Japan's peace and security," (3) "cooperation for regional and global peace and security," (4) "space and cyberspace cooperation," as well as (5) "bilateral enterprise." In the second point, both sides agreed on "actions in response to an armed attack against a country other than Japan," including "operations involving the use of force," such as "asset protection," "search and rescue," "maritime cooperation," "operations to counter ballistic missile attacks," as well as "logistics support" (Ministry of Foreign Affairs 2015).

The reinterpretation of Article 9 and the new Guidelines for Japan–US Defense Cooperation changed the nature of the Japan–US alliance to a more equal one, which was in line with decades-long pressure from Washington. While exercise of collective self-defense by Japan was still subject to several conditions, the policy shift enabled Tokyo to conduct a more active foreign and security policy in the region and on a global scale.

Passage of the security bills

The new interpretation of Article 9 created the necessity to revise a range of bills related to the SDF and their international activities. The Bill on Partial Revision of the SDF Law etc. Contributing to Peace and Maintenance of Security of Our Country and International Society (*Waga Kuni oyobi Kokusai Shakai no Heiwa oyobi Anzen no Kakuho ni Shi Suru Jieitai Hōtō no Ichibu o Kaisei Suru Hōritsu*) modified ten other legislative acts, while the Bill on Cooperative Support Actions Conducted by Our Country towards Armies of Other Countries etc. during Joint International Peace Operations (*Kokusai Heiwa Kyōdō Taisho Jitai ni Sai Shite Waga Kuni ga Jisshi Suru Shogaikoku no Guntaitō ni tai suru Kyōryoku Shien Katsudōtō ni kan suru Hōritsu*) became a new permanent law.[4] They were popularly called security bills (or "war bills" by their severest critics), and met with strong resistance from the opposition parties and pacifist NGOs.

In order to draft the controversial legislation, the Kantei mobilized two-thirds of the National Security Secretariat staff under the direction of Kanehara and Takamizawa (Toshikawa 2019: 195). Abe intended to entrust general coordination on security bills to Ishiba Shigeru, who, however, refused to assume the post of minister charged with this task. Instead, during a cabinet reshuffle in September 2014, Ishiba was nominated as minister for overcoming population decline and vitalizing local economy. As Ishiba (2018: 34–49) explained, he could not promote the new legislation as he had long been a supporter of Japan's full right to collective self-defense, not a limited version. As such, he wanted to avoid a difference of opinions on that issue in the cabinet.

The LDP–Kōmeitō coalition agreement signed after the December 2014 House of Representatives election put emphasis on promotion of an "active peace diplomacy that takes a panoramic perspective of the world map" (Kōmeitō 2014). Both sides promised to swiftly pass the security bills that contained the new interpretation of Article 9 of the Constitution. During a policy speech to the Diet in February 2015, Abe stressed he would "secure fully and resolutely the lives and peaceful livelihood of the Japanese people by developing security legislation that enables seamless responses to any situations" (Prime Minister of Japan and His Cabinet 2015). Negotiations between the LDP and Kōmeitō on the details of the security bills were started on February 13, 2015. One month later, the two sides achieved a preliminary agreement. The greatest problem was Kōmeitō's request that any dispatch of the SDF abroad should be subject to a UN resolution. Eventually, the coalition partners agreed to authorize Japan's participation in international operations based on any UN resolution related to the international problem in question. It paved the way for sending the SDF not only as a part of a UN peacekeeping operation, but also to provide logistics support to US forces involved in any military operation that could be vaguely connected to a UN resolution that referred to the concerned situation (Watanabe 2016: 94–99).

Apart from consistency with international law, the Kantei agreed to two other conditions for SDF dispatch overseas requested by Kōmeitō: maintenance of civilian control and public support, as well as ensuring the safety of the SDF personnel. As a result, deployment of the SDF abroad under the new permanent law was to be subject to the Diet's approval (Akimoto 2018: 73).

On May 12, 2015, the LDP General Council unanimously acknowledged the security bills project. Nevertheless, one member, Murakami Seiichirō, left the room before voting, arguing that revision of the Constitution was necessary to allow collective self-defense. Murakami thus respected the unwritten code of conduct in the ruling party. As he admitted, had he voted against the project, he would have had to leave the LDP (interview by the author, Tokyo, October 17, 2019). While only a symbolic resistance against the bills appeared in LDP decision-making bodies, retired LDP politicians were much more vocal in criticizing the prime minister. Former Kōchikai leader Koga Makoto stressed that the previous interpretation of Article 9 had not been imposed by the Cabinet Legislation Bureau alone, but rather that it was the fruit of the accumulated knowledge of generations of politicians. As such, he called on Abe to display more modesty toward this heritage. Koga found it particularly unacceptable to create the possibility of applying collective security to situations involving countries with which Japan had not even signed an alliance treaty. He deplored the fact that LDP decision-making bodies no longer sufficiently played a controlling role over governmental policy. As he stressed, since politicians who expressed any concerns regarding the Kantei's plans were automatically treated as a force of resistance, discussions focused on the technical details of applying collective self-defense instead of the questions regarding the necessity of the reform. Another former faction leader, Yamasaki Taku, who had been one of the authors of the legislation allowing dispatch of the SDF to Iraq under the Koizumi administration, noted that Japan's foreign policy was founded on three principles: UN rules, alliance with the US, and belonging to the community of Asian countries. According to him, Abe's policy destroyed the balance between these principles by putting an excessive emphasis on alliance with the US alone (Koizumi & Makino 2015: 18).

On May 14, 2015, the bill projects were approved by the NSC and authorized as a cabinet decision. On the next day, they were submitted to the House of Representatives Special Committee on Peace and Security System of Our Country and International Society chaired by Hamada Yasukazu. The opposition parties claimed that due to the gravity of the set of bills, they should be discussed for longer than a single parliamentary session. Nevertheless, to limit the political cost of the revision, Abe was determined to finish the legislative process as fast as possible. The deliberations in the Committee became an opportunity for the opposition parties to indicate the deficiencies in the reasoning of the government. The ruling coalition exposed itself to criticism when at the beginning of June 2015, three constitutional experts, including Waseda University Professor Hasebe Yasuo, who was summoned to the parliament by the LDP and Kōmeitō, said that the security bills violated the Constitution. In addition, DPJ lawmaker Tsujimoto Kiyomi found inconsistencies in the statements of Minister of Defense Nakatani Gen, who was the main person in charge of preparing the security bills. It turned out that in an interview from July 2013, Nakatani had claimed that usage of collective self-defense was impossible under the current Constitution and that such a policy shift necessitated revision of the Constitution itself (Shiota 2016: 180–190). Cabinet Legislation Bureau Director-General, Yokobatake Yūsuke, defended the constitutionality of the security bills. During the deliberations, DPJ lawmaker Terata Manabu compared the exercise of collective self-defense to an inedible, partially rotten miso soup. Yokobatake, however, evoked a different metaphor – of a balloon fish (*fugu*) that becomes edible after the removal of its poisonous organs. He thus referred to the fact that the security bills did not allow unrestrained exercise of the right to collective self-defense, but only a limited version (Akimoto 2018: 76).

Following discussions in the Diet, the LDP General Council authorized the final version of the security bills on July 1, 2015. Once more, only Murakami absented himself from voting by leaving the room. By doing so, he respected the unwritten principle that decisions of this body should be made unanimously. As he emphasized, he did not want to block the proceedings. Murakami felt powerless in the face of the institutional strength of the Kantei. He deplored the fact that even those LDP lawmakers who were lawyers did not want to endanger their political careers and turned a blind eye to the over-interpretation of the ruling in the Sunagawa case. Murakami (2016: 9–55) claimed that free discussion in the LDP was less welcome than in the Imperial Rule Assistance Association that replaced political parties during the Second World War. He criticized the fact that the Diet devoted only 200 hours to deliberations on as many as 11 bills and that the government failed to fully explain the significance of the policy change to the Japanese people.

The public remained largely critical of the security bills. According to an opinion poll conducted by *Asahi Shinbun* (2015c: 3) in mid-July 2015, 57% of respondents opposed and only 29% supported the legalization of collective self-defense and the broadening of the SDF's international activities. Moreover, 74% thought it was improper for the government to change the interpretation of the Constitution without revising the Constitution itself (10% thought otherwise). In addition, 72% found the prime minister's explanations of the bills insufficient and 69% claimed it was unnecessary to pass the controversial laws during the current parliamentary session. In total, 79% thought that under the new legislation the risk of the SDF being involved in combat would increase, while only 35% considered the bills a way to increase Japan's deterrence power. At the same time, 69% held a negative and only 17% a positive view on the fact that the ruling coalition voted on the security bills in the House of Representatives Commission despite the absence of the opposition parties. On the other hand, only 21% positively evaluated the reaction to the controversial legislation by the opposition politicians. As a result of these moods, the support rate for the Abe cabinet decreased to a record low of 37%.

The opposition parties applied a range of delaying tactics in the Diet. In the lower house, the JIP together with the DPJ submitted their own versions of security bills, but they were rejected by the ruling coalition. In the upper house, Yamamoto Tarō from the PLP accused Abe of bending to US pressure. He argued that Washington had influenced the judgment on the Sunagawa case and that legalization of collective self-defense reflected the conclusions of the "Third Armitage–Nye Report" that postulated the SDF dispatch to the South China Sea for monitoring and to the Hormuz Strait for minesweeping activities. On September 17, 2015, suspecting that the opposition politicians would try to block the door to the deliberation room, House of Councilors Commission Chairperson Kōnoike Yoshitada changed the room without notifying the security bills' opponents. This move antagonized the opposition lawmakers even further. During the plenary session, they used an array of techniques to physically disturb the proceedings. For example, in order to delay the voting, Yamamoto Tarō applied the "cow's walk" strategy and a filibuster speech (Akimoto 2018: 79–86).

Meanwhile, massive demonstrations took place in front of the Diet. The protest movements had gradually intensified since the 2014 cabinet decision that allowed collective self-defense. In December 2014, three organizations involved in the protests – 1000 People Committee Resisting War (Sensō o Sasenai 1000 Nin Iinkai), Don't Violate Article 9 of the Constitution Through Interpretation! Executive Committee (Kaishaku de Kenpō 9 Jō o Kowasuna! Jikkō Iinkai), and Cooperative Center for Protection and Revival of the Constitution (Kenpō o Mamori Ikasu Kyōdō Sentā) joined forces creating the Combined Action Executive Committee Resisting War and Violation of Article 9 (Sensō Sasenai 9 Jō Kowasuna Sōgakari Kōdō Jikkō Iinkai). Protests intensified even further after the submission of the security bills to the Diet in May 2015, with the newly-founded Students Emergency Action for Liberal Democracy (SEALDs, Jiyū to Minshushugi no tame no Gakusei Kinkyū Kōdō) taking the lead. The number of participants in the demonstrations abruptly rose after constitutional scholars admitted the bills violated Article 9 in June. The largest demonstration on August 30, 2015, gathered as many as 120,000 people. The scale of protests was reminiscent of the student demonstrations against the revision of the Japan–US security treaty by Abe's grandfather Kishi Nobusuke in 1960. In addition, since 2013, 405 local authorities councils had expressed their opinions on legalization of collective security, with as many as 393 of them holding negative or cautious views (Watanabe 2016: 198–221). Moreover, in June 2015, Japan Federation of Bar Associations submitted to the prime minister and to speakers of both houses of the Diet a petition against the security bills signed by more than 260,000 people. Apart from opposition

228 *Revision of interpretation of Article 9*

lawmakers, their initiative was supported by Murakami Seiichirō from the LDP (*Asahi Shinbun* 2015a: 34). In addition, statements against the security bills were issued by Middle East specialists, including former ambassadors, and five former prime ministers: Hosokawa Morihiro, Hata Tsutomu, Murayama Tomiichi, Hatoyama Yukio, and Kan Naoto (Mark 2016: 106).

Despite these protests, the security bills were passed by the House of Representatives on July 16, 2015, by the votes of the LDP, Kōmeitō, and the PFG. Abe initially hoped for passage of the security bills in both houses by mid-August.[5] Nevertheless, due to the strength of protests by opposition politicians and civic movements, he extended the ordinary parliamentary session until September 27, 2015, by a record 95 days. Abe presumably hoped that even if the upper house could not vote on the bills, they would be automatically approved 60 days after their passage in the House of Representatives (Watanabe 2016: 201–204). However, on September 19, 2015, the ruling coalition entered into an agreement on the security bills in the House of Councilors with three small opposition parties: the PFG, Assembly to Energize Japan (Nihon o Genki ni Suru Kai), and the New Renaissance Party (Shintō Kaikaku). The agreement facilitated the successful voting through of the security bills in the upper house (Shiota 2016: 186–189). The members of the ruling parties remained disciplined – none of Kōmeitō lawmakers and only two LDP politicians – Murakami Seiichirō and Wakasa Masaru – were absent from voting in the House of Representatives, citing health reasons (*Asahi Shinbun* 2015b: 4). Eventually, the security bills entered into force in March 2016.

Conclusion

Legalization of collective self-defense attested to the institutional strength of the Abe cabinet. As the interpretation of Article 9 from the 1950s had been sanctified by more than half century of practice, its revision encountered strong opposition from the Cabinet Legislation Bureau staff and pacifist civic movements. Knowing that the policy change would damage the high popularity of the government, Abe waited with this task until the victory in the House of Councilors election in July 2013. Afterwards, he accelerated his efforts. He played MOFA off against the Cabinet Legislation Bureau by ignoring the unwritten rule on the appointment of the Bureau's director-general, and partly circumvented LDP decision-making bodies through the Headquarters for Reconstruction of the Legal Basis for Security under the LDP president's direct control. In fact, resistance from LDP backbenchers was almost non-existent. Only one senior politician, Murakami Seiichirō, consistently warned against violation of the Constitution, but his protests did not exceed such gestures as abstention from voting on the controversial decision in the LDP General Council and the Diet. The most difficult task for Abe was convincing Kōmeitō to comply. In order to please his coalition partner, the prime minister agreed to limit the extent of Japan's right to collective self-defense, but he also did not exclude a temporary policy alliance with conservative opposition parties.

Strong protests by civic movements and opposition parties temporarily damaged the positive image of the prime minister, but Abe was strong enough to simply wait them out. Thanks to the weakening of LDP factions and the skillful use of layering and conversion strategies toward governmental and party institutions, none of Abe's critics in the LDP openly challenged the prime minister's leadership. Abe thus avoided the fate of his grandfather who had to sacrifice his prime ministership to pass the revised Japan–US security treaty through the Diet in 1960.

Notes

1. According to the government's view from 1981, "Japan as a sovereign state inherently possesses the right of collective self-defense under international law, but the exercise of the right of self-defense as allowed under Article 9 of the Constitution is limited to what is minimum and necessary to defend the country, and exercise of the right of collective self-defense exceeds that range and therefore is not permitted under the Constitution." In addition, according to the government's stance from 1985, the exercise of the right to self-defense was subject to three requirements: "1) there is an imminent and unlawful infringement against Japan; 2) there is no other appropriate means available to repel this infringement; and 3) the use of force should be limited to the minimum and necessary level." See The Advisory Panel on Reconstruction of the Legal Basis for Security (2008: 6).
2. Komatsu showed irritation toward lawmakers and he violated the prohibition of bringing mobile phone to the proceedings. See Makihara (2017: 266).
3. Abe rejected interpretations of the Constitution that referred to the so-called Ashida view. In 1946, Ashida Hitoshi presumably inserted the expression "In order to accomplish the aim of the preceding paragraph" at the beginning of Paragraph 2 of Article 9 to prohibit only those wars that served as "means of settling international disputes." Under this interpretation, Japan possessed unlimited right of self-defense, both individual and collective. See Watanabe (2016: 77–80).
4. The modified acts were SDF Law, International Peace Cooperation Law or UN Peacekeeping Operations Cooperation (PKO) Act, Law Concerning Measures to Ensure Peace and Security of Japan in Situations in Areas Surrounding Japan, Ship Inspection Operations Law, Legislation for Responses to Armed Attack Situations, Act on Measures Conducted by the Government in Line with US Military Actions in Armed Attack Situations, Law Concerning the Use of Specific Public Facilities, Marine Transport Restriction Act, Prisoner Treatment Act, and National Security Council Establishment Act. See Akimoto (2018: 70–73).
5. Abe probably wanted to pass the security bills before implementation of three controversial decisions in mid-May 2015: restart of Sendai Nuclear Power Plant, announcement of a statement on the 70th anniversary of Japan's surrender in 1945, and continuation of Futenma-replacement facility's construction in the Henoko Bay despite the expected revocation of land reclamation permit by Okinawa Governor Onaga Takashi. According to Watanabe (2016: 201–204), in order not to incite the protests in front of the Diet, Abe decided to temporarily suspend construction works in the Henoko Bay and issue a more accommodative version of the anniversary statement than had been anticipated.

References

Abe, Shinzō (2006) *Utsukushii Kuni e* [Towards a Beautiful Country], Tokyo: Bungei Shunjū.
Abiru, Rui (2016) *Sōri no Tanjō* [Birth of Prime Minister], Tokyo: Bungei Shunjū.
Akimoto, Daisuke (2018) *The Abe Doctrine. Japan's Proactive Pacifism and Security Strategy*, Singapore: Palgrave Macmillan.
Asahi Shinbun (2014a) "Shushō Hatsugen, Tsuyomaru Hihan. Kenpō Kaishaku 'Saikō Sekininsha wa Watashi.' Yatō Hanpatsu, Kantei Tsuyoki" [Prime Minister's Statement, Intensifying Criticism. "I Am the Highest Person in Charge" of Interpretation of Constitution. Resistance by the Opposition Parties, Bold Kantei], February 15, morning edition, 4.
Asahi Shinbun (2014b) "Asahi Shinbunsha Yoron Chōsa. Shitsumon to Kaitō" [Opinion poll by Asahi Shinbun. Questions and answers], June 23, morning edition, 3.
Asahi Shinbun (2015a) "Anpo Hōsei Hantai, Shomei 26 Man Ninbun. Nichibenren, Shushō, Shū San Gichō Ate" [Opposition Against the Security Bills, Signed by 260,000 People. Addressed to the Prime Minister and Speakers of the Houses of Representatives and Councilors], June 11, morning edition, 34.
Asahi Shinbun (2015b) "Jimin 2 Giin, Saiketsu Kesseki. Anzen Hoshō Kanren Hōan" [Two LDP Lawmakers, Absent from Voting. Security Related Bills], July 17, morning edition, 4.
Asahi Shinbun (2015c) "Anpo Hōan no Susumekata, Shijisō demo Gimonshi. Asahi Shinbunsha Kinkyū Yoron Chōsa" [The Way of Handling the Security Bills, Doubts Even Among the Supporters. Urgent Opinion Poll by Asahi Shinbun], July 20, morning edition, 3.
Asahi Shinbun Seijibu Shuzai Han (2015) *Abe Seiken no Ura no Kao. "Kōbō Shūdanteki Jieiken" Dokyumento* [Back Face of the Abe Administration. Document on "the Battle over the Right to Collective Self-Defense"], Tokyo: Kōdansha.
Cabinet Secretariat (2014) "Cabinet Decision on Development of Seamless Security Legislation to Ensure Japan's Survival and Protect its People" (July 1). Online. Available: http://www.cas.go.jp/jp/gaiyou/jimu/pdf/anpohosei_eng.pdf (accessed August 7, 2017).
Hughes, Christopher W (2015) *Japan's Foreign and Security Policy Under the "Abe Doctrine": New Dynamism or New Dead End?* London: Palgrave Macmillan.
Ishiba, Shigeru (2014) *Nihonjin no tame no "Shūdanteki Jieiken" Nyūmon* [Introduction on "Collective Self-Defense" for the Japanese], Tokyo: Shinchōsha.
Ishiba, Shigeru (2018) *Seisaku Shijōshugi* [Policy Supremacy], Tokyo: Shinchōsha.
Klein, Axel (2016) "Komeito – Rock 'n' Row the Coalition Boat," in Robert J. Pekkanen, Steven R. Reed & Ethan Scheiner (eds.), *Japan Decides 2014. The Japanese General Election*, Basingstoke and New York: Palgrave Macmillan, 72–86.
Koizumi, Kōhei & Makino, Megumi (2015) "Jimintō Jūchintachi ga Abe-ryū o Shikaru. Yamasaki Taku-shi, Koga Makoto-shi" [LDP Heavyweights Speaking of Abe. Mr. Yamasaki Taku, Mr. Koga Makoto], *Shūkan Asahi*, March 6, 18.
Kōmeitō (2013) "Kōmeitō no Kenpō Kaisei" [Kōmeitō's Revision of Constitution]. Online. Available: https://www.komei.or.jp/campaign/sanin2013/ig/kp.html (accessed July 24, 2019).

Kōmeitō (2014) "Jimin-Kōmei Renritsu Seiken Gōi (Zenbun)" [LDP-Kōmeitō Ruling Coalition Agreement (Full Text)] (December 16). Online. Available: Online. Available: https://www.komei.or.jp/news/detail/20141216_15770 (accessed July 17, 2019).

Kōmeitō (2015) "Security Bills and Komeito," *Kōmei Shinbun* (May 16). Online. Available: https://www.komei.or.jp/en/policy/stands/20150516.html (accessed July 30, 2019).

Kōmura, Masahiko (2017) *Furiko o Mannaka ni. Watashi no Rirekisho* [Pendulum to the Center. My Curriculum Vitae], Tokyo: Nihon Keizai Shinbun Shuppansha.

Kōno, Yōhei (2015) *Nihon Gaikō e no Chokugen. Kaisō to Teigen* [Frank Talk about Japan's Diplomacy. Memoirs and Suggestions], Tokyo: Iwanami Shoten.

Kumagai, Shin'ichirō & Murakami, Seiichirō (2014) "Intabyū. Nihon wa 'waimāru no Rakujitsu' o Kurikaesu na" [Interview. Let Japan Not Repeat the "Late Days of Weimar"], *Sekai*, May, 856: 11–16.

Liberal Democratic Party (2013) "Sangiin Senkyo Kōyaku 2013. Nihon o Torimodosu. Jimintō" [House of Councilors Electoral Manifesto 2013. Restore Japan, LDP]. Online. Available: https://jimin.jp-east-2.storage.api.nifcloud.com/pdf/sen_san23/2013sanin2013-07-04.pdf?_ga=2.191251374.564274348.1564660730-757367699.1564660730 (accessed August 1, 2019).

Liberal Democratic Party (2014) "Anzen Hoshō Hōsei Seibi Suishin Honbu. Dai 2 Kai, Shūdanteki Jieiken ni tsuite (Ishiba Shigeru Honbuchō)" [Headquarters for Reconstruction of the Legal Basis for Security. 2nd Meeting, On Collective Self-Defense (Chairperson Ishiba Shigeru)] (April 7). Online. Available: https://www.jimin.jp/policy/policy_topics/national_security_act/124377.html (accessed August 1, 2019).

Makihara, Izuru (2017) "Kenpō Kaishaku no Henkō. Hōsei Shitsumu no Tenkan" [Change of Interpretation of Constitution, Shift in Legal System Work], in Takenaka Harukata (ed.), *Futatsu no Seiken Kōtai. Seisaku wa kawatta no ka* [Two Alternations of Power. Has the Policy Changed?], Tokyo: Keisō Shobō, 245–272.

Makihara, Izuru (2018) *Kuzureru Seiji o Tatenaosu. 21 Seiki no Nihon Gyōsei Kaikaku Ron* [Reorganizing the Crumbling Politics. Discourse on Administrative Reform in the 21st Century Japan], Tokyo: Kōdansha.

Mark, Craig (2016) *The Abe Restoration. Contemporary Japanese Politics and Reformation*, Lanham–Boulder–New York–London: Lexington Books.

Ministry of Foreign Affairs (2015) "The Guidelines for Japan-U.S. Defense Cooperation" (April 27). Online. Available: https://www.mofa.go.jp/files/000078188.pdf (accessed July 22, 2020).

Miwa, Sachiko (2014) "Shūdanteki Jieiken, Semegiai. Jimin, Kyōgi Kikan o Setchi. Honbuchō ni Ishiba Kanjichō" [Collective Self-Defense, Fierce Competition. LDP Establishes a Consultation Body. Secretary-General Ishiba as Chair], *Asahi Shinbun*, March 26, morning edition, 4.

Miyazawa, Kiichi (1995) *21 Seiki e no Ininjō* [Mandate for the 21st Century], Tokyo: Shōgakukan.

Mizuno, Hitoshi (2017) *Naikaku Hōseikyoku wa "Kenpō no Bannnin" ka? Nichibei Anpo kaishaku o Kenshō Suru* [Is the Cabinet Legislation Bureau a "Guard of Constitution?" Analyzing the Japan–US Security Treaty], Tokyo: Namiki Shobō.

Murakami, Seiichirō (2016) *Jimintō Hitori Ryōshikiha* [One Member of the LDP Faction of Common Sense], Tokyo: Kōdansha.

Nakano, Jun (2016) "'Kōmei Kirai' no Shushō ga Tsuyomeru Kōmei Izon. Kantei to Kōmeitō, Sōka Gakkai o meguru Kihon Kōzu" [Dependence on Kōmeitō Strengthened by a Prime Minister Who "Hates Kōmeitō." Basic Connections Between the Kantei, Kōmeitō and Sōka Gakkai], in Nakano Kōichi (ed.), *Tettei Kenshō. Abe Seiji* [Comprehensive Examination. Abe Politics], Tokyo: Iwanami Shoten, 48–61.

Prime Minister of Japan and His Cabinet (1946) "The Constitution of Japan" (November 3). Online. Available: https://japan.kantei.go.jp/constitution_and_government_of_japan/constitution_e.html (accessed July 18, 2019).

Prime Minister of Japan and His Cabinet (2014a) "Policy Speech by Prime Minister Shinzo Abe to the 186th Session of the Diet" (January 24). Online. Available: https://japan.kantei.go.jp/96_abe/statement/201401/24siseihousin_e.html (accessed July 30, 2019).

Prime Minister of Japan and His Cabinet (2014b) "Press Conference by Prime Minister Abe" (May 15). Online. Available: https://japan.kantei.go.jp/96_abe/statement/201405/0515kaiken.html (accessed July 30, 2019).

Prime Minister of Japan and His Cabinet (2014c) *Rinji Kakugi oyobi Kakuryō Kondankai Gijiroku* [Proceedings of the Extraordinary Cabinet Meeting and Ministers' Discussion] (July 1). Online. Available: https://www.kantei.go.jp/jp/kakugi/2014/__icsFiles/afieldfile/2014/07/22/260701rinjigijiroku.pdf (accessed January 30, 2020).

Prime Minister of Japan and His Cabinet (2014d) "Press Conference by Prime Minister Abe" (July 1). Online. Available: https://japan.kantei.go.jp/96_abe/statement/201407/0701kaiken.html (accessed July 31, 2019).

Prime Minister of Japan and His Cabinet (2015) "Policy Speech by Prime Minister Shinzo Abe to the 189th Session of the Diet" (February 12). Online. Available: https://japan.kantei.go.jp/97_abe/statement/201502/policy.html (accessed August 1, 2019).

Samuels, Richard J. (2004) "Politics, Security Policy, and Japan's Cabinet Legislation Bureau: Who Elected These Guys, Anyway?," JPRI Working Paper, No. 99. Online. Available: http://www.jpri.org/publications/workingpapers/wp99.html (accessed July 19, 2019).

Shiota, Ushio (2016) *Abe Shinzō no Kenpō Sensō* [Abe Shinzō's Constitutional War], Tokyo: Purejidentosha.

Soeya, Yoshihide (2016) *Anzen Hoshō o Toinaosu. "Kyū Jō – Anpo Taisei" o Koete* [Asking Again About the Security. Going Beyond the "Article 9 – Security Treaty System"], Tokyo: NHK Shuppan.

Stockwin, Arthur & Ampiah, Kweku (2017) *Rethinking Japan. The Politics of Contested Nationalism*, Lanham–Boulder–New York–London: Lexington Books.

Tamura, Shigenobu (2014) *Abe Seiken to Anpo Hōsei* [The Abe Administration and Security Laws], Tokyo: Naigai Shuppan.

The Advisory Panel on Reconstruction of the Legal Basis for Security (2008) "Report of the Advisory Panel on Reconstruction of the Legal Basis for Security" (June 24). Online. Available: https://www.kantei.go.jp/jp/singi/anzenhosyou/report.pdf (accessed July 23, 2019).

The Advisory Panel on Reconstruction of the Legal Basis for Security (2014) "Report of the Advisory Panel on Reconstruction of the Legal Basis for Security" (May 15). Online. Available: https://www.kantei.go.jp/jp/singi/anzenhosyou2/dai7/houkoku_en.pdf (accessed July 23, 2019).

Toshikawa, Takao (2019) *Seiji no Riarizumu. Abe Seiken no Yukue* [Political Realism. Whereabouts of the Abe Administration], Tokyo: Kadensha.

Watanabe, Osamu (2016) *Gendaishi no Naka no Abe Seiken. Kenpō, Sensō Hō o meguru Kōbō* [The Abe Administration in Modern History. Battle over the Constitution, War Legislation], Tokyo: Kamogawa Shuppan.

Yomiuri Shinbun (2014) "Beikan Bōgo 'Sansei' 75% Hōjin Yusō. Kirai Sōkai mo 74%. Honsha Yoron Chōsa" [75% "Agree" with Protection of US Ships When Rransporting Japanese. Minesweeping 74% As Well. Our Opinion Poll], June 2, Tokyo morning edition, 1.

Summary and conclusions

When Abe Shinzō formed a government in December 2012, it was hard to predict that he would become the longest-serving prime minister in Japanese history. Despite extensive competences, heads of government in Japan had a reputation as weak decision makers. Even after the electoral and administrative reforms of the 1990s, it was personal skills that were considered the crucial factor that enabled a prime minister to take advantage of the institutional instruments at his/her disposal. After his disastrous first administration, Abe had gained extensive knowledge on the factors that decided about the failures and successes of the heads of government. Being the first prime minister who returned to the post since the establishment of the LDP in 1955, Abe skillfully avoided the errors that could endanger his political survival. The prolonged term in office, in turn, enabled him to lead gradual institutional change without conducting a full-scale institutional reform. Instead of trying in vain to establish a new decision-making system from scratch, he preserved it almost unchanged, but undermined it through layering and conversion strategies. While avoiding antagonizing all veto players, he played one ministry or group of LDP backbenchers off against another.

Long-lasting administration as a precondition for gradual institutional change

The history of Japanese politics in the post-war period teaches us about the factors that decide about prime ministers' failures and successes in remaining in power. Despite theoretically broad competences, the head of government in Japan was traditionally subject to many unofficial constraints on the exertion of power. In order to realize their policy agenda, prime ministers first had to overcome resistance from two kinds of veto players: LDP backbenchers and bureaucrats. The necessity to maintain harmony between different groups in the ruling party and keep balance between distinct ministries explains why most heads of government failed to remain in office for more than two or three years, and only a handful succeeded. The electoral reform of 1994 and the administrative reform implemented in 2001

Summary and conclusions 235

strengthened the prime minister's position vis-à-vis veto players, but it did not guarantee a top-down decision-making process.

Among the factors that weakened the head of government's powers were such determinants as strong political rivalry, backstage dependence on a powerful faction boss, low popularity of the cabinet, lack of charisma and clear policy agenda, overly ambitious policy goals, and electoral defeats in the House of Councilors elections. While divisions in the LDP put the strongest constraints on prime ministers until the 1990s, due to the weakening of factionalism as a result of the electoral reform, their importance waned over time. Instead, the public image of political leaders started playing a more important role in elections of LDP presidents and their ability to remain in power. It was the low popularity of the cabinet, often coupled with a lack of or an overloaded policy agenda, which decreased the electoral chances of the ruling party, which could lead to losing a majority of seats in the upper house. As the cabinet support rate dropped, intra-party pressure on the heads of government to resign increased, which translated into short prime ministerships.

The factors that facilitated the prime minister in remaining in office longer than average included exploitation of factional base of support, high popularity among the public, charisma, bold economic policy agenda, and successive electoral victories. Until the 1990s, it was almost exclusively faction bosses who were chosen as LDP presidents, but after the weakening of factionalism, it became more efficient to rely on a supra-factional basis of support. Those prime ministers who managed to maintain high popularity of the government, either through charismatic performance or through inspiring the people with ambitious economic policy goals, proved the most efficient in quelling voices of discontent from veto players. Successive electoral victories strengthened their position even further, enabling them to become real power brokers.

Due to the nature of the Japanese political system, it was the most efficient to implement lasting institutional reforms in an incremental manner. Only an extended administration created favorable conditions for a gradual institutional change. The prime ministers who exerted the greatest impact on the decision-making process tended to plan implementation of their policy agenda over the long term. Thanks to remaining in office longer than average, they were able to enhance their support base in the ruling party and strengthen the Kantei's institutions. Only when veto players perceived the prime minister's leadership as stable did they start to cooperate within the new institutional framework. Interestingly, the most successful decision makers, such as Satō Eisaku, Nakasone Yasuhiro, and Koizumi Jun'ichirō, did not implement many reforms on governmental and ruling-party levels. Instead of wasting political capital on abolishing the preexisting institutions and replacing them with new ones from scratch, it was more efficient to circumvent them or redefine their role.

236 *Summary and conclusions*

Under his first administration in 2006–2007, Abe committed most of the errors of his predecessors. He overloaded his policy agenda with difficult policy goals without proper preparation. He antagonized both the bureaucrats by passing anti-*amakudari* legislation, and a large part of the electorate by hastening right-wing initiatives. At the same time, Abe improperly reacted to numerous scandals of his cabinet members, which translated into a drop in the popularity of his government. The inability to swiftly resolve the missing pension records problem further increased the scale of LDP's defeat in the upper house election in July 2007. The loss of majority of seats in the House of Councilors translated into bolder voices of discontent in the ruling party, which, along with health problems, prompted Abe to resign suddenly after a single year in office.

Having learned his lesson, under his second administration, Abe prioritized remaining in power against rushing implementation of his policy agenda. Instead of devoting too much energy to realizing his long-cherished goals regarding constitutional revision and the security field, he focused on economic and social policies that were welcomed by a majority of voters. Abe polished the electoral strategy, tactically chose the moment of Diet dissolution, and quickly reacted to any scandals involving the members of his cabinet. Thanks to maintaining the high popularity of the government, he quelled voices of discontent in the ruling party and kept LDP's coalition partner, Kōmeitō, in check. At the same time, Abe fully exploited propitious political conditions, such as the weakening of LDP factions and fragmentation of opposition parties. Abe's subsequent electoral victories, despite the Moritomo Gakuen and Kake Gakuen controversies, contributed to the creation of the myth of his invincibility, which further solidified his power. Not only did Abe become the longest-serving prime minister in Japanese history, but he also created favorable conditions for record-long tenures of Chief Cabinet Secretary (CCS) Suga Yoshihide, Vice-Premier Asō Tarō, LDP Vice-President Kōmura Masahiko and LDP Secretary-General Nikai Toshihiro. The exceptional stability of the Abe administration, in turn, was a precondition for redefining decision-making rules in a gradual manner.

Gradual strengthening of the Abe Kantei

Once Prime Minister Abe stabilized his government, he proceeded to the realization of his policy vision in an incremental way. Without conducting a full-fledged overhaul of governmental institutions, he started redefining the traditional decision-making patterns in the government and in the ruling party through a mixture of layering and conversion strategies. Creation of new organs was pinpointed at changing the balance of power between the Kantei and veto players. The Cabinet Bureau of Personnel Affairs enabled the disciplining of the bureaucrats, the National Security Council (NSC) strengthened the head of government's control over security and foreign affairs, while the multiplication of headquarters under the LDP president's direct jurisdiction led to a marginalization of influential backbenchers in the ruling party.

Not to repeat the errors of his first administration, Abe paid great attention to maintaining policy coherence in his closest entourage. To improve communication within the Kantei, he started holding unofficial daily meetings with the CCS, three deputy CCSs, and the prime minister's executive secretary. He entrusted the post of CCS to Suga Yoshihide, who proved very efficient in coordinating policies with the ministries and the ruling parties. At the same time, the Kasumigaseki know-how of Administrative Deputy CCS Sugita Kazuhiro and Prime Minister's Executive Secretary Imai Takaya facilitated control over the bureaucrats in a top-down manner. The selection of appropriate people as his direct staff and the delegation of responsibilities to them enabled the prime minister to avoid excessive micro-management, thus allowing him to focus on polishing the policy agenda.

The top-down leadership of the prime minister and the Kantei became unquestioned. The previously powerful Administrative Vice-Ministers' Liaison Council did not return to its role from before the Democratic Party of Japan (DPJ) government. Instead of authorizing policies for submission to cabinet meetings, it served as a forum for weekly discussion on the ways of implementing cabinet decisions. Moreover, disclosure of cabinet proceedings contributed to the petrifaction of cabinet meetings, thus leaving more room for the prime minister and the CCS to use their discretionary powers. Only a few cabinet members, such as CCS Suga Yoshihide and Vice-Premier Asō Tarō, were admitted to the inner group of decision makers and consequently reappointed in successive government reshuffles. Most ministers were left little room for independent decisions, as the decision-making process was centralized under the Kantei.

Along with the unofficial daily meetings of the prime minister's direct staff, it was the Cabinet Secretariat that became the central decision-making organ, often identified as the core executive. The Cabinet Secretariat's competences were broadened due to the fact that the Cabinet Bureau of Personnel Affairs, the National Security Secretariat, and a large number of the advisory council offices were created within its structures. As a result, the number of the Cabinet Secretariat's administrative staff was increased by 20% between 2012 and 2015. A lot of experienced, ambitious bureaucrats were dispatched from ministries to the Kantei, which further changed the balance of power in favor of the prime minister.

Interestingly, instead of completely abolishing bureaucratic guidance, to some extent, Abe relied on civil servants to keep his ministers in check. After the establishment of the Cabinet Bureau of Personnel Affairs in 2014, the distribution of more than 600 high-ranking bureaucratic posts was centralized under the Kantei. CCS Suga used the new rules to reward those civil servants who remained loyal toward the prime minister, who displayed initiative in line with the government's policy agenda and strategy, and whose background fitted Abe's key policies, such as the empowerment of women. At the same time, the Cabinet Bureau of Personnel Affairs was used to punish those civil servants whose convictions differed from the policy of the government or who simply were deemed insufficiently loyal toward the Kantei.

Prime Minister Abe was particularly active in the security and foreign policy fields, which was facilitated by the creation of the NSC in 2013. Its core meetings were attended by the prime minister, the CCS, and the ministers of foreign affairs and defense. Abe established the NSC both to facilitate a swift response to emergency situations and to formulate long-term strategies, such as the National Security Strategy announced in December 2013. The new organ was assisted by the National Security Secretariat headed by Abe's trusted foreign policy adviser, Yachi Shōtarō. Abe used the NSC extensively to hold discussions on current security matters as well as to promote his key policy initiatives, including legalization for collective self-defense. To some extent, a centralization of foreign policy making was implemented at the expense of the competences of foreign ministers, whose individual initiatives were less visible under the second Abe administration than under previous governments.

Abe used advisory councils extensively to impose the pace of the decision-making process on crucial policies. Apart from the revived Council on Economic and Fiscal Policy (CEFP), he established a record-high number of new councils and arbitrarily selected their members so as to ensure their loyalty. As the councils' competences largely overlapped, it was the prime minister who became the ultimate arbiter in case of policy differences between them. The councils were subordinated to the Kantei to such an extent that sometimes their reports followed, rather than influenced, cabinet decisions. A large group of special advisers to the cabinet further enabled Abe to gain access to professional knowledge independently of the bureaucrats.

A similar network of advisory councils and headquarters was established in the ruling party. As the new bodies were controlled directly by the LDP president, they enabled the bypassing of traditional intra-party decision-making organs, such as the Policy Research Council and the General Council. As a result, while advance screening of all bill projects was preserved, instead of shaping intra-party consensus, it served to legitimize the Kantei's decisions. Policy projects were imposed on backbenchers along with schedules of deliberations that left almost no room for amendments. Acceleration and simplification of decision-making procedures met with dissatisfaction from party officials, but no one dared overtly challenge Abe's leadership. What additionally favored maintaining discipline in the LDP was the fact that it took some time for parliamentary tribes to restore their former connections and absorb new knowledge after three years in opposition under the DPJ administration. The LDP Research Commission on the Tax System, composed of the most influential senior backbenchers, put up the strongest resistance, but even it had to cede to the Kantei's pressure when preparing the annual tax system outlines, and was eventually penetrated by new members loyal to Abe.

Similarly to neglecting consensus-seeking activities in the LDP, Abe made light of the long-standing, but uncodified parliamentary traditions. Without conducting any major reform of the Diet, the Kantei's control over the legislative process was strengthened through establishment of special parliamentary committees, strict application of party discipline, and flexibility in scheduling Diet sessions. Despite the highly controversial character of many of the bills promoted by the government, they encountered only minimal resistance in the LDP. To further limit the possibility of criticizing the government during deliberations in the Diet, Abe did not waver from refusing to hold extraordinary sessions in 2015 and 2017. Gradually, Abe's domination over LDP backbenchers was reflected in official party rules. To enable the continuation of his prime ministership, in March 2017, the LDP Convention approved an extension of the allowable number of consecutive three-year long terms of the LDP president from 2 to 3.

Thanks to the new institutional tools and the general conviction about Abe's invincibility, different actors from the Kantei started applying pressure on veto players by simply referring to the prime minister's authority. As a side-effect, the transparency of the decision-making process was weakened. Not to endanger their careers, bureaucrats started paying excessive attention to the intentions of the Kantei, which led to violations of procedures or covering up evidence of scandals that involved their superiors. The bending of rules by the Ministry of Education, Culture, Sports, Science and Technology to allow Kake Gakuen to establish a veterinary faculty and the forgery of documents concerning the Moritomo Gakuen issue by the Ministry of Finance (MOF) exposed the detrimental effects of bureaucrats' complete subordination to the will of actors from the prime minister's direct entourage. At the party level, the overwhelming strength of the Kantei quelled voices of discontent together with individual initiative. The safest choice for LDP backbenchers was simply to follow Abe's instructions, which detrimentally influenced intra-party democracy.

The institutional reforms were implemented by Abe in an incremental manner. Instead of simply replacing old organs with new ones, new institutions were added to the preexisting structures through a layering strategy. The Cabinet Bureau of Personnel Affairs did not undermine the role played by the National Personnel Authority, but it simply provided the prime minister with instruments for exerting his previously existing power regarding bureaucratic nominations. The NSC, in turn, did not replace the old nine-member Security Council, but rather integrated it into a more comprehensive structure, while delegating other responsibilities to meetings in a four-member format. Similarly, the establishment of new advisory councils and headquarters under the LDP president's direct control did not lead to the abolition of the other intra-party decision-making bodies. While preserving the preexisting structures almost intact, Abe bypassed them through new ones, thus accelerating, simplifying, and steamrolling the decision-making process under the Kantei.

Major effects of minor changes

The empowered Kantei enabled Abe to act as a power broker vis-à-vis veto players. Through *divide et impera* rule, the prime minister played one ministry or group of LDP backbenchers off against another. Regarding implementation of Abenomics and postponement of consumption tax increase, he pacified the MOF and tax system parliamentary tribe by the use of Ministry of Economy, Trade and Industry (METI) and newly elected lawmakers. At the same time, the prime minister broke the Cabinet Legislation Bureau's opposition to a reinterpretation of Article 9 of the Constitution thanks to assistance from Ministry of Foreign Affairs (MOFA). The longer Abe served as prime minister, the greater was the impact of gradual institutional reforms on formal and informal decision-making mechanisms, and the more prone veto players became to pressure from the Kantei.

The MOF and METI had been rivals long before Abe assumed prime ministerial office. While the former ministry appealed for the maintenance of budgetary balance, either through limiting expenses or increasing taxes, the latter put greatest emphasis on achieving a high rate of economic growth. As it was METI's goals that better fitted Abe's policy agenda, it is natural that the prime minister took advantage of its institutional backing to realize his policy vision. He intentionally employed a number of former METI bureaucrats, such as Prime Minister's Executive Secretary Imai Takaya, in the Kantei. Their Kasumigaseki know-how and reform-minded attitude proved useful in imposing controversial decisions on other ministries, especially the MOF.

METI officials not only actively supported Abenomics, but also participated in formulating this bold set of policies. All "three arrows" – monetary easing, expansive fiscal policy, and structural reforms to encourage private sector investments – were in line with METI's policy of stimulating economic growth. Abe charged the newly established Headquarters for Japan's Economic Revitalization with the microeconomic aspects of Abenomics, and the revived CEFP with the macroeconomic. The "first arrow" was implemented through pressure on the Bank of Japan (BOJ). Despite the formal independence of the Bank and criticism of governmental plans by Governor Shirakawa Masaaki, in January 2013, the BOJ agreed to pursue a 2% inflation target, as requested by Prime Minister Abe. Kuroda Haruhiko, nominated as the new BOJ governor in March 2013, was much more willing to cooperate with the Kantei regarding anti-deflation policy than his predecessor. Under his chairpersonship, the BOJ initiated massive purchases of Japanese government bonds.

As the "second arrow" resembled traditional "pork barrel politics," it was eagerly embraced by most LDP backbenchers. Increasing expenses for public works met with concerns from the MOF, but the nomination of Vice-Premier Asō Tarō, a supporter of an active fiscal policy, as finance minister facilitated the preparation of successive supplementary budgets. To stimulate the economy, trillions of yen were devoted to large infrastructure projects. Reconstruction from the Great East Japan Earthquake and preparations for the Tokyo Olympic Games provided additional arguments to increase the scale of public works. The Kantei maintained the position of power broker, balancing between the LDP construction *zoku*'s requests to bolster budget spending and the MOF and CEFP private-sector members' insistence on maintaining budgetary balance.

The targets of the "third arrow" of Abenomics remained the least clearly defined. The prime minister relied on the expert knowledge of the members of the Industrial Competitiveness Council under the Headquarters for Japan's Economic Revitalization in preparing successive growth strategies. Some of their ideas were realized by newly established organs, such as the National Strategic Special Zone Advisory Council that introduced different kinds of facilitations for investors in National Strategic Special Zones. A lot of reforms conducted under the "third arrow," e.g. accession to the Trans-Pacific Partnership (TPP), closely followed METI's policy, which reflected its strong position in the government. In order to weaken the solidarity of the agricultural parliamentary tribe in the LDP, which remained the main opponent of TPP accession, Abe offered influential party and governmental posts to one of its leading members, Nishikawa Kōya, thus gaining his loyalty. The prime minister invested much of his political capital into ratification of the TPP treaty, which, however, did not enter into force in its original version due to withdrawal from the agreement by US President Donald Trump in January 2017. Other initiatives, such as promotion of women's empowerment, were imposed by the prime minister and his closest entourage and used to bolster the government's popularity.

While in the case of Abenomics, the MOF ceded ground to the Kantei and METI without much struggle, it put up a much tougher fight over the consumption tax increase. This time, it could count on support from Vice-Premier Asō Tarō, LDP Secretary-General Tanigaki Sadakazu, and the powerful tax system parliamentary tribe. Nevertheless, the prime minister leaned toward the stance of his economic advisers and METI bureaucrats who claimed that a value-added tax (VAT) hike would endanger Japan's economic recovery. On the party level, the Association for the Success of Abenomics, composed of young lawmakers who were prone to popular sentiments against the tax reform, proved instrumental in counterbalancing the powerful LDP Research Commission on the Tax System. Eventually, in light of the information that Japan's GDP had contracted for the second quarter in a row, in mid-November 2014, the prime minister announced his decision to postpone the second stage of the VAT hike until April 2017, and dissolved the House of Representatives. The only concession to veto players from Abe was the abolition of the clause according to which a sufficient economic growth rate should be attained to proceed with the reform.

LDP's landslide victory in the December 2014 election further enhanced the prime minister's position vis-à-vis veto players. The Kantei imposed its own version of the tax reform outline for FY 2015 on the LDP Research Commission on the Tax System. When, in October 2015, Commission Chairperson Noda Takeshi opposed the Kantei and Kōmeitō's plan to introduce a special reduced tax rate system together with the VAT hike, Abe simply removed him from office. Noda's successor, Miyazawa Yōichi, proved more willing to cooperate with the prime minister. Pacification of the LDP Research Commission on the Tax System facilitated the second postponement of the consumption tax increase, announced at the beginning of June 2016. This time, the decision was made despite opposition even from some of Abe's closest associates, such as LDP Policy Research Council and Special Committee for Financial Reconstruction Chair Inada Tomomi. Just as in 2014, the prime minister used economic data provided by METI to justify his decision. As he claimed, a slowdown in emerging economies could cause another global crisis, which created unfavorable conditions for the tax reform. Just as in 2014, the VAT hike postponement was strategically used before an election, this time to the House of Councilors.

Abe became a real power broker not only in the field of economic policy. While Abenomics and the postponement of the consumption tax increase were aimed at bolstering LDP's electoral results, the prime minister never abandoned the policy agenda of his first administration. This time, however, he implemented right-wing initiatives in an incremental manner, after having ensured that his position was strong enough to trade some of his popularity for achieving part of his long-cherished goals. The best example was the legalization of collective self-defense. Due to difficulties with revising the Constitution, Abe chose to reinterpret Article 9. In order to do that, he had to assuage the Cabinet Legislation Bureau's opposition against reinterpretation of the Constitution. After LDP's victory in the House of Councilors election in July 2013, Abe violated an unwritten rule that the director-general of this important organ should be recruited from the ministries related to internal affairs, and selected former MOFA bureaucrat, Komatsu Ichirō, for this post. As at least since Operation Desert Storm, MOFA had been promoting Japan's contribution to global security through legalization of collective self-defense, the change of the Bureau's head eliminated a major obstacle to the realization of Abe's plans. The prime minister strategically entrusted preparation of the new interpretation of the Constitution to as many as four former MOFA Treaties Bureau (International Legal Affairs Bureau) heads: Advisory Panel on Reconstruction of the Legal Basis for Security Chairperson Yanai Shunji, National Security Adviser Yachi Shōtarō, Assistant CCS Kanehara Nobukatsu, and Cabinet Legislation Bureau Director-General Komatsu Ichirō.

Summary and conclusions 243

At the party level, discussions took place in the LDP Headquarters for Reconstruction of the Legal Basis for Security and the General Council. By referring to the ruling on the Sunagawa case, LDP Vice-President Kōmura Masahiko managed to persuade most opponents to the Kantei's stance. In the LDP General Council, only a single member, Murakami Seiichirō, dared voice opposition, warning Abe against violating the Constitution. The most difficult task was to persuade LDP's coalition partner to accept the reform. In order to soften Kōmeitō's stance, the Kantei did not waver from examining the possibility of cooperation with conservative opposition parties or even threatening that Kōmeitō's relationship with Sōka Gakkai could be found illegal due to a violation of the constitutional principle of the separation of the state and religion. After long negotiations, Kōmeitō agreed to a limited version of collective self-defense. The cabinet decision from July 2014 was followed by the passage of a set of security bills in summer 2015. At the cost of arousing a wide popular movement against reinterpretation of the Constitution that led to a temporary drop in the government support rate, Abe thus managed to implement a revolutionary change in Japan's security policy.

Abe failed to achieve all of his long-cherished goals, such as a comprehensive revision of the Constitution, until his sudden resignation in August 2020. Nevertheless, thanks to the efficiently functioning Kantei, he still became one of the most successful prime ministers in Japanese history. While the electoral and administrative reforms of the 1990s prepared the ground for top-down leadership, it is a full understanding of the methods of conducting a gradual institutional change that paved the way toward Abe's record-long term in office. A skillful adaptation of political strategy to the strength of veto players and the level of discretion in interpretation or enforcement of rules proved crucial in enhancing the Kantei's position vis-à-vis the bureaucrats and LDP backbenchers. Power shifts in the Japanese government, in turn, enabled Abe to implement a lot of his ambitious plans in an incremental manner. While it remains to be seen if Abe's successors repeat his success, the initiation of a gradual change in bureaucratic ethics and LDP backbenchers' political culture can surely form the foundation of new path-dependent processes toward a durable redefinition of the balance of power between the main institutional players in Japanese politics.

Index

Abe Akie 61
Abe Shintarō 33, 41, 66, 74
Abe Shinzō: factional politics 69–73; first administration 14–15, 23–25, 27–28, 30–31, 48–49; government support 24–25, 57–64; policy agenda 55–57, 166–168, 187–188, 207–208; *see also* Abenomics; Abenomics 2.0; Seiwa Seisaku Kenkyūkai
Abenomics 8, 55–56, 76, 80, 139–140, 145, 152, 164–171, 179–182, 189–191, 193–194, 199, 240–242; "first arrow" 171–173; "second arrow" 173–175; "third arrow" 175–179; *see also* National Strategic Special Zones; women's empowerment
Abenomics 2.0 180–181; *see also* "dynamic engagement of all citizens"; "employment ice age generation"
Academy of Hope 82
administrative deputy chief cabinet secretary 16; *see also* Furukawa Teijirō; Ishihara Nobuo; Matoba Junzō; Sugita Kazuhiro
administrative reform 2–3, 18–19, 44, 46, 90, 92–94, 103, 114, 120, 169, 234
Administrative Reform Promotion Committee 43
Administrative Vice-Ministers' Council 16, 27, 43, 100; *see also* Administrative Vice-Ministers' Liaison Council
Administrative Vice-Ministers' Liaison Council 100, 178, 237
advance screening 46, 75, 132–136, 151–152, 238
Advisory Panel on Reconstruction of the Legal Basis for Security 124, 210–211, 213–214, 216–219

Afghanistan 210
Akagi Munenori 135
Akagi Norihiko 24
Akaishi Kōichi 121
Akihito 101
Algerian crisis 115, 127n5
amakudari 14, 49n1, 91, 146, 177–178; anti-*amakudari* law 27, 100, 236
Amari Akira 60, 106, 120–123, 139, 142, 153, 189; as decision-maker behind Abenomics 103, 168, 170–171, 175, 177
Aoki Mikio 30
APEC 191
Arc of Freedom and Prosperity 119, 127n8
Armitage, Richard L. 114–115, 227
Article 9 of the Constitution 65, 76, 206–211; reinterpretation of 118, 124, 211–212, 214–221, 223–225, 227–229, 242
"artificial alternation of power" 69
ASEAN 117, 192, 217
Asia's Democratic Security Diamond 119, 127n9
Asō Tarō: as faction boss 66, 70–71, 97; as foreign minister 119; as prime minister 24–25; as vice-premier 61, 67, 103, 107, 121, 170, 173, 192, 236–237, 241
Association Demanding Prompt Withdrawal from TPP Accession 143
Association for the Success of Abenomics 191, 198, 202, 241
Association of Shintō Shrines 73
Association Pondering Article 20 of the Constitution 74
Association Seeking Recovery Funds Without Tax Increase 166, 191
Association to Consider the Tax System for the Next Generation 141

Association to Protect the National Interest During TPP Negotiations 143
Aum Shinrikyō 74, 114

backbenchers 2–3, 14, 17, 132–137; *see also* parliamentary tribes; two-track decision-making
Banchō Seisaku Kenkyūjo 66, 67, 71
Bank of Japan (BOJ) 55, 92, 121, 164–166, 171–173, 175, 179–181, 191, 240
Basic Policies for Economic and Fiscal Management and Reform 121–122, 140, 169, 174
Belt and Road Initiative 96, 127n3
"Big-Boned Policy" *see* Basic Policies for Economic and Fiscal Management and Reform
Bill Concerning Reform of National Public Service System 109
Bill Establishing Political Leadership 28, 120
Bill on Protection of Specially Designated Secrets 95, 101, 118–119, 140, 156, 158
Budget Committee 157, 197, 213
budget compilation 45–48, 92, 140, 170, 182
bureaucrats 2–3, 13–16, 27–28, 89–93; *see also amakudari*; Cabinet Bureau of Personnel Affairs; sectionalism

Cabinet Bureau of Personnel Affairs 7, 89, 97–98, 108–113, 236–239
Cabinet Committee for Protection and Oversight 119
Cabinet Law 15, 18
Cabinet Legislation Bureau 90, 206, 208–215, 222, 225–226, 228, 242
cabinet meetings 16, 18, 27, 100–102, 126, 209, 237
Cabinet Office 12, 18, 92, 103, 106, 119–125
Cabinet Secretariat 2–3, 12, 15, 18, 43–44, 47, 93–94, 101, 104, 113–117, 119–121, 193, 213, 237; organizational structure 98–100, 124–125
Cameron, David 200
censure motion 29, 80
central government reform *see* administrative reform
Central Union of Agricultural Cooperatives 111, 143–144, 178

charisma 26–27, 35–36, 39, 59, 235
chief cabinet secretary (CCS) 3, 12, 15–16, 18, 73, 97–101, 104, 108–117, 237–238; *see also* Fukuda Yasuo; Gotōda Masaharu; Suga Yoshihide
China 3, 115, 117, 142, 148, 199–200, 216
Civil Service Reform Basic Law 109
civil servants *see* bureaucrats
civil service reform 46, 108–109
collective security 210, 212–213, 218–219, 222, 225
collective self-defense 55, 72, 156, 211–221, 224–229, 242–243; decision on legalization of 221–223; political stances on 206–211
Combined Action Executive Committee Resisting War and Violation of Article 9 229
"comfort women" 80, 85n5
Comprehensive Security Ministerial Council 113
"conservative mainstream" 32, 65
Constitutional Democratic Party of Japan (CDPJ) 78, 83, 207
consumption tax 22, 29, 145, 166–167, 173–174, 186–190, 240–242; first hike postponement 141, 190–196; hike decision under the Noda cabinet 21, 165, 187; second hike postponement 196–201
conversion 4–8, 229, 234, 236
core executive 2–3, 237
coronavirus 63, 84n2, 145, 175
corporate tax 36, 122, 139–141, 158, 167, 175–176, 189–190, 195
Council for Implementation of House of Representatives Reform "by the End of Heisei Era" 157
Council for Protection of Information 119
Council for Regulatory Reform 169–170
Council for Science and Technology 169
Council for Science, Technology and Innovation 169
Council on Economic and Fiscal Policy (CEFP) 28, 44, 46–47, 120–123, 238; and Abenomics 168–170, 172–174, 181, 240–241; and VAT hike postponement 188, 190
Council on Strengthening the Functions of the Kantei Regarding National Security 114

Council to Conceive Economy and Society After 2020 157
"cow's walk tactic" 137, 159n4, 227
Creation "Japan" 70, 73
Crimea 111, 118
critical juncture 4, 7

Democratic Party (DP) 81–83, 199
Democratic Party For the People (DPP) 83
Democratic Party of Japan (DPJ) 6–7, 20–21, 25–26, 28, 30–31, 38, 58–59, 77–81, 107, 112, 145; and Abenomics 164–165, 172, 177; and VAT hike postponement 187–188; and reinterpretation of Constitution 207, 226–227
deputy chief cabinet secretary for crisis management 17, 114, 116
Diaoyu Islands *see* Senkaku Islands
Diet Members' Alliance for Promoting the Assessment of the Constitution 208
displacement 5, 7
Doi Takako 29
Dōko Shigeru 157
Dokō Toshio 46
drift 5–6
"dynamic engagement of all citizens" 56, 180

earmarked funds for road improvement 139
Eda Kenji 80–81
Eda Satsuki 30
Edano Yukio 83
electoral reform 14, 17, 21, 64, 137, 148, 234–235
electricity retail market 176–177
"employment ice age generation" 56
Environment Agency 45
Etō Seiichi 106–107
Etō Seishirō 143
Experts' Council for Establishment of the NSC 115

factionalism 17, 20–22, 64, 148, 235
Financial Services Agency 92
Fujiyama Aiichirō 20
Fukuda Jun'ichi 62
Fukuda Muneyuki 106
Fukuda Takeo 20, 66
Fukuda Yasuo 15, 23, 66; as CCS 43, 97; as prime minister 26, 70, 149, 211

Fukushima 20, 27, 112, 177
Furukawa Teijirō 16, 43
Furutachi Ichirō 60
Furuya Kazuyuki 95
Fushiya Kazuhiko 47
Futenma 28, 194, 229n5
Future Investment Council 124, 169; *see also* Industrial Competitiveness Council

gentan 144
Gotōda Masaharu 15, 43, 97
Government Headquarters for TPP Measures 143
Government Revitalization Unit 28, 120
Government-Ruling Parties Liaison Council 75
Great East Japan Earthquake 60, 75, 139, 145, 156, 166, 174–176, 197–199, 241
Great Hanshin Earthquake 114
Guidelines for Japan–US Defense Cooperation 223

Hadley, Stephen J. 114
Hagiuda Kōichi 95, 109
Hamada Kōichi 125, 166, 189, 198
Hamada Yasukazu 70, 150, 225
Harada Minoru 201, 218
Hasebe Yasuo 226
Hasegawa Eiichi 106, 112, 165
Hasegawa Yasuchika 178
Hashimoto Gaku 145
Hashimoto Ryūtarō 29, 44, 65, 108, 186
Hashimoto Tōru 77, 79–81
Hata Tsutomu 65, 228
Hatoyama Ichirō 19
Hatoyama Yukio 21–22, 25, 28, 228
Hayashi Makoto 111
Hayashi Yoshimasa 58, 70–72, 79, 101, 123, 142, 151
Headquarters for Japan's Economic Revitalization, in the government 120–121, 123, 153, 167–170, 172, 181, 240–241; in the LDP 152, 154, 168, 170
Health Promotion Law 146
Heisei Kenkyūkai 64
Heiseikai *see* Heisei Kenkyūkai
Hiranuma Takeo 80
historical institutionalism 4; *see also* critical juncture; theory of gradual institutional change

Index   247

hometown tax 56, 97, 111
Honda Etsurō 125, 166, 189, 191, 198
Horiuchi Mitsuo 65
Hosoda Hiroyuki 66, 71, 149–150, 153–155
Hosokawa Morihiro 44, 186, 228

Ibuki Bunmei 195
Iijima Isao 43, 125, 220
Iizuka Atsushi 121
Ikeda Daisaku 74
Ikeda Hayato 20, 31–32, 36, 41, 65
Ikōkai 66
Imai Takaya 96, 112, 139, 165, 180, 189–200, 237, 240
Imamura Masahiro 60
Imperial Household Agency 101
"important policy councils" 18, 44
Inada Tomomi 60, 70, 122, 140, 150, 198, 242
Industrial Competitiveness Council 121, 123–124, 168–169, 175, 241; see also Future Investment Council
Information Oversight Audit Committees 119
Information Security Oversight Division 119
Initiatives from Osaka 81
Inoue Yoshihisa 197, 218
Inoue Yoshiyuki 94, 104
interest groups 14, 138, 145
International Monetary Fund (IMF) 192
Iraq 37, 209–210, 225
"iron triangle" 15
Ise-Shima summit 200
Ishiba Shigeru 58, 65, 67, 70–73, 146–147, 153–154, 180; as LDP secretary-general 149–150, 215–216, 218–219; as minister 56, 106, 224
Ishihara Nobuo 16
Ishihara Nobuteru 58, 67, 70, 171
Ishihara Shintarō 70, 79
Ishii Masafumi 212
Ishii Mitsujirō 20
Isozaki Yōsuke 106, 115
Itō Motoshige 122
Itō Tatsuya 65, 106
Iwata Kikuo 172–173, 179, 189
Izumi Hiroto 62, 106

JA Zenchū see Central Union of Agricultural Cooperatives

Japan Business Federation 96, 188
Japan Conference 73
Japan Defense Agency 207, 211
Japan Development Bank 92
Japan Innovation Party (JIP) 81, 227
Japan Medical Association 138, 140, 145
Japan Post 17, 23, 37–38, 40, 47–48, 69, 120, 193
Japan Restoration Association (JRA) 77, 79–81, 172, 218, 220
Japan Revitalization Strategy 169, 176, 181
Japan Socialist Party (JSP) 29, 38, 74, 78, 186, 207
Japan Tobacco 45, 146
Japanese Communist Party (JCP) 81, 207
Japanese Democratic Party 19
Japanese Heart 80
Japanese Liberal Party 19
Japanese National Railways 37, 45, 47–48

Kadomatsu Takashi 112
Kagoike Yasunori 61
Kaieda Banri 80–81
Kaifu Toshiki 21–22, 33, 209
Kajiyama Hiroshi 150
Kajiyama Seiroku 97, 108, 192
Kake Gakuen 62–63, 82–83, 109, 112, 157, 178, 239
Kake Kōtarō 62
kaken 209, 218
Kamoshita Ichirō 149–150
Kan Naoto 20, 26, 34, 187, 228
Kanehara Nobukatsu 95, 110, 212–213, 216, 220, 224, 242
Kantei 3, 7–8, 12, 15–17, 42–44, 216; and the government 93–97, 102–108, 110–115, 124–126, 169–170; and the LDP 73, 133–135, 151–158, 195–196; see also Cabinet Office; Cabinet Secretariat
Kasumigaseki 92; see also bureaucrats
Katō Katsunobu 56, 95, 109, 146, 150, 178, 180
Katō Kōichi 65, 97, 208
Kim Jong-il 94
Kim Jong-un 118
Kinmirai Seiji Kenkyūkai 67
Kishi Nobusuke 20, 66, 69, 89, 208, 219, 227

Kishida Fumio 65, 70–72, 103, 119, 147, 150, 154
Kishii Shigetaka 60
Kitagawa Kazuo 196, 218–220, 223
Kitamura Shigeru 95, 116
Kitaoka Shin'ichi 216
Kōchikai 64–66, 68, 72, 97, 208, 225
kōenkai 75, 188
Koga Makoto 65, 79, 208, 225
Koga Nobuaki 188
Koike Yuriko 66, 82–84, 104, 114
"Koizumi's children" 42, 67
Koizumi Jun'ichirō 4, 16–17, 29–31, 33–38, 40–48, 65–66, 75, 120–123, 187, 210, 235
Koizumi Shinjirō 66, 72, 142, 144, 157
Komatsu Ichirō 212–213, 220, 242
Kōmeitō 46–47, 74–77, 79–81, 83–84, 138; and reinterpretation of Constitution 208–209, 211, 216, 218–226, 228, 243; and VAT hike 187, 190, 192, 195–197, 199, 200–201
Kōmoto Toshio 66
Kōmura Masahiko 66, 71, 147, 189, 198–199, 214–216, 218–220
Kōno Ichirō 32
Kōno Tarō 95, 97, 101, 119
Kōno Yōhei 65–66, 208
Kōnoike Yoshitada 227
Kosaka Kenji 65
Kōzuki Toyohisa 111
Kumamoto Earthquake 95, 175, 198–199, 201
Kuniya Hiroko 60
Kuroda Haruhiko 172–173, 188, 191, 240
Kurokawa Hiromu 111
kuromaku 21–22, 33
Kyūma Fumio 24

Lagarde, Christine 192
layering 4–8, 115, 151, 155, 229, 239
LDP Diet Affairs Committee 136
LDP Disaster Resilient Japan General Research Commission 140
LDP Election Strategy Committee 149
LDP General Affairs Deliberative Council 214
LDP General Council 15, 47, 132–133, 135, 151, 153, 214, 225–226
LDP Headquarters for Reconstruction of the Legal Basis for Security 152, 215, 243
LDP Headquarters for the Party and Political System Reform 147
LDP Headquarters for the Promotion of Revision of the Constitution 153–155
LDP House of Councilors Caucus 29–30, 66
LDP Policy Council 151
LDP Policy Research Council 15, 132–135, 142, 151–155, 177, 221, 238
LDP Public Relations Headquarters 149
LDP Research Commission on Comprehensive Agricultural Policy and Trade 143
LDP Research Commission on the Tax System 24, 122, 134, 138–142, 176, 188–191, 195–199, 241–242
LDP Research Council for Regional Diplomatic and Economic Partnership 143
LDP secretary-general 17, 68, 73, 133, 149–150; *see also* Ishiba Shigeru; Nikai Toshihiro; Tanigaki Sadakazu
LDP Shadow Cabinet 151
LDP Special Committee for Financial Reconstruction 122, 198, 242
legislative initiative 133, 136
legislative process 3, 28, 80, 135–137, 155–159, 239
Lehman Brothers 174, 191, 197–200
Liaison Council of All Ministries 100
Liberal Democratic Party (LDP): decision-making bodies 15, 132–137, 151–155; establishment of 19–20; factions 14, 20–22, 31–33, 41–42, 64–73
Liberal Party (LP): Yoshida's 19, 133; Ozawa's 74, 83
"logic of the pendulum" *see* "artificial alternation of power"

Machimura Nobutaka 58, 66, 71, 109, 188, 195
Maehara Seiji 83
Maekawa Kihei 62, 112
Management and Coordination Agency 43
Masuda Hiroya 82
Masuda Kaneshichi 133
Masuzoe Yōichi 82
Matoba Junzō 27, 30, 94, 210
Matsui Ichirō 81
Matsuno Yorihisa 81

Matsuoka Toshikatsu 24
Matsushima Midori 60, 194
middle-sized constituencies 64; *see also* electoral reform
Miki Takeo 20, 66
minister's assistants 106
ministers of state for special missions 18, 103, 105
Ministry of Agriculture, Forestry and Fisheries (MAFF) 112, 142–143
Ministry of Defense (MOD) 27–28, 115–117, 211–212
Ministry of Economy, Trade and Industry (METI) 17, 92–93, 111–112, 120–121, 142; and Abenomics 164–170, 177–182, 240–241; and VAT hike 190, 200–202, 241–242
Ministry of Education, Culture, Sports, Science and Technology 62, 109, 112, 169, 239
Ministry of Health, Labor and Welfare 14, 28
Ministry of Home Affairs 16, 93, 95
Ministry of Internal Affairs and Communications 47, 56, 109, 111
Ministry of International Trade and Industry (MITI) 17, 92
Ministry of Justice 111
Ministry of Finance (MOF) 16–17, 46–48, 92–93, 120–122, 146; and Abenomics 164–166, 170–176, 181–182, 240–241; and Moritomo Gakuen scandal 61–63, 107, 112, 239; and VAT hike 186–193, 195–196, 201–202; *see also* budget compilation; consumption tax
Ministry of Foreign Affairs (MOFA) 16–17, 28, 96, 98, 110–111, 116, 142; and reinterpretation of the Constitution 206, 208–210, 212–213, 228, 242
Ministry of Land, Infrastructure, Transport and Tourism 75
Ministry of the Treasury 32, 46
Miyazaki Reiichi 210
Miyazawa Kiichi 22, 33, 41, 65
Miyazawa Yōichi 142, 194, 196, 242
Momii Katsuto 59
Mori Masako 107
Mori Yoshirō 22–23, 30, 66, 79
Moritomo Gakuen 61–63, 72, 82–83, 107, 111–112, 157, 239
Moriyama Hiroshi 143

Motegi Toshimitsu 71, 119, 146, 150, 168, 171, 177
Murakami Seiichirō 69, 71, 147, 153, 156, 180, 199, 214, 225, 228
Murata Renhō 82
Murayama Tomiichi 186, 228

NAIS 70
Nakae Motoya 96
Nakagawa Hidenao 66, 166, 188
Nakagawa Shōichi 25, 70
Nakaima Hirokazu 194
Nakasone Hirofumi 66
Nakasone Yasuhiro 4, 33, 35–47, 147, 156, 235
Nakatani Gen 219, 226
Nakayama Kyōko 104
National Defense Council 43, 113–114
National Federation of Agricultural Cooperative Associations 142, 144
National Personnel Authority 90, 110, 178, 239
National Police Agency 16–17, 95, 98, 116
National Public Service Law 104, 106
National Security Council (NSC): in Japan 104, 113–119, 216, 225, 238–239; in US 114, 118
National Security Secretariat 98, 116–117, 216, 222, 224, 237–238
National Security Strategy 117–118, 238
National Strategic Special Zone Advisory Council 124, 164, 176, 241
National Strategic Special Zones 62, 122, 140, 176, 178–179, 181–182, 241
National Strategy Unit 28, 120
National Tax Agency 92
Nemoto Takumi 70, 104, 107
New Economic Growth Strategy Workshop 70
New Frontier Party (NFP) 74
NHK 59–60, 98
Nikai Toshihiro 67, 71, 96, 140, 147, 150, 236
Nippon Keidanren *see* Japan Business Federation
Nippon Telegraph and Telephone Corporation 45
Nishikawa Kōya 143, 158, 241
Nishimura Akihiro 95
Nishimura Yasutoshi 95, 171
no-confidence motion 20, 29, 97, 199
Noda Seiko 70–71, 73, 150, 153, 180, 214

Noda Takeshi 139, 141, 153, 180, 188–189, 195–196, 214
Noda Yoshihiko 20–21, 80, 82, 167, 187
Nogami Kōtarō 95
North Korea 34, 63, 76, 82, 94–95, 98, 114, 117–118, 216
Northern Territories 18, 111
Nuclear Regulation Authority 112
"nuclear village" 145
Nukaga Fukushirō 65, 139, 188, 191
Nye, Joseph S. 115, 227

Obuchi Keizō 65, 74, 97
Obuchi Yūko 60, 194
Official Development Assistance (ODA) 117
Ōhira Masayoshi 20, 65, 135, 186
Okada Katsuya 81–82
Okada Naoki 95
Okamura Tadashi 178
Okazaki Hisahiko 210
Okuhara Masaaki 111
Onaga Takeshi 194
Ōno Banboku 20, 32
Operation Desert Storm 209, 242
Osaka Metropolis plan 77, 79, 81
Osaka Restoration Association 79, 81
Ōshima Tadamori 67, 156
Ōta Hiroko 47, 169
Ozato Sadatoshi 65
Ozawa Ichirō 21, 25, 65, 74, 83, 209

pandemic *see* coronavirus
Parliamentary League to Renew Challenges 70
parliamentary tribes 2–3, 14–15, 132–133, 137–146, 238; agricultural 142–146, 158, 241; commerce and industry 164–166, 187; construction 65, 140, 145, 173; financial 186, 192; labor and welfare 140, 145; road 139; tax system 134, 138–139, 142, 196–197, 202
Party Cherishing Japanese Heart *see* Japanese Heart
Party for Future Generations (PFG) 80, 228
Party Reform Promotion Investigation Committee 73
Party of Hope (PH) 82–83
path dependence *see* historical institutionalism
peacekeeping operations 115, 210–211, 222
People's Council for Dynamic Engagement of All Citizens 170, 180
People's Life Party (PLP) 81, 227
Personnel Examination Council 108, 110
"plan of doubling the income" 36
Policy Research Council *see* LDP Policy Research Council
"pork barrel politics" 173, 240
Prime Minister's Office 15, 18
prime minister's special advisers 12, 104, 106, 108
Proactive Contribution to Peace 117, 119
Public Employees Law 91

question time 157

Reagan, Ronald 34
Reconstruction Agency 103
Recruit scandal 21–22, 29, 49n3
Regulatory Reform Promotion Council 145, 169
ringi 2, 90
rule of dispersed management 13, 18
Ruling Coalition Conference on Reconstruction of the Legal Basis for Security 219
Ruling Parties Policymakers' Council 75
Russia 96, 111, 116, 118, 148

Sagawa Nobuhisa 61
Saitō Ken 112, 142
Sakata Masahiro 210
Santō Akiko 67
SARS-CoV-2 *see* coronavirus
Sasaki Toyonari 121
Sata Gen'ichirō 24
Satō Eisaku 1, 31–32, 38, 41, 64, 89, 235
Satō Hiroshi 77
Satō Shun'ichi 196
Second Provisional Administrative Reform Council 46–47
sectionalism 13, 15, 18, 47, 90, 97, 107; *see also* bureaucrats
Security Council 43, 114–115, 239
Seiwa Seisaku Kenkyūkai 64, 66
Seiwakai *see* Seiwa Seisaku Kenkyūkai
Sekō Hiroshige 95, 104, 221
Self-Defense Forces (SDF) 37, 60, 115, 117, 207, 209–212, 221–227
Senkaku Islands 115

seniority: among bureaucrats 90–91, 113; in LDP 45, 92
Shikōkai 66–67
Shimomura Hakubun 70, 106, 147
Shionoya Ryū 150
Shiozaki Yasuhisa 70, 94, 104, 139, 146, 187, 189
Shirakawa Masaaki 171–172, 240
Shisuikai 67–68
single-seat constituencies 17, 74–75, 78, 80–82, 137, 148, 200; *see also* electoral reform
Situation Management Specialist Committee 116
Social Democratic Party (SDP) 28, 81, 207
Sōka Gakkai 74–75, 77, 84n4, 196–197, 200–201, 218, 220–221
sontaku 61
South Kuril Islands *see* Northern Territories
Special Committee on Peace and Security System of Our Country and International Society 156, 225
special parliamentary committees 155–156, 159, 239
Steering Committee 30, 135–136
Stiglitz, Joseph 198
Students Emergency Action for Liberal Democracy (SEALDs) 227
Study Group on Financial, Fiscal, and Social Security Problems 180
Suga Yoshihide 94, 149; as CCS 77, 95–98, 100–101, 107, 110–111, 126, 189, 191–192, 197, 236–237; as minister 98, 115
Sugawara Ikurō 165, 200
Sugawara Isshū 150
Sugita Kazuhiro 95, 101, 109, 121, 177, 237
Suigetsukai 67
Sunagawa case 214, 216–217, 220, 226–227, 243
Sunrise Party 79
Supreme Court 12, 90, 209, 212, 214–215, 217
Suzuki Hiroshi 96
Suzuki Kan 106
Suzuki Zenkō 21, 26, 65

Tachibana Keiichirō 157
Taiyūkai 66
Takahashi Yōichi 187

Takaichi Sanae 60, 66, 70, 73, 139, 150, 170, 189
Takamizawa Nobushige 212, 216, 220, 224
Takenaka Heizō 46, 121, 123, 125, 141, 177
Takeshima Kazuhiko 47
Takeshita Noboru 21–22, 33, 64–65
Takeshita Wataru 65, 106, 150
Tamaki Yūichirō 83
Tanahashi Yasufumi 139
Tanaka Kakuei 21–22, 33, 64
Tanaka Kazuho 139, 192, 196
Tanaka Makiko 91
Tango Yasutake 47, 125, 169
Tani Kōichi 106
Tanigaki Sadakazu 23, 58, 97, 156; as LDP president 65, 70; as LDP secretary-general 150, 192, 197, 215, 241
Tanigawa Shūzen 66
Tanigawa Yoshiki 218
Taniguchi Tomohiko 57, 96, 98
Terata Manabu 226
"three political officials" 107
theory of gradual institutional change 1, 4–5
Tokuchi Hideshi 212
Tokyo Olympic Games 63, 103, 145–147, 152, 174, 241
Tokyo Stock Exchange 37, 167, 173
Tokyoites First Association 82
Trans-Pacific Partnership (TPP) 26, 57, 142–144, 178, 241
Truly Conservative Policy Research Association 70
Trump, Donald 63, 118, 178, 241
Tsujimoto Kiyomi 226
Tsushima Yūji 65
"twisted Diet" 29, 80, 83, 109
two-track decision-making 15, 45, 133, 151–153

ulcerative colitis 59, 63
UN Charter 117, 208, 210, 217, 223
United Kingdom (UK) 2, 6, 118, 135–136
United States (US) 5, 28, 35, 76, 89, 93, 142, 176; role in Japan's security 19–20, 114–118, 206–212, 217, 221–225
Unity Party (UP) 80–81
Uno Sōsuke 22–23

Value Added Tax (VAT) *see* consumption tax

veto players 1–2, 4–8, 13–15, 46–48, 89, 132, 181, 202, 208–209, 234–236; *see also* backbenchers; bureaucrats
Vision of Reform 81

Wakasa Masaru 228
Waki Masashi 215
Watanabe Tsuneo 119, 189
Watanabe Yoshimi 27, 109
Westminster system 2–3, 12, 45
women's empowerment 56, 82, 177–178, 241
World Economic Forum 144

Xi Jinping 96

Yachi Shōtarō 96, 110, 116, 125, 213, 238, 242
Yamada Makiko 111, 178
Yamaguchi Natsuo 76, 196, 218
Yamaguchi Taimei 150
Yamamoto Ichita 66, 70
Yamamoto Kōzō 166, 191
Yamamoto Tarō 227
Yamamoto Tsuneyuki 211
Yamamoto Yūji 70
Yamasaki Taku 137, 225
Yamatani Eriko 104
Yanagisawa Hakuo 24
Yanai Shunji 213, 242
Yanase Tadao 96, 111
Yasukuni Shrine 37, 49n5, 107
Yokobatake Yūsuke 212–213, 220, 226
Yonekura Hiromasa 178, 188
Yoshida doctrine 65–66, 208
Yoshida Shigeru 19, 31–32, 35, 41, 44, 65
Young Diet Member's Group to Consider Japan's Future and History Education 69
Your Party (YP) 77, 80, 172, 218, 220
Yūrinkai 65

zoku see parliamentary tribes

Printed in the United States
By Bookmasters